Guide to Passing the AMP Real Estate Exam

FOURTH EDITION UPDATE

JOYCE BEA STERLING, DREI

This publication is designed to provide accurate and authoritative information in regard to the subject matter covered. It is sold with the understanding that the publisher is not engaged in rendering legal, accounting, or other professional advice. If legal advice or other expert assistance is required, the services of a competent professional should be sought.

President: Dr. Andrew Temte
Chief Learning Officer: Dr. Tim Smaby
Vice President, Real Estate Education: Asha Alsobrooks
Development Editor: Julia Marti
Creative Director: Kelly Utesch

GUIDE TO PASSING THE AMP REAL ESTATE EXAM 4TH EDITION UPDATE
© 2009 by Dearborn Financial Publishing, Inc.®

Published by DF Institute, Inc., d/b/a Dearborn™ Real Estate Education
1905 Palace Street
La Crosse, WI 54603
www.dearbornRE.com

Printed in the United States of America

10   11   10   9   8   7   6   5   4   3

ISBN: 1-4277-8564-3
PPN: 1970-114B

CONTENTS

PREFACE

It is with pride that we present the fourth edition of *Guide to Passing the AMP Real Estate Exam*. This was the first exam guide on the market that was designed specifically for the licensing exam administered by Applied Measurement Professionals, Inc. The AMP exam questions are complex, and we believe this book will provide you with the testing edge to help you pass the exam.

Other than attending class, one of the most effective ways to prepare for your state exam is by studying exam topics and answering practice questions. *Guide to Passing the AMP Real Estate Exam* contains a streamlined review of the areas covered on the exam and more than 800 questions to help you prepare for your exam.

In writing the exam guide, the author has assumed that the reader is attending a real estate prelicensing class and that this book is being used as a review of the material covered in class. Specific state information regarding fair housing, transfer of deeds, and so on should be obtained from your classroom instructor.

ABOUT THE AUTHOR

Joyce Bea Sterling, DREI, has been teaching real estate principles, practices, and law since 1986, and has helped thousands of students pass their exams. Her instructional career includes being an adjunct professor at Northern Kentucky University (an AMP state) and teaching continuing education classes for the Kentucky Association of REALTORS® in 2003, 2004, and 2006, the Northern Kentucky Real Estate School, and numerous real estate boards and brokers in Kentucky and Ohio. She was a presenter at the National Association of REALTORS® in 2004 and 2005. She has a Bachelor of Arts in Education from Northern Kentucky University, a Suggestive Accelerated Learning and Teaching Certificate from Iowa State University, and is a Distinguished Real Estate Educator.

As an instructor she has taught every grade level from kindergarten through college and is considered a specialist in learning. Her credentials also include loan origination, Reverse Mortgage Specialist, Senior Housing Specialist, General Housing Specialist, e-Pro, public speaking, and stress management consultation. She is the coauthor of *Modern Real Estate Practice in Illinois*, Third Edition, and exam review audiotape sets for the states of North Carolina, New York, and Pennsylvania, all published by Dearborn™ Real Estate Education. She's also the coauthor and on-camera cohost of the *Mastering Real Estate Math* video, also published by Dearborn™ Real Estate Education.

ACKNOWLEDGMENTS

We wish to thank those who participated in the preparation of the fourth edition of *Guide to Passing the AMP Real Estate Exam* by serving as reviewers. We appreciate their insight and suggestions.

- Douglas Deratany, SHS, ARC, Associate Broker, Real Estate One Academy, Southfield, Michigan

- Kerry Kidwell, ABR, CRB, CRS, GRI, DREI, e-PRO, Realty Plus, Inc., Heyworth, Illinois

- Laurie MacDougal, Laurmac Learning Center, Oak Park, Illinois

- Dawn M. Svenningsen, Director, Dabbs Academy of Real Estate, Inc., Orland Park, Illinois

This book is dedicated to Jan Zalla, a truly amazing woman. Thank you for being the person that you are and for being a part of my life.

INTRODUCTION
ABOUT YOUR EXAM!

Knowledge is power . . . and knowledge of real estate can make you or save you thousands of dollars in the future. Congratulations on your decision to secure a real estate license! To get started, you must pass the AMP exam; then you can begin your career as a real estate licensee.

Applied Measurement Professionals, Inc. (AMP), of Lenexa, Kansas, began in 1990 with the goal of supplying professional testing for future real estate agents. This introduction will help you review basic reading and study skills, understand the format of the questions, and develop an exam strategy. The remaining chapters will guide you through a review of the six areas covered on your real estate exam.

AMP provides a candidate's handbook that contains your exam application. It is available through your school or the real estate commission and provides you with specific information regarding your own state exam. It is also available at *www.goamp.com*. Please read it carefully. This guide was written to be a streamlined review of the material presented in the classroom. More in-depth information about each subject is contained in the textbook.

USING THIS GUIDE TO PREPARE FOR YOUR EXAM

This comprehensive exam prep guide contains a variety of study tools to help prepare you for your examination. Chapters 1 through 6 follow the subject areas presented on the national AMP outline found in the candidate's handbook (available at *www.goamp.com*). The seventh chapter is a comprehensive math review covering financing, appraising, brokerage, area, and settlement math.

National AMP Outline	Number of Items
1. Listing Property	31
2. Selling Property	21
3. Property Management	14
4. Settlement/Transfer of Ownership	14
5. Financing	10
6. Professional Responsibilities / Fair Practice Administration	10

In the chapters, a **light bulb icon** is placed next to the material that is vital for you to know.

At the end of each chapter is a **Matching Quiz** covering important concepts covered in the chapter and 70 **Chapter Review Questions**. Both are designed to assess your knowledge of key concepts and exactly where you need to return for further review and study.

Sample salesperson and sample broker examinations, each offering 110 questions and rationales, follow the chapters. In addition, the **CD-ROM** packaged with this textbook allows computer practice with 50 additional salesperson and 50 broker questions. A computer is used when testing in all states where the AMP exam is given.

The complete **Glossary** includes all topics covered in the AMP exam.

A removable **Key Point Review-To-Go** is contained at the end of the book. The pages are perforated, so tear them out and take them with you wherever you go. Even if you only have 10 to 15 minutes to study, the repetition of reading the Key Points will help you commit them to memory. Also, review this section in the final days or hours before your exam. They are very effective for last-minute studying!

BROKER EXAM INFORMATION

You will notice that some of the headings and practice questions throughout the book are designated with a bull's-eye in the margin. This means that the particular topic appears on the broker examination only. However, broker-level candidates should still be able to answer all of the questions in the book. There is also a 110-question broker practice examination beginning on page 237.

Effective in 2009, the national portion of the brokers exam will be taken in a simulation format. The state section of the exam will be in the multiple choice format. The purpose of the simulation format is to provide realistic scenario problems to determine the level of competency of the candidate.

The simulation will include eight scored problems plus two pretest problems.

A primary issue and a property type will be designated in each simulation. The eight simulations will cover the following subjects: ethics, negotiation, document preparation, fair housing, environmental issues, representation of services, valuation, advertising, finance, agency/nonagency relationships, disclosures, property representation, trust accounts, training and supervision of licensees, and risk management. The property type will be designated as residential, commercial, property management, and unspecified.

Please check with your school or *www.goamp.com* and download the Candidate Handbook for your state for up-to-date information.

TIPS FOR EFFECTIVE STUDYING

Listening Effectively

Most real estate students have work, family, and many other responsibilities. That's why it is so important to concentrate intently on the information the instructor presents in class. Here are three basic rules for listening effectively.

Rule 1. Listen to what the instructor is saying, as well as to the inflections in the instructor's voice. An instructor's voice will change as important material is presented.

Rule 2. Instructors do not know what will be on any given test. However, some material is more important than other material. Listen carefully for the material that the instructor indicates you must know for the state and national exams.

Rule 3. Your time is valuable. Make the most of it while you are in class. A student who doodles, reads other material, or goes on a mental vacation during class time is missing valuable information.

Reading Effectively

Comprehensive reading is a skill that takes practice. Here are some steps to help you develop this essential skill for studying and passing the test.

Step 1. Begin preparation for your exam with your textbook or other instructional materials. Most text authors provide a preview of the material, as well as a summary at the end of each chapter. Read the preview, skim the headings, and read the summary to grasp the author's plan of presentation of the material. Then, with an understanding of what is to be learned, read the chapter.

Step 2. Highlight important words and terms while you are reading. Be sure to learn the words that you do not understand or ask your instructor their meanings. Be sure you learn the vocabulary words. This is essential for passing your exam.

Step 3. If possible, relate the material to your own life experiences. Recall listing your property with an agent, as well as what occurred during the real estate transaction. Read the important material at least three times. Then take the test at the end of the chapter. Read the material until you understand why you missed any of the questions.

Step 4. Next, use this guide to help you review the important material until you sit for your exam. Even if you have only a few minutes to review, it will help keep the material fresh in your mind. Remember. . . *repetition is the key to learning*.

Step 5. When you have completed your classes, read the most important material in this guide at least three times, then answer as many test questions as you can. You will find test questions at the end of every review area and sample salesperson and broker tests at the end of this guide. Go ahead and take the broker test, even if you're sitting for the salesperson exam. The more questions you can answer, the easier the state exam will be.

Other Study Tips

Read the class assignment before attending class to help you identify the areas in which you want to ask questions.

Find a quiet place to study. When studying at home, resist answering the phone or engaging in any other activities that can be distracting, such as having the television or radio on in the background. Most schools have a library or classroom available for study. If you make the effort to go to the library, you will probably be able to better focus on learning the material.

Consider forming a study group or finding another individual with whom you can study. Each individual should commit to reviewing the material independently before attending the study session. Determine your goals for each group meeting, and appoint a group leader to keep you on target.

Sometimes one person may try to dominate the study group. Be aware of any people who want to control the entire group or who think they have all the right answers. Studying in groups should be a joint effort.

UNDERSTANDING QUESTION FORMATS

The following question formats can be found on your AMP exam. Many students miss questions because they do not take the time to read them carefully.

When approaching a question on your state exam, read and answer each question three times. Read the first time to identify the format of the question being asked and its content. Read the second time to create in your mind a scenario of what the question is asking and to identify key words and phrases. Then, read each question a third time to make sure that you understand exactly what is being asked.

Answer the question in your mind, then read the answers to find that answer. Read each answer three times. There may be a key word or phrase in one of the answers or in the question that indicates the right answer. There should be ample time to read each question and each answer three times, but pace yourself. Keep track of the time and complete the test. Let's explore some of the types of questions that you may encounter on your exam.

The EXCEPT Format

When the word *EXCEPT* appears at the end of the question, it means you are looking for the *opposite* of what your logic tells you is correct.

"All of the following are true EXCEPT" means you are looking for the one answer that is false.

"All of the following are false EXCEPT" means you are looking for the one answer that is true.

The NOT Format

When *NOT* is found in a question, it means you are looking for the one answer that should not be included. This format is used to see if you really understand what is involved in a certain law or principle.

The SITUATIONAL Format

With a *SITUATIONAL* format, a scenario is created and the possible answers may include two Yes answers and two No answers. Questions in this format test your comprehension of the material, as well as your ability to analyze each answer. There may be only one word or phrase in the answer that will make it correct.

A situational format question can be very long. Read it carefully and create the situation in your mind before answering the question.

The DEFINITION or RECALL Format

These test questions are easy. . . as long as you know the definitions of the vocabulary words. A definition is given in the question, and you must match it with the answer.

The MOST IMPORTANT Format

In questions of this type, a key word or concept makes one answer more important than another.

The LEAST Format

The *LEAST* format could include the terms *LEAST INFLUENCE* or *LEAST LIKELY*. Look for the answer that is least probable.

Example: Which of the following would LEAST LIKELY be found in an abstract of title?

The BEST Format

The word *BEST* means the most advantageous or, as it relates to the test question, the better choice. This format also can be used for recall questions.

Example: A tenancy in common interest that grants the right to interval ownership of the property would BEST describe a(n). . .

The key words in this question are *interval ownership*, which would be best described as a time-share.

The TRUE Format

"Which of the following is *TRUE*?" means there are three wrong answers and one true answer. This format may be combined with the situational format to test your understanding of the meaning of a concept.

The FALSE Format

"Which of the following is *FALSE*?" means there are three true answers and one false answer.

The DIFFERENCE Format

With the *DIFFERENCE* format, you will make comparisons or look for the distinction between two words or concepts.

Example: The MAJOR DIFFERENCE between actual eviction and constructive eviction is. . .

Knowing the definitions of actual and constructive eviction, as well as the proper process for each eviction, is essential to correctly answer this question.

The HAVE IN COMMON Format

Questions using this format ask what a group of words have in common.

Example: What do the terms *possibility of reverter*, *right of reentry*, and *remainder* have in common?

To correctly answer this question, you must know the definitions of *possibility of reverter*, *right of reentry*, and *remainder*.

The MOST LIKELY Format

The *MOST LIKELY* format is asking for what would normally happen in a given situation.

Example: In a real estate transaction, the agent would MOST LIKELY represent whom?

The APPLICATION Format

The *APPLICATION* format tests to see if you can apply the information you have learned.

Example: If the net income on a property remains constant and the cap rate increases 1 percent, the value of the property will. . .

This question tests your knowledge of an appraising formula.

The ACCOUNTABLE Format

This question will set up a scenario or a situation and then ask who can be held accountable or if a certain party is accountable.

Example: A broker was asked to list a property by the executor of an estate. When the broker asked if the property was zoned commercial, the executor replied, "I think so."

Without additional verification, the broker listed and sold the property as having commercial zoning. The purchaser hired an architect to design a building and attempted to secure a building permit. The buyer was informed that the property was zoned residential. Who can be held ACCOUNTABLE for the damages?

To correctly answer this question, you must understand the law of agency.

This concludes the review of the question formats, and now you're ready to study. Remember, if you find yourself struggling with a concept, ask your instructor for additional clarification.

Listing Property

This chapter reviews the listing of property, assessment of property value, and services to the seller.

AMP Outline—Listing

I.	**Listing Property**		6.	Type of construction
	A. Listing		7.	Encumbrances
		1. Legal descriptions	8.	Compliance with building codes
		2. Lot size	9.	Ownership of record
		3. Physical dimensions of structure	10.	Homeowners association bylaws and fees
		4. Appurtenances	11.	Brokerage fee
		5. Utilities		

LEGAL DESCRIPTIONS

In some states, a street address is sufficient to identify the property in a listing and sales contract. Other states require the legal description in these contracts, as well as in deeds, mortgages, notes, and other real estate documents. Metes and bounds, lot and block, and the rectangular or government survey are the legal descriptions commonly used.

Metes and Bounds

The **metes-and-bounds** survey method or the **boundary survey** involves describing land by the **metes** (**distance**) and **bounds** (**direction**). A starting point must be identified that future surveyors can use, and it is known as a **point of beginning** (**POB**) or a **point of commencement** (**POC**). The surveyor travels around the property being described until the lot closes, that is, the surveyor returns to the point of beginning.

A metes-and-bounds legal description typically uses *feet and inches* as the units of measurement to describe the distance between monuments. Direction is given by the bearing of one monument in respect to another monument, described by using north, south, east, and west in relationship to degrees, minutes, and seconds.

FIGURE 1.1

Reading a Bearing

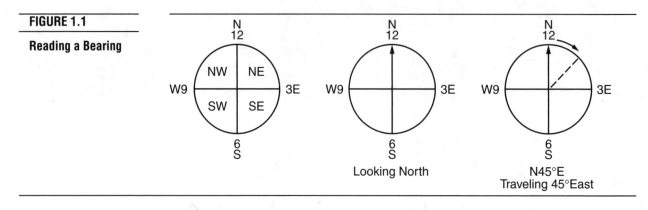

Looking North

N45°E
Traveling 45°East

For example, imagine a circular clock with a line drawn from 12 to 6 and another line from 9 to 3. North is 12 o'clock, east is 3 o'clock, south 6 o'clock, and west 9 o'clock. The four quadrants, then, are NE, NW, SE, and SW. A legal description reading N45°E means that a surveyor is moving 45° eastward from due north. On the imaginary clock, the surveyor is facing the position of the hour hand at 1:30 pm. (See Figure 1.1.)

Other survey terms are

- **monuments**—used to physically identify the POB and the intersections of the boundary lines of the area being surveyed;

- **benchmark**—a permanent reference point used to establish elevations and altitudes above sea level; and

- **datum**—a point, line, or surface from which elevations are measured to determine such things as the heights of structures or grades of streets.

Lot and Block

The **lot-and-block** method of legal description is used on maps and plats of recorded subdivided land (also known as a *recorded plat* or a *recorded map*).

When a developer subdivides a tract of land for the development of a subdivision, the surveyor's plat map is recorded in the county courthouse where the property is located. Each **parcel (lot)** of land is assigned a lot number and each group of contiguous lots is given a **block number**. A description might read, "Lots 5 and 6 of Block 9 of the Brentwood Subdivision." Because all states use this method, a description must include the county and state to distinguish it from another area.

FIGURE 1.2

Sections of a
Township

N

6	5	4	3	2	1
7	8	9	10	11	12
18	17	(16)	15	14	13
19	20	21	22	23	24
30	29	28	27	26	25
31	32	33	34	35	36

W   E

S

Government, Rectangular, or Geodetic Survey

The **government** (*rectangular* or *geodetic*) **survey** is based on a system of imaginary lines called **principal meridians**, which run north and south, and **base lines**, which run east and west.

- The largest square is called a *check* and measures 24 miles by 24 miles. Each check has 16 townships.

- A **township** measures 6 miles by 6 miles. Each township has 36 sections. (See Figure 1.2.)

- A **section** measures 1 mile by 1 mile and contains 640 acres.

- **Correction lines** are used to compensate for the earth's curvature.

- **Oversized** or undersized sections are called *fractional sections*.

A government survey description could read "The NW¼ of the NE¼ of the SW¼ of Section 32, Township 12 North, Range 3 West of the tenth Principal Meridian." When asked to locate the legal description of a parcel of land using the government survey, read the description *backward*. Use Figure 1.3 as an example to locate the N½ of the SE¼ of the SW¼: begin by locating the SW¼, then locate the SE¼ of the SW¼, then the N½ of the SE¼ of the SW¼.

To compute the acreage of the N½ of the SE¼ of the SW¼, remember there are 640 acres in one section of land. Divide 640 by the denominators: $640 \div 4 \div 4 \div 2 = 20$ acres of land.

If a question asks to compute the acres in the SW¼ of the NE¼ of the NE¼ and the N½ of the SE¼ of the SW¼, the words *and the* indicate that there are two parcels of land, as shown in Figure 1.4. Again, divide 640 acres by the denominators, but compute the acreage for the two tracts separately. Thus, $640 \div 4 \div 4 \div 4 = 10$ acres and $640 \div 4 \div 4 \div 2 = 20$ acres; $10 + 20 = 30$ acres of land.

FIGURE 1.3

Locating a Parcel of Land in the Government Survey

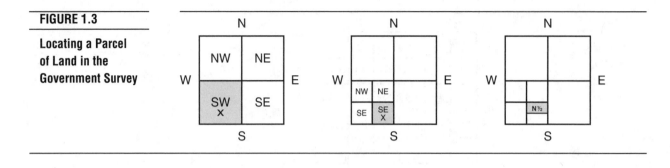

LOT SIZE

The accuracy of the lot size is essential in both residential and commercial properties. If there is a discrepancy between the lot size quoted in the listing contract or deed and the actual lot size, the *actual lot size* found by the survey will prevail.

Other terms associated with lot size are

- **floor area ratio**—the ratio of the floor area to the land area on which the building sits;

- **livability space ratio**—requires a minimum square footage of nonvehicular outdoor area in a development for each square foot of total living area;

- **front footage**—the linear measurement of a property along the street line or water line is always given first when dimensions are stated (if a lot measures 100' × 200', then the first dimension given [100'] refers to the front footage); and

- **setback**—the amount of space required between the lot line and the building line.

PHYSICAL DIMENSIONS OF STRUCTURE

Unless custom dictates otherwise, the general rule of thumb is that when an agent or appraiser measures a building to compute the **gross living area** (**GLA**), only the area above grade (ground) level is used. The *external dimensions* of the building are measured, excluding the garage, porch, or patio. The below-grade level that is finished is included in a different section of the appraiser's report.

FIGURE 1.4

Locating Two Parcels of Land in the Government Survey

The American National Standards Institute (ANSI) has established a standard measurement for computing the square footage of single-family homes that is used by many appraisers. Many real estate regulatory agencies are adapting the ANSI standards so agents and appraisers will be quoting the same square footage of the property.

APPURTENANCES

Listing contracts and sales contracts usually identify the appurtenances that will be transferred in the deed. The word **appurtenant** in real estate means rights, benefits, or attachments that transfer with real property.

- **Tangible** (touchable) **property** includes physical improvements on the property; fixtures, such as lighting, heating, and plumbing equipment, are appurtenances. A listing contract should identify fixtures that "go with the property" and fixtures that a seller intends to take with him or her after the sale.

- **Intangible** (cannot touch) **property** includes *rights and privileges* that belong to and pass in the deed from the grantor to the grantee. Easements and water rights are intangible appurtenances.

An **easement** is the *right to use* the land of another, but it *does not include* the right of possession. Among the various types of easements are the following:

Appurtenant Easement

- Benefits a parcel of real estate
- Involves two tracts of land owned by two different people
- The dominant estate benefits from the easement
- The servient estate is burdened by the easement (See Figure 1.5.)

Easement in Gross

- Benefits a person or a legal entity
- Involves one tract of land
- Personal gross easements terminate on the sale of the property or death of the easement owner (e.g., the billboard)

FIGURE 1.5

Appurtenant Easement

FIGURE 1.6

Easement in Gross

- Billboard
  (Personal Gross Easement)

- Water Line Easement
  (Commercial Gross Easement)

■ Commercial gross easements are usually assignable when the property is sold or on the death of the easement owner (e.g., a utility) (See Figure 1.6.)

Easement by Necessity

■ Created when a buyer purchases a landlocked property

■ Buyer must be given the access rights to **ingress** (enter) and **egress** (exit) the property

Easement by Prescription

■ Created when a claimant uses a property for a statutory period of time

■ Use must have been open, notorious, continuous, exclusive, and without the owner's approval

A **license** is the **personal privilege** to enter the land of another and use it for a specific reason, such as attending a sporting event, parking your car in a parking garage, or going to the movies. A license *can be revoked* at any time and terminates on the death of either party or the sale of the land.

A **profit a prendre** is the right to take crops, soil, or profit from the land of another. (Also known as *profit*.)

UTILITIES

A **utility** is a *service provided* to a property, such as supplying gas, electricity, telephone service, or water. Depending on the custom in the community, the company providing the service may be able to place a lien on the property if fees for such services are not paid. The listing contract should contain the utility services available on the property.

TYPE OF CONSTRUCTION

Agents should have a working knowledge of construction to help determine the quality, upkeep, and flaws of a property. This includes such details as identification of the type of foundation, exterior structural walls and framing, interior walls and finishing, and style and type of roof, windows, and doors.

An **encumbrance** is any claim, lien, charge, or liability that affects the value or the use of a property and is held by someone other than the owner of the property.

Encumbrances that affect the *title*: liens, mortgages, and judgments.

Encumbrances that affect the *use*: deed restrictions, encroachments, and easements.

COMPLIANCE WITH BUILDING CODES

To ensure the health, safety, and welfare of homeowners, there are local, state, or municipal building and construction standards that must be met. These standards include the regulation and control of design, construction, quality, use, occupancy, location, and maintenance of all buildings and structures.

A *building permit* must be issued for the construction of a new building or other improvement and for any substantial repair of an existing structure or the demolition of a building. The purpose of the permit is to ensure compliance with the **building code**, or *minimum standards of construction*. A violation of code and failure to disclose violations may constitute misrepresentation and make the contract voidable. When the building "meets code," a **certificate of occupancy** is issued. Building codes are established by local governments, but it should be noted that not all areas have building codes.

OWNERSHIP OF RECORD

When a property is purchased, most buyers record their deed at the courthouse, or at the Torrens office if the property is registered land. Recording the deed in public records gives notice to the world of ownership of the property.

HOMEOWNERS ASSOCIATION BYLAWS AND FEES

Bylaws are established by condominiums and subdivisions for the administration and management of the community. The bylaws also establish the homeowners association, the power given to the board, and the responsibilities of each homeowner. Anyone living in a community with homeowners' association fees is required to pay the fee or a lien will be placed on the property. The listing contract should include the bylaws and fees that must be paid.

BROKERAGE FEE

The brokerage fee that is paid to a listing company for the services of marketing, advertising, and securing a ready, willing, and able buyer is negotiated between the broker and the seller. Should a contract be entered into with a buyer, the payment of commission also should be established in that agreement. The *Sherman Antitrust Act* is a federal law that prohibits price fixing. Commissions are always negotiable. Most states also have antitrust laws.

AMP Outline—Assessment of Property Value

I.	**Listing Property**		3.	Depreciation
	B.	Assessment of Property Value	4.	Improvements
			5.	Economic trends
		1. Location	6.	Market data
		2. Anticipated changes		

LOCATION

The location of a property is one of the major factors in determining its value. *Location*, or **situs**, is the preference people have for a certain area. When determining the value of a property, an adjustment may be necessary to compensate for locational differences within the neighborhood.

ANTICIPATED CHANGES

The *principle of anticipation* says that the value of a property will adjust with any anticipated change. If the anticipated change is considered positive, such as a change of zoning from residential to commercial, the value of the property generally increases. If the anticipated change is considered negative, such as the expansion of an airport that will increase the noise level within the neighborhood, the value of the property generally decreases. An anticipated zoning change may increase or decrease the value of the property.

DEPRECIATION

Depreciation is a loss of property value due to any cause. This could include ordinary wear and tear, damage caused by fire or vandalism, or damage caused by acts of nature such as hurricanes, floods, earthquakes, and so forth. The three types of depreciation that the appraiser determines are physical, functional, and external. Please remember that *land does not ordinarily depreciate*; only the improvements are depreciated.

Terms Associated with Depreciation

- **Depreciation** causes a loss of property value.

- **Curable depreciation** is reasonable and economically feasible to correct.

- **Incurable depreciation** is not economically feasible to correct.

- **Physical depreciation** may be curable or incurable and is caused by lack of maintenance and ordinary wear and tear. Depreciation of the property can occur through deterioration, which may be the effect of either normal wear and tear or natural elements.

■ **Functional obsolescence** may be curable or incurable and occurs because of poor floor plan, outdated items, or changes in technology. Examples: low ratio of bathrooms to bedrooms; older home with limited electrical outlets in a room; new home built with a one-car garage.

■ **External obsolescence** is incurable and occurs because of factors located *outside the property*. External obsolescence is also known as *economic, locational,* or *environmental obsolescence*. Examples: nearby nuclear power plant, pig farm, or rising interest rates.

IMPROVEMENTS

Improvements are added to the land and will usually increase the value of the property. Improvements *to* land include buildings, additions such as a family room, or the replacement of a roof. Improvements *of* land include streets, sidewalks, and utilities.

ECONOMIC TRENDS

The life cycle of a community includes *growth, stability, decline,* and *gentrification* or *revitalization*. An appraiser evaluates the community to determine which cycle the property is in and how that affects the value of the property. Other economic factors that will affect a property's value include interest rates, taxes, employment levels, and population.

MARKET DATA

The first step of the appraisal process is to state the problem or the purpose for conducting the appraisal. Is the property being appraised to determine the market value because it is being sold? Is it being appraised to determine the cost to rebuild for insurance purposes? The second step of the appraisal process is to collect market data and to classify the data by type and by source.

General data refers to information that would be appropriate for many properties. This includes outside factors such as social, economic, environmental/physical, and government forces that would affect the value of the property. Other examples of general data include labor statistics, weather studies, transportation studies, and so forth.

Specific data refers to the information used in the analysis of the subject property and the comparable properties that will be used in the valuation process. The legal description, environmental reports, and survey would be gathered on the subject property.

Specific data on comparable properties is found under the Value Adjustments section of the appraisal report. (See Figure 1.7.) The sources of data include the primary and secondary data. *Primary data* are collected directly by the appraiser and include sketches, office files, and sales information. *Secondary data* are prepared by someone other than the appraiser, but they are used by the appraiser in determining value. Information from the multiple-listing service, conversations with other appraisers, and publications of all sold properties in the county are examples of secondary data.

Sales Comparison Approach	**Value Adjustments**
	Sales or Financing Concessions
	Date of Sale/Time
	Location
	Leasehold/Fee Simple
	Site
	View
	Design and Appeal
	Quality of Construction
	Age
	Condition
	Above Grade Room Count Gross Living Area
	Basement & Finished Rooms Below Grade
	Functional Utility
	Heating/Cooling
	Energy Efficient Items
	Garage/Carport
	Porch, Patio, Deck, Fireplace(s), etc.
	Fence, Pool, etc.
	Net Adj. (total)
	Adjusted Sales Price of Comparable

AMP Outline—Services to the Seller

I.   Listing Property
    C.   Services to the Seller
        1.   Responsibilities of the licensee and the listing firm
        2.   Property subdivision and selling of parcels
        3.   Hidden defects known by the owner
        4.   Information about required disclosures
        5.   Property included in or excluded from the sale
        6.   Personal and real property differences
        7.   Net proceeds estimation
        8.   Completion of listing agreement, provision to seller, explanation
        9.   Determination that parties holding title have signed listing agreement

10.   Showing of house and safeguarding property
11.   Methods of marketing property
12.   Presentation of offers to the seller
13.   Transaction files
14.   Deed restrictions and covenants
15.   Forms of ownership interests in real estate
16.   Issues related to conveyance of real property
17.   Fair housing laws
18.   Comparative market analysis and appraising
19.   Independent appraisal necessity
20.   Inspection necessity
21.   Nonownership interests in real property

RESPONSIBILITIES OF THE LICENSEE AND THE LISTING FIRM

When the property owner hires a broker to find a buyer, an agency relationship is created. The owner (**principal**) has delegated to the brokerage (**agent**) the right to act on the owner's behalf. This creates a **fiduciary relationship** wherein the agent owes the seller certain duties. Sales associates represent their brokers, and their primary fiduciary relationship is with their broker. In some states sales associates act as subagents for their brokers. A subagent is an agent of an agent. However, in states where brokers may designate salespeople to be the agents of buyers or sellers, the agency responsibility passes to the designated agents.

State laws will vary regarding the duties the brokerage firm and listing agent are required to perform when a listing is secured. In some states, the seller may waive agency duties wherein the brokerage will provide minimum services, such as only placing the property in the Multiple Listing Service. Other states require, if a property is listed, the agent to schedule appointments to show the property; advertise the property; communicate, negotiate, and deliver all written offers and counteroffers; accept earnest money; help the seller fulfill contract contingencies; attend the closing, etc. Unless the state allows a "waiver of duties," the brokerage and listing agent are required to follow the law of agency as discussed below.

The payment of compensation or its source does not create the agency relationship. A contract creates the agency relationship. Please see Figure 1.8 for a review of the types of agents, creation of agency, and types of agencies.

A **listing agreement** is a personal service contract securing the employment of a brokerage firm to find a ready, willing, and able buyer. The types of listing agreements are exclusive-right-to-sell, exclusive-agency, open, net, and option. See page 18 for a review of some of these listings.

Responsibilities of an Agent

The acronym COALD represents the duties of the agent to the principal. The broker must act with care, obedience, accountability, loyalty, and disclosure.

- **Care**—A broker is to exercise reasonable care and skill as a professional while transacting the business of the principal. For a client who is a seller, this includes establishing the correct list price, properly representing the property, informing the seller of tax consequences, and properly marketing the property. Tax or legal advice, however, should come from experts in these fields. For a client who is a buyer, this means helping the buyer find suitable property, negotiating the offer, and directing the buyer to a lender and other experts for inspections and advice.

- **Obedience**—The agent is to act in good faith and obey the principal's instructions given in the contract; however, the agent must not obey illegal instructions.

FIGURE 1.8

Agency

Types of Agents

1. **General agent**—When the principal delegates a broad range of powers. Examples: a property manager or a real estate agent with the agent's broker.
2. **Special agent**—When the principal delegates a specific act or business transaction. Example: a listing agent or a party with a durable power of attorney; a listing broker with the broker's seller.
3. **Universal agent**—A party given full power of attorney to represent another person.

Creation of an Agency Relationship

1. **Express agency**—When the parties state the contract's terms and express their intention either orally or in writing. Example: a listing agreement.
2. **Implied agency**—When the actions or conduct of the parties communicate that there is an agreement. Example: an implied agency established by the agent when talking with a buyer. "Take this deal. It's the best one for you."

Types of Agencies

1. **Single agency**—When a broker is representing the seller or the buyer in the transaction, but not both.
2. **Dual agency**—When an agent represents two principals in the same transaction.
3. **Facilitator or transaction broker**—One who does not represent either party in a transaction. Both parties are customers.
4. **Designated agency**—Created when an agent is appointed by a broker to act for a specific principal or client. This is used when one agent with the company listed the property and another agent within the company secured the buyer for the property. The listing agent would be the designated agent of the seller and the buyer's agent would be the designated agent of the buyer. In many states, the broker is the dual agent of the seller and buyer, but this is determined by state law. This can occur only with the written permission of both parties. Both parties are clients.

- **Accountability**—The agent is accountable for all funds or property of others that come into his or her possession.

- **Loyalty**—The agent must be loyal, putting the principal's interests above those of all others. This includes obtaining the best offer from a buyer when representing a seller, explaining offers to a client, and representing only the interests of the client.

- **Disclosure**—The agent must keep the principal informed, disclosing all facts and information that could affect the transaction. If representing a seller, the agent must disclose if the buyer is willing to offer more for the property. If representing the buyer, an agent needs to disclose all defects and if the seller would take less for the property.

Agents must use reasonable care and skill in performance, be honest, and disclose facts that materially affect the value of the property, regardless of whom they are representing.

Ministerial acts are those acts that a licensee may perform for a consumer that are informative in nature and do not rise to the level of active representation.

Puffing is the exaggeration of a fact.

Each state now has mandatory agency disclosure laws that stipulate when, how, and to whom disclosures must be made. Generally, the agency disclosure statement must be in writing. The purpose is to make sure buyers and sellers understand whether they are customers or clients in a transaction. Agency disclosure usually occurs before confidential information is given.

Selling

Once the listing is obtained, the agent will begin marketing and showing the property. The sellers' instructions are to be followed, such as the placement of a For Sale sign in the yard or a lockbox on the property. The seller may look to the agent for suggestions to make the property more marketable. *Unless directed otherwise by the seller*, all offers are to be presented to the seller. The agent may need to explain any contract terms the seller may not understand. Most sales contracts contain contingencies or conditions that must be satisfied before the contract is fully enforceable. Common contingencies include property inspection, pest inspection, loan approval, and a marketable title. The sales contract should have provisions for canceling the contract. If the buyer defaults, the seller may be able to retain the earnest money as liquidated damages. If the seller defaults, the earnest money is returned to the buyer. The contract may contain other steps to be followed when canceling the contract.

PROPERTY SUBDIVISION AND SELLING OF PARCELS

The control of land use and development is influenced by public (government) and private (nongovernment) restrictions and public ownership of land by federal, state, and local governments. Public controls include state regulations aimed at protecting the public health, safety, and welfare.

A developer places private restrictions on real estate to control and maintain the desirable quality and character of a subdivision or property. This is done through the use of deed restrictions and restrictive covenants. It only takes one person to enforce a deed restriction.

HIDDEN DEFECTS KNOWN BY THE OWNER

An agent must be aware of two types of defects in a property:

1. **Latent defects** are hidden structural defects not easily discovered by inspection.

2. **Patent defects** are easily visible when inspecting a property.

Most state laws require sellers to disclose property defects, hidden defects, and major repairs resulting from fires, hurricanes, or other natural disasters. An agent is liable for not disclosing known defects and may be liable for defects the agent "should have known" about. **Misrepresentation** occurs when property defects are not disclosed to the buyer. The buyer may be able to rescind the sales contract or receive **compensatory damages**, which are actual damages for the repair of the defect. **Punitive damages** are damages assessed as punishment.

INFORMATION ABOUT REQUIRED DISCLOSURES

A *lead-based paint disclosure statement* must be given when selling or leasing a residential property constructed prior to 1978. Purchasers or tenants must be given a lead hazard pamphlet as well as records and reports regarding prior tests for lead. Purchasers must be given 10 days in which to conduct an inspection, and they may waive this inspection.

Most states require that the seller complete a *seller's disclosure of property condition statement*, which provides information regarding the house systems (plumbing, electrical, heating and cooling, etc.), foundation, structural damage, leaking basement, the roof, drainage problems, boundary issues, source of water supply, source of sanitation, improvements to the property, and environmental issues such as mold, lead-based paint, and radon.

- The property disclosure statement should be completed by the seller or a person with the legal authority, such as the executor of an estate.

- Licensees should review the document to ensure that the seller has accurately and totally completed the form. (Did the seller sign the form? Have all the boxes been checked?)

- The property disclosure form is not intended to be a warranty or substitute for the buyer's securing an independent property inspection.

- If a licensee questions the accuracy of the property disclosure form, it should be discussed with the seller. Remember, the law of agency requires the disclosure of any material facts that would affect the transaction.

- Generally, the form is given to the buyer before the offer is made. If the buyer is purchasing a "For Sale by Owner" property, the law may allow the disclosure to be given after the offer is accepted.

Just as players on a team wear uniforms so they know who is on their side, an *agency disclosure* is given to buyers and sellers to inform them if the agent is on their team. The listing brokerage firm and listing agent are on the seller's team. Buyers need to understand when and if they have an agent on their team in the transaction.

- Generally, the agency disclosure form is given to the seller when the property is listed and given to the buyer before confidential information is disclosed. Check your state laws to determine when the agency disclosure form or other documents must be given to potential buyers and sellers.

- A dual agency may be created only with the knowledge of and written permission by both the buyer and seller.

- The sellers must be provided a copy of any documents they have signed, and the length of time a broker is required to keep copies of documents is determined by state law.

PROPERTY INCLUDED IN OR EXCLUDED FROM THE SALE

The offer to purchase should stipulate the real and personal property that will be conveyed at closing. The words *land, real estate,* and *real property* are often interchanged but have distinct definitions. (See Figure 1.9.) Real property can be a *divided interest*; that is, one party can own the air and surface rights while another party owns the subsurface or mineral rights. Unless a contract stipulates otherwise or mineral rights have been previously sold or leased, air, surface, and subsurface rights are purchased with the property.

FIGURE 1.9

Land, Real Estate, and Real Property

Land
Earth's surface to the center of the earth and the airspace above the land, including the trees and water

Real Estate
Land plus permanent human-made additions

Real Property
Real estate plus "bundle of legal rights"

Water Rights

Riparian rights are water rights granted to owners of land along the course of a river, stream, or lake. **Flowing water rights**: Land adjoining navigable rivers is usually owned to the water's edge, while land adjoining nonnavigable streams and lakes is owned to the center of the stream or lake.

Littoral rights are water rights of owners whose land borders on large, navigable lakes, seas, and oceans. **Nonflowing water rights**: Ownership ends at the mean high-water mark.

The action of water may affect the quality of land ownership. An owner is entitled to all land that is accumulated by **accretion** or the increase in land resulting from the deposit of soil by the water's action. The deposits are called **alluvion** or *alluvium*.

When water recedes, new land is acquired by **reliction**. **Avulsion** is the *sudden loss* of land as a result of an act of nature, such as an earthquake. The *gradual wearing away* of land is called **erosion**.

Physical and Economic Characteristics of Real Estate

The physical characteristics of real estate can be remembered by the acronym **HID**.

- **H**—*Heterogeneity* or nonhomogeneity—means that every parcel of land is different.

- **I**—*Immobility*—the geographic location of a parcel of land can never be changed.

- **D**—*Durable*—land is indestructible, meaning improvements can depreciate or be destroyed but the land still remains.

The economic characteristics of land that affect its value are scarcity, improvements, permanence of investment, and area preference.

- **Scarcity** means that when the supply is limited, the price will increase. This could be the scarcity of land in a given location or the scarcity of a certain type of zoning (e.g., multifamily).

- **Improvements** will increase or decrease the property value. For example, building a four-bedroom home on a vacant lot would increase value; an announcement that a nuclear power plant will be built nearby will probably decrease the surrounding property values.

- **Permanence** of investment refers to the capital and labor used to develop a large fixed investment. Examples: water lines, sewage systems, electricity, and roads.

- **Area preference** or **situs** refers to the location of the property and is based on factors such as reputation, aesthetic beauty (e.g., a river view), geography, and convenience. People will pay more for location.

Emblements

Trees, grasses, and perennial shrubbery that do not require annual cultivation are considered real property (*fructus naturales* or fruits of nature).

Emblements, or crops that require annual planting, are considered personal property. When a farm is being sold, the contract should stipulate who will have the right to harvest and profit from the annual crop. Usually, former owners and tenants are entitled to harvest the crops that are a result of their labor.

Fixtures and Trade Fixtures

A **fixture** is an item that was once personal property but has become affixed to the land or improvement so that the law construes it to be a part of the real estate. Most items that are a permanent part of a building are considered fixtures.

A fixture can be excluded from the sale of the property. "What goes" and "what stays" should be discussed in detail with the seller when the property is listed. To reach a meeting of the minds, the buyer must have an understanding of the contents of the listing agreement.

A **trade fixture** (*chattel fixture*) is an item that is owned by the tenant and attached to a rented space to conduct business. Trade fixtures usually can be removed from the property before the lease expires. If trade fixtures remain on the property *after the lease expires*, they generally belong to the landlord.

PERSONAL AND REAL PROPERTY DIFFERENCES

Personal property, also known as *personalty* or **chattels**, is all property that does not fit the definition of real property. It includes movable items not attached to real estate, such as furniture, cars, and clothing. It also includes items that were once attached but have been severed from real estate, such as trees, crops, and chandeliers.

Should a question arise as to whether an item is real or personal property, the courts use five tests to determine the status of the property. The acronym **MARIA** will help you remember the tests to determine if an item is real or personal property.

- **M**—*Method of annexation*—Was the item permanently attached? Can it be removed without causing damage?

- **A**—*Adaptation to real estate*—Is the item custom made? For example, house keys are movable but are considered to be real property because of their adapted use to the property.

- **R**—*Relationship to the parties*—Emblements are considered the personal property of the tenant, but in the purchase of a farm, emblements could belong to the seller or buyer, depending on what is negotiated.

- **I**—*Intention*—What was the intention of the owner when the item was installed? Did the owner intend for it to remain permanently or to take it when he or she sold the property? (Courts have ruled that this is the most important factor in determining if an item is real or personal property.)

- **A**—*Agreement*—What was the agreement in the sales contract?

NET PROCEEDS ESTIMATION

Seller expenses are determined by custom and will vary from community to community. Figure 1.10 lists *possible expenses* the seller could incur. Chapter 7 will provide practice questions to calculate the net proceeds estimation.

COMPLETION OF LISTING AGREEMENT, PROVISION TO SELLER, EXPLANATION

A **listing agreement** is a personal service contract securing the employment of a brokerage firm to find a ready, willing, and able buyer. Most states require that this agreement be in writing to be enforceable, but in some states oral listings are legal.

The typical listing contracts are exclusive-right-to-sell, exclusive-agency, open, and net. (See Figure 1.11.)

FIGURE 1.10	
Typical Closing Costs for Sellers	Mortgage payoff and outstanding interest
	Prorations for real estate taxes
	Prorations for utility bills, condo dues, and other items paid in arrears
	Closing fees charged by closing agent
	Survey charge
	Transfer tax
	Title policy fees
	Attorney's fees
	Inspection fees
	Brokerage commission
	Other government registration fees
	Other
	Total

FIGURE 1.11	
Types of Listing Agreements	1. **Exclusive-right-to-sell listing**—One broker lists the property and other brokers have the right to sell the property, if there is a cobrokerage arrangement. The listing broker is paid, no matter who sells the property.
	2. **Exclusive-agency listing**—One broker lists the property and the seller retains the right to sell the property. Other brokers may sell the property through a cobrokerage arrangement. If the seller sells the property without the services of a broker, a commission is not due.
	3. **Open listing**—In this agreement, the seller enters into listing agreements with any number of brokerage firms and retains the right to sell the property. The broker that sells the property is paid the commission, but if the seller sells the property, no commission is due any broker.
	4. **Net listing**—This listing does not contain a specified sales price or commission. Net listings are illegal in most states.

Listing agreements normally include the
a. type of listing;
b. broker's authority and responsibilities;
c. names of all parties to the contract;
d. brokerage firm;
e. listing price;
f. real and personal property descriptions;
g. term or length of time of the agreement;
h. commission;
i. termination and default provisions;
j. broker protection or extender clause;
k. warranties by the owner;
l. nondiscrimination wording;
m. antitrust wording;
n. authorizations for subagency or designated agency, use of lockbox, For Sale signs, and so forth;
o. other provisions as provided by state law;
p. signatures of the parties; and
q. unusual deed conditions or restrictions.

Listings may be **terminated** by

a. expiration;
b. fulfillment of the contract;
c. mutual consent or a rescission;
d. abandonment by either party;
e. death of the broker or seller;
f. destruction of the premises; and
g. eminent domain.

If the seller terminates the agency agreement *without cause*, the seller may be liable for the expenses incurred by the broker. The seller may refuse to sell the property even if the full list price is offered. However, the broker would be due a commission under this circumstance.

DETERMINATION THAT PARTIES HOLDING TITLE HAVE SIGNED LISTING AGREEMENT

When scheduling the listing appointment, the agent should ask the sellers for a copy of the deed, which will show who owns the property and has the right to sign the listing agreement. Only a person with the proper legal authority can authorize the sale of the property. Normally, this would be the owner, but it could also include a person with power of attorney, a guardian, a trustee, or a person authorized by the incorporation to sell a corporation's property.

Please note: Upon a divorce, one spouse may use a quitclaim deed to transfer that spouse's ownership to the other party. The quitclaim deed should be recorded, and the divorce decree will contain provisions for the transfer of the property. Should the couple decide to continue to own property after the divorce, both parties would be required to sign the deed. If the deed is in the name of one spouse only, both parties should sign the listing agreement.

SHOWING OF HOUSE AND SAFEGUARDING PROPERTY

When a buyer is interested in seeing a listed property, the appointment is made through the listing brokerage firm. Many brokerage firms have videos or checklists for sellers that include advice on how to make their property more marketable, thus selling faster. The information could include marketing tips on areas such as landscaping, lawn manicuring, painting, repairing the roof, cleaning or replacing carpet, cleaning closets, and renting furniture (if the property is vacant).

Safety guidelines that should be followed when showing a property include pointing out any potentially dangerous physical conditions of the property to the buyer; agents should always be prudent regarding their own personal safety.

The listing agent has duties to safeguard the property. This includes proper management of keys, caring for the property if the owner is out of town for extended periods of time, and recommending that the sellers remove all valuables prior to showing.

METHODS OF MARKETING PROPERTY

The brokerage firm and agent have a variety of media in which to market a listed property:

- Multiple-listing service
- Yard sign
- Brokerage Web site
- Virtual tours
- Classified advertising
- Property information sheet
- Agent Web site
- Public open house and company tour

- Direct mail or e-mail to past clients, customers, and neighbors
- Internet advertising
- Display advertising
- Broker open house
- Property Web site
- Radio and TV commercials
- Home book or magazine

Many states require that all listed property be advertised through the broker. This includes an exclusive-listing contract.

PRESENTATION OF OFFERS TO THE SELLER

To *offer* means to put forward for acceptance, rejection, or consideration. In real estate, an offer demonstrates the *intention* to enter into a contract. *An offer does not become a contract unless it is accepted without changes*. The party making the offer is the *offeror*, and the party receiving the offer is the *offeree*.

The terms of the offer must be clear and definite and typically will state a time period for acceptance. *An offer can be revoked at any time before acceptance.* Notice of revocation by the offeree, death of either party, insanity of either party, or a counteroffer will terminate an offer.

A change in terms voids the offer, and a **counteroffer** is created. The legal positions of the parties are reversed; that is, the offeror becomes the offeree and the offeree becomes the offeror.

In real estate, *unless there is a specific direction otherwise from the seller*, all offers are presented to the seller. Until the seller signs the offer there is no legally binding contract. It is also wise to note the time of the acceptance in writing. If state laws permit facsimile or electronic contracts, those laws should be followed regarding the acceptance and delivery of the contract.

Because a listing contract is considered an employment contract, if the seller is offered the full list price of the property and does not accept the offer, a commission is still due the broker. The duties of finding a ready, willing, and able buyer were fulfilled.

TRANSACTION FILES

State law determines how long transaction files must be kept by the brokerage firm. Generally, these documents include the listing contract, sales contract, property disclosure form, agency and/or dual disclosure form, inspection reports, HUD-1 settlement statement, and any other document that is a part of the transaction. Parties should *immediately* receive a copy of any document that is signed.

DEED RESTRICTIONS AND COVENANTS

Deed restrictions are provisions placed in deeds to control the future uses of the property. The restriction may be either a deed *condition* or a deed *covenant*.

A **condition** creates a conditional fee estate, which means that if the condition is breached, the title may revert to the grantor or the grantor's heirs. Deed restrictions normally "run with the land," meaning they transfer from one owner to the next.

A **covenant** is a promise between two or more parties in which they agree to perform or not to perform specified acts on the property. Restrictive covenants set the standards for all the parcels within a defined subdivision. These restrictions are available in public records, so any potential buyer has the right to review them before purchasing a property. If a deed covenant is breached, there can be a suit for money damages or injunctive relief.

Deed restrictions may be found in the deed, in the subdivision rules and regulations created by the developer or the homeowners' association of a condominium community. Private restrictions may also be placed on the property by the owner, and these restrictions would be found in the deed. (The word private means the property owner, not the builder-developer or other legal entity.) These restrictions may be enforced by other property owners, the developer, or the homeowners' association. Any unusual deed restrictions should be included in the listing contract.

FORMS OF OWNERSHIP INTERESTS IN REAL ESTATE

An **estate in land** refers to a party's legal interests or rights to a property. *To be an estate, an interest must be possessory or may become possessory in the future*, and the ownership is measured in *terms of duration*. Estates in land can be freehold or nonfreehold. Freehold estates include fee simple estates and life estates. (See Figure 1.12.) A freehold estate is considered to exist for an *uncertain duration* because no one really knows how long that person is going to own the property. (For the right amount of money, would you sell today?)

Nonfreehold estates include **leasehold estates**, which are usually based on calendar time.

A lease with a definite duration is an *estate for years*. A leasehold estate also can be for an uncertain duration, such as a *tenancy at will*. Leasehold estates are discussed on page 82.

FIGURE 1.12

Freehold Estates

Fee Simple Estates

1. Fee Simple Absolute
   A. The highest form of ownership that the law recognizes
   B. Ownership is for an indefinite duration
   C. Ownership is freely transferable
   D. It is an inheritable estate
2. Fee Simple Defeasible
   A. Special Limitation with Possibility of Reverter
      a. Title transfers "so long as" the property is used for a particular purpose.
      b. There is automatic reversion to the grantor or the grantor's heirs if the land ceases to be used for that purpose.
      c. The possibility of reverter is the possible future interest the grantor's heir(s) could have if the property ceases to be used for that purpose.
   B. Condition Subsequent with Right of Reentry
      a. Title is transferred "on the condition that" there is an activity that the grantee must not perform.
      b. The grantors must take legal steps to get the property back.
      c. The right of reentry is the possible future interest of the grantor.

Life Estates

1. Conventional Life Estate
   A. Ordinary with Remainder or Reversion
      a. Set up by a grantor.
      b. Life tenant has full use and enjoyment of property for tenant's life.
      c. Property reverts to grantor on the death of the life tenant (reversion).
      d. Property is transferred to the remainderman or a party other than the grantor.
   B. Life Estate Pur Autre Vie with Remainder or Reversion
      a. Set up by grantor but based on the life of a third party. *A* conveys title to *B*, based on the life of *C*.
      b. Should *B* predecease *C*, *B*'s heirs would have a life estate interest in the property as long as *C* is alive.
      c. Property reverts to *A* (grantor) on the death of the person by whose life it is measured.
      d. Property may transfer to *D*, a remainderman.
2. Legal Life Estates—Set Up by Law
   A. Dower—A wife's interests in her husband's property
   B. Curtesy—A husband's interests in his wife's property
   C. Homestead—A portion of the value of the real estate is protected from unsecured creditors

---

An *interest in land* may not be an estate. For example, an easement is an interest in land, but it is not an estate because it does not allow for possession of the property.

The three basic types of ownership in real estate are *severalty*, *co-ownership*, and *trust*. (See Figure 1.13.) Because the interpretation of these forms of ownership varies from state to state, specific questions regarding ownership should be directed to an attorney.

Issues Related to Conveyance of Real Property Trust

A *deed in trust* or *trust* is established to manage a property for an owner. The three parties in a trust agreement are the **trustor** (grantor), who conveys property into the trust; the **trustee** (holds legal title and manages the property); and the **beneficiary** (party benefiting from the trust). Trusts are usually established as an estate-planning tool to maintain privacy, avoid probate, and limit estate taxes. Laws regarding setting up a trust vary from state to state, and an attorney should be consulted to establish the trust. If the trust is established during the lifetime of the owner, it is known as a *living trust*. A trust established by will or after the death of the owner is known as a **testamentary trust**.

FIGURE 1.13

Types of Ownership

Characteristic	Tenancy in Severalty	Tenancy in Common	Joint Tenancy	Tenancy by the Entirety
Number of Owners	One person or legal entity	Two or more	Two or more with right of survivorship	Husband and wife only; law presumes they are one
Title	One title	Each co-owner has separate legal title to that co-owner's undivided interest	One title	One title
Interest	100% ownership	Shares may be unequal; law will interpret them as equal unless stipulated otherwise	Shares must be equal	Each owns 100% of the property
Conveyance	Yes, to whomever the owner stipulates	Yes, without the consent of the other owners	Yes, without the consent of the other owners	When both owners agree
Right to Partition	Not necessary; there are no co-owners	Yes	Yes	No
Status on Death	Passes to heir(s) or devisees(s)	Passes to heir(s) or devisees(s)	Passes to surviving owners	When one spouse dies, the other spouse owns it in severalty
Probate Necessary	Yes, if there is a will	Yes, if there is a will	No	No
Unities	Possession Interest Time Title	Possession	Possession Interest Time Title	Possession Interest Time Title Person
Termination	By sale or death of the owner	By sale or death of the owner	When any of the unities are broken	By consent of the parties; death of either party; or on divorce/ common ownership

Community Property

In **community property** states the laws are based on the idea that a wife and husband are *equal partners* in a marriage. Thus, any property acquired during the marriage is deemed to have been obtained by mutual effort. Listings, deeds, and mortgages require the signatures of both spouses.

When a spouse dies, the surviving spouse automatically owns one half of the community property, and the other half of the estate is inherited by the decedent's heirs.

Separate Property

Separate property includes not only property owned by either spouse before marriage but also property inherited during marriage or received by gift. Separate property can be sold or mortgaged without the signature or permission of the non-owning spouse.

Partnership

A **partnership** is an association of two or more persons who establish a business for profit as co-owners. A *general partner* is personally liable for business losses and obligations and is responsible for the operation and management of the business.

A *limited (passive) partner* is liable for business losses only to the extent of that partnership investment. A limited partner does not participate in the operation of the business.

Many states have adopted in whole or in part the *Uniform Partnership Act*, which provides that realty may be held in the name of the partnership. It also establishes the legality of the limited partnership form of ownership and provides that realty may be held in the name of the limited partnership.

A **suit for partition** is filed to break up a joint tenancy or tenancy in common ownership. This may be done by dividing the property, but if necessary the court will order a sale and divide the proceeds from the sale.

Condominiums

Condominium ownership is a way of owning real estate that blends severalty and tenancy in common ownership. (See Figure 1.14.) In a condo, the air space of the unit is owned in severalty, and there is shared ownership of the common areas.

- A *master deed* conveys the land to condominium use.

- The *declaration* allows the developer to create a condo community.

- *Bylaws* govern the operation of the homeowners association, which manages the community.

- Each condo owner must pay a *maintenance fee* for the expenses of managing the community. A lien can be placed against individual units, which may be foreclosed if this fee is not paid.

- *Special assessments* are improvements to the property that are not covered by the maintenance fee and must be paid by the owners.

- Each unit owner has a fractional undivided interest in the common areas and facilities.

- Areas outside the individual's condo are known as *common areas* or *elements* and are owned and used by everyone in the community.

- *Limited* common areas, such as a designated parking space, can be used only by the individual with the right to do so.

FIGURE 1.14

Condominium Ownership

The owner of unit 4 owns his or her unit, plus an undivided one-fifth share of the elevator, lobby, grounds, and structure.

Elevator

5
4
3
2
1

Grounds

Lobby

Condominium

Cooperative

- In **cooperative** ownership, a corporation holds title to the property.

- The purchasers (tenants) of the cooperative receive shares of **stock** in the corporation and a **proprietary lease** that grants occupancy of a specific unit in the building.

- Cooperative tenants *do not own real estate* and will pay a maintenance fee to cover a prorated share of the mortgage payment, property taxes, insurance, and maintenance.

- A co-op owner has the tax benefits that arise from the owner's share of the mortgage interest and property taxes paid on the property.

- A cooperative interest can be sold, but the new lessee must meet the qualifications of the co-op before the stock and lease can be transferred.

- If one owner fails to pay a maintenance fee to the cooperative, then the other co-op owners are responsible for the payment. If the mortgage payment is not made by the cooperative, the *entire building* can be foreclosed on.

- A co-op tenant may be *evicted* for nonpayment of the monthly fee or for not following the rules and regulations.

Time-Shares

A time-share is also known as **interval ownership** because the buyer of a **time-share estate** receives a deed for the property that allows possession for an allotted time each year.

The buyer of a **time-share use** has the *right to occupy* the property and use the facilities for a certain number of years. The developer retains ownership to the property, and when the specified time has expired, all interest reverts to the owner.

Town House or Row House

A town house or row house is an attached single-family dwelling normally with two floors. Owners of a town house purchase their residential structure and the land underlying the structure. The surrounding land, including sidewalks, open spaces, and recreational facilities, is owned in common with other members of the community.

Conversion is the procession of changing one form of ownership to another, such as converting an apartment building to a condominium.

Many town house developments are **planned unit developments**. A planned unit development is designed for a high density of dwellings and a maximum use of open space.

FAIR HOUSING LAWS

The *Civil Rights Act of 1866* was the first law written to prohibit discrimination based on race. The law reads:

> All citizens of the United States shall have the same right in every state and terri-tory as is enjoyed by white citizens thereof to inherit, purchase, lease, sell, hold, and convey real and personal property.

Currently, the federal Fair Housing Act prohibits discrimination based on *race, color, religion, sex, national origin, familial status*, and *disability*.

Many state laws are stricter than the federal regulations, and a licensee should be aware that failure to comply with these laws is a criminal act and grounds for disciplinary action.

The **federal Fair Housing Act** regulates the sale or rental of residential dwellings and any vacant land offered for sale for residential construction or use. The follow-ing actions have been found to be discriminatory:

- *Refusing* to sell, rent, negotiate, or deal with a person, or telling a person that a dwelling is not available for inspection, sale, or rent when it is

- *Changing or misrepresenting* the terms or services for buying or leasing housing

- Discriminating through any statement or *advertisement* that indicates a pref-erence for a certain race, color, sex, familial status, religion, national origin, or disability (See Figure 1.15)

- *Blockbusting*, or panic peddling, which means *inducing owners* to sell or rent now because minority groups are moving into the neighborhood

- *Steering* or channeling, which is *directing buyers* into or out of certain neighborhoods

■ *Denying or altering any terms* or conditions for a loan to purchase, construct, repair, or improve a dwelling

■ *Limiting or denying membership* in any real estate organization, such as the MLS or any other facilities related to the selling or renting of housing

■ Any act considered *intimidation or influence* by using fear, such as threatening or evicting a tenant who filed a complaint against the management for possible discriminatory acts

■ *Charging higher rents* and *higher deposits* to families with children

■ Deliberately *slowing down the processing* of a contract to hinder the sale or lease of a property

■ *Recording racially restrictive covenants* in order to screen out minorities

■ *Checking the credit* of a member of a minority group only

■ *Eviction* of tenants because of interracial marriage

■ *Appraisal reports* that state that population transitions are illegal

■ *Failure to display the equal housing opportunity poster*

■ *Redlining,* the practice of lenders refusing to negotiate loans in certain geographic areas, even when the borrower qualifies

FIGURE 1.15

HUD's Advertising Guidelines

Characteristic	Rule	Permitted	Not Permitted
Race Color National Origin	No discriminatory limitation/preference may be expressed	"master bedroom" "good neighborhood"	"White neighborhood" "no French"
Religion	No religious preference/limitation	"chapel on premises" "kosher meals available" "Merry Christmas"	"no Muslims" "nice Christian family" "near great Catholic school"
Sex	No explicit preference based on sex	"mother-in-law suite" "master bedroom" "female roommate sought"	"great house for a man" "wife's dream kitchen"
Disability	No exclusions or limitations based on handicap	"wheelchair ramp" "walk to shopping"	"no wheelchairs" "able-bodied tenants only"
Familial Status	No preference or limitation based on family size or nature	"two-bedroom" "family room" "quiet neighborhood"	"married couple only" "no more than two children" "retiree's dream house"
Photographs or Illustrations of People	People should be clearly representative and nonexclusive	Illustrations showing ethnic races, family groups, singles, etc.	Illustrations showing only singles, African American families, elderly white adults, etc.

Familial Status

Familial status protects the head of a household from discrimination when the head of household is responsible for a minor child or children and includes protection for a pregnant woman.

Unless exempt, a landlord cannot say "no children." The prospective tenant may be rejected if the number of people occupying the apartment exceeds occupancy codes.

The **exemptions** to the familial status law are any housing occupied or intended to be occupied solely by persons aged 62 or older; or if 80 percent of the units are occupied by someone 55 years of age or older, the building is exempt.

Exemptions to the Federal Fair Housing Act

The sale or rental of a single-family home is exempt if

- an owner who is not occupying the home has only one sale in 24 months;

- no more than three homes are owned at any one time;

- the services of a broker or any other person who is engaged in the business of selling or leasing real estate are not used; and

- no discriminatory advertising is used.

Other exemptions include the following:

- A one- to four-family dwelling is exempt if the owner occupies one of the units, no discriminatory advertising is used, and no agent is used.

- A nonprofit religious organization can discriminate on a religious basis only. Membership in that religious organization cannot be discriminatory.

- A nonprofit private club may restrict rentals or occupancy of lodgings to members only. Membership in the nonprofit private club, such as the YMCA, cannot be discriminatory.

There are *no exemptions* to the Civil Rights Act of 1866 and there are *no limits* to punitive damages against those found guilty of discrimination because of race. *Jones v. Mayer* is a 1968 Supreme Court case that upheld the Civil Rights Act of 1866.

Complaints of violations of the federal Fair Housing Act may be filed with the Department of Housing and Urban Development (HUD) or taken directly to a federal district court. Action also may be taken by the attorney general of the United States. An aggrieved party or the secretary of HUD must file a complaint *within one year* of the discriminatory act.

Penalties include

■ a fine of up to $100,000 and imprisonment for up to one year for failure to attend or provide testimony at a hearing or failure to answer lawful inquiries;

■ a fine of up to $11,000 for the first offense, up to $27,500 for the second offense within five years of the filing date of the complaint, and up to $55,000 for the third offense within seven years;

■ a fine of up to $1,000 and/or up to one year in jail for intimidation; and

■ a fine of up to $10,000 and/or up to 10 years in jail for bodily injury; for death, the penalty can be any jail term up to life.

Affirmative Marketing

An affirmative marketing program is designed to inform all buyers in a minority community of the homes for sale without discrimination. The purpose of affirmative marketing is to encourage the integration of minority groups into housing.

APPRAISING

When listing a property, an agent will develop a comparative market analysis (CMA) to help the seller determine the "fair market value" of the property. The CMA is developed by finding and analyzing recent sales of comparable properties that have sold in the recent past. Comparable sales are also used by an appraiser to calculate the value, or the present worth of future benefits.

An **appraisal** is the process of developing and communicating an objective opinion of an *estimate* of a property's **market value**. (See Figure 1.16.) The *market value* is the most **probable price** a buyer will pay for the property in an arm's-length transaction. That is, a transaction wherein the buyer doesn't have to buy, the seller doesn't have to sell, both have a knowledge of the market, and there is no other relationship between them (such as being relatives). **Market price** is the actual selling price of the property. **Cost** is the actual dollars spent to produce an asset. Value, price, and cost could be the same, but they are usually different.

Appraisal Terms

The principles of value that an appraiser will use in the appraisal process are the following:

■ **Competition**—the interaction of supply and demand wherein excess profits attract competition

■ **Conformity**—the maximum value is achieved when the property is in harmony with its surroundings

■ **Contribution**—the value of any part of the property is measured by its effect on the value of the whole

■ **Highest and best use**—the most reasonable, probable, and profitable use of the property

■ **Increasing returns**—when money spent on an improvement increases the property value

■ **Decreasing returns**—when adding improvements to the land does not produce a proportional increase in property values

■ **Plottage**—the value that is created when two or more tracts of land are merged into a single, larger one; **assemblage** is the process of merging the parcels of real estate

■ **Progression**—the value of a modest home will increase if it is surrounded by larger, more expensive properties

■ **Regression**—a larger, more expensive home will be adversely affected if it is surrounded by smaller, more modest homes

■ **Substitution**—the foundation for all approaches to appraising; the maximum value of a property tends to be set by the cost of purchasing an equal substitute property

■ **Supply and demand**—the amount of goods available in the market to be sold and the demand or need for the good

---

FIGURE 1.16

Approaches to Appraising

1. **Name: Sales Comparison Approach**
   Used to Appraise: Residential Property; Vacant Land
   Also Known As: Market Data Approach; Direct Sales Comparison
   Description: The value of subject property is determined by comparing it with at least three comparable properties that have recently sold.
   - ■ **SBA—Subject Better Add**—If the subject property has an amenity the comparable does not, add the value of the amenity to the comparable property.
   - ■ **CBS—Comparable Better Subtract**—If the comparable property has an amenity the subject does not, subtract the value of the amenity from the comparable property.

2. **Name: Income Approach**
   Used to Appraise: Investment or Income-Producing Property
   Also Known As: Capitalization
   Description: The appraiser capitalizes or determines the present net worth of future benefits or income the property will generate.

3. **Name: Cost Approach**
   Used to Appraise: Special Purpose Properties: Houses of worship, libraries, new properties used at their highest and best use
   Also Known As: Replacement or Cost Estimate
   Description: The value of the improvement is computed using the reproduction or replacement cost. The **reproduction cost** is the dollar amount required to construct an exact duplicate of the subject property. **Replacement cost** is the dollar amount required to construct improvements of equal utility using current materials. Land value is determined by the sales comparison approach to appraising.

See Chapter 7, Math Review, for the formulas for each of the above approaches.

DUST is the acronym to help you remember the four elements of value.

D—*Demand* is the number of properties (goods) that people are willing and able to buy at a given price.

U—*Utility* asks the question, "How has the land and improvement been utilized?" (A one-bedroom home versus a three-bedroom home.)

S—*Scarcity* means that when the supply is limited, the price will increase.

T—*Transferability* means that there must be a good and marketable title to the property.

The steps in the appraisal process:

1. State the problem.

2. List the data needed and the sources.

3. Gather, record, and verify the necessary data.

4. Determine the highest and best use.

5. Estimate the land value.

6. Estimate the value by the three approaches.

7. Reconcile the estimate of value received from the direct sales comparison, cost, and income approaches to arrive at a final value estimate for the subject property.

8. Report the final value estimate.

NEED FOR INDEPENDENT APPRAISAL

When an agent lists a property with unusual circumstances, an independent appraisal should be recommended. For example, there has been major growth in a community within the past three years. The agent is listing a 100-acre farm surrounded by this growth. There are no comparable properties, so determining the highest and best use of the farm requires an appraisal.

Also, some sellers may seek an independent appraisal before a property is listed because they want to know the estimated value before contacting an agent. This could happen if the property has historic value.

INSPECTION NECESSITY

Listing agents should inform owners of residential property built prior to 1978 of the necessity of a lead-based paint disclosure statement; provide property disclosure statements if required by state law; inform the seller that the buyer may want a third-party inspection; and inform the seller that lenders will require an appraisal and may require a pest inspection.

Buyers or lenders may also require radon, arsenic, or other environmental inspections.

Buyers' agents should recommend that the offer to purchase include a contingency for the buyers to have their own property inspector provide an independent analysis of the property. The contingency should be specific regarding the status of the contract and the return of the earnest money based on the outcome of the property inspection.

NONOWNERSHIP INTERESTS IN REAL PROPERTY

Agents should be aware of nonownership interests in real property. Examples would be easements, leases, and licenses, which are discussed in other sections of this review.

QUESTIONS

1. All of the following are true about condominiums EXCEPT
   A. a declaration must be filed before any units may be sold.
   B. each unit owner has a fractional undivided interest in the common areas and facilities.
   C. each owner usually receives a separate tax statement.
   D. each owner has a proprietary lease with the association covering the unit.

2. Horace owns a lot and, in writing, gives his neighbor, Martha, the right to use his driveway to reach Martha's garage. What is Martha's interest or right called?
   A. Lease
   B. Easement
   C. Encroachment
   D. Prescriptive right

3. Victor receives possession of property under a deed that states that he shall own the property so long as the present building standing on the property is not torn down. The type of estate Victor holds is which of the following?
   A. Life estate
   B. Nondestructible estate
   C. Fee simple estate
   D. Special limitation with possibility of reverter

4. The owner of property located along the banks of a stream or river MOST LIKELY has water rights known as
   A. littoral rights.
   B. reliction rights.
   C. riparian rights.
   D. avulsions.

5. How many acres are in a description reading "The NW¼ of the SE¼ and the S½ of the SW¼ of the NE¼ of Section 4"?
   A. 40 acres
   B. 50 acres
   C. 60 acres
   D. 80 acres

6. Which of the following BEST describes a legal life estate?
   A. Homestead estate
   B. Estate conveyed by one party to a second party for the second party's life
   C. Estate created by will
   D. Estate conveyed to a second party subject to a condition

7. In the sale of a time-share
   A. the selling broker must be a licensed security broker.
   B. each of the owners of the unit has the right to occupy it for a specific period each year.
   C. the seller is the vendee.
   D. the selling agent must be an employee of the developer.

8. All of the following are false regarding a property that is held by tenancy by the entirety EXCEPT
   A. the cotenants must be husband and wife.
   B. the property in question must be Torrens property.
   C. on the death of a cotenant, the decedent's interest passes to his or her heirs.
   D. in the event of a dispute, the property must be partitioned.

9. All of the following are false regarding a community property state EXCEPT
   A. the property that a person accumulated prior to marriage is called *separate property*.
   B. the property that a person received as a gift during marriage is known as *community property*.
   C. all property owned by a married person is called *community property*.
   D. the property paid for by the earnings of one spouse during marriage is known as *separate property*.

10. The cost approach would MOST LIKELY be used to appraise a
    A. single-family home.
    B. 20-unit apartment building.
    C. condominium.
    D. house of worship.

11. Broker Carl obtained an exclusive-agency listing from Rochelle Green. The broker would NOT be entitled to a commission if
    A. Carl sold the property himself.
    B. the property were sold through another broker.
    C. the property were sold through the multiple-listing service.
    D. the seller sold the property to a neighbor across the street who had her property listed with another broker.

12. Mr. and Mrs. Singleton signed a listing agreement with Agent Carl of Redford Realty. Under a standard listing agreement, the brokerage duties would require the performance of all the following duties EXCEPT
    A. market and advertise the property.
    B. use due diligence to find a ready, willing, and able buyer.
    C. present offers to the seller.
    D. prepare title for closing.

13. Which of the following is NOT associated with fee simple absolute ownership?
    A. It is an inheritable estate.
    B. The estate is freely transferable.
    C. It is the highest ownership recognized by law.
    D. The right of reentry can only be acquired by an heir.

14. Depreciation is said to be incurable if it
    A. is economically feasible to correct.
    B. affects only the land, but not the improvements.
    C. affects only the improvements, but not the land.
    D. is not economically feasible to correct.

15. Suzie just purchased a condominium. Which of the following statements is MOST LIKELY true regarding her ownership?
    A. Suzie owns her airspace in severalty and holds a tenancy in common ownership in the common areas.
    B. Suzie owns her condo in a fee simple defeasible estate and holds a joint tenancy ownership in the common areas.
    C. Suzie's ownership is in the airspace and subsurface space only.
    D. Suzie's ownership is held as a conventional life estate.

16. When a developer subdivides a tract of land for a subdivision, the developer must record which of the following in the county courthouse where the property is located?
    A. Plat map
    B. Listing contract
    C. Sales contract
    D. Benchmarks

17. A house with outdated plumbing is suffering from
    A. functional obsolescence.
    B. curable physical deterioration.
    C. incurable physical deterioration.
    D. external depreciation.

18. Agent Brayden listed the property of an 85-year-old who is selling because health issues require her to move into an assisted living facility. He is now acting as a dual agent, and the buyers have asked why the owner is selling. Can Brayden disclose this information to the buyers?
    A. Yes, it is permissible because he is a dual agent.
    B. Yes, if his broker gives permission.
    C. No, because it is confidential information and could reduce the negotiating position of the seller.
    D. No, because the buyers have no right to know anything about the seller.

19. A real estate listing contract is created when it has been signed by which of the following parties?
    A. Buyer
    B. Buyer and seller
    C. Seller
    D. Broker and seller

20. Which of the following is a protected class under the federal Fair Housing Act?
    A. Age
    B. Marital status
    C. Military status
    D. National origin

21. The buyers took possession of the property 30 days after closing. The 300-gallon aquarium that had been attached to the family room wall was missing. The wall had not been repaired. Under these circumstances is the aquarium real property?
    A. No, because all aquariums, no matter how large, are personal property.
    B. No, because it was movable.
    C. Yes, because the sellers took it with them.
    D. Yes, because the method of annexation caused damage when the aquarium was removed.

22. When a buyer records a deed to a property, the buyer is giving
    A. actual notice.
    B. notary notice.
    C. constructive notice.
    D. agency notice.

23. The MAJOR DIFFERENCE between a latent defect and a patent defect is that a
    A. latent defect is found by inspection, while a patent defect is a hidden defect.
    B. latent defect must be disclosed in a listing contract, while a patent defect is found in a property disclosure statement.
    C. latent defect is a hidden defect, while a patent defect is found by inspection.
    D. latent defect need not be disclosed, but all patent defects must be disclosed.

24. Which of the following is exempt under the federal Fair Housing Act?
    A. A real estate agent or broker selling the agent's own home is exempt if the property is not listed with a brokerage firm.
    B. An owner not occupying a duplex is exempt when the owner refuses to rent to a potential tenant because of race.
    C. A private club operating a senior citizens home for profit is exempt.
    D. A religious organization is exempt if it gives preference to its members in leasing church-owned property, as long as discrimination does not occur in becoming a member of the organization.

25. A conventional life tenant has the right to
    A. devise the life estate.
    B. commit waste to the property.
    C. sell, mortgage, or lease the life estate.
    D. refuse to pay property taxes.

26. Mr. Homeowner has given a company the right to erect a billboard on his property. Mr. Homeowner has MOST LIKELY given a(n)
    A. implied easement.
    B. easement appurtenant.
    C. prescriptive easement.
    D. gross easement.

27. Sam, Pam, and Jerome are joint tenants. Sam sells his interest to Joyce. How is the ownership now held?
    A. Pam, Jerome, and Joyce are joint tenants.
    B. Pam, Jerome, and Joyce are tenants in common.
    C. Pam and Jerome are joint tenants, and Joyce is a tenant in common with them.
    D. Pam and Joyce are joint tenants, and Jerome is a tenant in common with them.

28. John, Paul, and David decided to enter into a partnership. John is the general partner. This means
    A. his liability is limited to the money he has invested.
    B. all three are personally liable.
    C. Paul and David are personally liable.
    D. John is personally liable.

29. A seller would like to retain the right to sell his property while listing it with only one real estate brokerage firm. The seller should execute a(n)
   A. exclusive-right-to-sell listing.
   B. open listing.
   C. net listing.
   D. exclusive-agency listing.

30. When personal property that is used in a business is attached to real estate by the tenant, the personal property would MOST LIKELY
   A. belong to the landlord until the lease expires.
   B. belong to the tenant if removed before the lease expires.
   C. automatically become real property.
   D. stay with the property under any circumstances.

31. Jackie, Karen, and Laura own property as joint tenants. Laura dies and her property interest will be
   A. inherited by her heirs if she had a will.
   B. devised to her heirs if she died intestate.
   C. bequeathed to Jackie and Karen in her will.
   D. automatically conveyed to Jackie and Karen.

32. An agent involved in conducting a single business transaction under detailed instructions of a principal is considered a(n)
   A. general agent.
   B. special agent.
   C. implied agent.
   D. universal agent.

33. Which of the following would NOT be an encumbrance to property?
   A. Fence that is four feet across the boundary line
   B. Foreclosure suit
   C. Utility easement
   D. License

34. All of the following would affect the value of a property EXCEPT
   A. title insurance.
   B. situs.
   C. zoning.
   D. location.

35. Linda and Brad just got married and purchased their first home. They MOST LIKELY own the property
   A. as tenants in common.
   B. in severalty.
   C. in joint tenancy.
   D. in tenancy by the entirety.

36. Which form of ownership does NOT allow the right of partition?
   A. Tenancy in severalty
   B. Tenancy in common
   C. Joint tenancy
   D. Tenancy by the entirety

37. A broker would NOT have to prove that she was the procuring cause of the sale in which of the following listing agreements?
   A. Exclusive-agency listing
   B. All-inclusive listing
   C. Open listing
   D. Exclusive-right-to-sell listing

38. All of the following are true regarding an exclusive-right-to-sell listing EXCEPT
   A. an exclusive-right-to-sell listing usually contains provisions for cobrokerage.
   B. the contract may be terminated with liability.
   C. the seller can withdraw the contract at any time without liability.
   D. if the seller sells the property, a commission is still due.

39. Which of the following is necessary to create an estate in land?
   A. A valid deed must be conveyed to create an estate in land.
   B. A certificate of title must be issued to create an estate in land.
   C. A certificate of occupancy must be issued to create an estate in land.
   D. An interest must be possessory or may become possessory in the future to create an estate in land.

40. Yvonne gave a life estate to Mindy based on the life of Jayne and named Jodi as the remainder. This legal arrangement is BEST described as a(n)
    A. life estate.
    B. estate for years.
    C. legal life estate.
    D. life estate pur autre vie.

41. An appraiser who takes into consideration the reproduction cost of a building and then considers depreciation is MOST LIKELY using the
    A. cost approach.
    B. market approach.
    C. income approach.
    D. gross rent multiplier approach.

42. When making adjustments in the comparison of properties under the market data approach, which of the following is TRUE?
    A. If the subject is inferior, no adjustment is made in the comparable.
    B. If the comparable is inferior, an adjustment is made by subtracting from the comparable.
    C. If the comparable is superior, an adjustment is made by subtracting from the comparable.
    D. If the subject is superior, no adjustment is made in the comparable.

43. If a vacant city lot is to be listed, what would be the BEST way to describe the property in a listing contract?
    A. Lot and block
    B. Metes and bounds
    C. Street address
    D. Monument

44. All of the following are public controls of land use and development EXCEPT
    A. zoning.
    B. building codes.
    C. health and safety codes.
    D. deed covenants.

45. Which of the following would NOT be associated with life estates?
    A. Reversion
    B. Pur autre vie
    C. Possibility of reverter
    D. Remainder

46. The NW¼ of the SE¼ of the NE¼ and the S½ of the NE¼ contains how many acres of land?
    A. 10
    B. 60
    C. 90
    D. 80

47. The law that states that "All citizens of the United States shall have the same right in every state and territory as is enjoyed by white citizens thereof to inherit, purchase, lease, sell, hold and convey real and personal property" is
    A. President John Kennedy's executive order.
    B. the Civil Rights Act of 1964.
    C. the Civil Rights Act of 1866.
    D. Title VIII of the Civil Rights Act of 1968.

48. All of the following could be used by a real estate agent in helping a seller determine the value of a property EXCEPT
    A. a comparative market analysis.
    B. gross living area.
    C. private mortgage insurance.
    D. an independent appraisal.

49. Which of the following encumbrances would affect the use of a property?
    A. Easement
    B. Mortgage lien
    C. Judgment
    D. Tax lien

50. Which of the following is NOT an unlawful practice?
    A. Refusing to sell, rent, or negotiate with any person or otherwise make a dwelling unavailable
    B. Displaying the Equal Housing Opportunity Poster and providing all clients and customers with pertinent information in a transaction
    C. Altering the terms or conditions for a loan for the purchase, construction, improvement, or repair of a dwelling for a protected class
    D. Representing that a property is not available for sale or rent when in fact it is

51. All of the following are freehold estates that are inheritable EXCEPT a
    A. fee simple defeasible estate.
    B. fee simple absolute estate.
    C. special limitation estate.
    D. conventional life estate.

52. All of the following are associated with personal property EXCEPT
    A. chattels.
    B. personalty.
    C. bundle of legal rights.
    D. emblements.

53. A seller listed a property with ABC Realty. The broker for XYZ Realty has the legal right to contact the seller. ABC Realty MOST LIKELY has entered into a(n)
    A. net listing.
    B. open listing.
    C. exclusive listing.
    D. exclusive-right-to-sell listing.

54. The process of changing a building from an apartment to a condominium is known as
    A. conformity.
    B. conditional use.
    C. contingency ownership.
    D. conversion.

55. A person whose maintenance fee includes her portion of the mortgage payment, property taxes, insurance, and maintenance of the property MOST LIKELY owns a
    A. condominium.
    B. single-family home.
    C. duplex.
    D. cooperative.

56. Mr. and Mrs. Trapp sign an exclusive-right-to-sell listing that will expire in 4 months. Three weeks later it is determined they are not being transferred and they no longer want to sell their property. Can the listing be terminated?
    A. No, they signed an exclusive-right-to-sell listing and it cannot be terminated.
    B. No, the listing cannot be terminated because it is for 4 months.
    C. Yes, the listing can be terminated if the agent agrees.
    D. Yes, the listing can be terminated by mutual consent.

57. Upon the review of a survey the agent found a billboard easement, a utility easement, and a pipeline easement. These are examples of
    A. appurtenant easements.
    B. prescriptive easements.
    C. gross easements.
    D. easements by necessity.

58. Mr. and Mrs. Muething just purchased ocean-front property. The water rights attached to the property are
    A. accretion rights.
    B. reliction rights.
    C. riparian rights.
    D. littoral rights.

59. Which of the following statements regarding the lead-based paint disclosure is FALSE?
    A. The disclosure must be given when selling or leasing a residential property constructed prior to 1978.
    B. Tenants must be given ten days in which to conduct an inspection and they may waive this right.
    C. Purchasers or tenants must be given a lead hazard pamphlet.
    D. Purchasers or tenants must be given reports regarding a prior test for lead.

60. Which of the following would NOT terminate a listing agreement?
    A. Destruction of the premises
    B. Death of the sales agent
    C. Eminent domain
    D. Expiration

61. John, an agent of KMK Realty, listed his neighbor's house. Peggy also an agent of KMK Realty, secured the buyer for John's neighbor. The broker assigned John to be the exclusive agent for the seller and Peggy to be the exclusive agent for the buyer. John and Peggy are
    A. universal agents.
    B. attorneys-in-fact.
    C. dual agents.
    D. designated agents.

62. Which of the following would NOT be associated with the government survey?
    A. NW¼ of the NE¼ of the SW¼
    B. S16°E
    C. Meridians and base lines
    D. Fractional sections

63. Agent Pod has helped Mr. Cox purchase investment property for 10 years. Mr. Cox will be out of the country for the summer and has left Agent Pod in charge of the investment properties. Agent Pod is probably a(n)
    A. universal agent.
    B. special agent.
    C. general agent.
    D. designated agent.

64. The MAJOR DIFFERENCE between an appurtenance and an encumbrance is
    A. an appurtenance must be intangible; an encumbrance must be tangible.
    B. an appurtenance is attached to the deed; an encumbrance is attached to the land.
    C. an appurtenance may be tangible or intangible and is attached to the land or deed; an encumbrance is a claim or liability that affects the value or use of the property.
    D. an appurtenance may be tangible or intangible and can only be created by the current owner of the property; an encumbrance is a claim or liability that can be created by anyone.

65. Roger gave a life estate to his mother and named Brian as remainderman. Two years later, his mother sold the property to Jayce. Can Roger's mother legally transfer the property to Jayce?
    A. Yes, but the transfer would only be valid as long as Roger was alive.
    B. Yes, but the transfer would only be valid as long as Brian was alive.
    C. Yes, but the transfer would only be valid as long as Jayce was alive.
    D. Yes, but the transfer would only be valid as long as the mother is alive.

66. Bonnie, Brenda, and James co-own property. When Bonnie dies, her 50 percent interest passes to Brenda and James. Is this transference possible?
    A. Yes, if Bonnie left the property to Brenda and James in her will.
    B. Yes, if they owned the property as joint tenants.
    C. No, because property can never be left to co-owners.
    D. No, because Bonnie died testate.

67. Mr. and Mrs. Dennis made an offer of $500,000 on a property that was accepted by the seller. The sellers moved out on July 15, and the closing was to take place on July 31. On July 30, they met their agent at the property for a final inspection. When the agent opened the front door, they discovered three inches of water on the hardwood floors and mold covering the walls. Do Mr. and Mrs. Dennis have to purchase the property?
    A. Yes, because they signed a sales contract and have an approved loan.
    B. Yes, if the buyers' insurance will repair the water damage.
    C. No, because the property must be in the same condition it was on the day the offer was accepted.
    D. No, because the mold growing on the walls would terminate the sales contract.

68. Judy leased space for her real estate school. She installed a marker board, movie screen, and an LCD projector. Three years later the lease expired, and she did not renew her lease. Under general contract law, can she take the trade fixtures from the property?
    A. Yes, if the trade fixtures are removed before the lease expires.
    B. Yes, because she paid for the trade fixtures.
    C. No, if attached to the property the trade fixtures belong to the landlord.
    D. No, because the landlord wanted the trade fixtures for the next tenant.

69. Laura's hobby is making ceramic decorations. She custom made light-switch covers to match the wallpaper for every room in her home. When she listed the property, no mention was made of taking the items with her. Can she take the light-switch covers with her when she moves?
    A. No, because the removal might cause damage to the property.
    B. No, because it was not discussed when she listed the property.
    C. Yes, if they are removed before closing.
    D. Yes, if it is agreed upon between the buyer and seller in the sales contract.

70. Which principal of appraising is the foundation for all approaches to appraising?
    A. Supply and demand
    B. Highest and best use
    C. Substitution
    D. Conformity

MATCHING QUIZ

The column on the right contains a brief definition of important terms in this section.
Write the letter of the matching term on the appropriate line.

A. Functional obsolescence

B. Appurtenant

C. Constructive notice

D. Net listing

E. Fee simple absolute

F. Tenancy in common

G. Littoral rights

H. Replacement cost

I. Emblements

J. Profit a prendre

K. Situs

L. Joint tenancy

M. Fixture

N. Cooperative

O. Special limitation

P. Condominium

Q. Tenancy by the entirety

R. Income approach

S. Plottage

T. Patent defect

1. ___ Annual crops such as corn and tomatoes that are produced through labor and industry

2. ___ Stipulates that the seller will receive a specified amount of money, and anything over that amount is the broker's commission

3. ___ The value that is created when two or more tracts of land are merged into a larger tract

4. ___ Form of ownership in which the airspace is owned in severalty and the land and buildings are owned as tenants in common

5. ___ Location

6. ___ Legal notice or notice to the world by recorded documents

7. ___ A defect that is obvious and can be found by normal inspection

8. ___ Depreciation or loss of value due to inadequacies in features and design

9. ___ Form of ownership in which a corporation holds title and the owners purchase shares of stock in the corporation and receive a proprietary lease

10. ___ This word means attached and refers to tangible property or intangible rights and privileges that belong to the land

11. ___ Appraisal method used to appraise investment property; also known as the capitalization approach

12. ___ A fee simple defeasible estate with a possibility of reverter

13. ___ Highest form of ownership recognized by law; for an indefinite duration, freely transferable, and inheritable

14. ___ The owners' rights to use water when large lakes and oceans adjoin their property

15. ___ The right to take from the soil anything the soil produces

16. ___ Current construction cost to rebuild a building that is not an exact duplicate but serves the same purpose as the original

17. ___ Form of co-ownership by which each owner holds an undivided interest in real property as if he or she were the sole owner; characterized by unity of possession

18. ___ Form of joint property ownership held by a husband and wife during marriage; characterized by unities of time, title, interest, possession, and person

19. ___ Form of co-ownership that is characterized by unities of time, title, interest, and possession; on the death of a joint tenant, the decedent's interest transfers to the remaining joint owners

20. ___ Item of personal property that has been converted to real property because it is now permanently attached to the real property

ANSWERS

1. **(D)** A co-op owner has a proprietary lease; a condo owner does not.

2. **(B)** An easement gives the right to use the land of another.

3. **(D)** When a property is transferred "so long as" a condition is met or not met, it is transferred as a special limitation with the possibility of reverter.

4. **(C)** Riparian rights are the water rights of a property owner along a river or stream.

5. **(C)** $640 \div 4 \div 4 = 40$
   $640 \div 2 \div 4 \div 4 = 20$
   $40 + 20 = 60$ acres

6. **(A)** A homestead creates a legal life estate.

7. **(B)** By the definition of a "time-share."

8. **(A)** Tenancy by the entirety ownership can be held only by a husband and wife.

9. **(A)** Separate property is any property that is accumulated prior to marriage.

10. **(D)** The cost approach is used to appraise special-purpose properties such as houses of worship, museums, hospitals, fire departments, and so forth.

11. **(D)** In an exclusive-agency listing, the seller is not required to pay a commission if the seller sells the property without the assistance of the brokerage firm.

12. **(D)** The brokerage is not responsible for preparing the title for closing.

13. **(D)** The right of reentry is the possible future interest in a conditional subsequent, not fee simple absolute ownership.

14. **(D)** Incurable depreciation is not economically feasible to correct.

15. **(A)** The owner of a condo owns the airspace in severalty, meaning separate from the other condo owners, and is a tenant in common in the common areas.

16. **(A)** A plat map must be recorded by the developer.

17. **(A)** By definition of functional obsolescence.

18. **(C)** The purpose of the sale is confidential information and in this situation could reduce the negotiating position of the seller. If the seller gave permission, it would be acceptable for the agent to disclose the reason for the sale.

19. **(D)** The broker and seller are the principals in a listing contract.

20. **(D)** The seven protected classes under the federal Fair Housing Act are race, color, religion, national origin, sex, familial status, and disability.

21. **(D)** If the removal of a fixture will cause damage, it is generally considered real property.

22. **(C)** By definition of constructive notice.

23. **(C)** By definitions of latent and patent defects.

24. **(D)** Religious organizations can give preference to members only.

25. **(C)** By definition of conventional life estate.

26. **(D)** By definition of gross easement.

27. **(C)** A joint tenant does have the right to sell, mortgage, or lease the interest in the property without the consent of the other owners. The new owner would be a tenant in common with the other tenants, who still hold a joint tenancy.

28. **(D)** John is the general partner and is personally liable.

29. **(D)** By definition of exclusive-agency listing.

30. **(B)** Personal property of the tenant that becomes attached to the real property is known as a *trade fixture*. It belongs to the tenant and may be removed before the lease expires. If it remains on the property after the expiration of the lease, it belongs to the landlord.

31. **(D)** By the definition of joint tenancy. When one tenant dies, the property is automatically conveyed to the surviving joint tenant(s).

32. **(B)** By definition of special agent.

33. **(D)** A license is the privilege to use the property of another. It does not affect the value or use of the property.

34. **(A)** The value of property is not affected by an owner's having title insurance.

35. **(D)** Tenancy by the entirety is held by a husband and wife.

36. **(D)** Tenancy by the entirety does not allow partition.

37. **(D)** By definition of exclusive-right-to-sell listing.

38. **(C)** The contract could be terminated. However, the seller cannot withdraw at any time without liability.

39. **(D)** An estate must be possessory or may become possessory in the future for an estate to exist.

40. **(D)** A life estate *pur autre vie* is based on the life of a third party.

41. **(A)** By definition of the cost approach to appraising.

42. **(C)** When the comparable is superior, an adjustment is made by subtracting from the comparable. When the comparable is inferior, an adjustment is made by adding to the comparable.

43. **(A)** A lot-and-block method is the best way to describe this property in a listing contract.

44. **(D)** Deed covenants are not public controls; they are private controls placed on real estate.

45. **(C)** A possibility of reverter is a possible future interest found in a fee simple defeasible title with a special limitation.

46. **(C)** $640 \div 4 \div 4 \div 4 = 10$
    $640 \div 4 \div 2 = 80$
    $80 + 10 = 90$ acres

47. **(C)** The efforts of the federal government to guarantee equal housing opportunities to all U.S. citizens began more than 100 years ago with the passage of the Civil Rights Act of 1866.

48. **(C)** Private mortgage insurance would not be used in determining the value of a property.

49. **(A)** Generally, an easement affects the use of the property, but not the title.

50. **(B)** It is not unlawful to display the Equal Housing Opportunity Poster and to provide clients and customers with pertinent information.

51. **(D)** Conventional life estates are freehold estates that are not inheritable.

52. **(C)** The bundle of legal rights are the rights inherent with the ownership of real estate, not personal property.

53. **(B)** If a broker has entered into an open listing, other brokers can contact the seller directly because the seller has contracts with all brokers to sell property.

54. **(D)** Conversion is the process of changing from one form of ownership to another.

55. **(D)** The maintenance fee of co-op owners includes their portion of the mortgage payment, property taxes, insurance, and maintenance.

56. **(D)** The listing can be terminated with the mutual consent of the broker and the sellers.

57. **(C)** They are all examples of gross easements that benefit a person or legal entity.

58. **(D)** Littoral rights are water rights of owners whose land borders on large, navigable lakes, seas, and oceans.

59. **(B)** Purchasers must be given ten days to conduct an inspection, not tenants.

60. **(B)** Death of the sales agent would not terminate a listing. Death of the broker or seller would terminate the listing.

61. **(D)** John and Peggy have been appointed exclusive agents for the seller and buyer and are designated agents.

62. **(B)** S16° E would be associated with the metes-and-bounds description, not the government survey.

63. **(C)** The relationship is ongoing, and Agent Pod would be a general agent.

64. **(C)** By definitions of the words *appurtenance* and *encumbrance*.

65. **(D)** The life tenant has the right to sell, mortgage, or lease the property, but contracts are valid only while the life tenant is alive.

66. **(A)** Bonnie owned 50 percent of the property, so she, Brenda, and James were tenants in common. She can leave the property to whomever she wants to in her will, and that includes Brenda and James.

67. **(C)** Buyers are not required to purchase property that is not in the same physical condition that it was in the day the offer was accepted.

68. **(A)** Under general contract law, trade fixtures can be removed from the property before the lease expires.

69. **(D)** If an agreement is reached in the sales contract, Laura may take the light-switch covers.

70. **(C)** Substitution is the foundation for all approaches to appraising.

ANSWERS—MATCHING QUIZ

1. I	6. C	11. R	16. H
2. D	7. T	12. O	17. F
3. S	8. A	13. E	18. Q
4. P	9. N	14. G	19. L
5. K	10. B	15. J	20. M

CHAPTER 2

Selling Property

This chapter reviews the services to the buyer and includes buyer agency contracts, qualifying the buyer, showing properties, recommended inspections, preparing offers, need for homeowners insurance, and tax implications of ownership.

AMP Outline—Services to the Buyer

II. **Selling Property**
  A. Services to the buyer
    1. Relationship and responsibilities of licensees and selling firm to buyer
    2. Rights of ownership
    3. Determination of buyer's price range and eligibility for various types of financing
    4. Identification of property that meets buyers' needs and specifications
    5. Current market conditions
    6. Showing properties and property characteristics
    7. Material facts concerning property
    8. Physical condition of property
    9. Psychological impact related to property
    10. Income tax implications of home ownership
    11. Tax implications for real estate investments
    12. Sales contract forms and provisions, including contingencies
    13. Recommendation that buyer seek legal counsel
    14. Preparation of offers and counteroffers
    15. Presentation of offers and counteroffers
    16. Planning and zoning
    17. Availability of home protection plans

RELATIONSHIP AND RESPONSIBILITIES OF LICENSEES AND SELLING FIRM TO BUYER

When a real estate broker enters into a contract with a buyer, a buyer agency relationship is established and duties under the law of agency are applicable to the buyer client. If the sellers are represented by an agent, the sellers would be a client to their agent, but a customer to the buyer's agent.

When entering into a buyer agency agreement, the agent explains the parties' rights and responsibilities. At a minimum, a buyer agency agreement should contain

- purpose of agency,
- identification of the parties,
- property type description,
- compensation and method of payment,
- disclosure of any potential conflict of interest, and
- term of agreement.

It is important that the buyer understand the four options for compensating a buyer agent.

1.   The seller pays the fee to the listing brokerage, and a co-op fee is paid to the buyer brokerage.

2.   Buyer agents may be paid a *consultant fee*, which is an hourly rate or a flat fee for specific services.

3.   The buyers may agree to pay a *contingent fee*, whereby the buyer's agent is paid by the buyer only if the clients find and buy a home, and the seller does not agree to pay the compensation. This would be used if the buyer purchases a For Sale by Owner property.

4.   A noncontingency fee is paid to the agent whether or not the buyers purchase a home.

A brokerage and buyer agent's fiduciary duties must include visually inspecting the property and recommending that the buyer seek the necessary inspections of the property. Buyer agent duties also include a duty to inspect public records or permits concerning title or use of the property.

Types of Buyer Agency Agreements

Exclusive Buyer Agency—In this completely exclusive agency relationship, the buyer is legally bound to pay the agent when the buyer purchases the property described in the contract. This is true even if the buyer finds the property.

Exclusive-Agency Buyer Agency—This also creates an exclusive contract between the buyer and agent. However, the broker is entitled to payment only if the broker locates the property purchased by the buyer. The buyer can find suitable property without the obligation to pay the agent.

Open Buyer Agency Agreement—In this nonexclusive contract with the agent, the buyer can enter into similar agreements with any number of agents. The agent who finds the suitable property will be compensated.

RIGHTS OF OWNERSHIP

An *estate* is the bundle of rights associated with real property or the legal interest or rights in the land, but not the physical quantity of the land. At closing, the grantor transfers the bundle of rights to the grantee, allowing the grantee to possess, enjoy, control, exclude, and dispose of the property.

DETERMINATION OF BUYER'S PRICE RANGE AND ELIGIBILITY FOR VARIOUS TYPES OF FINANCING

Most real estate agents recommend that the buyers be preapproved for a loan. This will help determine the price range of the property for which they qualify, and it will also identify any credit issues to be resolved. If the buyer has not viewed a free credit report, the agent should recommend they do so by visiting *www.AnnualCreditReport.com* or by calling (877) 322-8228.

Assessing the buyer's price range depends on three basic factors: (1) stable income, (2) net worth, and (3) credit history. It seems like a simple process, but it involves more than just the use of mathematical formulas. The four basic steps for securing a loan for the purchase of real estate are

1. applying for the loan,
2. analysis of the borrower and the property,
3. processing the loan application, and
4. closing the loan.

To determine the **stable income** of the borrower, the lender may require paycheck stubs, tax returns, W2s, and verification of employment for the past two years. To determine the **net worth**, the borrower's liabilities are subtracted from the borrower's assets. On authorization, the loan officer will pull the credit report, which will include a **credit score** that takes into account the applicant's employment and credit history.

Loan processing involves ordering an appraisal, title search, termite inspection, or other inspections required for the loan. A completed loan package is sent to the underwriter, who will review all documentation and evaluate the risk of the loan. The loan will close when all underwriting conditions have been met. The two ratios that an underwriter analyzes are the mortgage-to-income ratio and the debt-service ratio.

1. The *mortgage-to-income ratio* is the ratio of the monthly housing expense (principal, interest, taxes, and insurance) to the gross monthly income. In many loans, the mortgage expense can be no more than 28 percent of the gross monthly income. This can also be known as the housing-to-income ratio or the *front-end ratio*.

2. The debt-to-service ratio expresses the relationship of the total monthly debt payments to the borrower's income. This is also known as the *debt-to-income ratio* or the *back-end ratio*.

In many conventional loans, the total debt-to-service ratio should be no more than 36 percent of the borrower's stable monthly income. FHA ratios are generally 29 percent and 41 percent, respectively. VA has no front-end ratio, and the back-end ratio is 41 percent of the gross monthly income.

To confirm the borrower's **assets**, the lender will require statements from checking, savings, stock, bond, retirement, and money market accounts.

The borrower must also disclose **liabilities** such as car payments, mortgage or rent payments, credit card debt, student loans, alimony or child support, and any other debts.

Fannie Mae developed the Desktop Underwriter (DU), an automated loan underwriting system that reduces time, cost, and subjectivity in the underwriting process. DU does not deny or approve loan applications, but assesses the credit risk of the application. Depending on the application package, the typical real estate loan will take somewhere between 10 and 30 days to close.

IDENTIFICATION OF PROPERTY THAT MEETS BUYERS' NEEDS AND SPECIFICATIONS

After the buyer's price range has been determined, other decisions the buyer will make include the importance of

- location near family, work, schools, houses of worship, transportation, and recreation;

- purchase of a single family home, multifamily home, or condo;

- purchase of a new home, existing home, or one that needs to be remodeled;

- accessibility considerations for a disabled person;

- style of home: Ranch, Tudor, two-story, and so forth;

- number and size of bedrooms, bathrooms, and so forth;

- special features such as hot tub, fireplace, pool, three-car garage; and

- lot size.

When a buyer is ready to make an offer, the buyer will want to know the

- possibility of assuming the mortgage or seller financing;

- down payment required, interest rate, and monthly payment if the offer is accepted;

- annual property taxes, insurance, and special assessments;

- average cost of water, sewer, gas, electric, and cable bills;

- reason for sale;

- age and condition of heating and air-conditioning, furnace, roof, and appliances;

- environmental issues, easements, and deed restrictions; and

- zoning or nonconforming use issues.

CURRENT MARKET CONDITIONS

An agent needs to be aware of current market conditions affecting the value and sale of real estate, including interest rates, employment levels, vacancy rates, demographics, and the absorption rate.

Demographics is the *statistical study of the population in reference to size, density, and distribution in a given area.* A company moving into or out of the area will have an impact on the employment levels, vacancy rates, supply and demand, and absorption rate.

The **absorption rate** is an *estimate of how quickly homes have sold in the neighborhood within the past year.* Because an agent cannot be certain exactly how and when demographic factors will affect current market conditions, he or she can never guarantee future profits from or appreciation of real estate.

In today's real estate market, many buyers are purchasing properties in foreclosure or in a short sale. **Foreclosure** is a *court process* brought about because the borrower has *defaulted* on the mortgage, typically because mortgage payments are not made. In a *short sale*, the lender *accepts a payoff for less than* the outstanding loan amount.

Agents should inform buyers making an offer on a short sale that this lender's process can take a long time. State laws should be reviewed to inform buyers of the process in a bankruptcy or short sale.

SHOWING PROPERTIES AND PROPERTY CHARACTERISTICS

Agents should be cautious in meeting strangers at properties. It is recommended that an agent have the potential buyers meet the agent at the office before taking them to a property. The National Association of REALTORS® Web site (*www.realtor. org*) features safety videos that should be viewed by any agent.

Once properties have been identified that meet the buyer's needs, the agent will call the listing brokerage firm or seller to schedule an appointment to visit the property. Because buyers rarely purchase the first home they see, the agent should have some system in place to help make notes on each property shown. This helps buyers decide if a property meets their needs.

Buyers should be given sufficient time to inspect the property, and the property disclosure statement should be available. Physical characteristics of the property, both good and bad, should be shown to the buyers. If the property is in foreclosure, is a short sale or an estate sale, or presents any other circumstance that might prevent the property from being readily transferable, this information should be disclosed to the buyer.

MATERIAL FACTS CONCERNING PROPERTY

A **material fact** is defined as a fact that is significant or essential to the issue or matter at hand. In a real estate transaction, a material fact can be anything from disclosure that a property is stigmatized to zoning verification, property taxes, building codes, building permits, certificates of occupancy, and other land-use restrictions that may apply. The local zoning administrator will assist the public in answering these questions. Any other encumbrances, such as deed restrictions and conditions, regulations of the homeowners' association, special assessments, or any other condition that would burden the use, enjoyment, or disposition of the property, also need to be disclosed.

PHYSICAL CONDITION OF PROPERTY

Many states require that an owner fill out property disclosure statements. Information is given about the house systems, foundations and structure, roof, land drainage, boundaries, water supply, sewer systems, construction or remodeling, homeowners association dues, and environmental hazards. (See Figure 2.1.)

FIGURE 2.1

Environmental Hazards

PSYCHOLOGICAL IMPACT RELATED TO PROPERTY

A property may be **stigmatized** if the history of the property makes it undesirable or if a sex offender lives in the neighborhood. A stigma may be created by a homicide, suicide, shooting, illegal drug sales, methamphetamine lab, or if the house is "haunted." Some states have laws requiring the disclosure of stigmatized properties. If there are no state laws, a broker should seek competent legal counsel when dealing with a stigmatized property.

According to the U.S. Drug Enforcement Administration, there were 7,050 seizures of methamphetamine labs (meth labs) in 2003. The illegal use of methamphetamine is a major drug threat in the United States. Meth labs can be set up almost anywhere and are often found in private residences, apartments, trailers, automobiles, campgrounds, and hotel and motel rooms.

According to the U.S. Department of Justice, the average meth lab produces five to seven pounds of toxic waste for every pound of meth produced. When a meth lab is found in a home, the site is deemed a toxic waste site. When these chemicals are dumped, contamination of soil and nearby water supplies is possible.

Most property disclosure documents do not specifically ask about the production of methamphetamine or other illegal drugs. A prudent buyer's agent would recommend that the buyer ask the seller to sign a statement that methamphetamine has never been made or used on the property.

INCOME TAX IMPLICATIONS OF HOME OWNERSHIP

One of the financial benefits of home ownership is that mortgage interest and property taxes are tax deductible. Here's an example.

Loan: $150,000   Interest: 6 percent   Term: 30 years
$150,000 × 6%   = $ 9,000 annual interest the first year
Property taxes   = $ 3,000
Total deduction   = $12,000

$12,000 × 28% = $3,360 tax savings if the borrower is in the 28 percent tax bracket.

Please note that mortgage interest may not be deductible on loans over $1.1 million.

Capital Gains

The Taxpayers Relief Act of 1997 established the exclusion of capital gains on the sale of the principal residence. **Single filers** may exclude up to $250,000 and **married** homeowners who file **jointly** may exclude up to **$500,000** from capital gains tax for profits on the sale of a principal residence. Homeowners whose gain exceeds the maximum for exclusion must pay tax on the amount over the exclusion. The exclusion can be taken more than once; however, to claim the exclusion, the home must have been used as a principal residence for two of the preceding five years. Homeowners may not have sold or exchanged a home during the two years preceding the sale. The rule does not apply to second homes or vacation property. Capital gains computations are covered in Chapter 7, Math Review, and a sample capital gain calculation is shown in Figure 2.2.

TAX IMPLICATIONS FOR REAL ESTATE INVESTMENTS

In the past, real estate investments were advantageous because tax laws allowed investors to use losses generated by these investments to shelter income from other sources. Present-day tax benefits include tax deductions for depreciation, the deferment of capital gains when property is exchanged, and deductions of losses from real estate investments. Because most agents are not Certified Public Accountants (CPAs), specific investment questions should be referred to the investor's CPA.

A capital gain is considered a short-term gain if the asset is owned for 12 months or less. It is considered long-term if the asset is owned for more than 12 months. The Tax Reform Act of 2003 reduced capital gains taxes. A short-term asset is taxed as regular income. If a taxpayer is in the 10 percent or 15 percent tax bracket, long-term gains are taxed at 5 percent. In 2008, this rate will be reduced to zero. For an asset held for more than 12 months, the maximum long-term gain is 15 percent.

A buyer of investment property should seek professional tax advice to keep abreast of the changing laws in this area.

A **capital gain** is the taxable profit realized from the sale or exchange of an asset.

Tax-Deferred Exchanges

Under **Internal Revenue Code Section 1031**, if an investor exchanges property instead of selling it, payment of the capital gain *may be deferred*. Usually the property exchanged is *like kind*; that is, real estate for real estate of equal or greater value. Other rules apply if real estate is exchanged for personal property. Please note that personal use property, such as a principal residence or vacation home, does not qualify for a like-kind exchange.

Sometimes additional money or personal property is given to make up the difference between the values of the exchanged properties. This money or personal property is known as boot, and capital gains must be paid immediately on the boot.

Following government guidelines, the seller may defer the gain on the sale of an investment property. The seller has 45 days from the close of escrow on the first property to "identify" a replacement property or properties. The close of escrow on the second property must occur within 180 days of the close of escrow on the first property. The 180 days must be within the time the taxpayer will file his or her tax return for the year of the sale. If this 180 days will extend beyond the standard April 15 filing deadline, the seller should obtain an extension of time to file his or her return. (April 15 deadline is for individuals and partnerships; March 15 is the deadline for a corporation.)

Reverse exchanges allow the replacement property to be acquired before the disposition of the relinquished property. The agent should advise the seller to seek advice from a CPA or other qualified tax professional or current guidelines.

FIGURE 2.2

Sample Capital Gain Calculation— Investment Property

Selling Price:			$125,000
Less:	7% Commission	$8,750	
	Closing costs	+ 800	
		$9,550	
			− 9,550
Net Sales Price:			$115,450
Basis:	Original cost	$60,000	
	Improvements	+ 5,000	
		$65,000	
Less:	Depreciation	−12,000	
		$53,000	
Adjusted Basis:			−53,000
Total Capital Gain:			$62,450

Depreciation

Depreciation, or *cost recovery*, is an income tax deduction that allows a taxpayer to recover the cost or other basis of certain property. It is an annual allowance for the wear and tear, deterioration, or obsolescence of the property. *Land cannot be depreciated; only the improvements on it can be depreciated.*

For investment properties purchased after 1987, the straight-line method of depreciation is used. This means *the depreciation is taken periodically in equal amounts.* Currently, residential investment property is depreciated for 27.5 years and commercial investment property is depreciated for 39 years. To compute the depreciation, the cost basis must be determined. See Figure 2.3 for a straight-line depreciation example.

When the investment property is sold, the depreciation that has been taken will be recaptured.

Because these laws are complicated, investors should obtain professional advice.

SALES CONTRACT FORMS AND PROVISIONS, INCLUDING CONTINGENCIES

A properly prepared contract legally binds **competent parties** to the terms of the contract. Real estate contracts include listing agreements, offers to purchase, sales contracts, options, binders, mortgages, notes, insurance policies, leases, and property management agreements. State law will determine whether agents are allowed to "fill in the blanks" of contracts without such an action being considered a practice of law. The creation or drafting of documents is considered a practice of law and can only be performed by an attorney.

FIGURE 2.3

Straight-line Depreciation Example

Purchase Price	$110,000
Closing Costs	+ 3,000
Total Acquisition Costs	$113,000
Percentage of cost that is a building	× 85%
Cost Basis	$ 96,050

$96,050 Cost Basis ÷ 27.5 years = $3,493—For Residential Investment Depreciation

$96,050 Cost Basis ÷ 39.0 years = $2,463—For Commercial Investment Depreciation

To be valid and enforceable, a contract must contain the following *essential elements*:

- The parties must be *legally and mentally competent and authorized to perform*. In most states, a person is legally competent at the age of 18. Other parties authorized to perform include executors, administrators, anyone operating under court order, a party with the proper power of attorney, or the party authorized by a corporation to enter into real estate contracts.

- There must be **offer and acceptance**, also known as *mutual assent* or *meeting of the minds*. An offer must be made by one party (offeror) and accepted without any qualifications or changes by the second party (offeree).

- The contract must be in *proper legal form*. Each state's *statute of frauds* determines the contracts that must be in writing. Generally, most real estate contracts must be in writing to be enforceable. In many states, leases and listings for *less than one year are not required to be in writing*.

- The contract must be entered into for a *legal purpose*. A contract entered into for an illegal purpose is *void*.

- There must be *legal* **consideration**, which is a *promise* made by one party to induce another party to enter into a contract. A gift is *good consideration*, while money or the promise to pay money is a *valuable consideration*. In a sales contract, the *consideration is the selling price* of the property; therefore, earnest money, or a good-faith deposit, is *not* necessary to create a binding sales contract.

- There must be **reality of consent**, which means the contract was entered into without duress, menace, misrepresentation, or fraud. The law protects a person who has been tricked or forced into entering a contract. That is, the contract is *voidable by the innocent party*, but valid as to the wrongdoer.

- For contracts that are required to be in writing, there must be the *signatures of the parties authorized to perform*. Thus, both the buyer and seller must sign the sales contract for it to be enforceable.

A list of the usual provisions that appear in a real estate sales contract is shown in Figure 2.4.

FIGURE 2.4

**Usual Provisions in a
Sales Contract**

- Identification of the seller, buyer, and property
- Type of deed being conveyed, with any restrictions
- The price of the property and how the purchaser will pay
- Amount of earnest money and remedies for breach of contract
- Provision for real estate taxes, hazard insurance, and rents, etc.
- Date for securing loan, closing, inspection, and possession
- Personal property to be left with the real estate
- Personal property the seller intends to remove
- Transfer or payment of any special assessments
- Provision stating time period for acceptance
- Dated signatures of all parties

Types of Contracts

- **Unilateral contract**—Only one party is obligated to perform in a unilateral contract. Examples: open listings and options.

- **Bilateral contract**—Both parties are obligated to perform in a bilateral contract. Exclusive listings, leases, and sales contracts are bilateral contracts.

- **Express contract**—The parties have specifically agreed, either orally or in writing, to enter into a contract.

- **Implied contract**—The parties by their actions or conduct enter into a contract. Examples of implied contracts include ordering food in a restaurant, securing the services of a taxi, or buying gasoline at a self-service gas station.

- **Executory contract**—One or both parties have duties to perform in an executory contract. A sales contract is executory because the buyer must financially qualify and the seller must produce a marketable title. Most contracts are executory contracts.

- **Executed contract**—All parties have fulfilled their duties and responsibilities in an executed contract. The sales contract becomes fully executed at closing when the deed has been conveyed and the buyer has paid the purchase price. Please note: The word *execute* means to *sign a document*. This is different from an executed contract.

Status of a Contract

- **Valid**—It meets *all* the essential elements and is an enforceable contract.

- **Void**—It is missing an essential element or is unenforceable by either party.

- **Voidable**—It may be rescinded by one or both parties. Contracts are voidable by the innocent party if entered into under duress, under undue influence, through misrepresentation, through fraud, with a minor, or with an incompetent person. A contract with a contingency that cannot be met is voidable.

- **Unenforceable**—When neither party can sue the other to force performance, the contract is said to be *unenforceable*. Because a real estate sales contract must be in writing, an oral agreement to purchase a property is unenforceable. A contract not performed within the statutory time period is unenforceable.

Following are other important terms associated with contracts:

- **Assignment**—An assignment is a transfer of rights and/or duties from one contract to another contract or from one person to another person. Most contracts include a clause that either forbids or permits assignment.

- **Novation**—When novation is granted, one contract is substituted for another contract with the intent to discharge the obligation of the original contract. It is a release of liability from the original contract.

- **Ambiguities**—Any ambiguities in a contract are construed against the writer of the contract. Contract terms must be clear and definite.

- **Contingency**—A contingency in a contract requires the completion of a certain act or promise before the contract is binding. A contingency that cannot be completed makes the contract *voidable*.

- **Equitable title**—In a sales contract, land contract, or trust deed, the buyer's interest in the property is called an *equitable title interest*. Though the legal title is held by another party, the buyer does have an insurable interest in the property.

- **Liquidated damages**—Damages or compensation that will be paid if one party breaches the contract. The *earnest money deposit* may serve as a *liquidated damage clause* in a sales contract. Generally, if the buyer defaults and the seller retains the earnest money deposit as liquidated damages, the seller may not sue for any further damages.

- **Right of first refusal**—This term can have two meanings. It can mean the right of a person to have the "first right" to purchase or lease a property, when the owner is ready to sell or lease. It can also be a contingency clause in a sales contract. For example, the seller has accepted an offer contingent on the buyers selling their house. If a seller's acceptance contained a right of first refusal, it means the seller can still market the seller's home. If a qualified buyer writes an offer, the seller must give the first buyers the right to buy. If the first buyers cannot buy, then they would release the seller from the contract so he could accept the offer from the "ready, willing, and able buyer."

- **Suit for specific performance**—A legal action to enforce the performance of the terms of a contract.

- **Caveat emptor**—Means "let the buyer beware."

- **Caveat venditor**—Means "let the seller beware."

- **Exculpatory clause**—A "hold harmless" clause that may be found in contracts excusing a party for injuries to another.

- **Indemnification clause**—A clause in which one party agrees to compensate another for a loss or damage that is sustained.

State laws determine the exact terms of a sales contract. Parties should immediately receive a copy of any signed contract.

Option Contracts

In an **option** contract, an **optionor** (seller) agrees *to keep open an offer to sell or lease* real property in return for option money. While the **optionee** (buyer) does not have to buy, the optionor must sell, should the buyer exercise the option. The option money given by the buyer may or may not apply toward the purchase price. (Typically, it does not.)

Option contracts typically contain the names and addresses of the parties, an identification of the property, the terms of the sale, the sales price, the date the option expires, the method of notice by which the option is to be exercised, and provisions for disbursement of the option money if the option is not exercised.

Unless the contract states otherwise, an option contract is assignable. On its creation it is considered a *unilateral contract* because only the seller is obligated to perform. Option contracts that have been exercised are *bilateral contracts* because the buyer is then obligated to buy and the seller is obligated to sell. These contracts are still enforceable on the death of either party.

Lease Option

In a **lease option**, the lessee (tenant) has the right to purchase the property under specified conditions or to renew or extend the lease at its end. The rent or a portion of the rent may be applied to the purchase price.

Land Contract

In a typical **land contract**, the **vendor** (seller) finances the property and retains title to it until the final payment is made or some other condition is met by the **vendee** (buyer). The buyer possesses the property and receives equitable title.

The vendee agrees to give the vendor a down payment and regular installments of principal and interest for a number of years. Typically, the buyer also pays for property taxes, insurance, repairs, and upkeep on the property.

A land contract is also known as a *contract for deed*, an *installment contract, articles of agreement for warranty deed, bond for title,* or *agreement of sale*.

RECOMMENDATION THAT BUYER SEEK LEGAL COUNSEL

Many buyers and sellers have the misconception that real estate agents are experts in everything from environmental issues to titles and deeds. For example, first-time buyers may ask how they should hold title to the property, but that is really a question for their attorney to answer. Agents must have a basic knowledge of many different aspects of real estate so they know when to recommend that a buyer seek legal counsel or other expert opinions that are needed. It is the agent's duty to inform a buyer that the offer should be reviewed by the buyer's attorney before it is presented to a seller. A buyer who refuses should sign a waiver indicating that the agent recommended that the buyer seek legal counsel.

PREPARATION OF OFFERS AND COUNTEROFFERS

To *offer* means to put forward for acceptance, rejection, or consideration. An offer does not become a contract unless it is *accepted without changes*, and the terms of the offer must be clear and definite. *An offer can be revoked at any time before acceptance*. Notice of revocation by the offeree, death of either party, insanity of either party, or a counteroffer all terminate an offer.

A time for performance of the following activities is typically found in the offer:

- Closing date

- Date of possession

- Date for property, termite, and lead-based paint inspections

- Date for loan application to be completed

- Date for loan approval

- Time for acceptance of the offer

If **"time is of the essence"** is found in the contract, it means the contract must be performed within the time limit specified. The party who does not perform on time may be liable for breach of contract. If a contract does not specify *time is of the essence* or a date of performance, then it is required to be performed "within a reasonable time."

One of the essential elements of a contract is offer and acceptance or the "meeting of the minds." Buyers and sellers need to be in agreement on the fixtures and personal property that is to be transferred at closing, if the seller will pay for any repairs that need to be made to the property, and the return of the earnest money if the offer is not accepted or if an inspection reveals a repair or issue the buyer finds unacceptable.

Typical contingency clauses found in an offer include that the appraised value must be equal to or greater than the offering price, that the property must pass inspections, that the contract be reviewed by an attorney, and that the buyer be able to obtain insurance on the property.

PRESENTATION OF OFFERS AND COUNTEROFFERS

Most buyers want their agent to present their offer to the sellers. The agent is in the position to explain the contract terms and the buyer qualifications. A buyer who has a sizable down payment, an earnest money check, and a preapproval letter from the lender will provide some assurances to the seller that the buyer is qualified and serious about purchasing the property.

If the property has been on the market for more than 30 days, it is recommended that the comparable market analysis of the property be updated. This will provide both the buyer and seller with recent sales of properties in the neighborhood.

The agent should go through each paragraph of the offer and how it affects the sellers. A buyer's agent should review the offer from the sellers' viewpoint and anticipate objections. Sellers want to know the bottom line, so have a worksheet to calculate the probable closing costs to determine the net to the sellers.

If any change in terms is made, the offer is void and a **counteroffer** is created. The legal positions of the parties are reversed; that is, the offeror becomes the offeree and the offeree becomes the offeror.

PLANNING AND ZONING

There are no federal zoning laws. Zoning is a police power conferred on municipal governments by state enabling acts. Many communities have a zoning and planning board to evaluate current needs and to project and plan for future growth in a stable manner.

Municipalities and counties develop a **master plan** or comprehensive plan to guide the long-term physical development of the area. **Zoning ordinances** are local laws that implement the comprehensive plan and regulate the land use and structures. A zoning board of appeals is established to hear complaints about the effects of zoning.

The following are terms associated with zoning:

- **Land use** is regulated by dividing the land into residential, commercial, industrial, and agricultural use districts.

- A **buffer zone** separates two different use districts. For example, a park could be planned between a residential district and a commercial district.

- **Bulk zoning** controls density or the ratio of land area to structure area. Bulk zoning is used to avoid overcrowding.

- **Aesthetic zoning** requires that new buildings conform to certain types of architectural styles.

- **Incentive zoning** requires that the street floors of office buildings be used for retail space.

- **Nonconforming property** is property in an area that was zoned for one use but for which the zoning has now changed. For example, when zoning changes the land use from residential to commercial, a residential owner usually is allowed to continue using the property as a residence until the property is sold or destroyed.

- A **variance** may be granted in cases where the zoning creates an unnecessary hardship on the owner, but the variance must not be detrimental to zoning. Variances may be granted for setback lines, height restrictions, and the like.

- When a *special-purpose property* that benefits the public, such as a hospital, library, or museum, is approved for construction, a **conditional-use permit** is granted.

- **Spot zoning** is a change of zoning for a particular spot or lot and is generally not permitted.

The federal or state government may, through special legislation, regulate land use in **special study zones**. This would be used to control development in high-risk flood-prone or geological areas. It could also include scenic easements, coastal management, and environmental laws.

AVAILABILITY OF HOME PROTECTION PLANS

It is the buyer's responsibility to conduct an inspection of the property to make sure the housing systems are functioning properly. **Home protection (warranty) plans**, in which insurance covers the repair or replacement of appliances and of electrical, plumbing, heating, air-conditioning, and other systems within the home, are available. The policy may be purchased by the agent, seller, or buyer. Typical coverage is for one year, but it can be renewed if desired. As with all insurance coverage, the policy should be reviewed for exclusions, deductibles, etc.

NEED FOR INSURANCE

Lenders require that the borrower purchase a homeowners insurance policy prior to closing but the sales contract should be reviewed to determine who is responsible for property insurance between the acceptance of the contract and the closing.

Due to recent changes in the industry, homeowners insurance policies may be difficult and expensive to obtain. Payments for claims involving mold, lead-based paint, hurricane damage, and terrorism are key factors in this change. Once an offer has been accepted, the agent should recommend that the buyers *immediately* contact their insurance agent to determine if there will be any insurance issues.

The Comprehensive Loss Underwriting Exchange (CLUE) is a database of consumer claims that insurance companies can access when they are underwriting or rating an insurance policy. The database contains property insurance claims for up to five years, and loss history from the prior owner of a home may affect the eligibility of the buyer to purchase insurance. Insurance companies use loss history because actuarial studies show a correlation between a consumer's prior *loss history* and the consumer's future insurance loss potential.

The determination to issue a policy is determined by not only the property's past history but the buyer's credit history as well. Typically, an insurance company will request credit information to determine whether to issue or renew an insurance policy and to rate the borrower to determine how much premium should be charged for the insurance coverage. Insurance companies believe that credit information is a good measure of financial responsibility and that consumers who show less financial responsibility will file more claims, so they should pay more for their insurance.

The three general categories of risk that a homeowner's policy should include protection against are (1) destruction of the premises, (2) injury to others on the premises, and (3) theft of personal property of the homeowner or family members. **Homeowners insurance policies** should be examined carefully to determine the terms if coverage includes repair or rebuilding the home in case of natural disaster; coverage of other structures, such as a garage, that are not attached to the house; coverage for personal property losses; additional living expenses; and liability against bodily injury or property damage lawsuits brought because of incidents that occurred on the property.

Insurance policies always include exclusions. Typically, mold, terrorism, damages from wind or hurricanes, flood damage or sewer backups, earthquakes or mudslides, falling objects, and damage caused by the weight of snow or ice are not covered.

To protect the lenders interest, the National Flood Insurance Reform Act of 1994 allows lenders to purchase flood insurance on behalf of borrowers/owners of properties in special flood-hazard areas and charge the cost back to the borrowers.

Most homeowners insurance policies contain a coinsurance clause that requires that the homeowner maintain insurance equal to at least 80 percent of the replacement cost of the dwelling. Please note: This coverage does not include the value of the land. A homeowner may choose to insure 100 percent of the value of the improvements. Lenders generally require insurance that covers the mortgage balance. Be sure to read coinsurance test questions carefully.

POLICY FOR COMPLYING WITH FAIR HOUSING LAWS

Early in the transaction, brokerage firms and agents should disclose to any party their commitment to comply with federal, state, and local fair housing laws. This includes providing equal professional services without regard to race, color, religion, sex, disability, familial status, or national origin. Agents should ask to review the brokerage policy manual to ensure compliance with fair housing laws. Licensees should refuse to tolerate an action or behavior that is against the law.

AMP Outline—Advising Buyers of Outside Services

II. **Selling Property**	2.	Surveys
B. Advising Buyers of Outside Services	3.	Appraisal reports
1. Inspection reports	4.	Environmental reports

INSPECTION REPORTS

Many buyers purchase property contingent on an inspection by an independent third party or property inspector. Lenders may require a pest control report showing that the property is free and clear of any live, visible infestation by wood-destroying organisms before a loan will be approved.

In the development of property, there must be an adequate and safe water supply, and the disposal of sewage must meet health and safety standards. Property owners who use septic tanks are required to have a *percolation test*, which tests the soil's absorption or drainage capacity. Only if the soil has the ability to absorb and drain water can the land be developed.

Many lenders also require a flood certification and environmental inspection before negotiating a loan on the property. This would determine if the property is in a flood-prone area, or if it is a site where any known environmental hazards have been disposed.

SURVEYS

The purpose of the survey is to determine the exact area of the land being purchased, to identify any existing encroachments and easements, and to determine compliance with setback and other zoning requirements. Most lenders require a **mortgage location survey** that assures the lender that the lot is as represented in the legal description and that the improvements are within the lot lines. A mortgage survey is *not a stake survey* as conducted by a civil engineer whereby boundaries are measured and land areas determined. A lender may also require buyers to purchase a title policy endorsement to protect the lender against survey problems.

The three major types of surveys are the geodetic or *government survey*, which measures the shape and size of the earth; the *cadastral survey*, used to determine the boundaries of parcels for defining ownership (used also in the tax assessment process); and the *topographic survey*, used to measure the features of the earth's surface and the location of roads.

APPRAISAL REPORTS

The lender orders the appraisal of the property, and typically the buyer will receive a copy of the report at closing. If a loan is being negotiated to purchase the property, buyers need to understand how the appraisal could affect their ability to secure a loan. Their offer should be made *contingent on* the appraisal being equal to or greater than the sale price because their loan is based on the appraised value or sale price, *whichever is less*. So, if they made an offer for $150,000 and the property was appraised for $148,000, the loan would be computed on the $148,000. The sellers should understand that if the appraised value is less than the sale price, the borrowers will want to renegotiate.

ENVIRONMENTAL REPORTS

Consumers are aware of environmental issues that can affect their health and the value of the property. Federal law requires the disclosure of lead-based paint in residential property built prior to 1978, and relocation companies typically require a radon inspection. Depending on the type of property being purchased, the buyer should ask the seller about disclosure of the following environmental hazards:

- **Urea formaldehyde**—used in building materials, especially insulation; emits gases that can cause respiratory problems and eye and skin irritations.

- **Asbestos**—used in building materials, especially insulation; microscopic fibers can result in respiratory diseases; harmful only if disturbed or exposed.

■ **Lead-based paint**—elevated levels of lead in the body can cause damage to the brain, kidneys, nervous system, and red blood cells; it is estimated that one in six children may have dangerously high amounts of lead in the body.

■ **Radon gas**—an odorless and tasteless gas that is produced by the natural decay of radium; breathing radon gas can cause respiratory problems and lung cancer.

■ **Carbon monoxide**—an odorless and colorless gas that occurs as a byproduct of incomplete combustion when burning fuels such as wood, oil, and natural gas; with improper ventilation, carbon monoxide inhibits the blood's ability to transport oxygen, which can cause nausea and even death.

■ **Underground storage tanks**—commonly found where gas stations, auto repair shops, printing and chemical plants, and dry cleaners used tanks for storage of chemicals; if used to store toxic wastes and the tanks are neglected, they could leak hazardous substances into the environment and thus contaminate the soil and groundwater.

■ **Mold**—found almost everywhere, but excess moisture allows mold to grow rapidly and mold can destroy property; some people are sensitive to mold, which can cause allergic reactions or more serious health problems.

■ **PCBs or Polychlorinated biphenyls**—formerly used in electrical transformers; equipment leaking PCBs should be replaced. PCBs are considered a health hazard.

QUESTIONS

1. Every enforceable contract for the sale of real estate must be in writing and signed by all parties, in accordance with the
   A. Real Estate License Act.
   B. Uniform Commercial Code.
   C. Statute of Frauds.
   D. Truth-in-Lending Act.

2. Sandra and Cyril entered into a one-year contract wherein Cyril agreed to provide complete lawn care and snow removal services for Sandra. However, after the first snowstorm of the year, Cyril decided he wanted to move south even though the contract had six months left. Eric wanted to provide the services Cyril had provided, and the parties agreed that Sandra and Eric would enter into a new contract and that the contract between Sandra and Cyril would be canceled. The above is an example of a(n)
   A. assignment.
   B. novation.
   C. unenforceable agreement.
   D. rejection.

3. If a prospective buyer has an option to purchase a certain parcel of real estate, the prospective buyer has
   A. paid consideration for the option right.
   B. the obligation to purchase the property at a reduced price.
   C. the right to subject the seller to a new mortgage.
   D. the obligation to pay existing liens.

4. Victor enters into a contract to sell certain land to Sally. During the course of the negotiations, Victor wrongfully represents the nature of the soil, claiming that a basement can be built. This contract is
   A. void.
   B. voidable by Sally because of misrepresentation.
   C. voidable by Victor because of mistake.
   D. voidable by neither because no harm was done.

5. The essential elements of a contract include which of the following?
   A. A notarial seal
   B. Mutual agreement
   C. A three-day cancellation right
   D. Equal bargaining power

6. What characterizes a bilateral contract?
   A. Only one of the parties is bound to act.
   B. Promises have been exchanged by two parties and both are obligated to perform.
   C. A restriction is placed by one party to limit the actual performance by the other party.
   D. A duty is to be performed by one party only.

7. What characterizes an executed contract?
   A. Only one party to the contract has made a promise.
   B. At least one party to the contract may still sue for specific performance.
   C. All of the parties have fully performed their duties.
   D. One of the conditions of the contract has been completed.

8. Charlene and Patricia enter into a contract wherein Charlene agrees to sell her house to Patricia. Charlene thereafter changes her mind and defaults. Patricia then sues Charlene to force her to go through with the contract. This is known as a suit for
   A. specific performance.
   B. damages.
   C. rescission.
   D. forfeiture.

9. To create a contract, the offeree must accept the offer
   A. immediately and cannot be given more than 24 hours to consider the offer.
   B. without changes.
   C. before the close of the tenth business day following the offer.
   D. only with the advice of the offeree's attorney.

10. When an offer has been signed by a purchaser and then given to the seller's broker with an earnest money check to present to the seller the
    A. transaction constitutes a valid contract in the eyes of the law.
    B. purchaser can sue the seller for specific performance.
    C. offer can be withdrawn any time prior to acceptance.
    D. earnest money will be returned if the buyer defaults.

11. Which of the following environmental issues would render a property a toxic waste site?
    A. Mildew found on a shower curtain
    B. Lead-based paint that is not chipped or peeling
    C. A methamphetamine lab
    D. Radon gas

12. An option contract that has been exercised is a(n)
    A. unilateral contract.
    B. bilateral contact.
    C. executory bilateral contract.
    D. executory unilateral contract.

13. After the snowstorm of the century, Warren offers to pay $6 to whoever will shovel his driveway. This is an example of which of the following?
    A. Implied contract
    B. Bilateral contract
    C. License
    D. Unilateral contract

14. Carl made a written offer on Kristen's property. After reviewing the contract with her attorney, Kristen accepted the offer in writing. At this point, what type of title does Carl have to the property?
    A. Legal
    B. Equitable
    C. Indefeasible
    D. Defeasible

15. As a general rule, an oral sales contract involving the sale of real estate
    A. can be enforced through a court action.
    B. can be assigned to a third party.
    C. can be subject to a real estate commission.
    D. is unenforceable.

16. Straight-line depreciation means
    A. investors can depreciate the value of the land for 27.5 years.
    B. homeowners may depreciate the purchase of a new furnace the year of purchase.
    C. homeowners must recapture the depreciation the year the property is sold.
    D. investors can depreciate the value of the improvements in periodic equal amounts.

17. Loss history and the buyer's credit are two factors that are considered when determining if
    A. the listing should be accepted by the brokerage firm.
    B. a homeowners insurance policy will be issued.
    C. an appraisal should be ordered.
    D. the seller should accept the offer.

18. An individual seeking to be excused from the dictates of a zoning ordinance should request a
    A. building permit.
    B. certificate of alternate usage.
    C. restrictive covenant.
    D. variance.

19. A buyer would MOST LIKELY be protected from destruction of the premises, injury to others on the premises, and theft of personal property if he or she purchased
    A. private mortgage insurance.
    B. long-term care insurance.
    C. homeowners insurance.
    D. life insurance.

20. Zoning ordinances control the use of privately owned land by establishing land-use districts. Which one of the following is not a usual zoning district?
    A. Residential
    B. Commercial
    C. Industrial
    D. Rental

21. The major intent of zoning regulations is to
    A. demonstrate the police power of the state.
    B. ensure the health, safety, and welfare of the community.
    C. set limits on the amount and kinds of businesses in a given area.
    D. protect residential neighborhoods from encroachment by business and industry.

22. All of the following are considered a part of the bundle of legal rights associated with real property ownership EXCEPT the rights to
    A. possess, enjoy, control, and exclude.
    B. sell, lease, devise, and improve.
    C. mortgage, mine, drill, and bequeath.
    D. trade, exchange, cultivate, and explore.

23. John and George have an arrangement in which George has agreed to let John make an offer on his property should he decide to sell. Which of the following BEST describes this arrangement?
    A. Offer and acceptance
    B. Mutual assent
    C. Land contract
    D. Right of first refusal

24. Which of the following is NOT a consideration in a buyer agency agreement?
    A. Description of the property the buyer desires to purchase
    B. Sales associate's compensation
    C. Broker's accountability to the buyer
    D. Disclosure of the dual agency relationship to the seller

25. Which of the following BEST describes a material fact that should be disclosed to buyers who do not have an agent representing them in a transaction?
    A. The seller is getting a divorce.
    B. The seller has AIDS.
    C. The seller owes special assessments on the property.
    D. The seller's spouse died on the property and that's why it's for sale.

26. A seller has set an appointment with an agent to list a property. The agent knows the property is stigmatized. What would be the BEST action for the agent to take?
    A. List the property and ignore the fact that the property is stigmatized.
    B. Secure the listing and advertise the property as stigmatized without the seller's permission.
    C. Disclose the fact that the property is stigmatized only to those buyers the agent thinks would be interested in knowing that the property is stigmatized.
    D. Discuss the matter with the broker and secure legal advice before listing the property.

27. The loan is negotiated on the
    A. appraised value or sale price, whichever is less.
    B. appraised value or sale price, whichever is greater.
    C. appraised value or assessed value, whichever is less.
    D. appraised value or assessed value, whichever is greater.

28. An underwriter is determining the desirability of a loan. The underwriter is LEAST LIKELY to take into consideration which of the following?
    A. The appraisal
    B. Pest control inspection
    C. Flood certification
    D. Home warranty plan

29. A zoning board is reviewing a request to build a factory in the community. In making the decision regarding the location of the factory, the board will MOST LIKELY consider
    A. the taxes to be paid by the employees.
    B. how far the employees will have to drive to work.
    C. the number of managers the factory will need.
    D. the performance standards that regulate air, noise, and water pollution.

30. Which of the following would be used to determine if soil has adequate absorption and drainage capacity to meet health and safety standards?
    A. Topography test
    B. Absorption test
    C. Percolation test
    D. Drainage test

31. The dwelling on a property has been valued at $95,000 and the land has been valued at $35,000. Fire destroys the dwelling. The homeowner with a standard insurance policy would MOST LIKELY file a claim for the maximum amount of
    A. $95,000.
    B. $130,000.
    C. $104,000.
    D. $76,000.

32. Which of the following documents would LEAST LIKELY be required by a lender for final approval of a loan?
    A. Pest control report
    B. The listing agreement
    C. Survey
    D. Title search

33. The terms *stable income*, *net worth*, and *credit history* describe three basic factors
    A. in assessing the sale price of the property.
    B. in assessing the buyer's qualifications.
    C. needed to appraise the property.
    D. that prove the seller has a good and marketable title.

34. The process of evaluating the loan to determine desirability of approving the loan is called loan
    A. underwriting.
    B. approval.
    C. application.
    D. officer.

35. The monthly principal and interest payment made on a loan is often referred to as the
    A. mortgage-to-income ratio.
    B. debt service.
    C. loan-to-value ratio.
    D. loan-to-income ratio.

36. The person who reviews all documentation and evaluates the risk of the loan is the
    A. real estate agent.
    B. loan officer.
    C. underwriter.
    D. processor.

37. *Time is of the essence* in a contract means that the
    A. duties and responsibilities of the contract must be fulfilled on or before a stipulated time indicated in the contract.
    B. buyer is obligated to fulfill all duties stipulated in the contract by a certain date, but the seller is not.
    C. seller is obligated to fulfill all duties stipulated in the contract by a certain date, but the buyer is not.
    D. agent is obligated to fulfill all duties stipulated in the contract by a certain date, but the buyer and seller are not.

38. At closing, a title is transferred to the buyer. Until that event occurs, a contract entered into by a buyer and a seller is
    A. executory.
    B. executed.
    C. void.
    D. unenforceable.

39. In most states, all of the following contracts would need to be in writing to be enforceable EXCEPT
    A. a three-month lease agreement on an apartment.
    B. a contract for the sale of air rights.
    C. the sale of an easement to the airport.
    D. a sales contract for a principal place of residence.

40. Carrie negotiated an option contract with Mindy, wherein Mindy had six months to purchase the property. In month four Mindy found another buyer for the property. If Mindy can transfer her option contract to the new buyer, she can do so because of the right of
    A. novation.
    B. first refusal.
    C. contingency.
    D. assignment.

41. After three extensions of a sales contract, the buyers and sellers finally met at the title company for closing. The primary role of the real estate agent at the closing is to
    A. explain the closing documents to the buyer.
    B. explain the closing documents to the seller.
    C. notarize documents.
    D. verify and receive the broker's fee.

42. When visiting a new subdivision, the buyers asked the agent if there would be commercial development "in their backyard" if they purchased a home on a particular street. The agent assured them the adjacent property was zoned residential. The BEST way for the buyers to confirm the agent's statement is to
    A. ask the agent's broker.
    B. ask a neighbor.
    C. check the plat map.
    D. check the master plan.

43. An agent forgot to get her buyer to sign the offer. What is the status of the offer?
    A. Valid
    B. Void
    C. Voidable
    D. Acceptable

44. Which of the following would LEAST LIKELY be found in a sales contract?
    A. The identity of the buyer and a description of the property being purchased
    B. The type of listing contract and its expiration date
    C. The identity of the seller and the type of deed being conveyed, including covenants, conditions, and restrictions
    D. Any appurtenances the seller intends to leave with the property

45. A contract entered into based on a misrepresentation is
    A. voidable by the aggrieved party.
    B. void between the parties.
    C. voidable by either party.
    D. a valid enforceable contract.

46. In a land contract, which of the following would MOST LIKELY happen?
    A. The vendor finances the property and makes installment payments.
    B. The vendee receives possession and the vendor retains an equitable title.
    C. The vendor pays the property taxes, insurance, repairs, and upkeep on the property until the final payment is made.
    D. The vendor retains the title to the property until the final payment is made.

47. A capital gain is
    A. a taxable profit that is realized from the sale or exchange of an asset.
    B. classified as long term if the asset is owned for more than six months.
    C. computed only on improvements.
    D. computed only on land.

48. A seller listed a property for $100,000. The buyer made an offer for the full list price and gave the seller three days to accept. Two days later the seller had not yet accepted. Regarding this situation, which of the following is true?
   A. The buyer cannot withdraw an offer for the full list price.
   B. The seller must accept the offer because it is for the full list price.
   C. The seller may reject the offer, but the commission is due the broker.
   D. The buyer must wait the entire three days before the offer can be withdrawn.

49. What do the terms *offer and acceptance*, *mutual assent*, and *meeting of the minds* have in common?
   A. The terms mean there is an unqualified acceptance of an offer, which is an essential element of a contract.
   B. The terms mean there is a qualified acceptance of an offer, which is an essential element of a contract.
   C. The terms affect only contracts for the transfer of easement rights in a lease agreement.
   D. The terms affect only contracts for the transfer of personal property at a foreclosure sale.

50. A husband in the military is currently stationed in Iraq. He and his wife decide to sell their house in the United States so she can join him. To provide a good and marketable title to the buyer, the wife should
   A. secure a specific, durable power of attorney from her husband and sell the property.
   B. sign her husband's name to all documents after showing her marriage certificate.
   C. let her husband's twin brother sign any necessary documents for him.
   D. sign all documents for him because she is his wife.

51. Which of the following is NOT true regarding tax-deferred exchanges?
   A. If an investor exchanges property instead of selling it, payment of the capital gain may be excluded.
   B. The seller has 45 days from the close of escrow on the first property to "identify" a replacement property.
   C. The close on the second property must occur within 180 days of the close of escrow on the first property.
   D. Reverse exchanges are allowed that allow the replacement property to be acquired before the disposition of the relinquished property.

52. A contract has written contingencies. The status of this contract is
   A. voidable.
   B. void.
   C. executed.
   D. fraudulent.

53. In a conventional loan, the usual debt-to-service ratio is
   A. 28 percent.
   B. 29 percent.
   C. 36 percent.
   D. 41 percent.

54. A buyer is going to attend a foreclosure sale. When discussing his possible purchase with a friend, his friend advised "caveat emptor." This means
   A. "let the seller beware."
   B. "let the bank beware."
   C. "let the neighbors beware."
   D. "let the buyer beware."

55. When purchasing a commercial property, the buyer placed $10,000 in an escrow account, and the offer stipulated the seller was to place $10,000 in an escrow account. If either party breached the contract, the aggrieved party was to receive the $20,000. This is BEST described as a(n)
   A. equitable damage clause.
   B. subordination clause.
   C. earnest money clause.
   D. liquidated damage clause.

56. When computing straight-line depreciation, an investor must depreciate
    A. residential investment property for 27.5 years.
    B. commercial investment property for 27.5 years.
    C. only the value of the land.
    D. the value of the land and the improvements.

57. A buyer's agent would NOT recommend the buyer seek expert advice if the buyer asked which of the following questions?
    A. "How should I take title to the property?"
    B. "Does the crack in the basement mean there is structural damage?"
    C. "How long has the property been on the market?"
    D. "Would you recommend a radon test?"

58. All of the following would render an offer voidable EXCEPT the contract that is
    A. missing an essential element.
    B. entered into under duress.
    C. entered into with misrepresentation.
    D. entered into through fraud.

59. The buyer's offer stipulated that the closing must take place by April 15. This clause is known as
    A. the settlement clause.
    B. time is of the essence.
    C. a contingency clause.
    D. transfer clause.

60. Recently, an ordinance was passed stating that no sign placed on a building may extend more than three feet above the highest point of the roof. Thomas wants to place a revolving sign nine feet high on the roof of his store. In order to legally do this, Thomas must get a(n)
    A. residual.
    B. variance.
    C. nonconforming use permit.
    D. aerial clearance.

61. Peggy made an offer of $250,000 on a For Sale by Owner property. Her offer contained an earnest money check for $1,000 and no contingencies. If the seller accepts her offer, is it a binding contract?
    A. Yes, because the offer included a $1,000 earnest money check.
    B. Yes, because the contract contained the consideration of her $250,000 offer.
    C. No, because she did not have an agent to present the offer.
    D. No, because the sales contract was not reviewed by an attorney.

62. "Broker will provide the owner with a list of names of all persons with whom the Broker or any other person negotiated concerning the above described property during the period of this listing no later than 14 days subsequent to the termination date of this listing agreement. If the property is sold to any person named in the list prior to the relisting of the property, without the services of another Broker, and within 180 days of the termination date of this contract, Seller agrees to pay the Broker a commission of seven percent." This is an example of a(n)
    A. contingency clause.
    B. extender or broker protection clause.
    C. right of first refusal clause.
    D. time is of the essence clause.

63. An offer was made contingent on the buyer's negotiating a 30-year fixed rate mortgage with an interest rate of no more than 7 percent. The buyer was to provide the seller with a preapproval letter from a lender by July 11 and the property was to close on July 31. On July 10, the seller's agent received another, higher offer on the property. Can the agent present the second offer to the seller, and what clause should be in the first contract to possibly release the seller from the first offer?
  A. Yes, the agent can present the second offer. If the first offer contains the "time is of the essence" clause and the buyer does not provide a preapproval letter from the lender by July 11, the seller will be released from the first offer.
  B. Yes, the agent can present the second offer. If the first offer grants novation to the seller, then the seller will be released from the first offer.
  C. No, the agent should not present the backup offer to the seller until July 12.
  D. No, once an offer has been accepted, the agent should never present additional offers to the seller.

64. A buyer entered into a buyer agency agreement. The buyer still has the right to enter into similar agreements with any number of agents. This describes a(n)
  A. exclusive buyer agency.
  B. exclusive-agency buyer agency.
  C. open buyer agency.
  D. designated buyer agency.

65. A sales contract had been negotiated between the buyer and seller. At the closing table, the seller received a phone call from his company and was informed that he was not being transferred after all. The seller has not signed the deed and no longer wants to sell his property. If he refuses to sell, does the buyer have legal action to force the sale?
  A. Yes, the buyer may file a suit for possession to enforce the sales contract.
  B. Yes, the buyer may file a suit for specific performance to enforce the sales contract.
  C. No, the seller has not signed the deed, and until that occurs, the buyer has no legal right to enforce the contract.
  D. No, the seller has not signed the deed and only then would the buyer have a right to file a suit to quiet the title.

66. Which of the following statements is FALSE regarding offer and acceptance?
  A. To offer means to put forward for acceptance, rejection, or consideration.
  B. An offer can be revoked at any time before acceptance.
  C. A counteroffer reverses the legal positions of the offeror and offeree.
  D. In real estate, an oral acceptance creates a binding contract.

67. Floyd owns 50 acres and has been presented with an option contract. The possible buyer included a $50,000 option money check with her contract. If Floyd signs the option contract and the buyer does not buy, does he have to return the $50,000 to the buyer?
  A. Yes, because option money is like earnest money and it is always returned to the buyer.
  B. Yes, because it is standard practice in an option contract to return the option money if the buyer does not buy.
  C. No, because it is standard practice in an option contract for the seller to keep the option money if the buyer does not buy.
  D. No, because option money should be placed in the broker's escrow account and given to the seller only if the option is exercised.

68. Which of the following is NOT required to create a valid sales contract?
    A. Offer and acceptance
    B. Consideration
    C. Signatures
    D. Earnest money

69. An executor called an agent to list a property to settle an estate. While showing the property to the agent, the executor commented that "Aunt Geneva always had tenants in the upstairs apartment." Without checking with zoning, the agent listed and sold the property as multifamily. If the property is not zoned multifamily, does the buyer have the right to rescind the contract?
    A. Yes, because the agent misrepresented the property and any contract entered into under misrepresentation is void.
    B. Yes, because the agent misrepresented the property and any contract entered into under misrepresentation is voidable.
    C. No, because the executor should have checked to determine the zoning of the property before listing the property.
    D. No, because the title company should have checked to determine the zoning of the property.

70. Which of the following federal tax rules BEST applies to a homeowner who sells a home?
    A. The homeowner may defer the payment of capital gains tax if another home is purchased within two years with a value equal to or greater than the adjusted sales price of the old residence.
    B. The homeowner may exclude the payment of capital gains tax if the homeowner has lived in the home two out of the last five years and the exclusion does not exceed the government allowance.
    C. The homeowner can depreciate the improvements on the property as long as the depreciation does not exceed $125,000.
    D. The homeowner must pay capital gains tax within nine months of the sale of the property.

MATCHING QUIZ

The column on the right contains a brief definition of important terms in this section.
Write the letter of the matching term on the appropriate line.

A. Novation

B. Caveat emptor

C. Absorption rate

D. Stigmatized property

E. Executory contract

F. Special study zones

G. Equitable title

H. Net worth

I. Assignment

J. Performance standards

K. Exculpatory clause

L. Radon

M. "Time is of the essence"

N. "Meeting of the minds"

O. Asbestos

P. Option contract

Q. Indemnification clause

R. Land contract

S. Voidable contract

T. Caveat venditor

1. ___ Another term for offer and acceptance, an essential element of a contract

2. ___ Used in building materials, especially insulation; harmful only if disturbed or exposed

3. ___ A "hold harmless" clause found in some contracts

4. ___ Estimate of how quickly new construction will be sold or occupied each year

5. ___ Substituting a new contract for an old one, which releases liability

6. ___ Term meaning "let the seller beware"

7. ___ The right to purchase property within a definite time at a specified price

8. ___ Agreement to compensate someone for a loss

9. ___ Term meaning "let the buyer beware"

10. ___ Regulate the air, noise, and water pollution allowed by manufacturing facilities

11. ___ Contract in which the seller finances the purchase of the property; also known as a contract for deed

12. ___ The past history of the property makes it undesirable

13. ___ The right to obtain absolute ownership to property when legal title is held in another party's name

14. ___ Transfer in writing of rights or interest in a bond, mortgage, lease, or other instrument

15. ___ Odorless, tasteless gas produced by the natural decay of other radioactive substances

16. ___ Contract that may be rescinded by one or both parties

17. ___ Regulation of land use to control development in high-risk flood-prone or geological areas

18. ___ In this contract, one or both parties have duties to perform

19. ___ Computed by subtracting liabilities from assets

20. ___ This clause in a contract means the contract must be performed within the time limit specified

ANSWERS

1. **(C)** Contracts for the sale of real estate must be in writing to be enforceable according to the statute of frauds.

2. **(B)** Novation is the substitution of a new party or contract for an existing one.

3. **(A)** In an option contract, the buyer must pay money or consideration for the option right.

4. **(B)** Victor, the seller, gave invalid information to the buyer, Sally. A contract entered into under misrepresentation is voidable by Sally, the aggrieved party.

5. **(B)** One of the essential elements of a contract includes mutual agreement between the parties.

6. **(B)** By definition of a bilateral contract.

7. **(C)** An executed contract exists when all parties have fully performed their duties.

8. **(A)** By definition of specific performance.

9. **(B)** An offer must be accepted without changes.

10. **(C)** An offer can be withdrawn at any time prior to acceptance.

11. **(C)** When a methamphetamine lab is found on a property, it is deemed a toxic waste site.

12. **(C)** When the buyer informs the seller that the buyer is going to purchase the property, the option is exercised and an executory bilateral contract exists.

13. **(D)** Because only one party, Warren, is obligated to perform, a unilateral contract exists.

14. **(B)** Equitable title is the buyer's interest in the property when legal title is held by another party.

15. **(D)** Real estate contracts must be in writing. An oral real estate contract is unenforceable by either party.

16. **(D)** Straight-line depreciation means that improvements are depreciated in periodic equal amounts.

17. **(B)** A property's loss history and the buyer's credit history will determine if an insurance company will issue a homeowners insurance policy.

18. **(D)** By definition of variance.

19. **(C)** Homeowners insurance protects from destruction of the premises, injury to others on the premises, and theft of personal property.

20. **(D)** Rental is not a land-use district. The land-use districts are agricultural, residential, commercial, industrial, and special-purpose properties.

21. **(B)** The major intent of zoning is to ensure the health, safety, and welfare of the public.

22. **(C)** The bundle of legal rights does not include the right to bequeath, which is to leave personal property in a will.

23. **(D)** A right of first refusal gives a person the first right to buy or lease a property.

24. **(B)** The broker's commission would be in the agreement, but not the agent's.

25. **(C)** This is a material fact that should be disclosed to the buyer.

26. **(D)** If a property is stigmatized, it should be discussed with the broker and the attorney before the listing.

27. **(A)** The loan is computed on the appraised value or sale price, whichever is less.

28. **(D)** The underwriter would least likely be concerned about the home warranty plan.

29. **(D)** Performance standards would be a major consideration in the location of the factory.

30. **(C)** By definition of a percolation test.

31. **(D)** A standard insurance policy covers 80 percent of the value of the dwelling.

32. **(B)** A copy of the listing agreement is not required for loan approval.

33. **(B)** Assessing the buyer's qualifications depends on stable income, net worth, and credit history.

34. **(A)** By definition of loan underwriting.

35. **(B)** By definition of debt service.

36. **(C)** The underwriter evaluates the risk and approves the loan.

37. **(A)** By the definition of time is of the essence.

38. **(A)** It is an executory contract because there are still obligations to be performed.

39. **(A)** In most states, leases for less than one year do not have to be in writing.

40. **(D)** An assignment is the transfer of rights and duties from one person to another person.

41. **(D)** The primary purpose of the agent at the closing is to collect the broker's check.

42. **(D)** The buyers should check the master plan to determine the zoning for the property.

43. **(B)** The offer is missing an essential element, the signature of the offeror, and is void.

44. **(B)** The type of listing contract would least likely be found in a sales contract.

45. **(A)** A contract entered into with misrepresentation is voidable by the aggrieved party.

46. **(D)** The vendor will most likely retain the title to the property until the final payment is made.

47. **(A)** The definition of capital gain is the taxable profit realized from the sale or exchange of an asset.

48. **(C)** An offer can be withdrawn at any time before acceptance. A seller does not have to accept the full list price for the property, but the commission is still due.

49. **(A)** By definition of offer and acceptance, mutual assent, and meeting of the minds.

50. **(A)** When one spouse cannot be present to sign documents, that spouse should create a power of attorney so documents can be properly transferred.

51. **(A)** The capital gain may be *deferred*, but it cannot be excluded.

52. **(A)** A contract with contingencies is voidable.

53. **(C)** In a conventional loan the debt to service ratio is normally 36 percent.

54. **(D)** Caveat emptor means "let the buyer beware."

55. **(D)** A liquidated damage clause is compensation agreed on in advance if one party breaches the contract.

56. **(A)** Using the straight-line method of depreciation, residential investment property is depreciated for 27.5 years and commercial property for 39 years.

57. **(C)** "How long has the property been on the market?" is not a question that would require the buyer to seek the advice of an expert.

58. **(A)** If an offer is missing an essential element, it is void (not voidable).

59. **(B)** *Time is of the essence* means the contract must be performed within the time limit specified.

60. **(B)** A variance grants relief from the harshness of a zoning ordinance.

61. **(B)** Contracts must contain consideration and the offer is the consideration in a sales contract, not the earnest money.

62. **(B)** By definition of extender or broker protection clause.

63. **(A)** Time is of the essence means the contract's terms must be performed with the specified time frame or the contract is null and void.

64. **(C)** By definition of open buyer agency agreement.

65. **(B)** If either buyer or seller does not perform after a sales contract has been signed and contingencies met, the other party may sue for specific performance.

66. **(D)** In real estate an oral acceptance does not create a binding contract.

67. **(C)** The option money is paid to the seller for taking the property off the market, and it is standard practice that it be retained by the seller.

68. **(D)** The consideration in a sales contract is the price. An earnest money check is not needed to create a valid sales contract.

69. **(B)** Any contract entered into under misrepresentation or fraud is voidable by the aggrieved party.

70. **(B)** In accordance with the new laws regarding exclusion of capital gains.

ANSWERS—MATCHING QUIZ

1. N	6. T	11. R	16. S
2. O	7. P	12. D	17. F
3. K	8. Q	13. G	18. E
4. C	9. B	14. I	19. H
5. A	10. J	15. L	20. M

3

Property Management

Residential property management includes single-family homes, multifamily apartment buildings, condominium communities, planned unit developments, cooperatives, mobile home parks, and housing for the elderly. Commercial property management includes office, retail, and industrial properties. This chapter reviews property management as it relates to the services to landlords and tenants.

AMP Outline—Leasing and Management

III. Property Management
  A. Leasing and Management
    1. Negotiation of property management agreements
    2. Negotiation of lease agreements used in property management
    3. Preparation and explanation of rental and lease agreements
    4. Methods of marketing property
    5. Rental market evaluation
    6. Disclosure of material facts to lessee
    7. Obtaining tenants
    8. Showing property and occupancy terms
    9. Applicant screening according to laws and regulations
    10. Complaints and conflict resolutions among tenants
    11. Operating budgets
    12. Trust accounts
    13. Financial statements for owners
    14. Income, expenses, and rate of return
    15. Environmental and safety hazards
    16. Compliance with federal requirements
    17. Eviction proceedings
    18. Maintenance and repair management
    19. Fees, security deposits, and rent collection
    20. Insurance coverage to protect tenant and owner

NEGOTIATION OF PROPERTY MANAGEMENT AGREEMENTS

The owner and the property manager negotiate the relationship between them. This relationship can be employer-employee, principal-agent, or trustor-trustee. A written management agreement between the parties stipulates whether payment is to be on a flat-fee basis or a percentage of the gross income. Whichever relationship or method of payment is negotiated, the property manager still has a fiduciary relationship with the owner.

A written management agreement is reached between the owner and the person or firm that will manage the property. States may have specific laws regarding such agreements, but generally the following must be included to establish the scope of the agent's authority:

- Identification of the parties

- Legal description of the property

- Statement of owner's purpose

- Duties and responsibilities of the manager

- Responsibilities of the owner

- Rate and schedule of compensation

- Accounting and report requirements

- Starting date, termination date, and provisions for renewal options

- Amount and method of determining the minimum security deposit to be collected from the tenants for each unit managed

- Procedure for returning or retaining the security deposit

- Provision setting forth the conditions under which the manager is authorized to pay expenses of the property being managed

- Signatures of the parties

The *property manager* has a *fiduciary relationship* with the *owner*, which includes the duties of care, obedience, accounting, loyalty, and disclosure.

- The *duty of care* means to use care and skill while managing the property and binding the owner to contracts and to be responsible in every way to the owner.

- The *duty of obedience* means to carry out, in good faith, the owner's instructions. The property manager should immediately terminate the relationship if asked to do something illegal or unethical.

- The *duty of accounting* means to maintain and accurately report to the owner the status of all funds received on behalf of or from the property owner.

- The *duty of loyalty* means to put the property owner's interests first and act without self-interest in every transaction.

- The *duty of disclosure* means to keep the owner informed of all material facts regarding the management of the property.

NEGOTIATION OF LEASE AGREEMENTS USED IN PROPERTY MANAGEMENT

Whether leasing residential, commercial, or industrial property, qualifying the tenant is one of the major responsibilities of the property manager. Filling out a lease application that may ask for verification of identity, authorization to secure a credit report, financial statement, special needs of the tenant, and securing rental history is a part of the process.

The lease negotiations could include concessions, such as free rent to influence a prospect to become a tenant, rent reductions and rebates, length of the lease period, tenant alterations, expansion options, noncompeting tenant restrictions, and lease buy-out, assumption, and subletting.

The provisions of a valid lease are essentially the same as for any valid contract. There must be an offer and acceptance by parties with the legal capacity to contract. The terms of a lease include

- names of the parties,

- description of the property,

- term of the lease,

- possession and use of the premises,

- rights and obligation of the parties,

- consideration (rent payments for the term of the lease),

- provisions for assignment and sublease,

- security deposit, and

- signatures of the parties.

A **lease** is an agreement that transfers exclusive possession and use of real estate from the landlord/owner/lessor to the tenant/lessee. This lease agreement can be oral or written. The owner has a **reversionary right** to retake the property on the expiration of the terms of the lease. Figure 3.1 lists the various types of leases used in property management.

Rental and Lease Agreements

The lessor's interest is called a **leased fee interest**, and the lessee's interest is called a **leasehold interest**. Owners are responsible for keeping the property habitable and for complying with local building and housing codes. These responsibilities include the upkeep of common areas and of electrical, heating, and plumbing systems; trash removal; maintenance of elevators; and any other services promised in the lease.

A *nondisturbance clause* in a mortgage states that the mortgagee agrees not to terminate the lease in event of foreclosure. However, the tenant must be in compliance with the lease terms.

FIGURE 3.1

Types of Leases—Nonfreehold Estates

Estate for Years or Tenancy for Years
- A lease with a definite time period or specified beginning and ending dates.
- No notice is needed to terminate the estate.
- A tenant who remains in possession after expiration is considered a holdover.

Estate from Period to Period/Periodic Tenancy
- A lease with an indefinite time period that automatically renews until proper notice to terminate is given.

Estate at Will or Tenancy at Will
- A lease that gives the tenant the right to possess the property with the consent of the landlord for an uncertain time period. The lease can be terminated at any time by the landlord or the tenant giving proper notice to the other party.
- Death of either party also terminates the lease.

Estate at Sufferance or Tenancy at Sufferance
- A tenancy created when a tenant remains in possession of the property without the consent of the landlord after the lease expires.
- If the landlord gives permission to a tenant to remain on the property after the expiration of a lease, the tenant may be treated as a holdover, and a tenancy at will or periodic tenancy may be created.

Assignment

Leases can be assigned or subleased *unless* there is a clause in the lease forbidding it. (See Figure 3.2.) A tenant who transfers *all* the leasehold interests *assigns* the lease. For example, the lessor executes a 20-year commercial lease with the lessee. Ten years into the lease, the business is sold. The new owner of the business (assignee) will be assigned *all the leasehold interests* and the landlord will receive the rent payment from the new tenant (assignee). Unless novation is granted, the previous owner (assignor) will not be released for the liability of the rent payments.

Sublease

A sublease is created when a tenant transfers *less than all the leasehold interests* by subleasing them to a new tenant. In this arrangement, there are *two landlord-tenant relationships*. For example, the lessor enters into a one-year lease on an apartment with a lessee. Six months into the lease, the tenant is transferred and decides to sublease the apartment. The original lease agreement between the lessor and lessee remains, but once the apartment is sublet, another landlord-tenant relationship is created between the lessee and the sublessee. The lessor expects a rent check from the lessee, and the lessee (sublessor) expects a rent check from the sublessee. The sublessor can charge more rent and retain the profit. The sublessor's interest is called a *sandwich lease*.

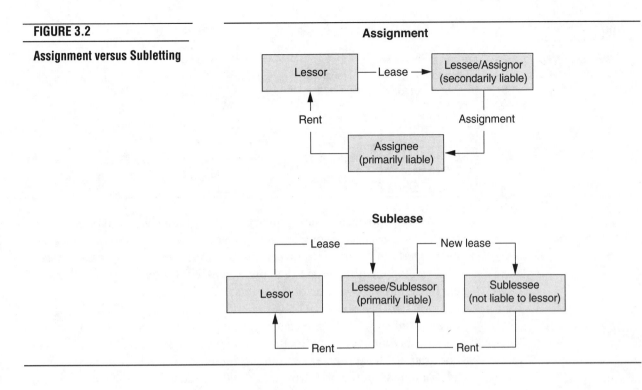

FIGURE 3.2

Assignment versus Subletting

Other types of leases are:

- **Lease option**—The tenant has the option to purchase the property at a specified price within a certain time. A portion of the monthly rental payment may be credited toward the purchase price.

- **Lease purchase**—The tenant agrees to purchase the property at a specified price within a certain period, which is usually the end of the lease.

- **Gross (straight) lease**—The tenant pays a fixed rental amount, and the owner pays all other ownership expenses for the property. The owner usually pays property taxes, insurance, and maintenance, while the tenant pays for the utilities.

- **Net lease**—The tenant agrees to pay ownership expenses such as utilities, property taxes, and special assessments. In a net-net lease the tenant pays for insurance as well. In a net-net-net lease, the tenant also pays for some agreed-on items of repair and maintenance. Thus, the terms *net, double net,* and *triple net* can be used to describe the lease, depending on the ownership expenses the tenant agrees to pay.

- **Percentage lease (used for retail space)**—The tenant agrees to pay a fixed base rental fee plus a percentage of the gross income in excess of a predetermined minimum amount of sales. The percentage lease also can be computed from the first dollar of sales. See Chapter 7 to learn how to compute the rent paid in a percentage lease.

- **Sale-leaseback**—The grantor sells the property to the grantee, and then leases it back. (See Figure 3.3.) For example, a buyer wants to purchase a unit being used as a model in a new condominium development. The developer had intended to use the unit as a model for the next six months. The developer and buyer enter into a sale-leaseback.

FIGURE 3.3

Sale-Leaseback

Sale-Leaseback

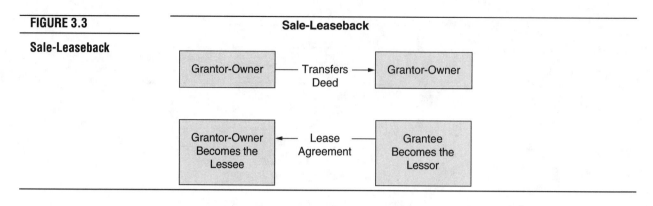

The developer/owner/grantor sells the property to the buyer/grantee. When the sales transaction is complete, the grantee becomes the lessor and leases the property to the previous owner, the developer, who becomes the lessee. The developer has the property to use as a model for the next six months and the buyer has the condo he or she wants.

- **Graduated lease**—The graduated lease is used to attract tenants to a property that is difficult to rent. It allows for a periodic step-up of rent payments. For example, tenants enter into a five-year lease in which they agree to pay $400 a month for the first two years, $450 for the next two years, and $500 for the final year.

- **Index lease**—The rent is tied to an index outside the control of both the landlord and the tenant. Index leases contain an **escalation clause** that allows the lease payment to change based on the index used, for example, the consumer price index. Index leases are more common in times of inflation, when the property manager does not want to enter into long-term fixed rentals that would cause the value of the property to decrease.

Termination of Leases

Leases may be terminated by the expiration of the term of the lease, proper notice as defined in the lease, surrender and acceptance, abandonment, merger, or destruction or condemnation of the property. **Death** of the lessor or lessee does not automatically terminate a lease. Should the property be **sold**, the grantee takes the title *subject to all existing leases*. Unless the leases indicate otherwise, the new landlord cannot make any changes until each lease expires.

PREPARATION AND EXPLANATION OF RENTAL AND LEASE AGREEMENTS

A lease agreement should be prepared to include the terms the manager and tenant agreed to during the negotiation process. The lease should be reviewed by the owner, tenant, and respective attorneys. The property manager should provide a reasonable explanation to the tenant regarding the terms of the lease agreement and advise the tenant to seek legal counsel before signing the lease.

Lease provisions may include

- the use of the premises,
- term of the lease,

- safekeeping and return of the security deposit,

- payment for tenant improvements to the property,

- payment for maintenance of the premises,

- parking space allotment,

- condemnation clause,

- compliance clause,

- insurance clause,

- noncompliance clause,

- renewals and rent increases,

- expansion options, and

- responsibilities of the landlord and the tenant.

METHODS OF MARKETING PROPERTY

A property manager can choose from a range of advertising media to reach a target audience. This could include a sign on the property identifying the management firm and the person to call for further information as well as flyers, newspaper advertising, regional magazines and trade journals, radio, television, direct mail and brochures, and Internet sites.

The first step in the development of a marketing plan is to determine if there is *a low or high vacancy rate* in the area for the type of property being leased. If there is a high vacancy rate, attracting tenants for immediate occupancy is the primary goal. *Concessions* such as free rent or reduced rent through a *graduated lease or rebates* may be offered to a tenant. If there is a low vacancy rate, an ad campaign would promote the many amenities of the property and the owner would analyze if potential tenants are willing to pay more rent.

RENTAL MARKET EVALUATION

A market is created when two or more people meet for the purpose of selling or leasing a commodity. These transactions occur at a national, regional, or local level. A property manager must be able to evaluate market trends to determine the rent that may be charged. This would include supply and demand and local economic conditions, as well as a neighborhood market analysis.

Regional Market Analysis

A regional market analysis should include demographic and economic information in the area where the property is located. This information includes population statistics, income and employment data, a description of transportation facilities, and supply and demand trends.

Neighborhood Market Analysis

Property managers rely on a neighborhood market analysis because much of their business is generated at a local level. The neighborhood market analysis would include boundaries and land usage, transportation and utilities, economy, supply and demand, and neighborhood amenities and facilities. Once the regional and neighborhood market surveys are complete, the property manager analyzes the data to determine the special features of the property and how it fits the needs of potential tenants.

DISCLOSURE OF MATERIAL FACTS TO LESSEE

Even though the property manager has a fiduciary relationship with the owner, the manager must disclose to the tenant material facts that would affect the lease. This would include location and return of security deposits, building rules, procedure for paying the rent and penalties for late payments, process for maintenance requests, steps for renewal, termination of the lease, and environmental disclosures.

OBTAINING TENANTS

The best method of renting property is to secure referrals from satisfied tenants. Many times an owner will pay cash or rental incentives (concessions) to current tenants for such referrals. Press releases sent to local newspapers and brokers may gain free publicity for the property when leasing new or large developments. The interest also provides a new media for advertising and obtaining tenants.

The property manager may also decide to work with a *leasing agent*, who is an independent contractor and whose primary function is to show the property and follow up on prospective tenants. Leasing agents may be paid a flat referral fee or a split-commission basis.

SHOWING PROPERTY AND OCCUPANCY TERMS

When the spatial needs have been determined and the prospective tenant has been qualified, the property manager should show property that best meets the needs of the prospective tenant. While showing the property, the manager describes the benefits of the space, building, and neighborhood as they meet the tenant's needs. If the property is occupied, the current tenant must be notified of the showing.

The occupancy terms to be negotiated include concessions, rent schedules, rebates, length of the leasing period, tenant alterations, expansion options, noncompeting tenant restrictions and the defraying of moving expenses. The property manager must negotiate these terms to meet the needs of both the owner and the tenant.

Once the lease agreement has been negotiated, the landlord must give exclusive possession of the property to the tenant. The **covenant of quiet enjoyment** means the landlord must honor the tenant's right of possession and may not enter the property without the tenant's permission unless it is an emergency, to provide services or make repairs, or other unusual circumstances.

The **warranty of habitability** requires that the landlord keep the property in good condition. This would include maintenance of the common areas and equipment, providing utilities, and being in compliance with state and local codes.

The tenant is obligated to use appliances in a safe manner and to keep the property in good repair.

APPLICANT SCREENING ACCORDING TO LAWS AND REGULATIONS

The property manager should develop (and the owner should approve) a screening process that provides equal professional services to all potential tenants. One of the first areas of qualification of potential tenants must be in meeting a tenant's needs as far as space requirements are concerned. The needs would be totally different for a residential tenant than for a commercial tenant. Other tenant considerations include

- motives for moving,
- when the current lease expires,
- projected budget for the new space,
- parking and transportation needs, and
- any special needs of the tenant.

Each prospective tenant should be required to fill out a lease application. For residential tenants, credit references, personal references, and rental history must be secured and checked by the property manager. In negotiating a commercial lease, the property manager must be sure that the person being interviewed has the authority to negotiate contracts for the company. This can be accomplished by asking for a copy of the articles of incorporation or partnership agreement.

For commercial property, a profit and loss statement of the company should demonstrate that the company is financially sound. All federal laws such as fair housing and the Americans with Disabilities Act must be obeyed when screening applicants.

COMPLAINTS AND CONFLICT RESOLUTION AMONG TENANTS

A property manager establishes communication with a prospective tenant during the initial interviewing process. This communication continues and is strengthened during the screening and the negotiation of the lease. Complaints that constitute an emergency would be handled immediately, while other complaints should be resolved in compliance with the lease. The property manager and owner should develop a complaint process that is either outlined in the lease or available to the tenant as a separate document.

Tenants must know that they cannot use their space in such a way as to infringe on the rights of others and that noncompliance with building rules, violations of the law, or any activities that disrupt other tenants are grounds for eviction.

OPERATING BUDGETS

An operating budget is based on the anticipated revenues and expenses. When the property manager develops the budget, it must reflect the owner's long-term goals. The budget will allocate money for continuous, fixed expenses such as employees' salaries, property taxes, and insurance. It will also establish a cash reserve fund for variable expenses such as repairs and supplies.

TRUST ACCOUNTS

Property managers may be required to maintain escrow or trust accounts in which security deposits are placed. Laws vary by state, but usually these accounts must be separate from business and personal accounts. The tenants are usually informed of the bank and the account number where their security deposits are located. State laws and the lease agreement also regulate the disbursement of security deposits and who may stipulate who receives credit for the interest earned from the security deposits (if the state laws allow the security deposits to be placed in an interest-bearing account).

FINANCIAL STATEMENTS FOR OWNERS

The property manager will develop a budget comparison statement, profit and loss report, and the operating budget. The purpose of the budget comparison is to compare the actual income and expenses with the projected budget.

Most owners require that the property manager create a monthly report of *income and expenses*. Quarterly, semiannual, or annual profit and loss statements are compiled from these monthly reports. From this, the owner can analyze how the property was managed, decide what changes should be made, and make projections for the next year.

Only the interest portion of each mortgage payment should be deducted as an expense on the profit and loss statement, whereas on the monthly reports the entire debt service is used.

The following is an example of a profit and loss statement:

Profit and Loss Statement
Period: January 1, XXXX, to December 31, XXXX

Receipts	$198,948.43
Operating Expenses	− 74,343.89
Operating Income	$124,604.54
Total Mortgage Payment	− 54,567.89
Mortgage Loan Principal Add-Back	+ 6,493.20
Net Profit	$ 76,529.85

The profit and loss statement may be compared with the operating budget that was prepared for the year. Such a comparison can measure the performance of the property manager and determine the changes that will need to be made in the future.

INCOME, EXPENSES, AND RATE OF RETURN

In developing a management plan for the owner, a property manager must include an operating budget for the property. The optimum rents for the property must be determined by the manager and adjustments made to reflect the specific advantages and disadvantages of the property.

Next, the manager computes the gross rental income of the property. The gross income of an apartment complex may be based on the room count of the space, whereas commercial properties may be computed by the square footage of the space. Projected vacancy rates and rent losses are subtracted from the gross rent, and the manager then adds income from other sources to arrive at the anticipated income of the property for the year.

Expenses such as real estate taxes, salaries, utilities, supplies, maintenance, repairs, insurance, administrative costs, management fees, and reserve funds are deducted to compute the net operating income before debt service. The debt service is subtracted to determine the before-tax cash flow of the property.

In summary, the basic formula used by property managers is

Potential gross income
− Vacancy and rent loss
+ Additional income
   Total anticipated revenue
− Expenses
   Net operating income before debt service
− Debt service
   Before-tax cash flow
− Taxes
   After-tax cash flow

The return on investment (ROI) is one way to measure the profitability of a property. The ROI is the ratio of the property's after-tax cash flow (ATCF) to the money invested (equity [E]) in the property. The formula for computing the return on investment is

$$\text{ROI} = \frac{\text{ATCF}}{\text{E}} \times 100\%$$

The ROI also may be computed on a before-tax basis.

A property with a $10,000 ATCF in which the owner has $100,000 invested would have an ROI of 10 percent. When this formula is used to analyze the owner's investment, it is called a cash-on-cash investment, and it may be computed on either a before-tax or an after-tax basis.

ENVIRONMENTAL AND SAFETY HAZARDS

Property managers and agents must have a working knowledge of hazardous substances and wastes and the laws regulating owners. A hazardous waste is a byproduct of a manufactured item, while a hazardous substance may include everyday items such as household cleaning products and paint. The Environmental Protection Agency (EPA) was established to centralize the federal government's environmental responsibilities.

The hazardous substances that a property manager most likely will come in contact with are asbestos, radon, contents of underground storage tanks, urea formaldehyde, polychlorinated biphenyls (PCBs), and lead paint.

A property manager is responsible for building security and handling emergencies. *Life safety* is the industry term for those responsibilities. The four goals of life safety programs are

1. preventing emergencies and security breaches by installing smoke detectors, sprinkler systems, paging systems, closed-circuit television, video camera, and security alarms;

2. detecting a breach as early as possible;

3. containing or confining the damage or intrusion; and

4. counteracting the damage by prompt and proper action.

This would also include the responsibility of hiring and training a life safety officer to assist in the evacuation of tenants and to enforce safety guidelines. Tenants should be educated so they know what to do in case of a disaster such as a hurricane, tornado, earthquake, fire, bomb threat, or other accident.

COMPLIANCE WITH FEDERAL REQUIREMENTS

Property managers must be in compliance with the antitrust laws, federal fair housing laws, Equal Credit Opportunity Act, Fair Credit Reporting Act, and the Lead-Based Paint Hazard Reduction Act, all of which are discussed in various chapters in this book. In addition to these laws, the property manager must be in compliance with the Americans with Disabilities Act, Megan's Law, and the Uniform Residential Landlord and Tenant Act.

The **Americans with Disabilities Act** (**ADA**) became effective in 1992. Its intention is to enable individuals with disabilities to become a part of the social and economic mainstream by mandating equal access to

■   public accommodations,

■   jobs,

■   public transportation,

■   telecommunications, and

■   government services.

A disability is a *physical or mental impairment or history of such impairment* that substantially limits one or more of a person's major life activities. An individual with AIDS or a person in an addiction recovery program is protected. The law *does not protect* anyone using an illegal drug or a controlled substance. A disabled individual is to be given full and equal enjoyment of goods and services in places of public accommodation, including hotels, shopping centers, commercial properties, and professional offices.

Private clubs and religious organizations are exempt from the Americans with Disabilities Act.

ADA stipulates that employers with 15 or more employees must adopt nondiscriminatory employment procedures, such as making reasonable accommodations to allow a qualified person with a disability to perform essential job functions. Any changes made are to be *reasonable* and are not to impose an undue burden on the business. Also, changes *cannot cause* a direct threat to the safety or health of others.

Property owners and managers need to know the priority guidelines for making buildings accessible to disabled individuals. All existing architectural and communication barriers must be removed, if doing so can be accomplished in a *readily achievable manner* at a low cost. Priorities have been set for these readily achievable changes.

ADA has affected the real estate business in several areas. Real estate brokerage firms must make the necessary changes to provide full and equal opportunities to disabled individuals. Property managers must have a solid understanding of the ADA so they can advise owners of necessary changes.

Megan's Law requires that information about certain sex offenders be available to the public. Sex offenders are required to register with state law enforcement authorities so their location is known.

The **Uniform Residential Landlord and Tenant Act** was designed to standardize and regulate the relationship between property owners and their tenants. Most states have enacted their own landlord and tenant laws, and the property manager should know the state and local laws.

Figure 3.4 is a summary of federal law as it affects landlords and tenants.

EVICTION PROCEEDINGS

Eviction procedures will vary by state, but the proper procedure must be followed by the property manager. A tenant is usually evicted or ejected because of nonpayment of rent, unlawful use of the premises, or noncompliance with health and safety codes.

Actual eviction is when the landlord files a suit for possession because the tenant has breached the lease. **Constructive eviction** is when the landlord breaches the lease and the tenant must leave the premises because they have become uninhabitable.

FIGURE 3.4

Federal Tenant and Landlord Rights and Responsibilities

Tenant's Protections	Owner's Responsibilities
No Abrogation Tenants cannot sign away their rights in advance of signing the lease.	**Keep the Premises Safe and Habitable** Establish building rules and regulations and make sure all tenants comply
Security Deposits Amount, location of, interest collected, and return of must be specified in the lease.	**Right to Reenter** The landlord must give reasonable notice to inspect, make repairs or improvements, or show the unit. The landlord may enter the unit without notice if there is an emergency.
Estate from Period to Period Unless the lease states otherwise, the lease is interpreted as an estate from period to period.	**Tenant's Noncompliance** The covenant of quiet enjoyment assures all tenants of the use of facilities in a reasonable manner. The landlord has the right to evict a tenant if the rules and regulations are not followed.
Fair Dealings The court may refuse to enforce all or part of a lease that is unconscionable or grossly unfair to the tenant.	
Effects of Unsigned Leases If only one party signs and delivers a written lease and the other party pays or accepts rent, the lease is considered binding even without the other party's signature.	**Abandonment of the Premises** A tenant who abandons the premises before the lease expires is liable for the remaining rent. The landlord is required to make a reasonable effort to rent the abandoned property.
Tenant's Right to Vacate The tenant may vacate the premises if the landlord breaches the lease agreement or if the unit becomes uninhabitable due to fire or other casualty.	**Use and Occupancy** This act covers only residential property and stipulates that unless there is an agreement otherwise, the tenant can only use the property for residential purposes. The tenant agrees not to conduct any illegal activities on the property.

MAINTENANCE AND REPAIR MANAGEMENT

The primary goals of a property manager are to generate the highest net operating income while maintaining the property. To preserve the physical condition of the property, the manager must be able to accurately assess the various levels of maintenance operations shown in Figure 3.5.

FEES, SECURITY DEPOSITS, AND RENT COLLECTION

The property manager must also be aware of state laws regarding limitations on the fees charged for rent application and credit reports, on security deposits, and on late payment penalties.

FIGURE 3.5 **Maintenance**	**Preventive maintenance**—preserves the physical building and eliminates costly problems before major repairs become necessary. **Corrective maintenance**—fulfills the owner's responsibilities to the tenant by keeping the building's equipment, utilities, and amenities functioning properly. **Routine maintenance**—includes routine housekeeping, such as maintenance of the common areas and grounds, and maintaining the physical cleanliness of the building itself. **New construction maintenance**—occurs to meet the needs of a tenant and could be something as simple as installing new carpeting or as complex as upgrading or remodeling the property to meet the tenant's needs.

Property managers must be aware of state laws regulating security deposits. These laws could include identifying the deposit in the lease, the bank and account number where the security deposit is located, the limit of the deposit to be collected, the interest that must be paid, and the procedure for the return and deduction of the deposit.

Rent

Rent is paid in advance, usually on the first of the month, and the property manager must know state and local laws regarding eviction procedures as they relate to rent. The lease agreement should specify the day the rent is due, the grace period and the late fee, and when eviction procedures will begin. If a lease agreement does not specify the due date, then rent is due at the end of the leasing period.

Rent control is a regulation by the state or local government agencies restricting the amount of rent landlords can charge their tenants. The primary purpose of rent control was to remedy high rents caused by the imbalance between supply and demand in housing.

INSURANCE COVERAGE TO PROTECT TENANT AND OWNER

One of the primary duties of the property manager involves risk management, which is usually done through the purchase of insurance. Risk management involves identifying the risk and deciding to avoid it, controlling it with safety programs, retaining the risk, or transferring the risk to third parties by the purchase of insurance. A property manager will monitor risks to determine the action that must take place in the future.

Types of insurance that may be purchased to protect the owner include

- property insurance—to cover natural disasters, fires, and vandalism;

- general liability insurance—to cover contractors and real and personal property;

- loss of income insurance—to cover loss of rents, profits, and commissions;

- replacement cost insurance—to cover the cost of a replacing a part of or the entire building;

- workers' compensation—to cover liability for injury to employees;

- commercial automobile liability—to cover injury and damage by vehicles; and

- machinery and equipment insurance—to cover machinery and equipment.

QUESTIONS

1. In assuming responsibility for the maintenance of a property, the manager is expected to do which of the following?
   A. Directly or indirectly supervise the routine cleaning and repair work of the building
   B. Execute an inverse severance contract
   C. Review all housing disclosure reports
   D. Approve all exchange agreements

2. The Uniform Residential Landlord and Tenant Act does not allow abrogation. This means
   A. the landlord must establish rules and regulations and make sure all tenants comply.
   B. if one party signs and delivers a written lease and the other party pays or accepts rent, the lease is considered binding even without the other party's signature.
   C. the amount, location of, and the interest collected on the security deposit must be specified in the lease.
   D. tenants cannot sign away their rights in advance of signing the lease.

3. A management agreement usually covers which of the following items?
   A. Authorization of payment of expenses
   B. Estoppel certificates
   C. Joint and several liability
   D. Waiver of subrogation

4. Cheryl leases a retail space to conduct her bookstore business and installs built-in bookcases. The built-in bookcases will become the property of the landlord
   A. automatically because they are considered permanent fixtures.
   B. on the expiration of the lease, if they are still attached to the property.
   C. only if removal will cause damage to the property.
   D. automatically on the expiration of the lease.

5. The landlord of tenant Carl has sold his building to the state so that an expressway can be built. Carl's lease expires, but the landlord is letting him remain until some unknown time when the building will be torn down. Carl continues to pay the same rent as was prescribed in his lease. What is Carl's tenancy called?
   A. Tenancy by the entireties
   B. Month-to-month tenancy
   C. Tenancy at sufferance
   D. Tenancy at will

6. The manager of a commercial building carries out many duties in connection with its operation and maintenance. The manager is usually the agent of the
   A. lessor of the building.
   B. lessee in the building.
   C. lessor and lessee.
   D. trustee.

7. Hobart entered into a five-year lease agreement. The premises have become too small for Hobart's business. Marcia is interested in possessing the premises for three years and paying Hobart directly. Which of the following agreements would Hobart and Marcia execute to effect Marcia's wishes?
   A. Assignment
   B. Novation
   C. Sublease
   D. Tenancy at sufferance

8. A property manager normally is charged with all of the following duties EXCEPT
   A. renting space to tenants.
   B. preparing a budget.
   C. developing a management plan.
   D. repairing a tenant's fixture.

9. Brenda is a tenant under an estate for years lease agreement. Under such an estate
   A. the term of the lease must be for at least one year.
   B. the lease will have a definite beginning and ending.
   C. a 30-day notice is required to terminate the lease.
   D. the lease is classified as a freehold estate.

10. A tenant and a property manager just executed a lease that begins on April 15, 2005, and ends on April 15, 2008. This lease is BEST described as a(n)
    A. estate for years.
    B. tenancy at will.
    C. periodic tenancy.
    D. estate from year to year.

11. Which of the following is the MOST IMPORTANT record kept by the property manager?
    A. Accounting report of income and expenses
    B. Tenants' complaints
    C. Property manager's personal expense account
    D. Utilities paid by the property manager

12. The tenant has agreed to pay a fixed monthly rent, a portion of the property taxes, and maintenance on a 1,200-square-foot retail space in a mall. This lease is BEST described as a
    A. percentage lease.
    B. gross lease.
    C. net lease.
    D. retail lease.

13. George leased a property to a college student. The lease expired on May 15. On May 16, George visited the property and discovered that the student was still residing in the apartment and hadn't even started packing. The student offered George a check for the next month's rent. Which of the following BEST describes this situation?
    A. The tenant is a trespasser and George may physically remove him from the property without any notice.
    B. A tenancy at sufferance is created if George accepts the check.
    C. An estate at sufferance is created if George refuses to accept the check.
    D. A tenancy by the entireties is created if George accepts the check.

14. Which of the following would a property manager LEAST LIKELY do?
    A. Screen and qualify tenants
    B. Place security deposits in the proper escrow account
    C. Accept a rebate from a service provider
    D. Negotiate a lease and present it to the owner for approval

15. Regarding a sublease, all of the following are true EXCEPT the
    A. sublessor's interest is called a sandwich lease.
    B. lessee has a leased fee interest and the lessor has a leasehold interest in the property.
    C. sublessor may charge a higher rent to the sublessee and make a profit on the lease.
    D. lessor expects the agreed-on rental payment from the sublessor.

16. Regarding an assignment, all of the following are false EXCEPT
    A. the lease between the assignor and the assignee is called a *transfer lease*.
    B. when the lease has been assigned, the lessee then expects payment from the assignee.
    C. the assignor transferred all the leasehold interests in the lease.
    D. when the lease has been assigned, there is a new landlord-tenant relationship between the lessor and the assignor.

17. Which of the following is the BEST method for attracting tenants to a property?
    A. Cooperating with brokers in the area
    B. Developing an advertising campaign
    C. Having press releases published in the local newspapers to create publicity
    D. Securing referrals from satisfied tenants

18. Harry has entered into a property management agreement with Sterling Properties, Inc. Harry's agreement MOST LIKELY stipulates that he will be paid a percentage of
    A. last year's net income.
    B. this year's potential income.
    C. this year's gross income.
    D. last year's gross income.

19. Which of the following criteria is the MOST IMPORTANT for a property manager to use to qualify and screen a potential tenant?
    A. The space requirements, financial history, and projected moving date
    B. Having lunch with the owner of the potential tenant's company
    C. Any special needs of the potential tenant
    D. The parking needs of the potential tenant

20. A percentage lease would MOST LIKELY be negotiated in all of the following spaces EXCEPT a(n)
    A. duplex.
    B. apparel shop.
    C. gasoline station.
    D. convenient mart.

21. Which of the following is LEAST LIKELY to terminate a lease agreement?
    A. The property is taken by eminent domain.
    B. The life tenant who had leased the property dies.
    C. The lessor sells the property.
    D. The lessee buys the land from the lessor.

22. The clause found in a mortgage that would protect the tenant should the landlord default on the mortgage payment to the lender is the
    A. constructive eviction clause.
    B. actual eviction clause.
    C. nondisturbance clause.
    D. nonfreehold clause.

23. Which of the following would LEAST LIKELY be necessary for a one-year lease to be enforceable?
    A. Notarization and recording of the lease
    B. Signature of the party authorized to perform
    C. Sufficient property description
    D. Consideration and term of the lease

24. The mayor rented an entertainment hall from April 30 to May 3. What type of leasehold estate does she have?
    A. Estate at sufferance
    B. Estate from year to year
    C. Estate at will
    D. Estate for years

25. What is the BEST way for a property manager to minimize problems with a tenant?
    A. To talk with the tenant about the tenant's conduct
    B. To tell the tenant to ask the other tenants how to behave
    C. To discuss and give a copy of the rules and regulations to the tenant
    D. To say nothing until there is a problem

26. A lease will MOST LIKELY be considered a(n)
    A. unilateral contract.
    B. bilateral contract.
    C. voidable contract.
    D. exculpatory contract.

27. The responsibilities of upkeep of the common areas, cleanliness of the buildings, and maintenance of the grounds BEST describes
    A. routine maintenance.
    B. preventive maintenance.
    C. corrective maintenance.
    D. new construction maintenance.

28. The primary goals of a property manager are to
   A. generate the highest net operating income for the owner while maintaining the investment.
   B. generate the highest gross income for the owner while maintaining the investment.
   C. negotiate the lowest rent possible for the lessee while providing as many amenities as possible.
   D. negotiate the highest rent possible for the lessor while providing as many amenities as possible.

29. Who is accountable for keeping the property habitable and for complying with local building and housing codes?
   A. Lessee
   B. Lessor
   C. Buyer
   D. Agent

30. A net lease usually includes payment by the lessee for all of the following EXCEPT
   A. property taxes.
   B. debt service.
   C. insurance.
   D. maintenance.

31. A lease agreement stipulates that the landlord is responsible for paying the water bill. The tenant came home one afternoon and discovered the water had been turned off. If the tenant chooses to leave the premises, this would be called
   A. constructive eviction.
   B. actual eviction.
   C. landlord eviction.
   D. tenant eviction.

32. The landlord's interests and rights in leased property are known as a
   A. leasehold interest.
   B. leased fee interest.
   C. leased indefeasible interest.
   D. leased defeasible interest.

33. In a lease agreement, the landlord guarantees that the lessee has exclusive possession of the property and that the landlord will not interfere with the tenant's possession or use of the property. This is known as the covenant of
   A. seisin.
   B. possession and use.
   C. warranty forever.
   D. quiet enjoyment.

34. In a sale-leaseback, the grantor becomes the
   A. lessor.
   B. lessee.
   C. new owner.
   D. landlord.

35. Which of the following would NOT be in a property management agreement?
   A. The duties and responsibilities of the manager and the owner
   B. The conditions under which the manager is authorized to pay expenses of the property being managed
   C. Starting date, termination date, and provisions for renewal options
   D. The amount and method of determining the good-faith deposit to be collected from the tenants for each unit managed

36. Which of the following is a responsibility of the property manager to the tenants that does NOT violate the manager's responsibility to the owner?
   A. Development of an operating budget
   B. Supervision of routine maintenance of the property
   C. Filing of proper federal and state income tax reports
   D. Accounting for security deposits

37. All of the following would MOST LIKELY be negotiated between the owner and the property manager in the management agreement EXCEPT the
   A. name of a tenant who just signed a 20-year lease with the owner.
   B. duties and responsibilities of the manager.
   C. beginning and termination dates of the contract and provisions for renewal.
   D. rate and schedule of compensation.

38. A property manager must take which of the following into consideration to determine the net operating income a property produces?
    A. Debt service
    B. IRS taxes
    C. After-tax cash flow
    D. Vacancy and rent loss

39. To compute the return on investment, a property manager must
    A. divide the before-tax cash flow by the after-cash tax flow.
    B. multiply the before-tax cash flow by the after-cash tax flow.
    C. divide the after-tax cash flow by the equity and multiply by 100 percent.
    D. multiply the after-tax cash flow by the equity and divide by 100 percent.

40. An agent has become a manager of a property that is difficult to lease. Which of the following leases would she MOST LIKELY use to secure a contract with a prospective tenant?
    A. Percentage lease
    B. Graduated lease
    C. Sublease
    D. Gross lease

41. The primary purpose of a profit and loss statement is to analyze
    A. how the property was managed, what changes should be made, and projections for the new year.
    B. if the property manager did a good job of following the operating budget.
    C. the ratio of the operating expenses to the operating income.
    D. the ratio of the rate of return to the debt service.

42. On a profit and loss statement, all of the following are entered EXCEPT
    A. mortgage loan principal add-back.
    B. receipts.
    C. operating expenses.
    D. property manager's compensation.

43. What do asbestos, radon, and urea formaldehyde all have in common?
    A. They are classified as environmental hazards, and a property manager must be aware of the identification and effect of them.
    B. They are all classified as hazardous substances.
    C. They are all produced as a result of the natural decay of radioactive substances.
    D. They are classified as environmental hazards, but a property manager need not be concerned about the effect of any such substances.

44. All of the following are grounds for actual eviction EXCEPT
    A. nonpayment of rent.
    B. unlawful use of the premises.
    C. the lessor's breach of the lease.
    D. the tenant's noncompliance with health and safety codes.

45. An operating budget allowed $2,500 for the property manager to buy new carpet. The property manager can negotiate a contract with a carpet company to purchase carpet for the property, as well as the manager's personal residence, all billed
    A. to the owner.
    B. to purchase carpet for the property and accept a rebate from the carpet company.
    C. if given that authorization in her or his employment contract.
    D. only after securing sealed bids from at least three companies.

46. KMK Law Firm just agreed to lease a space in downtown Cincinnati for the next 20 years. Which of the following terms BEST describes KMK's interest in the property?
    A. Tenant's interest
    B. Reversionary interest
    C. Leasehold interest
    D. Leased fee interest

47. Mr. Meade just offered to purchase an occupied fourplex. Should his offer be accepted, which of the following is TRUE regarding the current leases?
    A. The leases will be void.
    B. The leases will be unaffected.
    C. The lessee can cancel the leases.
    D. The lessor can raise the rent.

48. Which of the following would NOT be a factor in the development of a marketing plan by the property manager?
    A. Supply and demand
    B. Local economic conditions
    C. Location of the property
    D. Availability of good maintenance employees

49. The ABC Company agreed to lease a space for ten years. Five years later, ABC sold its company to XYZ. If the lease contains no provision regarding an assignment, ABC may
    A. assign the leasehold interest to XYZ.
    B. not assign the leasehold interest to XYZ under any circumstances.
    C. assign the leasehold interest to XYZ on the approval of its attorney.
    D. not assign the leasehold interest, but they may sublease the space to XYZ.

50. Which of the following is an environmental hazard associated with leakage near electrical equipment?
    A. Urea formaldehyde
    B. Radon
    C. Polychlorinated biphenyls (PCBs)
    D. Asbestos

51. All of the following occupancy terms are negotiated between a property manager and a prospective tenant EXCEPT
    A. expansion options.
    B. length of the leasing period.
    C. tenant alterations.
    D. the owner's profit.

52. The duties and responsibilities of a property manager would be LEAST LIKELY to include which of the following?
    A. Investing profits generated by the property for the owner
    B. Supervising the remodeling of the property
    C. Showing the property to prospective tenants
    D. Collecting the rent from current tenants

53. Sandy has shown a prospective tenant an available apartment. Which of the following would NOT be a consideration in qualifying the potential tenant?
    A. Credit history
    B. Race
    C. Space requirements
    D. Personal references

54. Which of the following does NOT normally terminate a lease?
    A. Death of the lessor
    B. Nonpayment of rent
    C. Constructive eviction by the lessee
    D. Condemnation of the property

55. A property manager is developing an operating budget. Which of the following is LEAST LIKELY to be considered an operating expense?
    A. Utility bills
    B. Debt service
    C. Maintenance expenses
    D. Management fees

56. Julie owns a fourplex. She lives in one unit and has an apartment available for rent. She would like for the new tenant to be a nonsmoker. Can she advertise the unit as a nonsmoking apartment?
    A. Yes, because smoking is behavior and not protected by federal fair housing laws.
    B. Yes, because the fourplex is owner occupied.
    C. No, because it would be discriminatory advertising.
    D. No, because only the owner of a duplex can discriminate because of smoking.

57. Brian just negotiated a property management agreement with Meade and Associates. The property management agreement
    A. is a personal service contract that terminates upon the death of either party.
    B. creates a special agency relationship.
    C. need not be in writing in most states.
    D. creates a universal agency relationship.

58. Rob is the owner of a 20-unit apartment building. He has just accepted an offer on his property. At closing, the security deposits will be
    A. returned to the tenants by Rob.
    B. prorated between Rob and the new owner.
    C. kept in Rob's name until each tenant leaves.
    D. transferred to the new owner.

59. An automatic renewal clause would MOST LIKELY be found in which of the following leases?
    A. Tenancy for years
    B. Periodic tenancy
    C. Estate at will
    D. Estate at sufferance

60. Melanie pays a fixed rental amount and the owner pays all other ownership expenses for the property. The lease agreement they have negotiated is MOST LIKELY a(n)
    A. index lease.
    B. percentage lease.
    C. net lease.
    D. gross lease.

61. Denny is a property manager and works for Phyllis, who died at 10 pm last night. Can Denny collect the rent checks that are due today?
    A. Yes, it is Denny's duty to collect the rent checks for her estate.
    B. Yes, Denny should collect the rent checks because it is his job.
    C. No, Denny should not collect the rent checks because his contract terminated upon her death.
    D. No, Denny should not collect the rent checks until the executor of her estate gives him permission to do so.

62. A hurricane destroyed several apartment buildings in a community, creating an imbalance between the supply and demand of rental units. If the local government imposes a law that restricts the amount of rent a landlord may charge, it is known as
    A. rent control.
    B. Uniform Landlord Tenant Act.
    C. fixed rent.
    D. gross rent.

63. Last night an apartment building was destroyed by fire. Are the tenants required to honor the remaining term of the lease?
    A. Yes, because a lease is not affected by destruction of the property.
    B. Yes, because the owner still has a mortgage payment to make next month.
    C. No, because a lease is terminated by destruction of the property.
    D. No, because the owner will file a claim with the insurance company and rebuild the property.

64. What is the MAJOR DIFFERENCE between an assignment and a sublease?
    A. When a lease has been assigned, the landlord expects payment from the assignor, but when the property has been sublet, the landlord expects payment from the sublessee.
    B. Only tenants of residential properties can assign leases and only tenants of commercial properties can sublease properties.
    C. A tenant who transfers all the leasehold interest assigns the lease, while a tenant who subleases transfers less than the leasehold interests in the property.
    D. An assignment is used for long-term leases, but a sublease is used for short-term leases.

65. Warranty of habitability is BEST defined as the
    A. landlord's responsibility to keep the property in good condition.
    B. landlord's reversionary right to occupy the property upon the expiration of the lease.
    C. tenant's duty to safeguard the property.
    D. tenant's duty to maintain insurance on the property.

66. All of the following terms are associated with a net lease EXCEPT
    A. double net.
    B. triple net.
    C. property taxes and insurance.
    D. property taxes and mortgage payments.

67. Which of the following terms could be found in a lease or a mortgage?
    A. Escalation clause
    B. Alienation clause
    C. Subordination clause
    D. Redemption clause

68. Steve signed a two-year property management agreement with Mary. Has an agency relationship been created and if so, what type of agent is the property manager?
    A. Yes, authority has been given for the property manager to act on the owner's behalf, and the property manager is a general agent.
    B. Yes, authority has been given for the property manager to act on the owner's behalf, and the property manager is a special agent.
    C. No, because to create agency the term of the agreement must be at least three years.
    D. No, because property management agreements do not create agency relationships.

69. To compute the return on investment, a property manager would need all of the following figures EXCEPT
    A. potential gross income.
    B. expenses.
    C. cap rate.
    D. debt service.

70. A property manager signed a lease agreement with a new tenant and collected a $500 security deposit check. She deposited the security deposit in the business bank account and did not disclose to the tenant the location of the money. Were her actions legal?
    A. Yes, if those were the instructions from the tenant.
    B. Yes, as long as the check was deposited within three business days.
    C. No, because the check should be deposited into a separate bank account for that purpose.
    D. No, because she did not inform the tenant of the location of the money.

MATCHING QUIZ

The column on the right contains a brief definition of important terms in this section.
Write the letter of the matching term on the appropriate line.

A. ROI

B. Rent control

C. Leasehold interest

D. Lease

E. Reversionary right

F. Estate for years

G. Estate from period to period

H. Estate at sufferance

I. Estate at will

J. Net lease

K. Percentage lease

L. Sale-leaseback

M. Graduated lease

N. Index lease

O. Actual eviction

P. Covenant of quiet enjoyment

Q. Sublease

R. Constructive eviction

S. Leased fee interest

T. Gross lease

1. ___ Landlord breaches the lease and tenant must leave the premises

2. ___ Grantor sells the property to the grantee and then leases it back

3. ___ The tenancy that is created when the tenant remains in possession of the property without consent of the landlord after the lease expires

4. ___ Tenant agrees to pay a fixed base rental fee plus a percentage of the gross income in excess of a predetermined minimum amount of sales

5. ___ Owner's right to retake the property on the expiration of the terms of the lease

6. ___ Lessor's interest in a leased property

7. ___ In this lease, the rent is tied to an index outside the control of the landlord and tenant

8. ___ Agreement that transfers exclusive possession and use of real estate from the lessor to the lessee

9. ___ Ratio of the property's after-tax cash flow to the money invested in the property

10. ___ In this lease, the tenant agrees to pay ownership expenses such as property taxes, insurance, and maintenance

11. ___ This lease allows for the periodic step-up of rent payments

12. ___ This lease is created when a tenant transfers less than all the leasehold interest to another tenant

13. ___ Landlord's promise to honor the tenants' right of possession and not enter the property without permission (unless it is an emergency)

14. ___ Lease that automatically renews until proper notice is given

15. ___ Regulation by the state or local government restricting the amount of rent landlords can charge tenants

16. ___ Lessee's interest in the leased premises

17. ___ Landlord files a suit for possession because tenant has breached the lease

18. ___ Lease with definite beginning and ending dates

19. ___ This is also known as a straight lease in which the tenant pays a fixed rental amount and the owner pays all other ownership expenses for the property

20. ___ Lease that can be terminated at any time by the landlord or the tenant giving notice

ANSWERS

1. **(A)** Being responsible for maintenance is one of the property manager's duties.

2. **(D)** Abrogation means the tenant cannot sign away his or her rights in advance of the signing of the lease.

3. **(A)** The authorization of the payment of the expenses would be a part of the agreement.

4. **(B)** The tenant has the right to take trade fixtures before the lease expires, but is expected to leave the property in good repair.

5. **(D)** A tenancy at will is a lease in which a person holds or occupies real estate for an uncertain duration, with the permission of the owner.

6. **(A)** The lessor is the owner and the property manager is an agent of the owner.

7. **(C)** Because less than all the leasehold interest is being conveyed, the parties negotiate a sublease.

8. **(D)** The property manager is not responsible for the repair of a tenant's fixture.

9. **(B)** An estate for years has a definite duration and no termination is required.

10. **(A)** By definition of an estate for years.

11. **(A)** An accounting report of income and expenses is used to develop all other reports the manager must provide the owner, including the profit and loss statement.

12. **(C)** By the definition of a net lease, the tenant agrees to pay ownership expenses.

13. **(C)** The tenant is in possession of the property after the expiration of the lease. George has not accepted the check; therefore, an estate at sufferance is created.

14. **(C)** A property manager may not accept a rebate from a service provider, unless the manager had the consent of the owner to do so.

15. **(B)** In any lease, the lessor's interest is a leased fee interest and the lessee's interest is a leasehold interest.

16. **(C)** In an assignment, all of the leasehold interest is transferred to the assignee.

17. **(D)** All the answers provide methods that a property manager can use to attract tenants. However, securing referrals from satisfied tenants is the best method.

18. **(C)** Property managers are typically paid a percentage of the gross income.

19. **(A)** When qualifying a potential tenant, a property manager must consider many factors. The space requirement, financial history, and projected moving date are the most important criteria.

20. **(A)** A percentage lease is used in the rental of commercial properties, not a duplex.

21. **(C)** When the lessor sells the property, the buyer must abide by the existing lease.

22. **(C)** A nondisturbance clause in a mortgage protects the tenant. If the owner defaults and the tenant pays rent to the lender, the tenant will not be evicted.

23. **(A)** Normally, a lease does not have to be notarized and recorded to be enforceable, though most states do have this requirement for long-term leases.

24. **(D)** The mayor entered into an estate for years with a definite beginning and ending.

25. **(C)** The property manager should discuss and give a copy of the rules and regulations to the tenant to minimize any problems.

26. **(B)** A lease is considered to be a bilateral contract wherein both parties are obligated to perform.

27. **(A)** By definition of routine maintenance.

28. **(A)** The primary goals of a property manager are to generate the highest net operating income on the property while maintaining the owner's investment.

29. **(B)** The lessor/owner is responsible for keeping the property habitable and for complying with local building and housing codes. These duties may be delegated to the property manager.

30. **(B)** The debt service is not normally paid by the tenant in a net lease.

31. **(A)** Constructive eviction is when the landlord does not fulfill his obligations and the tenant leaves the premises.

32. **(B)** The landlord's interest is a leased fee (ownership) interest, while the tenant's interest is a leasehold interest.

33. **(D)** By definition of covenant of quiet enjoyment as it pertains to leases. The covenant of quiet enjoyment in a deed guarantees that the grantee will have the property free from interference from third parties.

34. **(B)** The grantor or seller of the property becomes the lessee or new tenant at the end of the transaction.

35. **(D)** A property manager does not collect a good-faith deposit, which is another term for escrow deposit. The manager would collect a security deposit from the tenant.

36. **(D)** The security deposit belongs to the tenant, not the owner. Therefore, the primary accountability for the security deposit is to the tenant, but it does not violate the fiduciary relationship with the owner.

37. **(A)** The name of a tenant would not be found in the written property management agreement between the owner and the property manager.

38. **(D)** Potential gross income
    – Vacancy and rent losses
    + Additional income
      Total anticipated revenue
    – Expenses
      Net operating income before debt service

39. **(C)** The return on investment formula: after-tax cash flow ÷ equity × 100%.

40. **(B)** A graduated lease is used to attract tenants to properties that are difficult to lease.

41. **(A)** The purpose of a profit and loss statement is to analyze how the property was managed, what changes should be made, and projections for the new year.

42. **(D)** The property manager's compensation is not entered on a profit and loss statement.

43. **(A)** Asbestos, radon, and urea formaldehyde are all environmental hazards of which a property manager must be aware.

44. **(C)** Actual eviction occurs when the tenant has breached the lease.

45. **(C)** The property manager can act only within the scope and authority of the employment contract negotiated with the owner.

46. **(C)** KMK is a tenant, and the tenant's interest is best described as a leasehold interest.

47. **(B)** When the property is sold, the current leases remain binding and effective.

48. **(D)** The marketing plan does not consider the hiring of maintenance employees.

49. **(A)** Unless a lease forbids assignment and subleasing, the tenant may do so.

50. **(C)** PCBs can be found in electrical equipment.

51. **(D)** The owner's profit is not a term negotiated with a tenant.

52. **(A)** The property manager does not invest the owner's profit.

53. **(B)** The race of a potential tenant is not a consideration of the property manager when negotiating a lease.

54. **(A)** The death of the lessor does not affect the lease in any way.

55. **(B)** The debt service is not an operating expense.

56. **(A)** Smoking describes a behavior, not a person. Smoking is not a protected class under federal fair housing laws.

57. **(A)** A property management agreement is a personal service contract that would create a general agency relationship.

58. **(D)** The security deposits would be transferred to the new owner.

59. **(B)** A periodic tenancy would have an automatic renewal clause.

60. **(D)** In a gross lease the tenant pays a fixed rent, and the owner pays all ownership expenses.

61. **(C)** Property management contracts are personal service contracts and terminate upon the death of either party. The executor may hire Denny as a property manager, but the question does not provide that information and it should not be assumed.

62. **(A)** By definition of rent control.

63. **(C)** Leases normally expire upon the destruction of the premises.

64. **(C)** In an assignment, a tenant transfers all the leasehold interest. In a sublease, a tenant transfers less than the leasehold interest in the property.

65. **(A)** The warranty of habitability requires that the landlord keep the property in good condition.

66. **(D)** The tenant does not pay the mortgage payments in a net lease.

67. **(A)** An escalation clause is found in an index lease that will allow the lease payment to adjust. It is also found in an adjustable-rate mortgage to allow the interest rate to adjust.

68. **(A)** A property management agreement would create an agency relationship and the property manager would be a general agent, given a broad range of powers on behalf of the owner.

69. **(C)** An appraiser uses the cap rate to compute the value, but it is not used to determine the return on investment.

70. **(C)** Most states require that security deposit checks be placed in a separate escrow or trust account.

ANSWERS—MATCHING QUIZ

1. R	6. S	11. M	16. C
2. L	7. N	12. Q	17. O
3. H	8. D	13. P	18. F
4. K	9. A	14. G	19. T
5. E	10. J	15. B	20. I

4

Settlement/Transfer of Ownership

This chapter reviews settlement and the transfer of ownership, tax issues, titles, settlement procedures, and completion of the transaction.

AMP Outline—Tax Issues

IV.	**Settlement/Transfer of Ownership**	2.	Real property taxes
		3.	Tax shelters
	A. Tax Issues	4.	Capital improvements
	1. Tax implications of interest expenses		

TAX IMPLICATIONS OF INTEREST EXPENSES

The federal government encourages home ownership by providing income tax advantages such as tax deductions, deferments, and exclusions to buyers of homes. These tax benefits are different for a property used as a principal place of residence from those for property purchased for investment purposes.

In general, homeowners may deduct the following from their gross income to reduce their taxable income:

- Mortgage interest payments on first and second homes that meet the definition of "qualified residence interest"

- Real estate property taxes, but not interest paid on overdue taxes

- Certain loan discount points

- Certain loan origination fees

- Loan prepayment penalties

- Casualty losses to the real estate not covered by insurance

107

REAL PROPERTY TAXES

Real property taxes are **ad valorem taxes**. *Ad valorem* is Latin, meaning "according to valuation." Property taxes are computed on the assessed valuation of each property. To review the formulas for computing property taxes, see page 202.

Note that while property taxes are tax deductible, special assessments are not deductible!

Special assessments are for improvements that are made to the property such as sidewalks, water lines, and so forth.

An agent should keep informed of the rapid changes occurring in the industry. Current tax law allows first-time homebuyers to make a penalty-free withdrawal of up to $10,000 from their tax-deferred individual retirement funds (IRAs) for a down payment.

TAX SHELTERS

Tax shelters reduce current tax liability by offsetting income from one source with losses from another source. Real estate investments may be used as a tax shelter if IRS guidelines are met. Agents should always refer buyers, sellers, or owners to their CPAs for advice regarding the purchase of investment property for a tax shelter.

Under the Tax Reform Act of 1986 (TRA '86), income is classified as being generated from

- an active trade or business—salaries and commissions;
- portfolio activity—interest, dividends, royalties, gains, or losses from the sale of portfolio assets; or
- passive activity—nonmaterial participation of rental income or income from limited partnerships.

Prior to TRA '86, investors could write off passive losses against income generated by an active trade or business income. With the reform in 1986, investors could write off rental losses only if they had rental income.

Currently, taxpayers who earn less than $100,000 adjusted gross income may write off their real estate losses if they (1) actively manage their properties and (2) own at least 10 percent of the investment. If these two tests are met, they may write off up to $25,000 of real estate losses to offset active or portfolio income.

Taxpayers who earn $100,000 to $150,000 are limited in their deductions, and those who make more than $150,000 are not permitted to deduct any rental property losses against active income.

Regardless of the income bracket, real estate investors can take advantage of cost recovery or depreciation, which is discussed in another section.

CAPITAL IMPROVEMENTS

Any improvement that is made to extend the useful life of a property or add to its value is called a *capital improvement*. Major repairs such as replacement of a parking lot, roof, or building equipment would be a capital improvement. The costs of capital improvements to business property must be capitalized and may be depreciated.

Amp Outline—Titles

IV.	Settlement/Transfer of Ownership			
	B. Titles		6.	Preparation of title abstracts
		1. Need for title search	7.	Liens and order of priority
		2. Marketable title	8.	Importance of recording and types of notice
		3. Title insurance		
		4. Title problems		
		5. Legal procedures		

NEED FOR TITLE SEARCH

A deed transfers the title from the grantor to the grantee. The **title** is found within the deed and is used to show ownership of land. This means that the title represents facts that, if proven to be true, will enable a person to show ownership of real estate. A title search is conducted on the property to assure both buyer and lender that the seller can deliver a *marketable title* at the closing. The title search is carried out by a lawyer or abstractor who prepares a **chain of title**, which is a successive series of title transfers, as well as the *abstract of title*.

MARKETABLE TITLE

A **marketable title** or *merchantable title* is one that is free from *reasonable objections*, that is, one that will not place the buyer in a position *of legal liability* or threaten the buyer's right to quiet enjoyment of the property. If buyers accept a deed and then have a problem with the title, they may sue the seller based on the covenants found within the deed, if there are any, or call on their title company to defend the title if they have an owner's policy.

Easements, restrictions, violations of zoning ordinances, lis pendens notices, mortgages, liens, federal tax liens, property tax liens, and encroachments could render a title unmarketable, though slight encroachments usually do not. An unmarketable title does not prevent the property from being transferred by deed. The buyer may accept the property with certain defects that may limit or restrict ownership. However, a lender may refuse to negotiate a loan if the title is unmarketable.

FIGURE 4.1	Standard Coverage	Extended Coverage	Not Covered by Either Policy
Owner's Title Insurance Policy	Defects found in public records	Standard coverage plus defects discoverable through the following:	1. Defects and liens listed in policy
	1. Forged documents	1. Property inspection, including unrecordedd rights of persons in possession	2. Defects known to buyer
	2. Incompetent grantors	2. Examination of survey	3. Changes in land use brought about by zoning ordinances
	3. Incorrect marital statements	3. Unrecorded liens not known of by policyholder	
	4. Improperly delivered deeds		

TITLE INSURANCE

Title insurance *indemnifies* (*protects*) the policyholder against losses that arise from certain title defects that occurred before the policy was issued and that were not found in the title search. The title insurance company will defend any claim made against the policyholder. Whether purchasing an owner's or a lender's policy, the premium is paid only once, generally at closing. Title insurance *does not cover* all title defects. Figure 4.1 provides details of standard coverage, extended coverage, or defects not covered by either policy.

Owner's Policy

When a buyer purchases property, the buyer should seriously consider purchasing an owner's title policy to protect the buyer's interest. For a one-time premium, an owner's title insurance policy remains in effect as long as the insured, or the insured's heirs, retain an interest in the property. If the owner is a corporation, its successors by dissolution, merger, or consolidation are included.

Mortgagee's Policy

A mortgagee's (lender's) policy covers the loan balance and decreases as the balance is reduced. The coverage continues until the loan is repaid in full or the property is conveyed to a new owner.

TITLE PROBLEMS

Title problems occur when there is a hidden mistake in a prior deed, will, mortgage, or other document that may give someone else a valid legal claim against a property. These hidden defects include

- *incorrect information*, such as a wrong name, in a deed, mortgage, or other documents of public record that would affect the title;

- *a lien or claim against the property or seller* that could become the new owner's responsibility after the sale, such as unpaid mortgages, taxes, sewer and water assessments, or bills owed to workers or other creditors; it would also include attachments;

- *claims to ownership*, including a claim to a marital interest by the spouse of a former owner or by a child of former owners who was not mentioned in his or her parents' wills; and

- *the transfer of an invalid deed*, such as transfer by a previous seller who did not actually own the property, or by a previous owner who was not mentally or legally competent.

LEGAL PROCEDURES

Should there be a claim, the title insurance company negotiates with the claimant to settle the claim, defends the title in court (if necessary), satisfies any covered claim, and *pays for the costs incurred in defending the title*. When a title insurance company settles a claim, the company requires that the policyholder **subrogate** (**substitute**) rights to the claim to the title company. This means if compensation is paid to the policyholder, the title company now has the right to sue the claimant to collect any money it paid to cover the claim. The more common legal procedures that would affect the property are as follows:

- **Suit to quiet title**—A court action intended to establish or settle the question of ownership of or interest in a particular property. This could include the release of abandoned easements, dower or curtesy rights, adverse possession claims, foreclosures, bankruptcy, and judgments.

- **Bankruptcy**—A statutory process in which debtors obtain financial relief by a judicially supervised reorganization or liquidation of assets for the benefit of their creditors.

- **Foreclosure**—A legal procedure to terminate a defaulted mortgagor's interest in the property.

- **Judgment**—Court decision on the respective rights and claims of the parties in a suit; a general, involuntary, equitable lien on both real and personal property of the debtor that normally covers only the property in the county where the judgment is rendered.

- **Lis pendens notice**—Recorded to give constructive notice that an action affecting the property has been filed in court, meaning that a lawsuit has been filed, but a judgment has not been decreed; warns of a future lien on the property and renders a property unmarketable.

- **Writ of attachment**—Creditor asks the court to retain custody of the property while a court suit is being decided, thus preventing the debtor from transferring unsecured real estate before a judgment is rendered; ensures that the property will be available to satisfy the judgment.

- **Writ of execution**—A court order authorizing an officer of the court, such as a sheriff, to sell the property of a defendant to satisfy a judgment.

A *cloud on title* is any claim that creates a defect of title or casts doubt on the title's validity.

An example is when a mortgage has been paid in full but the mortgage release or satisfaction document has not been recorded to verify the payoff.

PREPARATION OF TITLE ABSTRACTS

An **abstract (of title)** is a condensed legal history of all transactions affecting the property; it includes conveyances, wills, records of judicial proceedings, recorded liens and encumbrances affecting the property, and their current status. The abstractor searches public records at the courthouse and then summarizes the information in chronological order.

An abstractor is liable for mistakes in the abstractor's search of the public records. The abstractor is *not* liable for forgery, missing heirs, or encroachments not found in the search.

LIENS AND ORDER OF PRIORITY

A **lien** is created when a debt is established when the **lienor (lender)** is given, by agreement, a claim to the property of the **lienee (borrower)** as security for a debt.

Terms Related to Liens

- **General lien**—claim against all property of the lienee, both real and personal property

- **Specific lien**—claim against a particular property only

- **Voluntary lien**—established intentionally by the lienee

- **Involuntary lien**—created by law without any action on the part of the owner (voluntary or involuntary liens may be statutory or equitable)

- **Statutory lien**—created by law, such as a judgment

- **Equitable lien**—created by the court based on "fairness," such as the payment of the balance on a delinquent charge account

- **Property taxes**—specific, involuntary liens placed on the owner's property

- **Special assessments**—levied for improvements made to property, special assessments are specific and statutory but may be either voluntary or involuntary liens

- **Mortgage lien (deed of trust)**—voluntary lien securing the loan for the lender until the debt is paid in full

- **Mechanic's lien**—placed on property by a party who performed labor or furnished material to improve the property (also known as *materialman's lien*)

- **IRS tax lien**—general, statutory, involuntary lien on all real and personal property owned by a debtor

The **priority** of liens is generally as follows:

- Real estate taxes and special assessments are paid first.

- The debtor in the first, or senior, lien position is paid next.

- The debtors in junior lien positions (second, third, and so on) are paid in the order of recording.

- Mechanics' liens generally become *effective on the day the work began*, the day the materials were delivered, the date the work was completed, the date the contract was signed or the work was ordered, or the date the lien was recorded.

- An IRS lien becomes effective from the date of filing or recording. It does not supersede previously recorded liens.

IMPORTANCE OF RECORDING AND TYPES OF NOTICE

For a lien to be established, it must be recorded in public records at the courthouse. **Recording** gives constructive notice of a party's interest in a property.

- **Constructive notice**—Legal notice created by recording documents such as deeds, mortgages, and long-term leases in the county where the property is located. *Physical possession* of the property also gives constructive notice of the rights of the parties that are in possession.

- **Actual notice**—A party has *actual knowledge* of the fact. When a party has actual notice of a third party's prior rights to a property and still accepts the deed to the property, the party accepts the deed subject to the third party's prior rights. For example, a person who accepts a deed with a judgment lien on the property becomes responsible for the judgment.

- **Torrens system**—A method of legal registration of land where title does not transfer and encumbrances are not effective against the property until the proper documents are registered at the Torrens office. In some states, this means that the title cannot be lost through adverse possession.

AMP Outline—Settlement Procedures

IV.	**Settlement/Transfer of Ownership**			5.	Types of deeds
	C.	Settlement Procedures		6.	Settlement Statement (HUD-1 Form)
		1.	Purposes and procedures of settlement	7.	Other settlement documents
		2.	Obligations of settlement agent	8.	Real Estate Settlement Procedures Act
		3.	Warranties associated with deeds	9.	Transfer tax
		4.	Essential elements of a valid deed		

PURPOSES AND PROCEDURES OF SETTLEMENT

A real estate settlement, or closing, takes place to consummate or finalize a real estate transaction. Before closing, the buyer makes a final inspection to ensure the property is in the same condition as promised in the sales contract. Both parties receive a copy of the settlement or closing statement, which they inspect to ensure that all monies have been accounted for properly. Each party may have an attorney present at the closing.

A face-to-face closing is a formal meeting of all parties involved, and a settlement agent presides over the closing. A closing in **escrow** means that a disinterested third party is authorized to act as an escrow agent for the buyer and the seller and to handle all closing activities.

OBLIGATIONS OF SETTLEMENT AGENT

The settlement agent sees that all documents are prepared for closing and conducts the closing. The settlement agent may file Form 1099-S with the IRS. A settlement agent could be a closing agent from the title company, an attorney, a lender, or a real estate agent. Proration calculations will be reviewed in Chapter 7.

Alienation is the act of *transferring* property to another. Alienation may be *voluntary*, such as by gift or sale, or *involuntary*, such as through eminent domain or adverse possession.

An alienation clause in a *mortgage* allows the lender to collect full payment when the property is conveyed.

WARRANTIES ASSOCIATED WITH DEEDS

A **deed** is the written instrument that transfers the title from the grantor/seller to the grantee/buyer. Different types of deeds can be used to convey the title, and the distinguishing characteristics are the covenants or promises made by the grantor. State laws have their own requirements for a deed.

ESSENTIAL ELEMENTS OF A VALID DEED

- The name of the **grantor** or party with the legal authority to transfer the property

- A **grantee** identified with reasonable certainty (a deed cannot be transferred to a deceased person or to a corporation that does not exist)

- **Consideration** will be stated and *may or may not be* the actual selling price

- A **granting clause** or words of conveyance

- An optional **habendum clause**, which means "to have and to hold" and defines ownership

- **Restrictions** or limitations placed on the conveyance of the property

- An accurate **legal description**
- The **signature of the grantor**
- **Delivery** and acceptance of the deed by the grantee

Acknowledgment

In most states, a deed must be acknowledged and attested to be recorded. The primary purpose of **acknowledgment** is to verify that the person who signed the written document did so voluntarily and of his or her own free will. The secondary purpose of acknowledgment is to verify the identity of the signer. **Attestation** is the act of witnessing a person's signing of a document.

TYPES OF DEEDS

A **general warranty deed** is the *best deed for the buyer to receive* because it contains five covenants or promises made by the grantor. They are the

1. **covenant of seisin**—promises the grantor owns the property and has the right to convey;

2. **covenant against encumbrances**—promises that there are no encumbrances other than those stated in the deed;

3. **covenant of quiet enjoyment**—promises that the grantor has a superior title and no one will object to the conveyance;

4. **covenant of further assurances**—promises that the grantor will correct any title defects found in the future; and

5. **covenant of warranty forever**—promises that the grantor will defend the title in disputes brought by third parties.

A **special warranty deed** contains three warranties. That the

1. grantor received title,

2. property was unencumbered by the grantor, and

3. grantor will defend the title for his or her period of ownership only.

A **bargain and sale deed**

- *implies* that the grantor *holds title and possession* but includes no express warranties.

A **quitclaim deed**

- contains *no express or implied covenants*; it conveys whatever interest the grantor has, *if any*, on that given day; and

- is used to correct an error in a deed or release an interest in the property.

Special purpose deeds include the following:

■ A **cession deed** is used to give property to the government, such as giving land for a park.

■ A **sheriff's deed** transfers the interest in a property that was foreclosed by the sheriff.

■ The **executor's** or **administrator's deed** is given by a court-appointed party to settle the estate of a deceased person.

■ A **tax deed** is given at property tax sale.

■ The **gift deed** is used to give property as a gift. The consideration would be stated as "love and affection." If the grantor gave the property as a gift in order to avoid creditors, the creditors could seize the property.

In a **deed in trust** the *trustor conveys title to a trustee*, who manages the property for the beneficiary.

■ An **inter vivos** means to set up a trust during one's life.

■ A **testamentary trust** means that the trust is established by will.

■ A **deed of reconveyance** is used in a deed in trust or a deed of trust to reconvey the title to the trustor. There are federal, state, and security regulations that govern trust agreements. (See Figure 4.2.)

When a person dies **testate** (with a will), the property will be *devised* or transferred to the devisee. When a person dies **intestate**, the *laws of descent and distribution* in the state where the property is located will determine who receives the property. If a person dies intestate and owns property in another state, the laws in the state where the property is located determine who receives the property.

SETTLEMENT STATEMENT (HUD-1 FORM)

See Figure 4.3 for a copy of a settlement statement.

OTHER SETTLEMENT DOCUMENTS

■ A **mortgage** is a pledge of property to the lender for security for the payment of the debt.

■ A **note** is the evidence of the debt and states the terms of repayment.

FIGURE 4.2	
Trust Deeds	

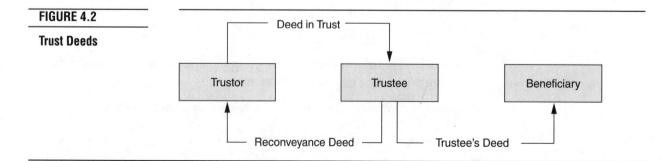

FIGURE 4.3

HUD-1 Uniform
Settlement Statement

A. U.S.DEPARTMENT OF HOUSING AND URBAN DEVELOPMENT	B.TYPE OF LOAN
	1. [ ]FHA 2. [ ]FMHA 3. [ ]CONV. UNINS.
	4. [ ]VA 5. [ ]CONV. INS.
	6. FILE NUMBER: KAREN	7. LOAN NUMBER:
	8. MTG. INS. CASE NO.:

C. NOTE: This form is furnished to give you a statement of actual settlement costs. Amounts paid to and by the settlement agent are shown. Items marked ("p.o.c.") were paid outside the closing: they are shown here for information purposes and are not included in the totals.

D. NAME OF BORROWER: JOHN SMITH, MARY SMITH

ADDRESS:

E. NAME OF SELLER: JOHN DOE, MARY DOE

ADDRESS: , Florence, KY, 41042   SELLER TIN:

F. NAME OF LENDER: NATIONAL LENDER, INC.
1 Wall Street
ADDRESS: New York, NY 10001

G. PROPERTY LOCATION: Lot
17-B Happy Hills Subdivision FLORENCE KY 41042

H. SETTLEMENT AGENT: ATI TITLE AGENCY OF OHIO,INC.   CLOSER: JAMES DWYER   PHONE NUMBER: NOT ON FILE
ADDRESS: 3980 RACE ROAD
CINCINNATI, OHIO 45211   SETTLEMENT AGENT TIN: 34-1766936
PLACE OF SETTLEMENT: ATI TITLE AGENCY
ADDRESS:

I. SETTLEMENT DATE
Closing date: 07/31/01
Proration date: 07/31/01

J. SUMMARY OF BORROWER'S TRANSACTION		K. SUMMARY OF SELLER'S TRANSACTION	
100. GROSS AMOUNT DUE FROM BORROWER:		400. GROSS AMOUNT DUE TO SELLER:	
101. Contract sales price	100,000.00	401. Contract sales price	100,000.00
102. Personal property		402. Personal property	
103. Settlement charges to borrower(line 1400)	2,099.50	403.	
104.		404.	
105.		405.	
Adjustments for items paid by seller in advance:		Adjustments for items paid for seller in advance:	
106. City/town taxes to		406. City/town taxes to	
107. County taxes to		407. County taxes to	
108. Assessments to		408. Assessments to	
109.		409.	
110.		410.	
111.		411.	
112.		412.	
120. GROSS AMOUNT DUE FROM BORROWER:	102,099.50	420. GROSS AMOUNT DUE TO SELLER:	100,000.00
200. AMOUNTS PAID BY OR IN BEHALF OF BORROWER:		500. REDUCTIONS IN AMOUNT DUE TO SELLER:	
201. Deposit or earnest money		501. Excess deposit(see instructions)	
202. Principal amount of new loan(s)	97,000.00	502. Settlement charges to seller(line 1400)	6,150.00
203. Existing loan(s) taken subject to		503. Existing loan(s) taken subject to	
204.		504. Payoff of first mortgage loan	46,425.58
205.		505. Payoff of second mortgage loan	
206.		506.	
207.		507.	
208.		508.	
209.		509.	
Adjustments for items unpaid by seller:		Adjustments for items unpaid by seller:	
210. City/town taxes to		510. City/town taxes to	
211. County taxes 01/01/01 to 07/31/01	815.67	511. County taxes 01/01/01 to 07/31/01	815.67
212. Assessments to		512. Assessments to	
213.		513.	
214.		514.	
215.		515.	
216.		516.	
217.		517.	
218.		518.	
219.		519.	
220. TOTAL PAID BY/FOR BORROWER:	97,815.67	520. TOTAL REDUCTION IN AMOUNT:	53,391.25
300. CASH AT SETTLEMENT FROM/TO BORROWER:		600. CASH AT SETTLEMENT TO/FROM SELLER:	
301. Gross amount due from borrower(line 120)	102,099.50	601. Gross amount due to seller(line 420)	100,000.00
302. Less amounts paid by/for borrower(line 220)	97,815.67	602. Less total reductions in amount due seller(line 520)	53,391.25
303. CASH [X FROM] [TO] BORROWER:	4,283.83	603. CASH [X TO] [FROM] SELLER:	46,608.75

SUBSTITUTE FORM 1099 SELLER STATEMENT-The information contained in Blocks E,G,H and I and on line 401 (or, if line 401 is asterisked, lines 403 and 404) is important tax information and is being furnished to the Internal Revenue Service. If you are required to file a return, a negligence penalty or other sanction will be imposed on you if this item is required to be reported and the IRS determines that it has not been reported.
SELLER INSTRUCTION-If this real estate was your principal residence, file Form 2119, Sale or Exchange of Principal Residence, for any gain, with your income tax return; for other transactions, complete the applicable parts of Form 4797, Form 6252 and/or Schedule D (Form 1040).

You are required by law to provide _____ with your correct taxpayer identification number.
If you do not provide _____ with your correct taxpayer identification number, you may be subject to civil or criminal penalties.
Under penalties of perjury, I certify that the number shown on this statement is my correct taxpayer identification number.

_____   _____
Seller   ATI Contact Person and Phone Number for 1099 Information

FIGURE 4.3

HUD-1 Uniform Settlement Statement (continued)

File KAREN — L. SETTLEMENT CHARGES			PAID FROM BORROWER'S FUNDS AT SETTLEMENT	PAID FROM SELLER'S FUNDS AT SETTLEMENT
700. TOTAL SALES/BROKER'S COMMISSION Based on $ 100,000.00@ 6.00 % = 6,000.00				
Division of Commission (line 700) as follows:				
701. $3,000.00		to XYZ		
702. $3,000.00		to ABC		
703. Commission paid at settlement				6,000.00
704.				
800. ITEMS PAYABLE IN CONNECTION WITH LOAN.				
801. Loan Origination fee	%			
802. Loan Discount	%			
803. Appraisal fee		to APPRAISALS "R" US	325.00	
804. Credit Report		to NATIONAL LENDER, INC.	50.00	
805. Lender's inspection fee		to		
806. Mortgage Insurance application fee		to		
807. Assumption Fee		to		
808. Tax Service Fee TAX SERVICE FEE		to NATIONAL LENDER, INC.		75.00
809.		to		
810.		to		
811. Flood Certification		to NATIONAL LENDER, INC.	15.50	
812.		to		
900. ITEMS REQUIRED BY LENDER TO BE PAID IN ADVANCE.				
901. Interest from 07/31/01 to 08/01/01 @$ 21.26027 /day 1 day			21.26	
902. Mortgage insurance premium for 12 mo. to JOHN SMITH -POCB 223.00				
903. Hazard insurance premium for yrs. to				
904.	yrs. to			
905.				
1000. RESERVES DEPOSITED WITH LENDER				
1001. Hazard Insurance	3 mo.@$	20.00 per mo.	60.00	
1002. Mortgage insurance	2 mo.@$	40.42 per mo.	80.84	
1003. City property taxes	mo.@$	per mo.		
1004. County property taxes	3 mo.@$	117.58 per mo.	352.74	
1005. Annual assessments (Maint.)	mo.@$	per mo.		
1006.	mo.@$	per mo.		
1007.	mo.@$	per mo.		
1008.	mo.@$	per mo.		
1009. Aggregate Reserve for Hazard & Flood Ins, City & County Prop. Taxes, Mortgage Ins. & Annual Assessments			(80.84)	0.00
1100. TITLE CHARGES:				
1101. Settlement or closing fee		to ATI TITLE AGENCY	250.00	
1102. Abstract or title search		to ATI TITLE AGENCY	175.00	
1103. Title examination		to		
1104. Title insurance binder		to ATI TITLE AGENCY	50.00	
1105. Document preparation		to		
1106. Notary fee		to		
1107. Attorney's fee to		to		
(includes above items No.:)				
1108. Title insurance		to ATI TITLE AGENCY	569.00	
(includes above items No.:)				
1109. Lender's coverage	97,000.00	$ 339.50		
1110. Owner's coverage	100,000.00	$ 229.50		
1111. Deed Preparation		to STEPHEN G. BRINKER, ATTY		75.00
1112.		to		
1113.		to		
1114.		to		
1200. GOVERNMENT RECORDING AND TRANSFER CHARGES				
1201. Recording fees: Deed $ 14.00 Mrtg $ 42.00 Rel. $			56.00	
1202. City/county tax/stamps: Deed $ Mrtg $				
1203. State tax/stamps: Deed $ Mrtg $				
1204.		to		
1205.		to		
1206.		to		
1300. ADDITIONAL SETTLEMENT CHARGES				
1301. Survey		to ATI TITLE AGENCY	130.00	
1302. Pest inspection PEST CONTROL		to PEST CONTROL	45.00	
1303.		to		
1304.		to		
1305.		to		
1400. TOTAL SETTLEMENT CHARGES (entered on lines 103, Section J and 502, Section K)			2,099.50	6,150.00

CERTIFICATION: I have carefully reviewed the HUD-1 Settlement Statement and to the best of my knowledge and belief, it is a true and accurate statement of all receipts and disbursements made on my account or by me in this transaction. I further certify that I have received a copy of HUD-1 Settlement Statement.

_____   _____
Borrowers   Sellers

The HUD-1 Settlement Statement which I have prepared is a true and accurate account of this transaction. I have caused or will cause the funds to be disbursed in accordance with this statement.

_____   _____
Settlement Agent   Date

WARNING: It is a crime to knowingly make false statements to the United States on this or any other similar form. Penalties upon conviction can include a fine and imprisonment. For details see: Title 18: U.S. Code Section 1001 and Section 1010.

- An **affidavit of the seller** is a document in which the seller affirms that from the time the sales contract was accepted until the date of closing, the seller has done nothing to burden the title that would not be revealed in the title search.

- A **bill of sale** is used to show the transfer of personal property.

- A **payoff statement** indicates the payoff of the seller's existing note(s).

- An **insurance policy** is required by buyer to show payment of homeowners insurance.

REAL ESTATE SETTLEMENT PROCEDURES ACT

The **Real Estate Settlement Procedures Act (RESPA)** is a federal act that requires that lenders disclose to the buyer and seller all settlement costs on *federally related mortgage loans*, and first and second liens for the *purchase or refinancing of one- to four-family dwellings*.

RESPA requires that lenders and settlement agents make certain disclosures at the time of the loan application and at the closing of the loan. These include the following:

- The booklet *Settlement Costs and You* must be given to a prospective borrower within three business days from the time that person receives or prepares a loan application.

- Within three business days of application, the lender must provide the borrower with a good-faith estimate of the settlement costs the borrower will likely incur.

- The Uniform Settlement Statement (HUD-1 Form) must be used to itemize all charges related to the transaction.

- The lender is prohibited from receiving any kickbacks or other referral fees from service providers.

- Lenders cannot charge a fee for the preparation of the settlement statement. The buyer and seller must receive a copy of the settlement statement at the closing.

- RESPA does not apply to a land contract; a purchase-money mortgage, wherein the seller is solely financing the property; or a transaction where the buyer is assuming the seller's existing loan and the lender charges less than $50 for the assumption.

A new good-faith estimate and HUD-1 statement must be used beginning January 1, 2010. Visit *www.hud.gov* for more information.

TRANSFER TAX

Real estate transfer taxes, or RETTs, are state, county, and/or municipal sales taxes most often used as general revenue. However, RETTs can be devoted to specific uses such as affordable housing development or open space protection. Transfer taxes are normally paid by the seller or lessor when the property is conveyed by a deed, contract for deed, lease, sublease, or assignment. The transfer tax may be paid by the purchase of tax stamps and are sometimes called documentary stamp taxes.

AMP Outline—Completion of the Transaction

IV.   Settlement/Transfer of Ownership
D.   Completion of the Transaction
  1.   Negotiations between buyers and sellers leading to an agreement
  2.   Contract requirements and fulfillment of contingencies leading to closing
  3.   Federal statutory requirements
  4.   Rights of home ownership (for example, homestead; rights of married people)
  5.   Rights of others related to property (for example, adverse possession, adjoining owners, encroachments)
  6.   Nature and types of common-interest ownership (for example, condominium, planned unit development, cooperative, townhouse)
  7.   Eminent domain proceedings
  8.   Securities law application and referral
  9.   Situations in which experts are required (for example, financial planning and legal advice)

NEGOTIATIONS LEADING TO A SALES AGREEMENT

When buyers decide to make an offer, the critical process of negotiating begins. Most buyers believe the seller is willing to take less than the list price and that the agent will help buyers arrive at a realistic offer and assist them in planning a negotiating strategy. Most sellers believe the buyer will pay more than their first offer if they really want the house and that the agent will assist the seller in accepting the offer or structuring a counteroffer. Usually, both parties understand they may have to give on certain points in order to reach an agreement. It is important for the buyer to understand that once an offer has been presented, the seller may accept, counter, reject, or do nothing with the offer. When the buyer and seller reach an agreement, an executory sales contract is created between the parties. An executory contract means that one or both parties have duties to perform. If nothing else, the buyer must bring cash to the closing, and the seller must provide a good and marketable title for the property to transfer.

CONTRACT REQUIREMENTS AND FULFILLMENT OF CONTINGENCIES LEADING TO CLOSING

It is essential that the buyer and seller understand the contract terms and the contingencies that must be fulfilled. Contingencies can include property, termite, radon, and lead-based paint inspections as well as finance and repair issues. The timelines for fulfillment of the contingencies should be reviewed by the agent to be sure the contingencies are met. Until the contingencies have been fulfilled, the contract is voidable. To change any of the provisions in the contract, the parties should create an addendum or supplement to the contract. Appropriate parties should sign the addendum.

FEDERAL STATUTORY REQUIREMENTS

In real estate transactions, agents should comply with the federal and state fair housing laws, Real Estate Settlement Procedures Act (RESPA), the Truth-in-Lending Act, the Patriot Act, and other laws that apply to the particular loan program.

RIGHTS OF HOME OWNERSHIP

Property can be transferred fee simple absolute, fee simple defeasible, or with a life estate interest. Please see Figure 1.12 in Chapter 1 for a review of these terms.

RIGHTS OF OTHERS RELATED TO PROPERTY

The individual's right to the ownership of property is subject to certain powers by the federal, state, and/or local governments. These powers include police power, eminent domain, taxation, and escheat.

Government Powers

- **Police power**—The right of the government to regulate for the purpose of promoting the health, safety, and welfare of the public (i.e., zoning, building codes, and subdivision regulations).

- **Eminent domain**—The right of a government, a quasi-government body, or a public company to take property for public use. Just compensation must be paid to the owner. The government exercises its right to take the property by the process of **condemnation**.

- **Taxation**—The right of the government to charge a property owner a fee to raise funds to meet the public needs.

- **Escheat**—When a property owner dies **intestate**, that is, leaves **no will and no heirs** can be found, the property reverts (escheats) to the state or the county.

PETE is the acronym to help you remember the government powers.

P—Police Power   **E**—Eminent domain   **T**—Taxation   **E**—Escheat

Private Powers

The individual's right to the ownership of property is also subject to certain private powers such as deed conditions and subdivision rules and regulations. Other rights could be acquired by adverse possession, encroachments, license, and the rights of adjoining owners.

Adverse Possession

If a person uses someone else's property for a statutory period and if the use is open, notorious, hostile, and continuous, the person may acquire title to the property through **adverse possession**. The rights of the party in possession are called **squatter's rights**.

To acquire a title through adverse possession, the squatter must file a **suit to quiet title** after the statutory period has been met. Periods of ownership by different squatters can be **tacked** or combined, enabling a party who has not been in possession for the entire time to establish a claim. Adverse possession is an involuntary alienation or conveyance of property. When a squatter receives a title through an adverse possession claim, it is called a *title by prescription* or a *prescriptive title*.

An **encroachment** is an unauthorized intrusion of an improvement onto the real property of another. This could be an intrusion into the air, surface, or subsurface space of the property's boundary lines or building setback lines. A survey is the best way for a buyer to determine if there are any encroachments on a property.

An **encroachment** is an unauthorized intrusion of an improvement onto the real property of another. This could be an intrusion into the air, surface, or subsurface space of the property's boundary lines or building setback lines. A survey is the best way for a buyer to determine if there are any encroachments on a property.

Lateral and Subjacent Support

A property owner has an incidental right to the lateral support provided by the adjoining neighbors' property and the right to the **subjacent support** the earth receives from its underlying strata. That is, a property owner cannot excavate or mine the land in such a way that it will cause a neighbor's land to collapse or sink.

NATURE AND TYPES OF COMMON INTEREST OWNERSHIP

Ownership that allows for a sharing of interests with other co-owners of real property includes condominiums, cooperatives, time-shares, and town houses. Such ownership provides the benefits of home ownership with a sharing of amenities and expenses. Condominiums, cooperatives, time-shares, and townhouses are reviewed in Chapter 1.

EMINENT DOMAIN PROCEEDINGS

Eminent domain is an *inherent right* of state and federal governments; public corporations, such as school districts and sanitation districts; and public utilities and public service corporations, such as railroads and power companies, to take privately owned property for a necessary public use when just compensation is given to the owner. **Condemnation** is the *process* for taking the land.

SECURITIES LAW APPLICATION AND REFERRAL

A **security** is defined as an act where a party *joins with others in the expectation of making a profit from the efforts of others*. Any pooling of money that attracts investors and meets the definition of a public offering may be federally regulated by the *Securities and Exchange Commission (SEC)* or by state **blue-sky laws**.

A **syndicate** is formed when two or more people unite and pool their resources to own, develop, and/or operate an investment. Syndication may take the form of a Real Estate Investment Trust (REIT), general partnership, limited partnership, corporation, tenancy in common, or joint tenancy.

Real Estate Investment Trust

The main advantage of a REIT is that investors can avoid double taxation when certain requirements are met. The trust does not have to pay corporate income tax as long as 95 percent of its income is distributed to its shareholders, 75 percent of the trust's income comes from real estate, and certain other qualifications are met. The trust sells certificates that are purchased by investors, and then the trust invests in real estate, mortgages, or both. Profits are distributed to investors.

SITUATIONS WHERE EXPERTS ARE REQUIRED

Unless an agent is also an attorney, appraiser, accountant, property inspector, termite inspector, environmental inspector, or any other professional who might be involved in a transaction, the agent should not give an opinion. However, the agent must have enough *basic* knowledge in these fields to know when to advise a client or customer to seek an expert's opinion.

In this section, we will analyze the different stages of the transaction when expert advice should be sought. This list is not complete. Any unusual circumstance should be discussed with the agent's broker or manager.

Listing

1. When listing an unusual property where there are no comparable sales, an agent should refer the seller to an appraiser.

2. The seller should be referred to a CPA to discuss the tax consequences of a profit made on the sale.

3. If the seller is interested in a 1031 tax-deferred exchange, the agent should refer the seller to a CPA.

4. An agent may recommend that the seller purchase a CLUE report, which can be given to a buyer as a means of assuring the buyer that property insurance can be obtained.

Showing

1. The buyer should be referred to a loan officer to determine qualifications for purchasing a property and to secure homeowner's insurance.

2. If the buyer has questions regarding the boundary lines of the property, the agent should recommend that the buyer have the property surveyed.

3. Questions regarding zoning should be referred to the zoning board.

4. Questions regarding the school district should be referred to the school board.

5. The agent should recommend that the buyers carefully review the sellers' property disclosure statement. If the buyers decide to write an offer, the agent should recommend that they have their own property inspection and that a contingency clause be a part of the offer.

Offers and Counteroffers

1. Questions such as "How should I take title to the property?" should be referred to an attorney.

2. The agent should refer buyers and sellers to their own attorneys to review contracts, contingencies, and addendums before signing the documents.

From Acceptance to Closing

1. Agents should recommend property inspections and other professional inspections in a timely manner to fulfill any contingency clauses in the contract. (Examples are radon, lead-based paint, water, well inspections, etc.)

2. Agent should recommend that buyers contact their own insurance agents to ensure that the buyers have a policy on property they are buying at closing.

Closing

1. The agent should recommend that the buyer and seller have their own attorneys to represent them at closing.

QUESTIONS

1. When land is to be condemned or taken under the power of eminent domain, which of the following must apply?
   A. The taking must be for a public purpose.
   B. Statutory dedication must be executed.
   C. Adverse possession claim must be taken.
   D. Constructive notice must be given.

2. What do the police powers of governmental authority include?
   A. Foreclosure
   B. Defeasance
   C. Building codes and zoning regulations
   D. Alienation

3. The Real Estate Settlement Procedures Act requires
   A. that closing of a real estate transaction be held within 90 days of the execution of the purchase agreement.
   B. that disclosure be made of all closing costs prior to the closing.
   C. the seller's approval of the buyer's statement.
   D. a qualified buyer.

4. Henry sold a parcel of real estate to Marlin and gave Marlin a quitclaim deed. On receipt of the deed Marlin may be certain that
   A. Henry owned the property.
   B. there are no encumbrances against the property.
   C. Marlin now owns the property subject to certain claims of Henry.
   D. all of Henry's interests in the property as of the date of the deed belong to Marlin.

5. Current tax laws do NOT allow which of the following as tax deductions?
   A. Interest paid on the mortgage for residential or income property
   B. Special assessments on residential property
   C. Property taxes on residential or income property
   D. Repairs made to a rental property

6. Which of the following is TRUE regarding a deed and title?
   A. A deed can be prepared only by an attorney, while a title can be prepared by an attorney or an owner.
   B. A deed is valid only if it is recorded, and a title does not have to be recorded to show ownership.
   C. The purpose of a deed is to transfer title from the grantee to the grantor.
   D. The purpose of a deed is to convey title from the grantor to the grantee.

7. Boris transfers property to David with a special warranty deed. Which of the following is TRUE?
   A. Boris is making additional warranties beyond those given in a warranty deed.
   B. Boris's property is Torrens property.
   C. Boris is warranting that no encumbrances have ever been placed against the property that have not been satisfied or released.
   D. Boris's warranties are limited to the time he held the property.

8. The state, county, and/or municipal sales tax is many times used as general revenue and is normally a debit to the seller on the HUD-1 statement. It is sometimes called a documentary stamp tax and may also be called a(n)
   A. recording fee.
   B. environmental tax.
   C. transfer tax.
   D. real estate tax.

9. Samantha sold her house to Buddy. Buddy, however, did not record the deed. Under these circumstances
   A. the transfer of property between Samantha and Buddy is ineffective.
   B. Buddy's interest is not fully protected against third parties.
   C. the deed is invalid after 90 days.
   D. the deed is invalid after six months.

10. For a deed to be valid, the
    A. grantor must be legally competent.
    B. signature of the grantor must be witnessed.
    C. documents must pass through the hands of an escrow agent.
    D. grantee must sign the deed.

11. A quitclaim deed
    A. carries no covenant or warranty.
    B. may not transfer the seller's title.
    C. carries full warranty.
    D. provides a limited warranty.

12. An investment that will allow the taxpayer to reduce current tax liability by offsetting income from one source with losses from another source is called a tax
    A. deduction.
    B. rate.
    C. liability.
    D. shelter.

13. Which of the following BEST describes a capital gain?
    A. A capital gain is the taxable profit that is realized from the sale of a capital asset.
    B. A capital gain is the difference between the sale price and the original investment.
    C. A capital gain is the taxable profit that investors must pay when as asset is sold.
    D. A capital gain is the difference between the sale price and the selling expenses.

14. Roger is selling limited partnerships in a real estate venture. The offering is being made within state lines, and all purchasers are residents of the state. The offering is MOST LIKELY regulated by
    A. the Securities and Exchange Commission.
    B. the real estate commission.
    C. blue-sky laws.
    D. white-sky laws.

15. A defect or cloud on the title to property may be cured by
    A. obtaining quitclaim deeds from all other interested parties.
    B. bringing an action to register title.
    C. paying cash for the property at the closing.
    D. bringing an action to repudiate title.

16. Sally is in the process of purchasing Jack's house. To protect its interest, her mortgagee decides to take out title insurance. The title insurance policy
    A. may act as the instrument of transfer.
    B. indemnifies the holder against some, but not all, of the possible defects in title.
    C. protects Sally from all defects in the title.
    D. protects Jack from a lawsuit.

17. Under the condominium form of ownership, the interest of the owner in the unit the owner possesses is normally a
    A. life estate.
    B. fee simple interest.
    C. proprietary leasehold interest.
    D. reciprocal proprietary easement interest.

18. Deed restrictions are a means whereby
    A. local zoning laws are enforced.
    B. the planning commission's work is made effective.
    C. villages and cities can control construction details.
    D. the seller can limit or control the buyer's use.

19. Normally, a deed is considered valid even if
    A. signed by an authorized attorney-in-fact rather than the seller.
    B. the grantor was an illegal alien.
    C. the deed was signed by a minor and not the guardian of the minor.
    D. the grantor did not deliver the deed.

20. George sold his house to Sylvia. In the deed used in the transaction, George guaranteed that the property was not encumbered during the time he held title except as noted in the deed. The type of deed George gave to Sylvia is a
    A. general warranty deed.
    B. quitclaim deed.
    C. special warranty deed.
    D. limited quitclaim deed.

21. Which of the following is NOT usually prorated between buyer and seller at the closing?
    A. Recording charges
    B. Property taxes
    C. Rents
    D. Utility bills

22. Tom has a claim affecting the title to Bill's property. Bill has no mortgages against the property and has been trying to sell it. Tom is concerned about the possibility of a bona fide purchaser buying it before he obtains a judgment. To protect himself during the course of the court action, Tom should
    A. publish a notice in a newspaper.
    B. seek an attachment.
    C. bring a quick summary proceeding.
    D. notify Bill that any attempt to sell the property will be considered fraud.

23. Which of the following transfers is an involuntary alienation of property?
    A. Quitclaim
    B. Inheritance
    C. Eminent domain
    D. Gift

24. All of the following are required by RESPA EXCEPT
    A. lenders must provide borrowers with a good-faith estimate of loan closing costs.
    B. a uniform settlement sheet must be used at closings.
    C. the borrower must be given five days to back out of the loan transaction after receiving the required settlement information.
    D. no kickbacks may be given to any party in connection with the loan transaction.

25. How may title to real estate be transferred?
    A. Descent and distribution
    B. Involuntary alienation
    C. Delivery of the deed
    D. All of the above

26. All of the following are intended to convey legal title to real estate EXCEPT a(n)
    A. warranty deed.
    B. deed of trust.
    C. trustee's deed.
    D. equitable title.

27. The words "to have and to hold" in a deed define the ownership that is being transferred. This phrase is known as the
    A. granting clause.
    B. habendum clause.
    C. alienation clause.
    D. distributor clause.

28. The deed MOST LIKELY to be used to correct errors in a deed is a
    A. quitclaim deed.
    B. warranty deed.
    C. bargain and sale deed.
    D. grant deed.

29. For a deed to be recorded, it must be acknowledged. The primary purpose of acknowledgment is to
    A. convey title to the grantee.
    B. ensure the identity of the grantee.
    C. verify that the deed was signed without duress.
    D. guarantee a marketable title.

30. All of the following are true regarding RESPA EXCEPT that it
    A. requires the disclosure of all closing costs.
    B. covers one- to four-family dwellings.
    C. sets the interest rate that the lender can charge.
    D. regulates the amount the lender can collect from the borrower to place in escrow.

31. Which of the following statements is true regarding title insurance?
    A. Title insurance is paid monthly and is included in the mortgage payment.
    B. Title insurance covers losses due to a defect in the title, but it does not pay for the cost of defending the title.
    C. There are two title polices that may be purchased. The owner's policy covers the owner, while the mortgagee's policy covers the lender.
    D. Title insurance normally does not cover defects caused by forgery.

32. Which of the following is FALSE regarding ad valorem taxes?
    A. Ad valorem is another term for property taxes.
    B. Unpaid ad valorem taxes could create a general lien on the property.
    C. Ad valorem taxes are tax deductible.
    D. Unpaid ad valorem taxes could create a specific lien on the property.

33. What is the MAJOR DIFFERENCE between a general lien and a specific lien?
    A. A general lien may be filed only on personal property, while a specific lien is filed on real estate.
    B. A general lien may be filed by a corporation, while a specific lien may be filed by a specific individual.
    C. A general lien may be filed by an attorney, while a specific lien can be filed by anyone.
    D. A general lien may be filed against real and personal property, while a specific lien may be filed against only a specific property.

34. In 1975 a person moved into an abandoned log cabin. Over the years he repaired the property and paid the property taxes. In 2005 another man appears with a deed to the property. Both claim to own the property. To settle this matter, there needs to be a
    A. suit for specific performance.
    B. suit for partition.
    C. suit to quiet the title.
    D. suit for exoneration.

35. When a property is abandoned, it may revert to the county or state by the process of
    A. escheat.
    B. eminent domain.
    C. testate.
    D. intestate.

36. Middleton decided he could make more money from his tree farm by dividing it into small parcels and selling them. Subsequently, Middleton entered into a series of purchase agreements, in connection with which he agreed to continue to operate the property and distribute proceeds from its income to the buyers. Under the circumstances, Middleton has sold
    A. real estate, because the object of the sale was land.
    B. securities, because the buyers were investors relying on Middleton's activities to generate a profit from the premises.
    C. real estate, because the property was subdivided before the sales took place.
    D. securities, because the object of the purchase was trees; the underlying land was merely incidental to the sale.

37. Steward entered into an agreement to sell his house to the Manders. The closing is scheduled to take place April 15. In January, Steward paid the taxes for the entire year, although the Manders are assuming responsibility for taxes attributable to the period following the closing. At the closing, on the settlement statement, the adjustment made for property taxes appears as a
    A. debit to the buyer and a credit to the seller.
    B. credit to the buyer and a debit to the seller.
    C. credit to the buyer.
    D. debit to the seller.

38. Harry and Edith entered into an agreement to sell their house. Some time ago, a special assessment was levied against their property for sidewalk and street improvements in front of their house. Under the agreement with the purchaser, the buyers will not assume the special assessment. If the assessment has not been paid off prior to the closing, the amount remaining due will appear as a
    A. credit to the buyer.
    B. debit to the seller.
    C. credit to the seller and a debit to the buyer.
    D. debit to the seller and a credit to the buyer.

39. Expenses involved in the closing of a real estate transaction are shown on the settlement as a
    A. debit to either the buyer or the seller.
    B. credit to either the buyer or the seller.
    C. debit to both the buyer and the seller.
    D. credit to both the buyer and the seller.

40. RESPA requirements apply to any residential real estate transaction
    A. in a state that has adopted RESPA.
    B. involving a federally related mortgage loan.
    C. involving any mortgage financing less than $100,000.
    D. involving any sale price less than $100,000.

41. A purchaser of property can be guaranteed of receiving good title to the property if at the closing she or he receives
    A. a general warranty deed.
    B. a quitclaim deed.
    C. a contract for deed.
    D. none of the above.

42. Broker Bonnie represented the seller in a transaction. Her client informed her that he did not want the deed to recite the actual consideration paid for the house. After seeking legal advice, Bonnie
    A. must inform her client that only the actual price of the real estate may appear on the deed.
    B. may show a price on the deed other than the actual price, provided it does not vary by more than 10 percent of the purchase price.
    C. may advise her client that he may show consideration of $10 on the deed if permitted by state law and advise him to seek legal counsel to answer any other questions.
    D. should inform the seller that either the full price should be stated or all references to consideration should be removed from the deed.

43. Any improvement that is made to extend the useful life of a property or add to its value is called a capital
    A. improvement.
    B. asset.
    C. gain.
    D. enhancement.

44. Which of the following is NOT an example of constructive notice?
    A. Recording a deed at the courthouse
    B. A legal notice in the newspaper
    C. An unrecorded lien
    D. Possession of the property

45. An agent just deposited a commission check into her bank account. Under IRS guidelines, this would be classified as
    A. active income.
    B. passive income.
    C. portfolio income.
    D. gift income.

46. Which of the following is TRUE regarding an abstract of title?
    A. It can be developed only by an attorney.
    B. It contains the names of missing heirs.
    C. It contains information taken from public records.
    D. It is necessary before a property can be listed.

47. Jayne decided to buy investment property. She negotiated a first and second mortgage on a property at the same time. What is the MAJOR DIFFERENCE between these loans?
    A. The second mortgage would have a higher rate of interest than the first mortgage.
    B. The second mortgage would have a lower rate of interest than the first mortgage.
    C. The second mortgage would be for a shorter term than the first mortgage.
    D. The second mortgage would be in a junior lien position, while the first mortgage would be in a senior lien position.

48. An owner's title insurance policy normally covers all of the following EXCEPT
    A. missing heirs.
    B. incorrect marital status.
    C. zoning restrictions.
    D. forgery.

49. RESPA regulates all of the following transactions EXCEPT a(n)
    A. FHA-insured mortgage.
    B. contract for deed.
    C. VA-guaranteed mortgage.
    D. conventional mortgage sold to Fannie Mae.

50. The process an airport would use to take property for public use while paying the owner just compensation is
    A. eminent domain.
    B. escheat.
    C. adverse possession.
    D. condemnation.

51. At a closing, Howard received a deed in which the grantor implied possession and ownership of the property. Howard MOST LIKELY received a
    A. general warranty deed.
    B. bargain and sale deed.
    C. special warranty deed.
    D. grantee's deed.

52. Lis pendens is BEST described by which of the following?
    A. A notice filed when the property is foreclosed
    B. Constructive notice that a property owner is in litigation that could result in a future lien on the property
    C. Actual notice that a judgment has been secured against a property owner
    D. A notice that allows the court to maintain custody of a property until it is sold in bankruptcy

53. Lucas wishes to take title to a property with a deed that BEST protects his interest. Lucas wishes a(n)
    A. fee simple interest conveyed by a quit-claim deed.
    B. estate for years interest conveyed by a bargain and sale deed.
    C. fee simple interest conveyed by a warranty deed.
    D. periodic estate interest conveyed by a grant deed.

54. Sandy signs a deed conveying her property to her friend Steve. She tells no one and places the deed in her safe-deposit box. Several months later, she dies intestate and the deed is found. Who receives the property?
    A. Steve, because the deed has been signed by Sandy.
    B. Sandy's heirs, as determined by the laws of descent and distribution.
    C. Another friend Sandy told could have the property three days before her death.
    D. The state, because she died intestate.

55. All of the following documents would MOST LIKELY be recorded EXCEPT a
    A. general warranty deed.
    B. mortgage.
    C. mortgage release.
    D. sales contract.

56. Joe just purchased his first investment property. His accountant has advised him that all of the following would be a tax deduction EXCEPT
    A. mortgage interest paid on the loan.
    B. principal paid on the loan.
    C. property taxes.
    D. discount points paid on the loan.

57. Which of the following would NOT be associated with testate?
    A. Will
    B. Devisee
    C. Probate
    D. Descent

58. Sterling wants to exchange her 20-unit apartment building for another investment property. Internal Revenue Code Section 1031 gives her how many days after the closing to identify another property for exchange?
    A. 30 days
    B. 45 days
    C. 90 days
    D. 180 days

59. Gary, Tom, and Angie have decided to pool their resources for investment purposes. This process is
    A. called syndication.
    B. a suit for performance.
    C. a limited partnership.
    D. illegal in most states.

60. Which of the following would NOT be associated with an adverse possession claim?
    A. Title by prescription
    B. Suit to quiet the title
    C. Squatter's rights
    D. A license

61. For 15 years Roger and Caroline have owned a single-family home that is used for investment purposes. The house is located off an expressway ramp, and a hotel chain has just made an offer on their property. If they sell the property, can they negotiate a 1031 exchange and exclude the payment of capital gains tax?
    A. Yes, if they follow the rules of a 1031 exchange, they can exclude the payment of capital gains.
    B. Yes, they can do a 1031 exchange because they have owned for more than 12 months.
    C. No, because the property they wish to exchange was not identified in the offer.
    D. No, because a 1031 does not allow the exclusion of the payment of capital gains tax, only the deferment of capital gains tax.

62. Which of the following statements is FALSE regarding depreciation?
    A. To investors, depreciation is also known as cost recovery.
    B. Land cannot be depreciated, only improvements can be depreciated.
    C. Depreciation on a primary residence can only be calculated using the straight-line method.
    D. When the property is sold, depreciation must be recaptured.

63. Mr. and Mrs. Buyer declined to purchase an owner's title policy, but the lender required them to purchase a lender's title policy. Six months after the closing a man knocked on their door. He explained that he had an ownership interest in the property because his wife sold the property while he was in another country. The man at the closing table, who said he was the husband, was not. If the man's claim is true, are the buyers covered under the lender's policy?
    A. Yes, because the closing took place only six months ago, they would be covered.
    B. Yes, the lender's policy would protect the buyer.
    C. No, the buyer declined to purchase an owner's policy and they are not covered by the lender's policy.
    D. No, because the buyers are a married couple they are not covered.

64. All of the following actions would create a cloud on the title EXCEPT
    A. undisclosed dower rights.
    B. lis pendens notice.
    C. writ of execution.
    D. mortgage release.

65. Which of the following covenants would NOT be found in a general warranty deed?
    A. Covenant of seisin
    B. Covenant to renew
    C. Covenant of warranty forever
    D. Covenant of quiet enjoyment

66. At the closing table the grantor executed a notarized deed. The grantee accepted the deed and possession was taken by the buyer after closing. Six months later, the grantor did a title check and noticed that the grantee had not recorded the deed. Is there a valid transference between the parties?
    A. Yes, the grantor signed and the buyer accepted a notarized deed, so the transference is valid between the parties.
    B. Yes, because the grantee took possession of the property the day of closing, there is a valid transference between the parties.
    C. No, because the grantee did not record the deed, there is not a valid transference between the parties.
    D. No, because the grantee did not record the deed within three days of closing, there is not a valid transference between the parties.

67. Which law requires that the booklet *Settlement Costs and You* be given to a prospective borrower within three business days of loan application?
    A. Truth-in-Lending
    B. Regulation Z
    C. Regulation B
    D. RESPA

68. Caryl lives in Chicago, and he purchased a 200-acre farm in Kentucky. The title search showed that the farm was located in Boone County, Kentucky, and Kenton County, Kentucky. The deed should be recorded in
    A. Chicago, Illinois, where he lives.
    B. Boone County, Kentucky.
    C. Kenton County, Kentucky.
    D. Boone and Kenton counties in Kentucky.

69. While searching the Internet, Vicky found a piece of property she was interested in buying. State laws require the seller to disclose in the deed the actual selling price of the property. Can Vicky go to the courthouse, conduct her own title search on the property, and determine what the seller paid for it?
    A. Yes, if her attorney goes with her.
    B. Yes, because recorded records are public documents.
    C. No, because she has not made an offer on the property.
    D. No, because only attorneys and abstractors can search public documents.

70. Mr. and Mrs. Schneider are a retired couple. They contracted with a builder to construct their retirement home and paid cash for the property. At closing they had their attorney represent them and they purchased an owner's title policy. Three months later, it was determined that the builder had not paid the subcontractors. Before the title company will make a payment to settle the claim, Mr. and Mrs. Schneider will need to
    A. pay an additional title insurance premium.
    B. subordinate their rights to their attorney.
    C. have their attorney negotiate with the subcontractors.
    D. subrogate their rights to the title company.

MATCHING QUIZ

The column on the right contains a brief definition of important terms in this section.
Write the letter of the matching term on the appropriate line.

A. Capital gain

B. Syndicate

C. Abstract of title

D. Chain of title

E. Cloud on title

F. Suit to quiet title

G. Special assessments

H. Lis pendens

I. Subrogate

J. General warranty deed

K. Special warranty deed

L. Bargain and sale deed

M. Quitclaim deed

N. Government powers

O. Adverse possession

P. Encroachment

Q. License

R. RESPA

S. Judgment

T. General lien

1. ___ Court decision on the respective rights and claims of the parties in a lawsuit

2. ___ This contains no express or implied covenants or warranties

3. ___ To substitute one party for another in a legal right or claim

4. ___ Deed that implies that the grantor holds title and has possession of the property

5. ___ Any claim that creates a defect of title or casts doubt on the title's validity

6. ___ Deed in which the grantor promises to defend the title for his or her period of ownership only

7. ___ The open, notorious, hostile, and continuous use of another's property for a statutory time, which may allow the squatter to claim the property

8. ___ Police power, eminent domain, taxation, and escheat

9. ___ Levees for improvements, such as sidewalks and waterlines, made to a property

10. ___ Formed when two or more people unite and pool their resources to own, develop, and/or operate an investment

11. ___ Ownership history of a parcel of land showing the owners in the successive series of title transfers

12. ___ Claim against all property of the lienee, both real and personal

13. ___ Condensed legal history of all transactions affecting the property, such as wills, liens, judgments, and so forth

14. ___ Real Estate Settlement Procedures Act, which requires the disclosure of closing costs on federally related mortgage loans

15. ___ Fixture, or structure, such as a wall or fence that invades a portion of a property belonging to another

16. ___ Taxable profit that is realized from the sale or exchange of an asset

17. ___ Legal action intended to establish or settle the title claim to a particular property

18. ___ This notice renders a property unmarketable because it means that litigation is pending

19. ___ Deed that contains five covenants and is the best type of deed the grantee can receive

20. ___ Privilege granted to a person for the temporary use of the land of another; can be revoked at any time

ANSWERS

1. **(A)** The government has the right to take private property through eminent domain, but the taking must be for the public benefit and just compensation must be paid.

2. **(C)** Police powers are the right of the government to regulate for health, safety, and welfare of the public. Building codes and zoning regulations are examples of police power.

3. **(B)** According to RESPA, a buyer must receive a good-faith estimate within three days of application, have the right to review the settlement sheet one day prior to closing, and receive a copy of the settlement sheet at the closing.

4. **(D)** A quitclaim deed makes no warranties. It transfers whatever interest the giver has, if any.

5. **(B)** Special assessments on a residential property are not tax deductible.

6. **(D)** A deed conveys the title from the grantor to the grantee.

7. **(D)** By definition of special warranty deed.

8. **(C)** By the definition of a transfer tax.

9. **(B)** When the grantee does not record the deed, his interests are not protected against third parties.

10. **(A)** The grantor must be legally competent when the grantor signs the deed. The signature must be acknowledged and attested if it is to be recorded.

11. **(A)** By definition of a quitclaim deed.

12. **(D)** By the definition of tax shelter.

13. **(A)** By definition of capital gains.

14. **(C)** Securities sold intrastate are regulated by blue-sky laws.

15. **(A)** Quitclaim deeds signed by the parties that have an interest in the property are the best way to perfect a title.

16. **(B)** Indemnification is an agreement to reimburse someone for a loss. The holder of title insurance is indemnified against some, but not all, possible defects.

17. **(B)** The owner's interest in the unit is normally a fee ownership interest, held in severalty, meaning separate from other owners.

18. **(D)** By the definition of a deed restriction.

19. **(A)** A deed must be transferred by a competent party. The attorney-in-fact is considered a competent party.

20. **(C)** By definition of special warranty deed.

21. **(A)** The recording fee is an expense of the buyer and is not prorated.

22. **(B)** By definition of attachment.

23. **(C)** Alienation in real estate means conveyance. Eminent domain is involuntary alienation of real estate.

24. **(C)** RESPA does not offer the buyer a five-day right of rescission in a sale contract.

25. **(D)** All are ways a title may transfer.

26. **(D)** An equitable title is an insurable title, but it does not transfer legal title.

27. **(B)** By definition of habendum clause.

28. **(A)** A quitclaim deed most likely would be used to correct an error in a deed.

29. **(C)** The primary purpose of acknowledgment is to verify that the document was executed without duress. The secondary purpose is to ensure the identity of the party signing the document.

30. **(C)** RESPA does not set interest rates.

31. **(C)** The owner's policy covers the owner, while the lender's policy covers the lender and decreases as the mortgage balance is reduced.

32. **(B)** Unpaid property taxes create a specific lien on the property, not a general lien.

33. **(D)** By the definition of general and specific liens.

34. **(C)** In an adverse possession claim, there needs to be a suit to quiet the title to determine who is the rightful owner of the property.

35. **(A)** When a person dies without a will and there are no heirs, the property is considered abandoned and reverts to the state by escheat.

36. **(B)** By the definition of an investment contract, which is a type of security.

37. **(A)** The taxes were paid in advance for the entire year; therefore, they are a debit to the buyer and a credit to the seller.

38. **(B)** The buyers will not assume the assessment; therefore, the entry will be a debit to the seller.

39. **(A)** Expenses could be a debit to either the buyer or the seller on a settlement sheet.

40. **(B)** RESPA regulates federally related mortgage loans.

41. **(D)** Nothing can provide a 100 percent guarantee of clear title.

42. **(C)** The actual consideration need not be stated in a deed unless state law requires it.

43. **(A)** By the definition of capital improvement.

44. **(C)** An unrecorded lien would not give constructive notice.

45. **(A)** Salaries and commissions are classified as active income.

46. **(C)** An abstract of title is a history or digest of information taken from public records.

47. **(D)** A lien position is established by the order of recording at the courthouse.

48. **(C)** Zoning changes or zoning regulations are not covered under title insurance.

49. **(B)** A contract for deed is a land contract and the transaction is financed by the owner. RESPA does not regulate such transactions.

50. **(D)** The right of the government to take the land is eminent domain. The process is condemnation.

51. **(B)** By definition of bargain and sale deed.

52. **(B)** By definition of lis pendens.

53. **(C)** A fee simple absolute ownership conveyed by a general warranty deed would best protect the grantee's interest.

54. **(B)** The deed was not delivered during the lifetime of the grantor; therefore, the property transfers to Sandy's heirs by the laws of descent and distribution in the state where the property is located.

55. **(D)** The sales contract is not recorded at the courthouse.

56. **(B)** The principal paid on the loan is not a tax deduction.

57. **(D)** When a person dies intestate, the state laws of descent and distribution determine who receives the property of the deceased person. Descent would not be associated with testate, which is the status of a party who has died with a will.

58. **(B)** Forty-five days is given to identify property for the exchange.

59. **(A)** By the definition of syndicate.

60. **(D)** A license is the personal privilege to be on the land of another and would not be associated with adverse possession.

61. **(D)** The 1031 exchange allows the deferment of capital gains tax, not the exclusion of it.

62. **(C)** Depreciation cannot be taken on a primary residence.

63. **(C)** The mortgagee's policy covers the lender, not the owner.

64. **(D)** A mortgage release would not create a cloud on the title.

65. **(B)** The covenant to renew is not found in the general warranty deed. It may be found in a lease.

66. **(A)** There is a valid transference between the parties. Usually buyers or their lenders will record the deed, but a buyer is not required by law to record the deed. It is the best way for the buyers to protect their interests in the property.

67. **(D)** RESPA requires distribution of the booklet *Settlement Costs and You*.

68. **(D)** The deed should be recorded in all counties where the property is located.

69. **(B)** Public records can be searched by anyone.

70. **(D)** The Schneiders will subrogate their rights to the title company.

ANSWERS—MATCHING QUIZ

1. S	6. K	11. D	16. A
2. M	7. O	12. T	17. F
3. I	8. N	13. C	18. H
4. L	9. G	14. R	19. J
5. E	10. B	15. P	20. Q

5

Financing

This chapter covers the following information regarding financing: sources of financing, types of loans, terms and conditions, and common clauses and terms in mortgage instruments.

AMP Outline—Sources of Financing

V. **Financing**	3. Assumption of existing financing
A. Sources of Financing	
1. Institutional	4. Other sources of financing
2. Seller financing	

I N S T I T U T I O N A L

The **primary mortgage market** and the **secondary mortgage market** are sources of funds for financing. Primary mortgage market lenders originate or make loans directly to borrowers, while the secondary mortgage market buys mortgages from primary market lenders.

Primary Mortgage Market

Savings and loans

- Specialize in long-term, single-family home loans

- May offer conventional, FHA, or VA mortgages

Mutual savings banks

- Located primarily in the northeastern United States

- State chartered, owned by their depositors, and originate FHA or VA loans

Commercial banks

- Have historically specialized in short-term loans (such as home improvement loans, mobile home loans, and commercial loans)

- Have become more active in the negotiation of long-term residential loans

Insurance companies

- Specialize in large-scale, long-term loans that finance commercial and industrial properties
- May require an equity kicker or participation financing in the loans they negotiate

Mortgage bankers

- Originate loans and package mortgages, selling them to investors and continuing to service them after they are sold

Mortgage brokers

- Do not loan their own money
- Bring borrowers and lenders together and are paid a percentage of the money borrowed

Credit unions

- Source of funds for their members

Pension funds

- Work through mortgage bankers and mortgage brokers in real estate financing

Rural Economic and Community Development

- Federal agency under the Department of Agriculture that negotiates loans to people in rural areas
- Negotiates loans for the purchase of property, to operate farms, or to purchase farm equipment
- Bases the interest paid on the loan on the income of the borrower
- Originates loans either through a private lender or directly by the agency

Federal Reserve

The Federal Reserve (the Fed) was established to stabilize the economy by controlling the money supply and credit available in the country. It does this by creating money, regulating reserve requirements, and setting the discount rate of interest.

- An oversupply of money creates inflation; an undersupply can cause a recession.
- When the reserve requirements are increased, the money supply shrinks, thus increasing interest rates.

■ If the reserve requirements are decreased, the money supply grows, thus decreasing interest rates.

■ The discount rate of interest is the rate the Fed charges for loans to its member banks, and it can move money into or out of commercial banks by buying or selling government bonds.

Real estate borrowers compete with other businesses for money. When the money supply is limited, interest rates are high and qualifying buyers can be difficult. When money is plentiful, interest rates are low and qualifying buyers is much easier.

SELLER FINANCING

Land Contracts

In a **land contract** the seller/vendor agrees to finance the sale of the property. Typically, the buyer/vendee makes a down payment, then monthly payments until the balance is paid in full. The seller normally retains title to the property until the final payment. Should the buyer default, the seller can evict the buyer and retain all money paid. Many states now have laws that give a defaulted buyer more legal protection, and the seller must foreclose on the property to reclaim it.

Be aware that there is no mortgage involved in a land contract. A mortgage is a *pledge of property to a lender as security for the payment of a debt*, but the land contract is itself the security instrument.

The buyer's interest in a land contract is an equitable interest or equitable title. An **equitable title** represents the buyer's interest in the property when the legal title is held by another party. It also is an insurable interest, meaning the buyer can secure insurance on the property. Most land contracts stipulate that the buyer secure insurance, pay property taxes, and maintain the property.

Purchase-Money Mortgage

A **purchase-money mortgage** (PMM) is a creative financing technique that developed when interest rates were high. Usually the seller agrees to finance a portion or the entire purchase price, as opposed to the land contract, where the amount financed is always the entire amount, less the buyer's down payment. A PMM is also known as a *take-back mortgage*.

Here is an example of a purchase-money mortgage: A buyer has a 5 percent down payment, and the seller agrees to loan the borrower 15 percent of the sale price. The lender will negotiate an 80 percent loan and will not require private mortgage insurance. This is known as an 80/15/5 loan. (There is also an 80/10/10 loan.)

At the closing, the seller pays off an existing loan and "takes back" a mortgage on the property just sold. To secure the loan, the seller establishes a junior lien on the property and receives payments from the buyer until the loan is paid in full. This occurs with the approval of the lender negotiating the 80 percent loan.

ASSUMPTION OF EXISTING FINANCING

FHA-insured and VA-guaranteed loans are assumable loans. For FHA-insured loans originated after December 1, 1986, and VA-guaranteed loans originated after March 1, 1988, the buyer must meet approval. A third party can buy the property subject to the mortgage or assume the mortgage.

Subject to the Mortgage

When a property is taken "subject to" the mortgage, the original borrower, or obligor, remains liable for the debt, even if the third party, or buyer, defaults. If a default occurs, the buyer loses the property and the original borrower can reclaim it either by buying the property or by buying the mortgage from the lender and foreclosing.

Assumption of the Mortgage

When a third party "assumes" the mortgage, the third party becomes liable for the debt. Should the new buyer default, that buyer is primarily liable for the debt and the original borrower is secondarily liable. A **novation** is a substitution of one contract for another. If the lender grants novation in the assumption of an existing mortgage, the original borrower is released from liability.

Other Sources of Financing

Changes in the mortgage and credit markets in 2008 make it essential for agents to be educated in the new lending guidelines. Agents should establish relationships with lenders and learn how to help sellers in foreclosure and buyers who are purchasing in a short sale.

"Green loans" are gaining popularity with buyers and owners who are willing to make homes energy-efficient.

AMP Outline—Types of Loans

V.   **Financing**
    B.   Types of Loans
        1.   Security for loans
        2.   Repayment methods—definitions
        3.   Forms of financing
        4.   Secondary mortgage markets
        5.   Down payment assistance programs

SECURITY FOR LOANS

Security Instruments

Security instruments (documents) are used to provide collateral for the Statute of Frauds requires security instruments to be in writing. These instruments consist of

■   mortgages, primarily used in lien-theory states;

- trust deeds, primarily used in title-theory states; and

- land contracts, used when the seller is financing the property.

Lien-Theory State

The lender's interest in the property can be a lien interest or a title interest. In a **lien-theory state**, the borrower receives the deed at the closing, and the lender establishes a lien position by recording the note and mortgage. Should the borrower default, the mortgage gives the lender the right to foreclose on the property, the note determines how much money the lender can collect, and the lien establishes the order in which the creditors are paid.

Title-Theory State

In a **title-theory state**, the law construes the lender to have *legal title* to the property and the borrower to have an equitable title. Because the lender holds the title to the property, the lender has the right to possession of the property on default.

Intermediate-Theory State

Intermediate-theory states are a combination of lien theory and title theory. The law interprets the lender as having a lien on the property unless the borrower defaults. On default, the title passes to the lender.

FIGURE 5.1

Deeds of Trust

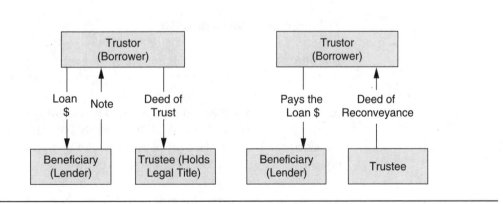

Deed of Trust

- A **deed of trust** is also known as a **trust deed**. (See Figure 5.1.)

- Legal title is conveyed to the **trustee** for the benefit of the **beneficiary**.

- A **defeasance** clause stipulates that when the final payment is made, the lender's interest is defeated and a **deed of reconveyance** is given from the trustee to the **trustor**.

- If the borrower defaults, the trustee will initiate **foreclosure**.

- This is a **nonjudicial foreclosure** or foreclosure by advertisement.

REPAYMENT METHODS—DEFINITIONS

- **Equity**—the difference between the market value and any liens on the property

- **Mortgage**—a pledge of property to a lender; collateral

- **Mortgagor**—the borrower

- **Mortgagee**—the lender

- **Note**—gives evidence of the debt and states the terms of repayment

- **Obligor/promissor**—the borrower in a note

- **Obligee/promisee**—the lender in the note

Conventional and Unconventional Mortgages

- **Conventional mortgage**—Not insured or guaranteed by the government.

- **Conventional uninsured mortgage**—Typically, the borrower has a 20 percent or greater down payment and the lender accepts the creditworthiness of the borrower and the property as security for the loan.

- **Conventional insured mortgage**—Typically, the borrower has less than a 20 percent down payment and the lender requires private mortgage insurance.

- **Unconventional mortgage**—FHA is *insured* by the government and VA is *guaranteed* by the government.

Private Mortgage Insurance

If a borrower has *less than a 20 percent down payment*, the lender may require that the borrower purchase **private mortgage insurance (PMI)**. Payment for PMI can be a one-time premium, but typically it is a percentage added to each monthly payment. When the loan balance is paid down to 80 percent of the total value, the PMI payment will be dropped. If the property is sold at foreclosure for less than the mortgage balance, the PMI pays the lender up to the amount of the insurance, typically the top 20 percent to 25 percent of the loan.

Amortization

To *amortize* means to repay the loan in monthly or other periodic payments that include principal and interest. A portion of each payment is applied to the principal balance and a portion is kept by the lender as interest on the loan.

In a **fully amortized loan** or direct reduction loan, at the end of the loan period the principal balance is zero. A 30-year fixed-rate mortgage is a fully amortized loan. If the payments are paid each month, the loan is paid in full on final payment.

In a **partially amortized loan**, or **balloon mortgage**, the principal and interest payments do not pay off the entire loan. A balance remains when the final payment is made.

In a **nonamortized loan**, periodic interest payments are made to the lender, but *nothing* is applied to the principal balance. These loans are called **term mortgages** or *straight mortgages*. A **construction loan** is an example of a nonamortized loan. With a construction loan, the borrower receives the money in stages, called *draws*, and makes periodic payments of interest. When the construction is complete, the borrower must have secured long-term financing and will pay off the entire principal balance.

Types of Mortgages

An **adjustable-rate mortgage (ARM)** contains an **escalation clause** that allows the interest to adjust over the loan term. Adjustable-rate mortgages are tied to an index such as the cost of funds index or to U.S. Treasury Securities (T-bills).

The premium charged by the lender and added to the index to determine the interest is called the *margin*. Over the life of an adjustable-rate mortgage, the margin remains constant. A *cap* sets the maximum limit to which the interest rate can increase over the life of the loan.

A **blanket mortgage** may be used by a builder or developer. This mortgage covers more than one tract of land and contains a *partial release clause*, which allows the borrower to obtain a release of any one lot or parcel and thus to give the buyer a marketable title.

A **buydown mortgage** allows the borrower to "buy down" the interest rate, thus reducing the monthly payment for a number of years. To buy down the interest rate, the borrower must pay interest in advance.

A **budget mortgage** includes principal, interest, taxes, and insurance payments (PITI). The tax and insurance portions of each monthly payment are put into an escrow account and paid when those payments are due.

A **construction loan** is used to finance the erection of improvements on land. The loan is received in a series of *draws* as each stage of construction is completed and inspected.

Construction loans are also known as *short-term* or *interim loans*.

A **graduated-payment mortgage (GPM)** is also known as a *flexible-payment plan*. The borrower makes lower monthly payments for the first few years and larger payments for the remainder of the loan term. If the lower monthly payments do not cover all the interest charges, the lender adds the unpaid interest to the principal balance. This creates **negative amortization** because the loan balance *increases* instead of decreases.

A borrower who has negotiated a **growing-equity mortgage (GEM)** realizes that there will be periodic increases in the monthly payment. However, the increase is applied directly to the principal, thus reducing the term of the loan.

Package mortgages are usually used in the sale of new homes in a subdivision or in condominium sales. Such a loan covers both real and personal property.

An **open-end mortgage** allows the mortgagor to borrow additional funds, up to a maximum dollar amount, all of which are secured by the same original mortgage.

In a **shared-appreciation mortgage (SAM)**, the lender agrees to originate the loan at below market interest rates in return for a guaranteed share of the appreciation the borrower will realize when the property is sold. This typically is used in the financing of commercial projects.

When a borrower negotiates a **straight mortgage (term loan)**, he makes periodic payment of *interest only* and the *principal is paid in full at the end* of the term. A construction loan is an example of a straight mortgage.

A **reverse annuity mortgage (RAM)** or *reverse mortgage* allows homeowners 62 years of age or older to borrow against the equity in their homes without income or credit ratio qualifications. The money may be taken in a lump sum, line of credit, monthly payment (to the owner), for a specified term, or a combination of the above. The loan comes due when the borrower no longer permanently resides in the property. Reverse mortgages are nonrecourse loans.

A **wraparound mortgage** is also known as an *all-inclusive* or *overriding loan*. It is a junior loan that wraps around an existing senior loan. For example, an owner has an existing mortgage and equity in his property. When he goes to the lender to negotiate a loan against the equity, the lender agrees to do so and "wraps it around" the existing first mortgage. The borrower makes only one monthly payment to the lender that is applied to both mortgages. To create a wraparound mortgage, the original loan must be assumable.

FORMS OF FINANCING

FHA-Insured Loans

The **Federal Housing Administration (FHA)** was established in 1934 to encourage improvements in housing standards, to encourage lenders to make loans, and to exert a stabilizing influence on the mortgage market after the Great Depression. FHA does *not* negotiate loans; FHA *insures* loans. FHA operates under the Department of Housing and Urban Development (HUD). An FHA-insured loan is backed by the government, meaning that should a borrower default and the lender foreclose on the property, the lender is insured against loss.

Lenders must be qualified to negotiate an FHA-insured loan. There are several FHA insured loan programs, with the most popular being the 203(b)B for owner-occupied one- to four-family dwellings.

Characteristics of an FHA loan are as follows:

- Every county has a maximum FHA lending limit. (This increases annually.)

- There is a one-time upfront mortgage insurance premium (MIP), which can be financed; ½ percent MIP is added to the monthly payments.

- There is a minimum down payment, and the borrower must have cash for it. The down payment may be a gift, but it cannot be a loan.

- Interest rates are negotiable, and as a rule, FHA does not set income limits for borrowers.

- Discount points may be paid by the buyer or seller.

- Prepayment penalties are not allowed, and the maximum origination fee a lender can charge is 1 percent.

- If an FHA-insured loan is assumed by another borrower, the borrower must meet FHA qualifying guidelines. (If a borrower is assuming an FHA-insured loan negotiated prior to December 15, 1989, the borrower would not have to meet FHA qualifying guidelines.)

- When the loan is assumed, the lender will issue a *certificate of reduction* to verify the existing principal balance.

VA-Guaranteed Loans

The *Serviceman's Readjustment Act of 1944* initially established the Veterans Administration, now the Department of Veterans Affairs (VA). One of its purposes was to make government-backed loans available to qualified veterans and unremarried widows or widowers of veterans. A qualified person can negotiate a VA or GI loan with a 100 percent **loan-to-value ratio**, or with a minimum down payment, at relatively low interest rates. The VA guarantees loans to lenders and normally does not make loans unless a qualified lender is not readily available, as in an isolated rural area.

Other characteristics of a VA-guaranteed loan are as follows:

- A qualified person can secure a VA-guaranteed loan on a *one- to four-family dwelling* that will be *owner-occupied*.

- The limit on the amount of loan that a veteran can obtain is determined by the lender.

- There is a limit on how much the VA will guarantee. Should the borrower default and the lender receive less than the mortgage balance after a foreclosure sale, the VA guarantees a certain amount based on a sliding scale of the value of the property.

- To determine the amount the VA will guarantee, a veteran must apply for a **certificate of eligibility**, which establishes the maximum guarantee entitlement of the veteran.

- A **certificate of reasonable value (CRV)** is issued by the VA for the property being purchased. The CRV states the current market value based on a VA-approved appraisal and places a ceiling on the amount of the VA loan allowed for the property.

- The borrower or seller also must pay a *funding fee* to the VA. This is a percentage of the loan amount and depends on the eligibility status and down payment of the veteran. The funding fee may be financed as a part of the loan.

- Discount points may be paid by the buyer or seller when a VA-guaranteed loan is negotiated.

- No prepayment penalties are allowed on VA mortgages.

- A VA loan is assumable. If another qualified veteran assumes the loan, that veteran's certificate of eligibility may replace the existing certificate. The original borrower is granted novation by the lender, and his or her full eligibility is reinstated by VA.

- If a nonveteran assumes the loan, the original borrower remains liable for the loan. Novation from the lender does not reinstate the eligibility of the veteran. Only the VA can reinstate the eligibility.

SECONDARY MORTGAGE MARKETS

The secondary mortgage markets were created to provide a "rollover of funds" to the primary mortgage market. When a loan has been negotiated by a local lender, the lender may sell the loan to the secondary market and have money available to meet the demands of its new borrowers. A loan cannot be sold on the secondary market unless it conforms to the secondary market guidelines. A **nonconforming loan** is one that does not meet secondary market specifications.

Loans that are purchased by the secondary market are pooled (packaged) and sold to investors in the form of **mortgage-backed securities (MBS)**. Investors purchase *pass-through participation certificates* that entitle the holders to pro-rata shares of all principal and interest payments made on the pool of loan assets.

Federal National Mortgage Association

The **Federal National Mortgage Association** (Fannie Mae) was established in 1938 for the purpose of buying FHA-insured loans from lenders; in 1945, Fannie Mae agreed to also purchase VA loans from lenders. Eventually, other types of loans were purchased from lenders, and in 1968, Fannie Mae became a government-sponsored enterprise (GSE), meaning that it was chartered by Congress as a private shareholder-owned company.

Fannie Mae's purpose today is to still provide liquidity and stability in the housing market by purchasing mortgages from lending institutions that negotiate loans that meet Fannie Mae guidelines. In September 2008, Fannie Mae was taken over by the federal government, and Director James Lockhart of the Federal Housing Finance Agency (FHFA) was appointed conservator.

Government National Mortgage Association

The **Government National Mortgage Association** (GNMA or Ginnie Mae) is a federal agency created in 1968 when Fannie Mae was reorganized. It is owned by the government and is a division of the Department of Housing and Urban Development (HUD). Ginnie Mae specializes in high-risk and special assistance programs, such as housing for the elderly. Ginnie Mae has a mortgage-backed securities program that sells guarantee certificates to investors. These Ginnie Mae passthrough certificates provide for a monthly "pass through" of principal and interest payments directly to certificate holders.

Through a tandem plan, Ginnie Mae also works with Fannie Mae in secondary market activities when money is tight. The tandem plan provides that Fannie Mae can purchase high-risk, low-yield loans at full market rates and Ginnie Mae will guarantee payment and absorb the difference between the low yield and current market prices. Ginnie Mae purchases FHA, VA, and certain Rural Development loans.

Federal Home Loan Mortgage Corporation

The **Federal Home Loan Mortgage Corporation** (FHLMC, or Freddie Mac) was established to assist savings and loan associations as a secondary market for conventional mortgages. Freddie Mac is a publicly owned corporation that purchases mortgages, pools them, and sells bonds in the open market as mortgage-backed securities.

Freddie Mac guarantees timely payments to investors of their mortgage-backed securities. In September 2008, Freddie Mac was also taken over by the federal government, and Director James Lockhart of the Federal Housing Finance Agency (FHFA) was appointed conservator.

DOWN PAYMENT ASSISTANCE PROGRAMS

The Housing and Economic Recovery Act of 2008 no longer allows sellers to participate in Down Payment Assistance (DPA) programs for loans backed by the Federal Housing Administration, such as AmeriDream. There may be other local and state grant programs to help buyers purchase homes. If certain conditions are met, these grants usually do not need to be repaid. Agents should work with reputable lenders when offering these programs to buyers.

AMP Outline—Terms and Conditions

V.   **Financing**
    C.   Terms and Conditions
        1.   Compliance with provisions of federal regulations
        2.   Loan origination costs
        3.   Lender requirements
        4.   Conditional approval
        5.   Default
        6.   Foreclosure and redemption rights
        7.   Nonrecourse provision

COMPLIANCE WITH PROVISIONS OF FEDERAL REGULATIONS

Truth-in-Lending Act

The **Truth-in-Lending Act** was passed as a part of the *Consumer Credit Protection Act*. This law, also known as *Regulation Z*, requires that lenders disclose the true cost of credit to borrowers, expressed as an *annual percentage rate (APR)*.

Loans covered by Regulation Z include all real estate financing for borrowers who intend to purchase one- to four-family dwellings and who are natural persons. Loans *not* covered by Regulation Z include loans for business, commercial, or agricultural purposes; personal property credit transactions over $25,000; and loans to the owner of a dwelling containing more than four units.

When negotiating a home improvement loan or refinancing, there is a *three-business-day right of rescission* mandated by Regulation Z. This right of rescission does *not* apply to first mortgages and trust deeds. Also under Regulation Z, full disclosure is required by the lender if any of the following trigger items appears in an ad:

- Amount of monthly payment

- Number of payments

- Amount of down payment

- Finance charges

- Term of the loan

If any of the above trigger items appears in an ad, full disclosure is required. The advertisement must include

- cash price;

- required down payment;

- number, amounts, and due dates of all payments;

- total of all payments to be made over the term of the mortgage (unless the advertised credit refers to a first mortgage or deed of trust to finance the acquisition of a dwelling); and

- annual percentage rate.

Finally, according to Regulation Z, a *creditor* is an entity that extends consumer credit more than 25 times a year, or more than 5 times a year if the transaction involves a dwelling as security. The credit must be subject to a finance charge or payable in more than four installments by written agreement.

As used above, "full disclosure" means that if any of the above items is used in an ad, the same ad must include the cash price; required down payment; number, amounts, and due dates of all payments; and the annual percentage rate.

Equal Credit Opportunity Act

The **Equal Credit Opportunity Act (ECOA)** prohibits discrimination based on *race, color, religion, national origin, sex, marital status, age, or source of income* in the granting of credit. This act requires that credit applications be considered only on the basis of income, net worth, job stability, and credit rating. If the applicant is rejected, lenders have 30 days to inform the applicant of the reasons why credit was denied. (This 30-day notice also applies to creditors that terminate existing credit.)

Community Reinvestment Act

The **Community Reinvestment Act** was passed to prevent *redlining* and disinvestment in central city areas. This act requires that lenders delineate the communities in which their lending activities take place, make available listings of the types of credit they offer in the communities, and make available appropriate notices and information regarding lending activities. It also gives lenders the option to disclose affirmative action programs designed to meet the credit needs of their communities.

Usury Laws

Some states have **usury** laws that limit the maximum interest rate that a lender can charge on certain types of loans. Please note: Usury laws do not set the interest rates; they establish the maximum rate that can be charged. In times of emergencies, the federal government can set aside usury laws.

LOAN ORIGINATION COSTS

The loan origination fee is charged by the lender to cover the administrative costs of making the loan. The fee is a percentage of the loan amount.

Other costs the borrower pays to originate the loan are for the credit report, appraisal, and points required by the lender. See pages 198-199 for more information on origination fees and discount points.

LENDER REQUIREMENTS

To approve the loan, typically the lender may require an appraisal, termite inspection, homeowners insurance, and escrow for tax and insurance payments, title search, and any other conditions the underwriter determines are necessary to close the loan.

CONDITIONAL APPROVAL

Approval of every loan is conditional on some terms being met by the borrower. Typically, the loan commitment letter states the loan has been approved pending resolution of the following items before or at the closing:

- Satisfactory title report
- Mortgagee's title insurance
- Homeowners insurance policy
- Survey
- Verification of job status
- Affidavit of marital status

- Copy of the settlement sheet of the house just sold

- Verification of bank accounts

- Payoff of a particular bill

- Inspection reports required by the lender

- Any repairs required by the appraiser

A **lock-in clause** in the loan application guarantees that the interest rate quoted the buyer on loan application is "locked" for a specific time.

The finance fees that must be disclosed include loan fees, finders' fees, service charges, interest, and discount points. Fees that do not have to be disclosed by Regulation Z include attorney's fees, escrow fees, appraisals, surveys, inspection fees, title fees, and closing expenses.

DEFAULT

The **default** clause in a note and mortgage protects the lender if there is a nonperformance of a duty or obligation of the part of the borrower. This clause requires the timely payment of the terms of the note, upkeep of the property, payment of property taxes and insurance, and permission from the lender for improvements to be made on the property. If the borrower defaults, the lender has the right to foreclose.

FORECLOSURE AND REDEMPTION RIGHTS

Foreclosure is the legal process whereby the property can be sold as security for the payment of a debt. State and local laws regulate foreclosure proceedings. The three types of foreclosure are judicial, nonjudicial, and strict.

Judicial Foreclosure

Foreclosure by **judicial sale** occurs in states that require that the lender go to court and prove that the borrower has defaulted. The judge orders an appraisal of the property and sets a foreclosure sale date. Creditors are notified, and the property is advertised. The property is sold, and when the paperwork is in order, the sale is confirmed. At that point, the owner's rights to the property have been foreclosed. A **deficiency judgment** is a personal judgment levied against the defaulted borrower when a foreclosure sale does not produce sufficient funds to pay the mortgage debt in full.

Nonjudicial Foreclosure

Nonjudicial foreclosure is used in states where the mortgage contains a power-of-sale clause. This clause allows the lender to sell the property without going through the court system. The defaulted borrower has a specified time in which to make up delinquent payments and costs. If the payments are not made, the property is advertised and sold.

Strict Foreclosure

Strict foreclosure allows the lender to foreclose on the property after appropriate notice has been given to the delinquent borrower and the proper papers have been filed in court. If full payment is not made within a prescribed time, the borrower's equitable and statutory redemption rights are waived, the property is sold, and the lender keeps all equity in the property, if there is any. (See Figure 5.2.)

FIGURE 5.2

Redemption

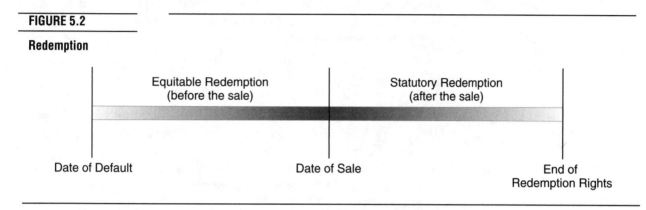

NONRECOURSE PROVISION

In a **nonrecourse loan**, the borrower is *not held personally liable* for the note. This occurs when the lender accepts the property as adequate security for the loan. This type of loan is typically made to real estate syndicates or other real estate investors, but reverse mortgages are also nonrecourse loans.

AMP Outline—Common Clauses and Terms in Mortgage Instruments

V.   **Financing**
      D.   Common Clauses and
            Terms in Mortgage
            Instruments

1.   Clauses and terms
      used in mortgages
2.   Escalation
3.   Acceleration
4.   Rescission

CLAUSES AND TERMS USED IN MORTGAGES

Prepayment

An **open mortgage** usually allows a borrower to pay off the loan at any time over the life of the loan *without a penalty*. This is allowed by a **prepayment privilege clause** in the mortgage. When a borrower repays the loan ahead of schedule, the lender collects less interest, so while some lenders allow the prepayment of the mortgage, others charge a prepayment penalty. This penalty may be a percentage of the remaining mortgage balance.

Interest Rates

The **interest** paid by the borrower is a charge for the use of money, and the lender normally computes simple interest on residential loans. A *fixed* interest rate is constant over the life of the loan. An *adjustable* interest rate can change over the life of the loan.

The *lock-in clause* in the note typically means that upon loan application, the lender has agreed to "lock" the rate for a specified time period, or it could mean that the loan cannot be prepaid unless all interest is paid.

Release

When the mortgage is paid in full, the lender must release its interest in the property. In lien-theory states, a *mortgage release* or *satisfaction piece* is recorded. In title-theory states, a *defeasance clause* provides that the lender release its interest in the title. If the mortgage document was a **trust deed**, the *reconveyance deed* must be recorded to release the lender's title interest.

If a lien is not released at settlement, the lien will "run with the land" or stay attached to the property. This is why a title search is conducted to protect the interest of the buyer and the lender.

Due-on-Sale

A **due-on-sale clause** in a mortgage allows the lender to collect full payment from the mortgagor when the property is sold. This clause prevents owners from selling the property to a buyer on a loan assumption or a land contract.

Alienation

Mortgages may also contain an **alienation clause** providing that if the property is conveyed to any party without the lender's consent, the lender can collect full payment.

Subordination

Under certain circumstances, a lender with a first lien position will agree to switch positions (**subordination**) and take a second lien position on the property. For example, a borrower has a first mortgage with lender XYZ and a line of credit with lender ABC. The borrower decides to refinance her loan with XYZ. When she refinances, her current mortgage with XYZ is paid in full, and technically ABC would move into a first lien position. XYZ will agree to refinance only if ABC will subordinate. Usually a subordination fee will be charged if an agreement to subordinate is reached.

ESCALATION

An **escalation clause** is found in an adjustable-rate mortgage and in certain leases. In a mortgage, it allows the interest rate to adjust over the life of the loan. In a lease, it allows the lease payment to adjust over the life of the lease.

ACCELERATION

Notes, mortgages, and security instruments contain an **acceleration clause** that allows the lender to call the note due and payable in advance of the loan term. Typical provisions that accelerate the payments are default of the mortgage, destruction of the premises, or the sale of the property to another party. If this clause were not in the note and/or mortgage, the lender would have to sue the borrower for each individual monthly payment.

Please note that the acceleration clause allows the lender to call the entire balance due, not just the months the borrower is behind.

RESCISSION

The process of **rescission** means that the contract has been canceled, terminated, or annulled and the parties have been returned to the legal positions they were in before they entered the contract. A contract may be rescinded due to mistake, fraud, or misrepresentation. For example, if the seller cannot provide a marketable title, the buyer is not required to purchase the property, and the contract may be rescinded.

Hypothecation means to pledge property to the lender as collateral without giving up possession of it.

QUESTIONS

1. Who is the individual who obtains a real estate loan by signing a note and a mortgage?
   A. Mortgagor
   B. Mortgagee
   C. Optionor
   D. Optionee

2. Which of the following describes a mortgage that uses both real and personal property as security?
   A. Blanket mortgage
   B. Package mortgage
   C. Purchase-money mortgage
   D. Wraparound mortgage

3. Which of the following describes a mortgage that requires principal and interest payments at regular intervals until the debt is satisfied?
   A. Term mortgage
   B. Amortized mortgage
   C. First mortgage
   D. Balloon mortgage

4. What is the clause in a note, mortgage, or trust deed that permits a lender to declare the entire unpaid sum due should the borrower default?
   A. Judgment clause
   B. Acceleration clause
   C. Forfeiture clause
   D. Escalator clause

5. A mortgage must include a power-of-sale clause to be foreclosed by
   A. action.
   B. advertisement.
   C. judicial procedure.
   D. the FHA.

6. In many states, by paying the debt after a foreclosure sale, the mortgagor has the right to regain the property. What is the right called?
   A. Equitable right of redemption
   B. Owner's right of redemption
   C. Vendee's right of redemption
   D. Statutory right of redemption

7. In a title-theory state, the
   A. mortgagee takes title to the mortgaged property during the term of the mortgage.
   B. mortgagor has a lien against the property for the full amount of the mortgage.
   C. mortgagor may foreclose only by court action.
   D. mortgagor holds title to the property during the term of the mortgage.

8. Gloria is qualified to obtain an FHA loan for the purchase of a new home. From which of the following may she obtain this loan?
   A. Federal Housing Administration
   B. Federal National Mortgage Association
   C. A qualified Federal Housing Administration mortgagee
   D. Federal Home Loan Mortgage Corporation

9. A mortgage instrument may include a clause that prevents the assumption of the mortgage by a new purchaser without the lender's consent. What is this clause called?
   A. Alienation clause
   B. Power-of-sale clause
   C. Defeasance clause
   D. Certificate of sale

10. The defeasance clause in a mortgage requires that the mortgagee execute a(n)
    A. assignment of mortgage.
    B. satisfaction of mortgage.
    C. subordination agreement.
    D. partial release agreement.

11. John enters into a contract with Wally wherein John will sell his house to Wally for $400,000. Wally cannot get complete financing, and at the closing John and Wally enter into a contract for deed. On signing the contract for deed, Wally's interest in the property is that of
    A. legal title.
    B. equitable title.
    C. joint title.
    D. mortgagee in possession.

12. Which of the following is a lien on real estate?
    A. Easement
    B. Recorded mortgage
    C. Encroachment
    D. Restrictive covenant

13. What is a mortgage loan that requires monthly payments of $1,175.75 for 20 years and a final payment of $25,095 known as?
    A. Wraparound mortgage
    B. Accelerated mortgage
    C. Balloon mortgage
    D. Variable mortgage

14. Which of the following relates to a mortgage loan?
    A. Acceleration clause
    B. Covenant of further assurances
    C. Writ of execution
    D. Vested interest

15. In a sale-leaseback arrangement, the
    A. seller/vendor retains title to the real estate.
    B. buyer/vendee gets possession of the property.
    C. sale is disallowed in most states.
    D. buyer/vendee is the lessor.

16. In which of the following markets may a lender sell a loan that a lender had previously originated?
    A. Primary market
    B. Secondary market
    C. Mortgage market
    D. Investor market

17. Fannie Mae and Ginnie Mae
    A. work together as primary lenders.
    B. are both owned by the federal government.
    C. are both private agencies.
    D. are both involved in the secondary market.

18. A deficiency judgment can take place when
    A. a foreclosure sale does not produce sufficient funds to pay a mortgage debt in full.
    B. not enough taxes have been paid on a piece of property.
    C. a foreclosure sale is not completed.
    D. All of the above.

19. When a buyer assumes the mortgage, which of the following is TRUE?
    A. If the mortgage has an alienation clause, this does not affect the assumption.
    B. Normally, the seller is released from all liability when the mortgage is assumed.
    C. The seller is primarily liable if the buyer defaults on an assumed mortgage.
    D. A buyer who assumes a mortgage is primarily liable for the debt, and the original borrower becomes secondarily liable for the debt.

20. An eligible veteran made an offer of $250,000 to purchase a home to be financed with a VA-guaranteed loan. Four weeks after the offer was accepted, a certificate of reasonable value (CRV) for $247,000 was issued for the property. In this case, the veteran may
    A. withdraw from the sale with a 1 percent penalty.
    B. purchase the property with a $3,000 down payment.
    C. not withdraw from the sale.
    D. withdraw from the sale on payment of $3,000.

21. In an FHA transaction
    A. points may be paid by the seller or the buyer.
    B. an origination fee must be paid by the seller.
    C. the mortgage insurance premium must be paid in cash at settlement.
    D. the mortgage insurance premium must be paid by the seller.

22. A government-backed loan that guarantees the lender against a loss is a(n)
    A. FHA mortgage.
    B. VA mortgage.
    C. adjustable-rate mortgage.
    D. graduated-payment mortgage.

23. As an entity operating in the secondary mortgage market, the Federal Home Loan Mortgage Corporation was established to assist
    A. the Federal Housing Administration.
    B. the Federal National Mortgage Association.
    C. savings and loans associations.
    D. federal banks.

24. Which of the following is TRUE about a term mortgage?
    A. All interest is paid at the end of the term.
    B. The entire principal is due at the end of the term.
    C. The debt is partially amortized over the term.
    D. The term is limited by state statutes.

25. Which of the following is TRUE regarding a purchase-money mortgage?
    A. The seller retains possession of the property.
    B. The seller executes and delivers a note at closing.
    C. The seller finances a portion of the purchase price and places a junior lien on the property.
    D. The seller agrees to repurchase the property if the buyer defaults.

26. Regulation Z applies to
    A. business loans.
    B. residential loans made to a person.
    C. commercial loans under $10,000.
    D. installment sales.

27. Terence lent money to Rena and in return took a mortgage as security for the debt. Terence immediately recorded the mortgage. Thereafter, Omar lent money to Rena, took a mortgage, and recorded it. Rena later defaulted, and a court determined that Omar's interest had priority over Terence's interest. Under these circumstances, chances are
    A. Terence knew Omar was going to make a loan prior to making his own loan.
    B. Omar's loan was larger than Terence's loan.
    C. Terence had signed a subordination agreement in favor of Omar.
    D. Omar had signed a satisfaction.

28. All of the following are agencies operating in the secondary market EXCEPT the
    A. Federal National Mortgage Association.
    B. Federal Savings and Loan Insurance Corporation.
    C. Government National Mortgage Association.
    D. Federal Home Loan Mortgage Corporation.

29. Brice and Judy Jones purchased their home three years ago. They made a $20,000 down payment and obtained a mortgage loan to finance the balance of their purchase. The Joneses have paid $14,400 in mortgage payments over the last three years, $10,000 of which has been used to pay the mortgage interest. The $24,400 that the Joneses have invested in their home over the last three years is referred to as their
    A. homestead.
    B. profit.
    C. redemption.
    D. equity.

30. A mortgagor can get direct financing from all of the following EXCEPT
    A. mortgage banking companies.
    B. savings and loans associations.
    C. commercial banks.
    D. Fannie Mae.

31. Which of the following would be the beneficiary in the deed of trust security instrument used in a title-theory state?
    A. Buyer
    B. Seller
    C. Lender
    D. Attorney

32. What is the MAJOR DIFFERENCE between conventional and unconventional loans?
    A. A conventional loan is guaranteed or insured by the government, while an unconventional loan is not.
    B. An unconventional loan is guaranteed or insured by the government, while a conventional loan is not.
    C. A conventional loan is sold on the secondary market, while an unconventional loan is not.
    D. An unconventional loan is sold on the secondary market, while a conventional loan is not.

33. On an adjustable-rate mortgage a margin is added to the index to determine the new interest rate. This margin will
    A. change every six months.
    B. decrease as the term of the loan decreases.
    C. change as the index changes.
    D. remain constant over the life of the loan.

34. A defaulted borrower's right to redeem property before a foreclosure is known as the
    A. statutory right of redemption.
    B. equitable right of redemption.
    C. borrower's right of redemption.
    D. lender's right of redemption.

35. Laws that determine the maximum interest rate a lender can charge are known as
    A. maximum interest rate laws.
    B. usury laws.
    C. truth-in-lending laws.
    D. borrower protection laws.

36. Developer Emil placed a mortgage on his housing development. When he sold a lot to purchaser Sandy, a partial release was obtained for the lot she purchased. The mortgage Emil obtained was a(n)
    A. blanket mortgage.
    B. purchase-money mortgage.
    C. package mortgage.
    D. open-end mortgage.

37. Which of the following instruments is given by the purchaser to a seller who takes back a note for part or all of the purchase price of the property?
    A. Installment contract
    B. Purchase-money mortgage
    C. FHA mortgage
    D. Contract for deed

38. Which of the following requires that finance charges be stated as an annual percentage rate?
    A. Regulation Z
    B. Real Estate Settlement Procedures Act
    C. Equal Credit Opportunity Act
    D. Fair Housing Act

39. In determining whether to extend a loan to the purchaser of a house, lending institutions MOST LIKELY consider most important the
    A. sale price.
    B. stability of the purchaser's financial position.
    C. appraised value.
    D. term of the loan.

40. The act that requires that lenders inform both buyers and sellers of all fees and charges is
    A. ECOA.
    B. REIT.
    C. RESPA.
    D. Truth-in-Lending.

41. A recorded lien was not removed from the property at a settlement table. What is the status of the lien?
    A. It follows the seller of the property because it was the seller's debt.
    B. It remains on record against the property.
    C. It is no longer valid because the property has transferred.
    D. It must be recorded again by the debtor since the property has transferred.

42. According to Truth-in-Lending, a lender must reveal all of the following EXCEPT
    A. discount points.
    B. interest rate.
    C. title fees.
    D. origination fee.

43. A buyer obtained a loan in which the interest can fluctuate, and if it does, there will be an adjustment in the principal payment. The buyer MOST LIKELY has secured a(n)
    A. partially amortized loan.
    B. unconventional loan.
    C. fixed-rate mortgage.
    D. adjustable-rate loan.

44. A buyer purchases a property through a loan assumption. The seller has requested that the old note and mortgage be substituted for a new note and mortgage in the buyer's name. If the lender allows this change, it is known as the granting of a(n)
    A. attachment.
    B. release of mortgage.
    C. satisfaction piece.
    D. novation.

45. A mortgage that has been sold to another party is said to have been
    A. assigned.
    B. transferred.
    C. deferred.
    D. purchased.

46. The financial market is made up of primary and secondary intermediaries. Which of the following is NOT a financial intermediary?
    A. Credit unions
    B. Pension funds
    C. FNMA
    D. HUD

47. An owner negotiated a home equity loan on his property. The owner's right to rescind this agreement within three days is provided by
    A. FHA.
    B. Regulation Z.
    C. Regulation B.
    D. VA.

48. Which of the following would restore a veteran's benefits?
    A. Novation from the lender
    B. Loan assumption by a buyer
    C. Subject-to mortgage taken by a buyer
    D. Substitution of eligibility by another veteran on a loan assumption

49. A borrower negotiated a second mortgage on her property. This mortgage is subordinate to the first mortgage and the borrower makes one monthly payment. She MOST LIKELY secured a
    A. shared-appreciation mortgage.
    B. purchase-money mortgage.
    C. wraparound mortgage.
    D. growing-equity mortgage.

50. The mortgage that will MOST LIKELY create negative amortization is the
    A. graduated-payment mortgage.
    B. shared-appreciation mortgage.
    C. adjustable-rate mortgage.
    D. growing-equity mortgage.

51. A retired couple would like additional spendable income. From their financial advisor, they learned they could negotiate a loan against the equity in their property and receive a monthly check from the lender for the rest of their lives as long as they reside in the property. This arrangement is known as a(n)
    A. open mortgage.
    B. closed mortgage.
    C. reverse mortgage.
    D. open-end mortgage.

52. A borrower has secured a guarantee from the lender that the interest rate quoted on loan application would not change prior to closing. This is known as a(n)
    A. fixed-rate mortgage.
    B. anaconda agreement.
    C. extender clause.
    D. lock-in agreement.

53. Which of the following parties must sign the note and the mortgage?
    A. Mortgagor/promisee
    B. Mortgagee/promisor
    C. Mortgagor/promisor
    D. Mortgagee/promisee

54. A buyer assumes and agrees to pay an existing loan on the property. Who is liable for the loan?
    A. The seller is primarily liable.
    B. The buyer is primarily liable.
    C. The buyer is primarily liable ,and the seller is secondarily liable.
    D. The seller is primarily liable, and the buyer is secondarily liable.

55. A trust deed or mortgage can be used to finance property. What is the MAJOR DIFFERENCE between these instruments?
    A. Both are security instruments.
    B. Both involve the buyer's signing a note.
    C. Both can be foreclosed on.
    D. A trust deed transfers a title interest, and a mortgage allows the lender to place a lien on the property.

56. Mr. Chalk is purchasing a duplex as a qualified veteran. Under these circumstances, the VA will
    A. set the rate of interest.
    B. determine the maximum loan amount.
    C. set the limit on the guarantee.
    D. determine the term of the loan.

57. Keith is a first-time homebuyer seeking advice from an agent regarding the difference between a mortgage broker and a mortgage banker. The agent will tell him that
    A. free checking is a typical incentive to negotiate a loan through a mortgage banker, but not a mortgage broker.
    B. mortgage bankers normally deal in conforming loans, but mortgage brokers deal in nonconforming loans.
    C. mortgage bankers normally hold their loans in portfolio, but mortgage brokers sell their loans on the secondary mortgage market.
    D. mortgage bankers originate loans, package them, and sell them to investors, while mortgage brokers bring borrowers and lenders together and are paid a percentage on the loan amount.

58. Branham is negotiating a home loan and the lender is requiring that he set up an escrow account for taxes and insurance. This is known as a
    A. buydown mortgage.
    B. budget mortgage.
    C. balloon mortgage.
    D. blanket mortgage.

59. An FHA-insured or VA-guaranteed loan is an example of a(n)
    A. conventional mortgage.
    B. conventional uninsured mortgage.
    C. conventional insured mortgage.
    D. unconventional mortgage.

60. The federal act that prohibits a lender from discriminating based on race, color, religion, national origin, sex, marital status, age, or source of income is the
    A. federal Fair Housing Act.
    B. Equal Credit Opportunity Act.
    C. Community Reinvestment Act.
    D. Truth-in-Lending Act.

61. Mr. and Mrs. Abrams are 70 years old. Their home is in excellent condition, and they have no liens on their property. They would like to negotiate a loan where they make no monthly payments and have no income or credit ratios to qualify. Is there a loan product that will meet their needs?
    A. Yes, because they own their home without liens they can negotiate a home equity line of credit with any lender.
    B. Yes, because they are over the age of 62, they can negotiate a reverse mortgage where they will make no monthly payments and have no income or credit ratios to qualify.
    C. No, there is no loan program where the borrower does not make monthly payments or have income or credit ratios to qualify.
    D. No, Truth-in-Lending does not allow anyone over the age of 65 to negotiate a loan.

62. The buyer assumed an existing mortgage and the lender issued a certificate of reduction to verify the loan balance. The buyer is assuming a(n)
    A. FHA-insured loan.
    B. VA-Guaranteed loan.
    C. Fannie Mae loan.
    D. Ginnie Mae loan.

63. A veteran is negotiating a GI loan. The appraiser will issue a
    A. certificate of reduction.
    B. certificate of reasonable value.
    C. certificate of deposit.
    D. certificate of indebtedness.

64. What is the MAJOR DIFFERENCE between an open mortgage and an open-end mortgage?
   A. An open mortgage is negotiated on fixed-rate mortgages, and the open-end mortgage is negotiated on adjustable-rate mortgages.
   B. An open mortgage is used to purchase new construction, and the open-end mortgage is used to purchase manufactured homes.
   C. An open mortgage allows prepayment of the loan during the loan term; an open-end mortgage is expandable by increments up to a maximum dollar amount, under the original security document.
   D. An open mortgage allows a prepayment not to exceed 5 percent of the loan balance if repaid within 5 years; an open-end mortgage does not allow a prepayment penalty.

65. Which of the following is NOT a way for lenders to secure their interest in the property?
   A. Lien-theory state
   B. Title-theory state
   C. Intermediate-theory state
   D. Hypothecation-theory state

66. Which government body is responsible for creating money, regulating reserve requirements, and setting the discount rate of interest?
   A. Federal Housing Administration
   B. Federal National Mortgage Association
   C. Federal Reserve
   D. Federal Register

67. A reverse mortgage is an example of a
   A. nonrecourse loan.
   B. blanket mortgage.
   C. package mortgage.
   D. Nehemiah loan.

68. Jon had been preapproved for a loan and his offer of $160,000 was accepted. Circumstances changed, and three weeks before the closing the seller did not want to sell and Jon did not want to buy. Can they release each other from the contract?
   A. Yes, they can release each other from the contract, and the process is known as rescission.
   B. Yes, they can release each other from the contract, and the process is known as reconciliation.
   C. No, once a sales contract is executed by both parties there can be no changes.
   D. No, because the broker fulfilled the terms of the listing agreement, the buyer and seller must fulfill the terms of the sales contract.

69. A lender that is in a first lien position on the property has agreed to move into a second lien position if it is paid a $400 fee. This process is known as
   A. subrogation.
   B. subordination.
   C. sublease.
   D. subterfuge.

70. While listening to the radio, a consumer heard *"For qualified borrowers we have 30-year fixed-rate mortgages with an annual percentage rate of 6.35 percent. This is a limited offer, so call today."* Is this loan in compliance with Regulation Z?
   A. Yes, this ad meets RESPA requirements.
   B. Yes, this ad meets Truth-in-Lending requirements.
   C. No, lenders are not allowed to advertise interest rates on the radio.
   D. No, the interest rate is a trigger item that requires full disclosure.

MATCHING QUIZ

The column on the right contains a brief definition of important terms in this section.
Write the letter of the matching term on the appropriate line.

A. Subject to the mortgage

B. Assumption of the mortgage

C. Title-theory state

D. Lien-theory state

E. Mortgagee

F. Reverse mortgage

G. Unconventional mortgage

H. Amortize

I. Federal Reserve

J. Blanket mortgage

K. Secondary mortgage market

L. Usury

M. Regulation Z

N. Alienation clause

O. Subordination clause

P. Acceleration clause

Q. Equitable redemption

R. Statutory redemption

S. Deficiency judgment

T. Rescission

1. ___ Original borrower remains liable for the debt if buyer defaults

2. ___ The practice of charging more than the rate of interest allowed by law

3. ___ Buyer becomes primarily liable for the debt and original borrower (seller) is secondarily liable

4. ___ The lender in a loan document

5. ___ The defaulted borrower's right to redeem the property after foreclosure

6. ___ The contract has been canceled and the parties have returned to the legal positions they were in before they entered into the contract

7. ___ Clause that allows the lender to call the note due and payable at once

8. ___ Clause that allows a lender to move from a first lien position to a second lien position

9. ___ When a loan is negotiated in this type of state, the law allows the mortgagee to place a lien on the property

10. ___ Clause in a mortgage that allows the lender to collect full payment if the borrower transfers the property to any party without lender's consent

11. ___ Personal judgment levied against a defaulted borrower when the foreclosure sales does not pay the debt in full

12. ___ The defaulted borrowers' right to redeem the property before the foreclosure sale

13. ___ A state in which the security instrument gives the mortgagee the title to the property

14. ___ Loan for seniors that does not require a monthly payment to the lender

15. ___ Also known as Truth-in-Lending, this federal law requires that lenders disclose the true cost of credit as an APR.

16. ___ Mortgage that covers more than one tract of land or property

17. ___ Market where mortgages are bought and sold; provides a rollover of funds to the primary mortgage market

18. ___ Established to stabilize the economy by controlling the money supply and credit available in the country

19. ___ To repay the loan in monthly or other periodic payments that include principal and interest

20. ___ Mortgage that is backed by the government as an FHA-insured or VA-guaranteed loan

ANSWERS

1. **(A)** The mortgagor is the borrower, the mortgagee is the lender.

2. **(B)** By definition of package mortgage.

3. **(B)** By definition of amortization.

4. **(B)** By definition of acceleration clause.

5. **(B)** A power-of-sale clause is found in mortgages or trust deeds in title-theory states. This clause gives the lender the right to sell the property by advertisement when the borrower defaults and other stipulations are met.

6. **(D)** Statutory right of redemption is the right a delinquent borrower has after the foreclosure sale to redeem the property, if all costs are paid.

7. **(A)** By definition of title-theory state.

8. **(C)** A lender must qualify to negotiate FHA-insured loans. FHA, FNMA, and FHLMC do not negotiate loans.

9. **(A)** The alienation clause allows the lender to call the note due if the property is transferred to another person.

10. **(B)** When the final payment is made, the lender must release its interest in the property. A deed of reconveyance would transfer the deed back to the buyer.

11. **(B)** When property is purchased under a land contract, the buyer's interest is an equitable title interest.

12. **(B)** A recorded mortgage places a lien on a property.

13. **(C)** By definition of a balloon mortgage.

14. **(A)** An acceleration clause in a mortgage allows the lender to call the entire balance due and payable on default of the borrower.

15. **(D)** The buyer or vendee becomes the lessor in a sale-leaseback agreement.

16. **(B)** Loans are bought and sold in the secondary mortgage market.

17. **(D)** FNMA and GNMA are both members of the secondary mortgage market.

18. **(A)** When a foreclosure sale does not produce sufficient funds to pay a debt in full, a deficiency judgment may be filed against the borrower.

19. **(D)** By definition of loan assumption.

20. **(B)** If the sale price was $250,000 but the CRV was $247,000, the veteran does not have to purchase. He could, however, purchase at $250,000 with a $3,000 down payment.

21. **(A)** Discount points may be paid by the buyer or seller in an FHA-insured loan. The origination fee and MIP are paid by the buyer. The MIP may be a one-time fee or a percentage added to the monthly payment.

22. **(B)** VA makes a guarantee to the lender; FHA insures the lender against a loss.

23. **(C)** FHLMC was established to buy mortgages from savings and loans.

24. **(B)** In a term mortgage, periodic interest payments are made and the principal is due at the end of the term.

25. **(C)** By definition of purchase-money mortgage.

26. **(B)** Regulation Z applies to residential loans made to a person, not to loans made for business, commercial, or agricultural purposes or properties sold under land contracts.

27. **(C)** By definition of subordination agreement.

28. **(B)** The FSLIC is not a member of the secondary market.

29. **(D)** Equity is the difference between the market value and any liens on the property.

30. **(D)** Fannie Mae is not a source of funds on the primary market.

31. **(C)** In the deed of trust document, the lender is the beneficiary, the trustor is the borrower, and the trustee holds the legal title for the lender.

32. **(B)** FHA and VA loans are unconventional loans that are backed by the government.

33. **(D)** The index may change on an adjustable-rate mortgage, but the margin will remain constant over the life of the loan.

34. **(B)** Equitable right of redemption is the right to redeem the property *before* foreclosure. Statutory right of redemption is the right to redeem the property *after* foreclosure.

35. **(B)** Usury laws determine the maximum interest rate that lenders can charge. They are normally state laws, but the federal government could set these rates as well.

36. **(A)** Blanket mortgages cover more than one tract of land and contain a partial release clause.

37. **(B)** By definition of purchase-money mortgage.

38. **(A)** Regulation Z, or Truth-in-Lending, requires the disclosure of the APR.

39. **(B)** Of these answers, the buyer's financial position is the major factor in determining if the lender should underwrite the loan.

40. **(C)** RESPA requires that a settlement sheet be given to the buyers and sellers, disclosing the fees paid by the parties.

41. **(B)** A lien not resolved at the closing remains with the property.

42. **(C)** Regulation Z does not require the disclosure of title fees. (RESPA does.)

43. **(D)** By definition of adjustable-rate mortgage.

44. **(D)** By definition of novation.

45. **(A)** A mortgage that has been sold is said to have been assigned to another party.

46. **(D)** HUD is a federal agency, but it is not a financial intermediary.

47. **(B)** Regulation Z provides for a three-day right of rescission on home equity loans and refinancing of property.

48. **(D)** The substitution of eligibility by another veteran on a loan assumption or the payoff of the loan would release the veteran's eligibility; then the VA could restore the veteran's benefits.

49. **(C)** By definition of wraparound mortgage.

50. **(A)** A graduated-payment mortgage can create negative amortization.

51. **(C)** By definition of reverse annuity mortgage.

52. **(D)** By definition of lock-in agreement.

53. **(C)** The buyer is the mortgagor in the mortgage and the promissor in the note. The buyer is required to sign these documents.

54. **(C)** When the buyer assumes a loan, the buyer is primarily liable and the seller is secondarily liable.

55. **(D)** A trust deed transfers a title interest to the lender (the beneficiary), while a mortgage allows the lender to place a lien on the property.

56. **(C)** The VA will set the limit on the guarantee to the lender.

57. **(D)** By definitions of mortgage bankers and mortgage brokers.

58. **(B)** A budget mortgage includes monthly payments of principal, interest, taxes, and insurance.

59. **(D)** Unconventional mortgages are backed by the government.

60. **(B)** The Equal Credit Opportunity Act prohibits lenders from discriminating when negotiating loans.

61. **(B)** The reverse mortgage would allow them to secure a loan against a percentage of the equity in their property without making monthly payments or having income or credit ratios to qualify.

62. **(A)** The certificate of reduction is given when an FHA loan is assumed.

63. **(B)** The appraiser would issue a certificate of reasonable value on a VA-guaranteed loan.

64. **(C)** By the definitions of open mortgage and open-end mortgage.

65. **(D)** Hypothecation means pledging property to the lender without giving up possession rights.

66. **(C)** Those are the responsibilities of the Federal Reserve.

67. **(A)** Reverse mortgages are nonrecourse loans.

68. **(A)** By the definition of rescission.

69. **(B)** By the definition of subordination.

70. **(B)** As long as the annual percentage rate is included in an advertisement, it meets Truth-in-Lending guidelines.

ANSWERS—MATCHING QUIZ

1.	A	6.	T	11.	S	16.	J
2.	L	7.	P	12.	Q	17.	K
3.	B	8.	O	13.	C	18.	I
4.	E	9.	D	14.	F	19.	H
5.	R	10.	N	15.	M	20.	G

6

Professional Responsibilities/Fair Practice/Administration

This chapter covers the following information regarding the real estate brokerage business: professional responsibilities, fair practice, and administration.
◎ *Topics that appear only in the broker's exam are designated by the bull's-eye in the margin.*

AMP Outline—Professional Responsibilities and Fair Practice

VI. Professional Responsibilities/ Fair Practice/Administration
- ◎ A. Terms of contract between salesperson and broker
- ◎ B. Trust accounts
- C. Complete and accurate records
- ◎ D. Required notifications and reports to real estate regulatory agencies
- ◎ E. Company policies, procedures, and standards
- F. Market trends and financing essentials
- G. Resolving misunderstandings
- H. Sales force training
- I. Sales force supervision
- J. Commissions from sales of real estate
- ◎ K. Appropriate distribution of commissions
- L. Accounting procedures in the office

◎ TERMS OF CONTRACT BETWEEN SALESPERSON AND BROKER

For a salesperson to be **operative**, a broker must hold the salesperson's license. The salesperson is authorized to perform real estate activities on behalf of the broker, and all activities must be carried out in the name of the broker. The broker is responsible for all of the salesperson's activities.

Independent Contractors

Most agents work as **independent contractors**. According to the Internal Revenue Code, the three requirements to meet the independent contractor status are

1. the individual must have a current real estate license;

2. the individual must have a written contract with the broker that contains the following clause: "The salesperson will not be treated as an employee with respect to the services performed by such salesperson as a real estate agent for federal tax purposes"; and

3. ninety percent or more of the individual's income as a licensee must be based on sales production, not on the number of hours worked.

An independent contractor assumes responsibility for paying the contractor's own income tax and Social Security. The agent cannot receive any employee benefits from the broker.

Unlike with the independent contractor, the broker *can* regulate the working hours, office routine, and attendance at meetings of *employees*. The broker withholds income tax and Social Security for the employee, and the employee may receive benefits from the broker.

◎ TRUST ACCOUNTS

A trust account also is known as an *escrow account* or *impound account*. The account is set up by a broker to hold the money of others until a transaction is closed. This includes earnest money checks in sales transactions and security deposits in property management. State laws regulate the establishment, maintenance, and auditing of the account or accounts that a broker is required to have.

Should the broker *deposit* the client's money into his or her personal, operating, or general account, **commingling** has occurred. Commingling is not allowed in most states. Should the broker *spend* the client's money, *embezzlement* has occurred. Embezzlement is illegal.

COMPLETE AND ACCURATE RECORDS

State laws determine the length of time that brokers must retain complete and accurate records of all business transactions. The documents that must be kept include but are not limited to copies of sales contracts, deeds, title searches, title insurance policies, homeowners insurance policies, surveys, inspection certificates, appraisals, and warranties or guarantees of heating, electrical, or plumbing systems.

◎ REQUIRED NOTIFICATIONS AND REPORTS TO REAL ESTATE REGULATORY AGENCIES

The following notifications and reports are usually required by state regulatory agencies. Please check your state laws to determine the details of these and other requirements.

■ **Transaction files**: State law determines how long brokers must keep transaction files. Generally, brokers are required to keep any documents associated with the transaction. These files include but are not limited to the listing contract, sales contract, escrow deposits and withdrawals, agency and property disclosures, HUD-1, and addenda.

■ **Licenses**: Issuance, renewal, transference from one broker to another broker, escrow of, change of surname, change of resident address.

■ **Brokerage business**: Opening, relocating, or closing an office; permission to use company name or name change; notification on death of the principal broker; and appointment of ancillary trustee or working with another broker to close an existing business.

■ **Escrow or trust accounts**: Providing name and location of the escrow account; permission to audit the escrow account.

◎ COMPANY POLICIES, PROCEDURES, AND STANDARDS

Company policies, procedures, and standards are set to establish a clear understanding of the relationship between the broker and the sales associate and thus to communicate the "rules of the game" to the sales associate to resolve as many controversies as possible *before* they arise, and to provide a framework and atmosphere in which people can work together and succeed. A manual of procedures, policies, and standards should include but not be limited to advertising and promotion, compensation, cooperative sales with outside brokers, escrow, floor duty, interoffice exchange of clients, listing, open houses, sales meetings, screening prospects, signs, and termination.

MARKET TRENDS AND FINANCING ESSENTIALS

Property managers and commercial and residential agents must be aware of national and international economic factors that affect their market. Agents should be aware of the projections of the Federal Reserve and how the lowering or raising of the discount rate will impact the ability of buyers to qualify for a loan.

On a local level, a residential agent may decide to specialize in a niche such as first-time buyers, new homes, or senior housing, to name three unique markets within the industry. Knowing the communities includes knowing neighborhoods, schools, transportation, houses of worship, shopping, industry, and recreation. Creating a relationship with lenders and keeping abreast of financing terms and rates is essential to the success of an agent. Even though most agents are not lenders, they should know basic loan qualifications, direct buyers to secure their free annual credit report, and have written authorization to secure credit if the position requires it. (Property managers may be required to secure the credit of a possible tenant.)

RESOLVING MISUNDERSTANDINGS

From time to time, disputes occur in any real estate office. A dispute may be between two agents, between the agent and the company, or between real estate firms. Issues vary, but often revolve around commission splits. Whenever possible, the agent and management should resolve such disputes as quickly as possible. Usually a dispute can be quickly resolved by a review of the agent's employment agreement.

In other cases, company policy and the procedures manual should be reviewed. When neither of these items exists, advice or even binding arbitration by an impartial, disinterested party from outside the firm may be sought. Local boards of REALTORS® require arbitration and offer mediation between members. If the dispute is between brokerage firms that are not REALTORS®, the dispute can be settled through the court system.

If the dispute involves a real estate transaction, the parties will be looking to the agents for professional advice. The agents' knowledge and expertise should be used every step of the way to avoid ambiguities and misunderstandings.

SALES FORCE TRAINING

The training of a new agent is often done by formal classroom instruction, on-the-job training, and attendance at sales meetings. The success of a real estate office or company depends on the skill and knowledge of the sales force. At a minimum the training should cover the following topics:

- Law of agency, state laws, ethical standards practiced by the company
- Completing documents needed in the transaction; listing, sales, and disclosures
- Making a listing presentation
- Creating a competitive market analysis
- Prospecting for sellers and buyers
- Handling objections
- Managing paper flow within the office
- Key and yard sign procedures
- Advertising and open houses
- Developing a contact database
- Communicating with clients, customers, and follow-through and follow-up procedures
- Working effectively with buyers, qualifying, showing properties, and writing an offer
- Negotiating contracts
- Telephone communication
- Internet marketing

SALES FORCE SUPERVISION

It is the broker's responsibility to supervise the licensees under the broker's control. The broker must ensure that the sales staff is well acquainted with the laws of agency and with federal, state, and local fair housing laws, as well as with state laws covering the general conduct of the licensee. Many brokers hire professionals to review listing and sales contracts, agency disclosure forms, property disclosure forms, and any other documents needed in transactions. The broker's license may be suspended or revoked because of an agent's illegal or inappropriate actions.

In some states, if the broker's license is suspended or revoked, all of the licenses held by the broker are immediately suspended until those licensees associate with another broker. *Check with your state to determine the status of an agent's license should a broker's license be suspended or revoked.*

A salesperson or broker who fails to adequately comply with required laws and regulations may be subject to disciplinary action by the real estate commission or by state and local courts. Actions against licensees may be brought by a buyer, a seller, another broker, or the real estate commission itself.

COMMISSIONS FROM SALES OF REAL ESTATE

Sherman Antitrust laws prohibit price fixing, allocation of customers or markets, tie-in arrangements, and group boycotting. Commissions are always negotiable between the brokerage and the seller or buyer. It doesn't matter if the company is a franchise, if one company listed a property and a cooperating broker sold the property, or if one brokerage listed and sold the property, *the commission check is always made payable to the brokerage.*

⊚ APPROPRIATE DISTRIBUTION OF COMMISSIONS

The agent who attends the closing returns to the office and gives the check to the broker, who computes the appropriate commission and pays the agent. If an agent is given a bonus by either party, the bonus is to be given to the broker, who will distribute it to the agent.

A **listing agreement** should state that the seller is responsible for the payment of the commission and whether the payment is to be from the proceeds of the sale.

Many states have laws under which real estate brokers may place a lien on the property for payment of the commission. If the state has not passed a broker lien law, the broker would have to take other legal recourse to collect the commission if the net proceeds are not sufficient to pay the commission.

When a **buyer agency relationship** is created, the agreement should state who is responsible for paying the commission. Typically, the seller still pays the commission on the purchase of a listed property. However, if the buyer purchases a

For-Sale-by-Owner property, the seller is under no contractual obligation to pay the commission, and the buyer may be required to pay.

 Most state laws require that, to earn a commission, an agent must be licensed at the time of the transaction, have an employment contract (listing contract or buyer agency agreement), and be the procuring cause of the sale. When a brokerage firm has secured a qualified buyer on the seller's terms, the broker is due a commission.

Each listing broker establishes the division of commission with cooperating brokers when the listing is shared or submitted to the local multiple-listing service. Each broker should have a written agreement with the broker's licensees stating how commissions received will be divided. Commissions may be divided in different ratios between listing and selling agents and brokers. A salesperson is allowed to receive a commission only from the salesperson's broker. For calculations of the commission, see pages 194-195.

ACCOUNTING PROCEDURES FOR THE OFFICE

A broker must maintain accurate accounting records of income and expense, commission records of agents, and payroll records for employees as well as bank and escrow account statements.

If the brokerage is engaged in property management, *operating funds* are used to maintain and to repair a property or to run credit checks and screen prospective tenants. The broker must provide an owner with a statement showing the receipt and disbursement of any funds. Escrow accounts are subject to the state real estate commission's regulation and examination. Mismanagement of escrow accounts can be cause for disciplinary action by the real estate commission.

The broker must maintain records showing the receipt and the disbursement of commission funds to and from other brokers as well as to salesperson licensees.

IRS Form 8300—Cash Payment Reporting Requirements

Each person engaged in a trade or business who, in the course of that trade or business, receives more than $10,000 in cash in one transaction or in two or more related transactions must file Form 8300 with the Internal Revenue Service. Any transactions conducted between a payer (or its agent) and the recipient in a 24-hour period are related transactions. Transactions are considered related even if they occur over a period of more than 24 hours if the recipient knows, or has reason to know, that each transaction is one of a series of connected transactions. A copy of Form 8300 must be kept for five years from the date it is filed.

Form 8300 requires the identity of the individual(s) from whom the cash was received, the person(s) on whose behalf the transaction was conducted, a description of the transaction and method of payment, and the business that received the cash. The form must be filed by the 15th day after the date the cash was received.

If that date falls on a Saturday, Sunday, or legal holiday, the form must be filed by the next business day.

Penalties may be imposed for

- failure to file a correct and complete form on time, unless a reasonable cause can be shown;

- failure to furnish a correct and complete statement to each person named in a required form;

- causing or attempting to cause a trade or business to fail to file a required report;

- causing or attempting to cause a trade or business to file a required report containing a material omission or misstatement of fact; or

- structuring or attempting to structure transactions to avoid the reporting requirements.

A minimum penalty of $25,000 may be imposed if the failure is due to an intentional disregard of the cash reporting requirements. These violations may result in imprisonment of up to five years or a fine of up to $250,000 for individuals and $500,000 for corporations or both.

See Appendix B for a copy of Form 8300.

QUESTIONS

1. Which of the following would NOT be a required notification that a broker must file with a regulatory agency?
   A. Change of location for a branch office
   B. Name of lending institution where escrow account is located
   C. Notification of death of the principal broker
   D. Notification of a new listing agreement

2. When the seller listed the property, she informed her agent that he was not to show the property unless the buyer was willing to pay a $300 showing fee, which would be applied to the purchase price. The sellers also instructed that an offer must be accompanied with a $10,000 earnest money check. Several weeks later, the agent presented an offer with a $5,000 earnest money check that was accepted by the seller. The check was deposited into the escrow account but was returned three days later due to nonsufficient funds. Is the broker liable to the seller for the $5,000?
   A. No, the broker is not liable but the agent is.
   B. No, neither the broker nor agent is liable.
   C. Yes, the broker is liable.
   D. Yes, the broker and agent are liable.

3. Which of the following laws gives an individual full and equal enjoyment of goods and services in places of public accommodation?
   A. Equal Credit Opportunity Act
   B. Regulation Z
   C. Americans with Disabilities Act
   D. Federal Fair Housing Act

4. Buyer Tina entered into buyer agency agreements in which the broker who finds her a suitable property is paid. Tina has MOST LIKELY entered into a(n)
   A. exclusive buyer agency agreement.
   B. exclusive-agency buyer agency agreement.
   C. open buyer agency agreement.
   D. net buyer agency agreement.

5. Which of the following BEST describes an independent contractor in the real estate business?
   A. An independent contractor has a current real estate license, and the contractor can receive employee benefits from the broker.
   B. An independent contractor has a current real estate license, and the broker assumes the responsibility for paying the contractor's income tax and Social Security tax.
   C. An independent contractor has a current real estate license, a written contract with the broker, and 90 percent or more of the individual's income as a licensee is based on sales production and not on the number of hours worked.
   D. An independent contractor has a current real estate license, a written contract with the broker, and the broker can regulate the working hours of the agent.

6. Which of the following laws prohibit price fixing and the regulation of commission rates?
   A. The federal Sherman Antitrust Act and state antitrust laws
   B. The federal Truth-in-Lending Act and state antitrust laws
   C. The federal Usury Act and state antitrust laws
   D. The federal Regulation B Act and state antitrust laws

7. Broker *M* received an earnest money check from Mr. and Mrs. Buyer. Broker *M* took the check and placed it in his business account. Broker *M* is guilty of
   A. embezzlement.
   B. commingling.
   C. fraud.
   D. misrepresentation.

◎ 8. The broker is accountable for which of the following?
   A. The payment of agents' income taxes
   B. The training and supervision of licensees under the broker's control
   C. The office hours that agents work
   D. The number of cold calls each agent makes each day

9. A principal broker's license has just been revoked, so all licenses held by the broker are MOST LIKELY
   A. revoked.
   B. suspended.
   C. placed on probation.
   D. canceled.

10. Mr. and Mrs. Buyer just entered into an exclusive buyer agency agreement. The agency relationship that has been created can be BEST described as a
    A. general agency.
    B. universal agency.
    C. dual agency.
    D. special agency.

11. Agent Amelia just received a $500 bonus check from a seller. What should she do with the check?
    A. The check is considered commission, and it should be written to and given to her principal broker.
    B. Tell the seller she can accept only cash and the broker cannot know about the bonus.
    C. Tell the seller that her broker does not allow any of the agents to accept bonus checks.
    D. Cash the check and say nothing to her broker.

12. Agent Jordon works for ABC Realty. She was the buyer's agent in a real estate transaction that was listed by XYZ Realty. The seller has agreed to pay the commission. Jordon will receive her commission check from the
    A. principal broker of XYZ Realty.
    B. principal broker of ABC Realty.
    C. seller.
    D. buyer.

13. To earn a commission, an agent must be
    A. licensed at the time of the transaction.
    B. licensed at the time of the transaction, have an employment contract, and be the procuring cause of the sale.
    C. licensed at the time of the transaction, be the procuring cause of the sale, and have met all continuing education requirements.
    D. licensed at the time of the transaction, be the procuring cause of the sale, and be a member of the multiple-listing service.

14. Under what circumstances may salespeople advertise a property for sale?
    A. If they personally listed the property
    B. If the name of their broker is listed in the ad
    C. If they personally pay for the ad
    D. If they are members of the local real estate board

15. Mary and Dick are salespeople in the brokerage firm of Farnsworth-Schmidt Realty. One day over coffee, they decide that Mary will specialize in houses on the east side of town and Dick will specialize in houses on the west side of town. Such a practice is
    A. legal, because the prohibition against allocation of market does not apply to salespeople working for the same broker.
    B. legal, because the agreement was not in writing.
    C. illegal, because only brokers may agree to restrict competition.
    D. illegal, because state laws prohibit such a division of the market.

◎ 16. Broker Carol has several salespeople employed at her office. Early one day, one member of the sales staff brings in a written offer with an earnest money deposit on a house listed with the broker. Later the same day, another salesperson brings in a higher written offer on the same property, also including an earnest money deposit. Carol, in accordance with the policy of her office, does not submit the second offer to the seller until the first has been presented and rejected, so the seller is not informed of the second offer. In this situation, the broker's actions are
   A. permissible, providing the commission is split between the two salespeople.
   B. permissible, if such an arrangement is written into the salespeople's employment contracts.
   C. not permissible, because the broker must submit all offers to the seller.
   D. not permissible, because the broker must notify the second buyer of the existence of the first offer.

17. Broker Sandra represents a buyer interested in a house listed with broker Jack. Sandra feels that Jack is often very difficult to negotiate with. Therefore, Sandra may inform her client to
   A. carry on negotiations with the seller directly.
   B. inform the buyer that Jack is difficult to deal with and to find another house.
   C. write an offer.
   D. say nothing about Jack being difficult to deal with and tell the buyer that the house just sold.

18. All of the following statements are false regarding a real estate broker's acting as the agent of the seller EXCEPT the broker
   A. can lower the sale price of the property without the seller's approval.
   B. must follow the legal instructions of the seller.
   C. can disclose the seller's personal information to a buyer if it helps secure an offer on the property.
   D. can accept a commission from the buyer without the seller's approval.

19. An exclusive-right-to-sell listing is BEST described as an
   A. executed express contract.
   B. executed bilateral contract.
   C. executory unilateral contract.
   D. executory bilateral contract.

20. The government agency established to control the supply and reserves of money as well as to establish a discount rate is
   A. Fannie Mae.
   B. Ginnie Mae.
   C. Federal Reserve.
   D. FDIC.

◎ 21. For a broker to open an office, the broker must hold a minimum of how many licenses?
   A. One
   B. Two to three
   C. Four to six
   D. None

22. Who must be licensed in a real estate office?
   A. The owner
   B. Anyone engaged in listing real estate
   C. All personal assistants
   D. Anyone giving information from the newspaper

23. What is the difference between an appraisal and a competitive market analysis?
   A. One is used for financing and the other for refinancing.
   B. One is used to determine market value and the other for land.
   C. They are the same.
   D. One is used for fair market value and the other for marketing.

24. When listing a property with a fee simple defeasible title, which of the following appurtenances should be in the listing agreement?
   A. House and furniture
   B. House and car
   C. House and landscaping
   D. House and deed conditions

25. Which of the following legal descriptions must include airspace above a datum?
    A. Survey of a cemetery plot
    B. Survey of a condominium
    C. Survey of a single-family home
    D. Survey of mineral rights

26. The principle of appraising that says the whole is worth more than the sum of its parts is referring to
    A. regression.
    B. progression.
    C. assemblage.
    D. plottage.

27. Which of the following is NOT true regarding a real estate settlement?
    A. Closing is the time when the title to real estate is usually transferred in exchange for payment of the purchase price and can be known as *passing papers*.
    B. The primary issues of a face-to-face closing are fulfilling the promises made in the sales contract, closing the buyer's loan, and the mortgage lender's dispersing the loan funds.
    C. An escrow agent is a disinterested third party who is authorized to act for both the buyer and seller and to coordinate the closing activities; the agent also may be called the *escrow holder*.
    D. If the buyer is assuming the seller's existing mortgage loan, the buyer will want to know the exact balance of the loan as of the closing date, and the lender will issue an estoppel certificate to verify the loan balance.

28. A buyer purchased a property, but did not record the deed. By taking possession of the property, the buyer is giving
    A. possessory notice.
    B. constructive notice.
    C. actual notice.
    D. implied notice.

29. Which of the following BEST describes a lis pendens notice?
    A. A recorded notice that allows all lien holders to collect before a judgment
    B. A recorded notice that is filed only when a property is in foreclosure
    C. A recorded notice that is filed on final determination of a suit to quiet title
    D. A recorded notice that a property is in litigation that could result in a future lien being placed on the property

30. Which of the following is NOT found in an abstract of title?
    A. Any restrictions found within the deed
    B. Guarantee of title
    C. Property description
    D. Existing mortgage on the property

31. What law requires that a real estate broker make his or her office accessible to all individuals?
    A. The Building Accessible Law of 1995
    B. The federal Fair Housing Act
    C. The Americans with Disabilities Act
    D. The Civil Rights Act of 1968

32. Which of the following would NOT be a factor influencing supply and demand in a real estate market?
    A. A new law regulating real estate agents
    B. The demographics of the area
    C. Rising interest rates
    D. The announcement of a new factory moving to the area

33. Which of the following statements is FALSE regarding the Federal Reserve?
    A. When the reserve requirements are increased, the money supply shrinks, thus increasing interest rates.
    B. When the reserve requirements are decreased, the money supply grows, thus decreasing interest rates.
    C. An oversupply of money creates inflation, and an undersupply can cause a recession.
    D. The Federal Reserve does not regulate the reserve requirements for depository institutions.

34. Which of the following is exempt from the ADA?
    A. Hotels, motels, and restaurants
    B. A church or synagogue
    C. A residential apartment building that is owner-occupied
    D. A shopping center

◎ 35. Which of the following is TRUE regarding a trust account?
    A. A trust account must be opened by a new agent within seven days of the receipt of his or her license.
    B. A trust account is set up by a broker to hold the money of others until a transaction is closed or released by proper procedure.
    C. Money from the trust account can be used by the broker at any time.
    D. If the buyer defaults on a sales contract, the agent may withdraw money from the trust account and pay the seller.

36. Which of the following deeds is MOST LIKELY used to transfer property at a foreclosure sale?
    A. General warranty
    B. Trustors'
    C. Special warranty
    D. Quitclaim

37. A father gave each of his six children quitclaim deeds to the same property with the instructions that the deed not be recorded until his death. None of the deeds was acknowledged or attested. His instructions were followed. In his will, the father left the property to his second wife. Who MOST LIKELY has ownership rights to the property?
    A. The six children because they received deeds first.
    B. The first child that received the quitclaim deed to the property.
    C. The second wife because she received the property in the will, and the deeds to the children were not acknowledged or recorded.
    D. The last child that received the quitclaim deed to the property.

◎ 38. The broker places a buyer's earnest money check into the firm's business account. This act is known as
    A. embezzlement.
    B. standard practice.
    C. commingling.
    D. redlining.

39. Broker Dee entered into an exclusive-right-to-sell listing with a seller and found a qualified buyer who agreed to buy the property at the listed price. The seller refused to sell. Which of the following is TRUE?
    A. The seller can refuse the offer and has no legal liability to anyone.
    B. The seller can refuse to sell, but a commission is owed the broker.
    C. The seller cannot refuse to sell because the listed price was offered.
    D. The seller cannot refuse to sell because he signed an exclusive-right-to-sell listing agreement.

40. A violent crime was committed in a home, and as a result the property is stigmatized. When listing the property, the agent should
    A. ignore the fact that the crime occurred and say nothing to the sellers.
    B. be aware of the status of the property but say nothing to potential buyers.
    C. show the property to out-of-town buyers who probably will not know to ask any questions.
    D. discuss the situation with the broker and seek competent counsel about how to best deal with the property.

41. Which of the following is NOT a responsibility of the agent when the agent is representing the buyer in a real estate transaction?
    A. To show properties that protect the broker's commissions and select the best times to show those properties
    B. To be fair and honest with the seller but safeguard the buyer's interest under all circumstances
    C. To suggest the minimum amount of earnest money deposit to be made and suggest that forfeiture of the deposit be the sole remedy if the buyer defaults
    D. To require that a seller sign a property condition statement and confirm representations of the condition of the property

42. Which of the following is the responsibility of a seller's agent to the buyer?
    A. Disclosure of any material fact pertinent to the property
    B. Disclosure of the lowest offer the seller will accept on the property
    C. Disclosure that the seller is near bankruptcy or foreclosure
    D. Disclosure that the seller has AIDS

43. A buyer made an offer and gave the seller three days to accept. On the following day, she found an FSBO property she liked better. The buyer called the agent to revoke her previous offer. The agent had no communication of acceptance from the seller. Regarding this situation, the buyer must
    A. make an immediate offer on the FSBO property before it is purchased by someone else.
    B. make sure the seller is notified of the revocation before making an offer on the FSBO property.
    C. do nothing more because she has notified the agent of her decision to rescind the offer.
    D. give the seller three days to accept or reject, as stated in the offer.

◎ 44. Which of the following would NOT be included in a manual of company procedures?
    A. Advertising and promotion policies
    B. Procedure for deposit of escrow check
    C. Fair housing policies
    D. How to best discuss commissions with competitive agents

45. Which of the following is NOT TRUE regarding an exclusive-agency agreement?
    A. It may contain a broker protection clause.
    B. It excludes the seller from selling the property.
    C. It excludes other brokers from listing the property.
    D. It excludes the property from being placed in the MLS unless permission is granted by the seller.

46. A seller agreed to list his house for $190,000, but he was not informed that the actual value of the property was $200,000. The agent purchased the property the next day. This is an example of a violation of which of the agent's responsibilities?
    A. Obedience
    B. Accountability
    C. Loyalty
    D. Discovery

47. The principal to whom an agent gives advice and counsel is a
    A. subagent.
    B. customer.
    C. client.
    D. fiduciary.

48. A testator devised a parcel of real estate with the restriction that it be used for single-family dwellings only. Zoning in this area allows multifamily dwellings. Which of the following would be upheld?
   A. The devisee can build single-family or multi-family dwellings because the grantor is dead.
   B. The zoning ordinance takes precedence, and the devisee can build multifamily dwellings.
   C. The deed restriction takes precedence and prevents the owner from building multi-family dwellings.
   D. The devisee can sell the property to someone else and that grantee can build single-family or multifamily dwellings.

49. A church was purchasing a property from a business. At the closing table, the attorney representing the church refused to accept the deed. Which of the following would permit the church to refuse the deed?
   A. The deed did not contain the correct consideration.
   B. The sales contract stated that the business would provide a general warranty deed, and a special warranty deed was presented for acceptance.
   C. The deed presented at the closing did not contain the signature of the grantee.
   D. The sales contract did not state that time is of the essence; therefore the church could refuse the deed because it did not close in a timely manner.

◎ 50. An agent worked for a company that provided a company jacket to be worn in all business transactions, provided health insurance, and withheld taxes. The employment relationship between the brokerage and the agent was MOST LIKELY that of a(n)
   A. independent contractor.
   B. employer/employee.
   C. joint venture.
   D. general partnership.

◎ 51. An agent listed and sold a property. If the seller paid a 7 percent commission, how much would the agent receive?
   A. An undisclosed dual agent would be paid 3.5 percent.
   B. A disclosed dual agent would be paid 4 percent.
   C. The agent was a dual agent and would not be paid a commission.
   D. The agent would be paid whatever was negotiated with the broker.

52. Which of the following is NOT true regarding the ECOA?
   A. It prohibits discrimination based on race, color, and religion.
   B. It prohibits discrimination based on national origin, sex, marital status, or age.
   C. It requires that credit applications be considered only on the basis of income, net worth, job stability, and credit rating.
   D. It requires that credit applicants disclose their childbearing intentions if income could be interrupted in the future.

53. Which of the following is NOT TRUE regarding the ADA?
   A. It is designed to eliminate discrimination against individuals with disabilities by mandating equal access to jobs, public accommodations, government services, public transportation, and telecommunications.
   B. Public accommodations include hotels, shopping centers, professional offices, private clubs, religious organizations, and private entities that own, lease, or operate virtually all commercial facilities.
   C. Any employer with 15 or more employees must adopt nondiscriminatory employment procedures and make reasonable accommodations to enable an individual with a disability to perform essential job functions.
   D. The definition of a person with a disability is one who has a physical or mental impairment that substantially limits one or more major life activities and includes disfiguration due to an accident.

54. A borrower's right to rescind within three business days an agreement to allow a lender to place a second mortgage on his or her property as security for the loan is provided by the
    A. Real Estate Settlement Procedures Act.
    B. Equal Credit Opportunity Act.
    C. Truth-in-Lending Act.
    D. Fair Credit Reporting Act.

55. The practice of lending institutions refusing to make loans in certain geographic areas is called
    A. blockbusting.
    B. redlining.
    C. channeling.
    D. steering.

56. Which of the following BEST defines the law of agency?
    A. The selling of another's property by an authorized agency
    B. The rules of law that apply to the responsi-bilities and obligations of a person who acts for another
    C. The principles that govern one's conduct in business
    D. The rules and regulations of the state licensing agency

57. Which of the following BEST defines blockbusting?
    A. Changing the zoning districts of a municipality
    B. Representing to homeowners that minori-ties are moving into the area
    C. Discriminating against minorities by lim-iting the housing available to them
    D. Removing property from the tax rolls

58. The federal Fair Housing Act applies to all of the following EXCEPT
    A. rental property.
    B. vacant land sales.
    C. single-family sales.
    D. commercial or industrial properties.

59. An offer was presented to a seller for acceptance one day prior to the expiration of the listing. The seller had three days to accept the offer. On day two, the seller did accept the offer. One day prior to closing the seller discovered the buyer was a relative of the listing agent and rescinded the contract. Does the seller have the right to rescind the contract?
    A. No. Disclosure of a relationship between the buyer and listing agent is not relevant.
    B. Yes. A seller can rescind a contract any time prior to closing.
    C. No. A seller cannot rescind a contract any time prior to closing.
    D. Yes. An undisclosed dual agency was created and the seller can rescind the contract.

60. Mr. and Mrs. Homeowner own their principal place of residence in Anytown, U.S.A. They own a condominium in Resort Beach, U.S.A. They are now 65 years of age and decide to retire. Under federal fair housing laws they may discriminate in the sale of their home if
    A. they use the services of a small broker.
    B. they own four or fewer properties and do not discriminate because of race in the transaction.
    C. they own no more than three homes at one time, do not use the services of a broker, and do not use discriminatory advertising.
    D. they are no longer living in the home and have not discriminated in the sale of a property within the last 36 months.

61. On a listing appointment the seller told the agent that he was learning disabled and illiterate. He asked he agent to read the listing agreement to him. After a lengthy discussion answering all of the seller's questions, the seller said he understood the terms and placed his X where the agent indicated. Is this a valid listing contract?
    A. Yes, because the seller is illiterate, not incompetent.
    B. Yes, but only if the seller has an attorney verify what the agent said.
    C. No, because an illiterate person can never enter into a valid contract.
    D. No, an illiterate person must have a guardian explain all documents to him.

62. When the agent scheduled an open house with the sellers she advised them to remove all jewelry, valuables, and medications that could be stolen. Several people came through the open house, one of whom asked permission to use the bathroom. The next morning the sellers called to inform the agent that three bottles of medication were missing from the medicine cabinet. Can the agent be held accountable for the missing medication?
   A. Yes, because the agent should have checked every visitor before they left the open house to see if they had stolen any property.
   B. Yes, because an agent is accountable for the money or property of others that comes into his or her possession.
   C. No, because the agent advised the sellers to remove all valuables before the open house, she is not liable.
   D. No, because the agent cannot watch every-one at an open house.

63. Mike's brokerage firm listed a property and was paid a flat fee to place it in the multiple-listing service. The following week the seller advertised the property in the local newspaper as a For Sale by Owner and there was no mention of the listing broker. Can the seller advertise his own property without mentioning the broker?
   A. Yes, if he signed an exclusive-agency listing or an open listing and state law permits it.
   B. Yes, if he signed an exclusive-right-to-sell or net listing and state law permits.
   C. No, because a seller can never advertise his property as a For Sale by Owner if it is listed with a brokerage.
   D. No, because the seller did not have permission of the broker to advertise the property, he cannot advertise the property.

64. Ken and Joyce listed their property for $249,500. They instructed their agent not to bring them any offers below the listed price. Six days later the agent received an offer of $245,000 from an agent with another company. Can she refuse to present the offer to the sellers?
   A. Yes, because the sellers' instructions are legal.
   B. Yes, but only if the sellers' instructions are in writing.
   C. No, because the offer is from an agent with another company.
   D. No, because all offers are to be presented to the seller.

65. The owner of an FSBO property agreed to let an agent show her property. Later, the agent presented an offer that was accepted by the seller. When the transaction closed, the brokerage commission was paid by the seller. Did the agent represent the seller in the transaction?
   A. Yes, because the brokerage was paid by the seller.
   B. Yes, if they entered into a listing contract.
   C. No, because an agent can never represent a For Sale by Owner.
   D. No, because the seller did not request representation.

66. Sally is an agent for ABC Realty and she has 15 listings. Jo is also an agent for ABC Realty and has a buyer for one of Sally's listings. The broker appointed Sally as the exclusive agent of the seller and Jo as the exclusive agent for the buyer. This arrangement is an example of
   A. express agency.
   B. implied agency.
   C. designated agency.
   D. undisclosed agency.

67. When the buyer made an offer on a property he gave the agent $500 in cash for the earnest money. After the offer was accepted the agent deposited the cash into his personal account and then wrote the broker a check for the $500 deposit. Is this action legal?
    A. Yes, if the broker told him follow that procedure.
    B. Yes, if the buyer gave permission for the agent to follow that procedure.
    C. No, because it is a commingling of funds.
    D. No, because it is embezzlement.

68. A landlord, who was also an attorney, owns a duplex. One of his tenants moved out, so he placed an ad in the local paper that read "For Rent: 2-bedroom apartment in duplex. Steep stairs. No children or pets." Is the ad legal?
    A. Yes, because he is an attorney so he does not have to follow fair housing guidelines.
    B. Yes. Because the property has "steep stairs," he is protecting children from getting hurt and that is legal.
    C. No, because a duplex is exempted from the fair housing laws.
    D. No, because landlords cannot advertise "no children" unless the property meets all the requirements to be designated as housing for older persons.

69. Which of the following documents would NOT create an agency relationship?
    A. Property management agreement
    B. Sales contract
    C. Listing contract
    D. Buyer agency contract

70. For their down payment the buyers brought $20,000 cash to the closing table. Which form must be filed with the Internal Revenue Service to report this transaction?
    A. 1099
    B. 1003
    C. 8300
    D. 8303

MATCHING QUIZ

The column on the right contains a brief definition of important terms in this section.
Write the letter of the matching term on the appropriate line.

A. Independent contractor

B. Commingling

C. Embezzlement

D. Escrow account

E. Arbitration

F. Sherman Antitrust Act

G. IRS Form 8300

H. Transaction files

I. Federal Reserve

J. Law of agency

1. ___ Federal law that prohibits price-fixing

2. ___ Document used to report receiving more than $10,000 in cash in a business transaction

3. ___ Outlines the duties and responsibilities of the principal and the agent

4. ___ Regulates the supply of money in the market

5. ___ The act of spending the client's money

6. ___ Files that must be kept by the broker for a number of years as required by state law

7. ___ Also known as impound account; an account for other people's money

8. ___ The act of depositing the client money into a personal or business account

9. ___ Party who assumes responsibility for paying the party's own income tax and Social Security

10. ___ Agreement to resolve a dispute by using a neutral third party whose decision is binding

ANSWERS

1. **(D)** A listing agreement is NOT a notification that must be sent to a regulatory agency.

2. **(B)** The seller accepted the offer with the $5,000 check, so the broker and agent are not liable.

3. **(C)** The Americans with Disabilities Act was passed in 1990 to enable individuals with disabilities to become a part of the social and economic mainstream.

4. **(C)** In an open buyer agency agreement, the agent who finds suitable property is paid.

5. **(C)** By definition of independent contractor.

6. **(A)** By definition of antitrust laws.

7. **(B)** A client's money must be placed in a separate escrow or trust account. When it is placed in the business account, commingling has occurred.

8. **(B)** A broker is liable for the training and supervision of activities of licensees under his or her control.

9. **(B)** When a principal broker's license is revoked or suspended, all licenses held by the broker are most likely suspended.

10. **(D)** A special agency is created when the principal delegates a specific act or business transaction.

11. **(A)** All commission checks must be given to the principal broker.

12. **(B)** An agent is paid by her or his principal broker.

13. **(B)** The three requirements for collecting a commission are (1) to be licensed at the time of the transaction, (2) to have an employment contract, and (3) to be the procuring cause of the sale.

14. **(B)** Properties listed by an agent must be advertised in the name of the brokerage firm.

15. **(A)** The antitrust laws prohibit price fixing in any way, but not how salespersons within a given office decide to divide a market.

16. **(C)** All offers must be presented to the seller.

17. **(C)** When representing the buyer, an agent must negotiate the best possible deal for the buyer.

18. **(B)** This is the true statement. A broker must follow the legal instructions of the seller.

19. **(D)** An exclusive-right-to-sell listing is an executory contract in that one or both parties have obligations to perform. It is a bilateral contract because both parties are obligated to perform.

20. **(C)** The Federal Reserve was established to control the supply of money to help stabilize the economy.

21. **(A)** A brokerage firm can be opened with one license, which can be the broker's.

22. **(B)** Anyone engaged in listing, selling, property management, or other activities regarded as the practice of real estate must be licensed.

23. **(D)** The appraisal is used to estimate market value, while a CMA is a marketing tool that helps the seller estimate the asking price of the property.

24. **(D)** If a fee simple defeasible title is being transferred, the deed conditions should be in the listing contract.

25. **(B)** A survey of a condominium must contain the legal description of the elevations of floor and ceiling surfaces and the vertical boundaries in reference to an official datum. Thus, it must include the airspace above the datum.

26. **(D)** The principal of plottage states that the whole should be worth more than the sum of its parts. The process of merging adjacent lots held by separate landowners into a larger lot is assemblage.

27. **(D)** When the buyer is assuming the seller's existing mortgage, the lender issues a mortgage reduction certificate to verify the loan balance, not an estoppel certificate.

28. **(B)** Constructive notice is notice that certain facts can be discovered by due diligence or inquiry. Even though the deed was not recorded, possession of the property grants constructive notice.

29. **(D)** By definition of lis pendens.

30. **(B)** An attorney will give certificate of title, but there is no guarantee of title.

31. **(C)** The Americans with Disabilities Act requires that all properties provide accessibility to the public.

32. **(A)** A new real estate law would NOT influence supply and demand in the real estate market.

33. **(D)** The Fed does regulate the reserve requirements for depository institutions.

34. **(B)** Private clubs and religious organizations are exempt from the ADA.

35. **(B)** By definition of trust account.

36. **(D)** A quitclaim deed most likely transfers property at a foreclosure.

37. **(C)** The second wife would most likely receive the property because most states require that a document be acknowledged before it can be introduced as evidence in a court of law. Most states will not allow a document to be recorded at the courthouse without its being acknowledged.

38. **(C)** By the definition of commingling.

39. **(B)** A listing contract is an employment contract. When the broker found the qualified buyer, the commission had been earned.

40. **(D)** State laws vary as to how to handle the sale of stigmatized properties, and the agent should discuss the situation with the broker and an attorney immediately.

41. **(A)** When an agent is representing a buyer, the agent must search for the best properties for the buyer to inspect, including FSBOs.

42. **(A)** A seller's agent is responsible for being honest and fair with the buyer and for disclosing all pertinent and material facts about the property.

43. **(C)** An offer can be revoked at any time before acceptance. Because the agent had no communication of acceptance from the seller, the buyer has no responsibilities for the offer once the revocation was communicated.

44. **(D)** It is against the Sherman Antitrust laws to discuss commissions with competitive agents.

45. **(B)** An exclusive agency permits the seller to sell the property and not pay a commission if the buyer was procured without the assistance of the broker.

46. **(C)** Loyalty means placing the principal's interest above the interest of all others, including self-interest. Because the agent did not disclose the true market value of the property, the agent did not fulfill his responsibility of loyalty.

47. **(C)** A client is a person to whom the agent gives advice and counsel.

48. **(C)** Whenever a deed restriction and a zoning ordinance conflict, the most restrictive is upheld.

49. **(B)** If a deed other than a general warranty deed is to be given by the grantor, it must be stated in the sales contract and should be stated in the listing contract.

50. **(B)** An employer would withhold taxes and provide health insurance.

51. **(D)** The agent would be paid whatever was negotiated with the broker.

52. **(D)** Credit applicants cannot be asked about their childbearing intentions or capability or about their birth-control practices.

53. **(B)** Private clubs and religious organizations are not included in the definition of public accommodations and are exempt from the ADA.

54. **(C)** Truth-in-Lending or Regulation Z provides the three-day right of rescission when a borrower is negotiating a second mortgage or refinancing the property.

55. **(B)** By definition of redlining.

56. **(B)** The rules of law that apply to the responsibilities and obligations of a person who acts for another is the law of agency.

57. **(B)** Blockbusting is representing to sellers that minorities are moving into a neighborhood.

58. **(D)** Federal fair housing laws do not apply to commercial properties.

59. **(D)** An undisclosed dual agency has been created and the seller would have the right to rescind the contract.

60. **(C)** Under federal fair housing laws the owners of a single-family home may discriminate in the sale of the home if they own three or fewer homes and do not use the services of a broker or discriminatory advertising.

61. **(A)** Illiterate persons can enter into binding contracts when they fully understand the terms.

62. **(C)** The agent advised the seller to remove valuables and under most circumstances has fulfilled her duty to them.

63. **(A)** The seller retains the right to sell the property in an exclusive agency or an open listing. Unless state law forbids the seller from advertising a listed property without mentioning the broker, it is legal.

64. **(D)** All offers are to be presented to the seller.

65. **(B)** If they entered into a listing agreement, the agent would represent the seller. Payment of commission does not create agency.

66. **(C)** By the definition of designated agency.

67. **(C)** By the definition of commingling.

68. **(D)** Only housing that meets the requirements of the designation of housing for the elderly can advertise no children. (The ad would probably read "Adult Community.")

69. **(B)** A sales contract does not create an agency relationship.

70. **(C)** IRS Form 8300 is used to report receiving more than $10,000 cash in a trade or business transaction.

ANSWERS—MATCHING QUIZ

1. F
2. G
3. J
4. I
5. C

6. H
7. D
8. B
9. A
10. E

7

Math Review

Depending on which test you receive, there could be between 8 and 20 math questions on your state examination. This chapter will show you how to use the "T" method for working math questions. It is a simple formula that can be used to solve most of the math questions that you encounter on the exam. The formulas for brokerage, financing, appraising, area, and settlement math will also be reviewed.

Answers may vary, depending on how many decimal places are carried out. When working these questions, please carry out the decimal to four places and round in the final step.

THE "T" METHOD

Here is a math question that you can work in your head. If an agent sold a property for $100,000 and the broker was paid a 7 percent commission, what was that commission? That's right. $7,000. Let's use this question to learn how the "T" formula works.

$$\frac{\text{Part}}{\text{Total} \mid \text{Rate}}$$
$$\times$$

In the "T," the *total* is placed on the bottom left, the *rate* on the bottom right, and the *part* at the top. Using the "T" for the above question, it gives us this:

$$\frac{\$7,000 \text{ Commission } \$}{\$100,000 \mid 7\%}$$
$$\times$$

Rule 1

When given the two numbers in the bottom of the "T," the *total* and the *rate*, the mathematical function is **multiplication**. $100,000 × 7 percent = $7,000.

Rule 2

When given the *part*, at the top of the "T," and the *rate*, at the bottom, the mathematical function is **division**. It helps to remember TGIF: **T**op **G**oes **I**nto the calculator **F**irst.

> Example: If a broker received a $7,000 commission check and the selling price was $100,000, what was the commission rate?

The $7,000 is the part and goes at the top of the "T." $100,000 is the sale price or total and goes in the lower left. Thus, $7,000 ÷ $100,000 = 7 percent.

÷ $7,000 Commission $	
$100,000	.07 or 7%
Sale Price	Commission Rate

Rule 3

When given the *part*, at the top of the "T," and the *total*, at the bottom, the mathematical function again is **division**. Remember TGIF.

> Example: The seller received $100,000 and the commission paid was 7 percent. What was the sale price of the property?

Notice how this question is different. Is the $100,000 a part or a total? It's a part, so it goes at the top of the "T." It is equal to 93 percent of the selling price, so 93 percent goes in the lower right of the "T." $100,000 ÷ 93% = $107,526.88.

$100,000 Seller's Net ÷	
$107,526.88	0.93 or 93%
Sale Price	Seller's %

Rule 4

When solving for the total, take the part and divide by the percent to which that part is equal.

For example: Commission $ ÷ Commission Rate = Sale Price and Seller's $ ÷ Seller's % = Sale Price.

BROKERAGE MATH PROBLEMS

Brokerage math questions include computing commissions and determining the sale price when given the seller's dollars and the commission rate.

÷ Commission $ ÷	
Sale Price	Commission Rate

Sale Price × Commission Rate = Commission $

Commission $ ÷ Commission Rate = Sale Price

Commission $ ÷ Sale Price = ~~Sale Price~~

÷ Seller's Dollars $ ÷	
Sale Price	Seller's %

Sale Price × Seller's % = Seller's Dollars $

Seller's $ ÷ Seller's % = Sale Price

Seller's $ ÷ Sale Price = Seller %

BROKERAGE MATH QUESTIONS

Beginner Level

1. Ms. Seller is interviewing agents to list her property. She has the following quotes from two different companies: XYZ Realty, 7 percent commission, and Redford Realty, 5.5 percent commission. If her house sells for $225,000, how much will she save if she lists her property with Redford Realty?
   A. $3,357
   B. $3,375
   C. $4,500
   D. $5,400

2. At closing the seller paid the broker $21,000, which was equivalent to 7 percent of the selling price. What was the selling price of the property?
   A. $147,000
   B. $210,000
   C. $300,000
   D. $400,000

3. Anne, a sales associate for XYZ Realty, listed and sold a $175,000 home. The seller paid a 6 percent commission of which Anne received 2 percent for listing the property and 1.5 percent for selling the property. How much was the broker share of the commission?
   A. $10,500
   B. $5,250
   C. $6,125
   D. $4,375

4. A property sold for $235,000 and the selling broker's half of the commission was $8,225. What was the commission rate?
   A. 4 percent
   B. 5 percent
   C. 6 percent
   D. 7 percent

5. A broker and sales associate split commissions on a 60/40 basis. How much commission will the sales associate earn if he sells a property for $125,000 and a 6 percent commission is paid?
   A. $7,500
   B. $3,000
   C. $4,500
   D. $3,500

Intermediate Level

6. When Branham of DF Realty listed a property, the seller agreed to pay a 7 percent commission. Tiffany of DF Realty sold the property sold for $190,000. If the listing agent was paid 2 percent and the selling agent was paid 1.5 percent, how much was the broker paid after paying his agents?
   A. $2,850
   B. $3,800
   C. $6,650
   D. $13,300

7. Judy listed her property with a XYZ Realty that charges a flat fee of $2,995 to list the property. If an agent within XYZ sells the property, the total commission paid is $2,995. However, if an agent from another company brings the buyer that purchases the property, Judy agreed to pay that company a 3 percent commission. Agent Dorothy from JFK presented an offer of $425,000. If the offer is accepted, the total commission that Judy will pay is
   A. $15,745
   B. $12,750
   C. $11,250
   D. $10,500

8. A broker sold a property for $250,000. She was paid 6 percent on the first $100,000, 5 percent on the next $100,000, and 4 percent on the balance. How much was the broker paid?
   A. $6,000
   B. $5,000
   C. $13,000
   D. $24,000

9. An agent was paid $2,500, which was half of the 7 percent that the broker collected. What was the sale price of the property?
   A. $71,248
   B. $35,714
   C. $35,417
   D. $71,428

10. A broker and a sales associate split commissions on a 60/40 basis. If the broker's share of the commission was $3,500 and the sale price was $83,333, what was the commission rate?
    A. 6 percent
    B. 10.5 percent
    C. 7.5 percent
    D. 7 percent

Advanced Level

11. Mr. and Mrs. Trapp sold their property and after paying a 6 percent commission, they received a check for $470,000. What was the selling price of the property?
    A. $500,000
    B. $783,333
    C. $800,000
    D. $900,000

12. Ms. Vollman sold her condo and paid 6 percent commission to the selling broker. If her net was $200,000, what was the sale price?
    A. $205,698.49
    B. $212,765.95
    C. $225,349.59
    D. $229,879.39

13. After closing expenses of $550 and a 6 percent commission was paid, the seller received a check for $149,850. What was the sale price of the property?
    A. $150,400
    B. $155,424
    C. $159,424
    D. $160,000

14. Mr. Seller wants to net a profit of $20,000 and agrees to pay a 7 percent commission. He also has selling expenses of $400 and a mortgage of $35,250. What is the minimum offer he could accept on the property?
    A. $59,839
    B. $59,545
    C. $58,565
    D. $59,656

15. Mr. and Mrs. Seller want to net a 12 percent profit after paying the brokerage firm a 6.5 percent commission. If the original purchase price was $104,500, what is the minimum offer they can accept?
    A. $125,716
    B. $117,040
    C. $125,176
    D. $124,647

PROPERTY MANAGEMENT MATH FORMULAS

An agent acting as a property manager may be paid a percentage of the gross or net income as commission. Normally, the manager is paid a percentage of the gross income, but read the question carefully.

Example: The annual gross rent collected on a building is $124,000. If the property manager is paid a 6 percent commission on the rents collected, how much is he paid annually?

$$\frac{\$7{,}440 \text{ Commission } \$}{\$124{,}000 \quad | \quad 6\%}$$

Gross Rent × Commission Rate = Commission $

Gross or Net Rent × = Commission $

Commission $ ÷ Commission Rate = Gross or Net Rent

Commission $ ÷ Gross or Net Rent = Commission Rate

Read the question carefully to determine if you are solving for the annual, semiannual, quarterly, or monthly commission.

The commission may also be computed as so many dollars per square foot of the space leased.

Example: A tenant leased a 60 ft. × 100 ft. space for $8 per square foot annually. If the property manager is paid 8 percent of the rent collected, how much is she paid annually?

Step 1   60' × 100' = 6,000 square feet

Step 2   6,000 square feet × $8 = $48,000 annual rent

Step 3
$$\frac{\$3{,}840 \text{ Commission } \$}{\$48{,}000 \quad | \quad 8\%}$$

Gross Rent × Commission Rate

Though there are several types of percentage leases, this is usually how they are negotiated: the tenant pays a fixed monthly rent or base rent, plus a percentage of all income over a certain amount. The rent could also be paid on all income.

Example: A shop owner entered into a percentage lease with the lessor in which she agreed to pay a fixed rental of $650 per month, and when gross sales reached $175,000, she pays 5 percent of sales over that amount. This year, her gross sales were $225,000. What was the total rent paid at the end of the year?

Step 1 $650 × 12 = $7,800 fixed rent

Step 2 $225,000 – 175,000 = $50,000 gross sales over $175,000

Step 3

$$\frac{\$2,500 \text{ Commission } \$}{\$50,000 \quad | \quad 5\%}$$

Gross Sales × Commission Rate

Step 4 $7,800 + 2,500 = $10,300 Total Commission Paid

In a graduated lease, the rents increase or "step up" on a gradual basis over the life of the lease.

Example: A tenant entered into a 12-year graduated lease with the owner of a building. He agreed to pay $400 per month for the first four years, $450 per month for the next four years, and $500 per month for the remaining term. If the property manager is paid 6 percent of the total rent collected, how much will he be paid at the end of the leasing term?

Step 1 $400 × 12 × 4 = $19,200
$450 × 12 × 4 = $21,600
+$500 × 12 × 4 = $24,000
$64,800

Step 2 $64,800 gross rent collected in 12 years

Step 3

$$\frac{\$3,888 \text{ Commission } \$}{\$64,800 \quad | \quad 6\%}$$

×

Gross Rent × Commission Rate

PROPERTY MANAGEMENT QUESTIONS

Beginner Level

16. Ms. Golz's pays rental of $15.50 per square foot annually for her office that measures 25' × 50'. If the leasing agent is paid 7 percent of her rent collected, how much is she paid?
    A. $19,375
    B. $14,233
    C. $3,345
    D. $1,356

17. A space was leased for $1,200 per month. The owner pays a property manager 8 percent of the gross income as commission. How much does the owner pay annually?
    A. $1,512
    B. $1,152
    C. $1,215
    D. $96

18. A property manager negotiated a 15-year graduated lease with the following terms. The lessee will pay $550 per month for the first five years, with a $50 a month increase every five years thereafter. If the property manager is paid a 6.75 percent commission, what will be the total commission paid at the end of the term?
    A. $7,290
    B. $7,087
    C. $7,429
    D. $7,920

Intermediate Level

19. The lease agreement for Julia's Fine Arts store was as follows: $1,200 fixed monthly rent plus 4 percent commission on all sales over $850,000. This year her gross sales were $1,500,000. How much was paid in rent?
    A. $14,400
    B. $26,000
    C. $40,400
    D. $35,000

20. Peggy entered into a 20-year graduated lease. She will pay $500 per month for the first five years, and $575 per month for the next fifteen years. The property manager is paid 6 percent of the total rent collected and he has another 5 buildings with the same agreement. How much will he be paid over the life of the leases?
    A. $40,050
    B. $48,060
    C. $50,260
    D. $55,350

21. The XYZ store leased a space in the mall with the following agreement: $575 fixed monthly rent, plus a 5.25 percent commission on all sales over $225,000. The gross sales were $389,250 for the year. What was the total rent paid by XYZ?
    A. $15,523
    B. $8,623
    C. $9,600
    D. $15,253

Advanced Level

22. The KLM store leased a space in the mall with a percentage lease and agreed to pay $425 monthly fixed rent and 6 percent on all sales over $175,000. This year, the total rent paid was $9,321. What were the gross sales?
    A. $184,849
    B. $213,350
    C. $213,530
    D. $245,350

23. VonTrapp Heirlooms' percentage lease read as follows: The tenant agrees to pay $800 per month fixed rent plus 4 percent on all sales over one million dollars. If the total rent paid was $49,600, the gross sales were
    A. $1,000,000.
    B. $1,500,000.
    C. $2,000,000.
    D. $2,500,000.

FINANCING MATH FORMULAS

Financing math questions include computing the loan amount, annual interest dollars, discount points, loan origination fees, and amortization of a loan. Remember, the lender negotiates the loan on the sale price or appraised value, whichever is less.

Example: A seller agreed to pay $85,000 for a property, but it appraised for $83,500. The lender agreed to negotiate a 90 percent loan. What was the loan amount?

$$\frac{\$75,150 \text{ Loan}}{\$83,500 \mid 90\%}$$

Appraised Value × Loan-to-Value Ratio

Sale Price or Appraised Value × Loan-to-Value Ratio = Loan

Loan ÷ Sale Price or Appraised Value = Loan-to-Value Ratio

Loan ÷ Loan-to-Value Ratio = Sale Price or Appraised Value

A question may ask for the annual, semiannual, quarterly, monthly, or daily interest that is due on a loan.

Example: Sterling negotiated a $125,000 loan at 8.75 percent annual interest. How much interest will she pay the first year?

$$\frac{\$10,937.50 \text{ Annual Interest } \$}{\$125,000 \mid 8.75\%}$$

Loan × Interest Rate

Loan × Interest Rate = Annual Interest $

Annual Interest $ ÷ Loan = Interest Rate

Annual Interest $ ÷ Interest Rate = Loan

Discount points are computed as a percentage of the loan amount: 1 point = 1 percent of the loan, 2 points = 2 percent of the loan.

Example: Fred secured an $89,000 loan and was required to pay three discount points. How much did he pay in points?

$$\frac{\$2,670 \text{ Discount Points } \$}{\$89,000 \mid 3\%}$$

Loan × Discount Points %

Loan × Discount Points % = Discount Points $

Discount Points $ ÷ Loan = Discount Points %

Discount Points $ ÷ Discount Points % = Loan

A lender's cash outflow is the loan minus the discount points percent.

Example: Ms. Buyer secured an $89,000 loan and had to pay one point. What was the cash outflow of the lender?

$89,000	Loan
− 1%	Discount Points %
$88,110	Cash Outflow

To determine the effective yield to the lender, remember this rule of thumb: For each discount point that the lender charges, the lender's yield is increased by $\frac{1}{8}$ percent on a 30-year loan.

Example: Warren negotiated an $80,000 loan for 30 years at an 8.25 percent rate of interest and had to pay two points. What was the effective yield to the lender?

Step 1 $1 \div 8 = 0.125$

Step 2 $0.125 \times 2 = 0.25$ increase

Step 3   8.25% interest + 0.25% increase = 8.5% effective yield
0.125 × Discount Points = Increase
Interest Rate + Increase = Effective Yield

The loan origination fee is also computed as a percentage of the loan amount.

Example: The buyer secured a $50,000 loan and had to pay a 1.5 percent origination fee. How much did the buyer have to pay for the origination fee?

$750 Origination Fee $	
$50,000	1.5%

Loan × Origination Fee $
Loan × Origination Fee % = Origination Fees $
Origination Fee $ ÷ Loan = Origination Fee %
Origination Fee $ ÷ Origination Fee % = Loan

The word *amortize* means to reduce the debt by making payments that include both principal and interest. The principal and interest payment is normally given in the question about loan amortization.

Example: Sandy negotiated a $100,000 loan at 10 percent interest for 30 years. Her monthly payments are $877.58 per month. What is her loan balance after the first payment?

Step 1

$10,000 Annual Interest $	
$100,000	10%

Loan × Interest Rate

Step 2 $10,000 Annual Interest $ ÷ 12 months = $833.33 Monthly Interest

Step 3 $877.58 P&I − $833.33 Monthly Interest = $44.25 Principal

Step 4 $100,000 − 44.25 = $99,955.75 Loan Balance after First Payment

FINANCING QUESTIONS

Beginner Level

24. Brayden purchased a property for $175,000. If his loan was $131,250, what was the loan-to-value ratio?
    A. 90 percent
    B. 80 percent
    C. 75 percent
    D. 70 percent

25. A lender negotiated an $82,250 loan, which was 80 percent of the appraised value. The appraised value of the property is
    A. $65,800.50
    B. $68,500.50
    C. $82,250.50
    D. $102,812.50

26. Mr. and Mrs. Buyer applied for a VA loan to purchase a property for $79,500. The property appraised at $79,000. They agreed to pay a 1 percent loan origination fee. How much did they pay in origination fees?
    A. $790
    B. $970
    C. $975
    D. $795

27. Peg's offer was accepted. Her lender agreed to a 90 percent loan-to-value ratio with an interest rate of 7 percent. With an annual interest of $17,640, what was the loan amount?
    A. $176,400
    B. $252,000
    C. $280,000
    D. $290,000

Intermediate Level

28. The semiannual interest paid on a loan was $4,387.50. If the interest rate is 6.5 percent, what was the loan amount?
    A. $67,500
    B. $135,000
    C. $270,000
    D. $540,000

29. Maggie is paid 45 percent of the origination fee that her company charges. She negotiated a reverse mortgage and her company was paid 2 percent of the appraised value of $190,000. How much as Maggie paid?
    A. $1,710
    B. $3,800
    C. $5,200
    D. $6,400

30. What is the rate of interest if the mortgagor makes quarterly interest payments of $1,340.63 on a $65,000 loan?
    A. 2.06 percent
    B. 8.25 percent
    C. 7.75 percent
    D. 9.25 percent

31. To secure a $100,000 loan, the buyer paid $3,000 in discount points and the seller paid $2,000 in discount points. How many points were charged?
    A. 3
    B. 2
    C. 5
    D. 4

32. A savings and loan agreed to make a $65,000 mortgage at 8 percent interest for 30 years and charged three points to negotiate the loan. What was the effective yield to the lender?
    A. 8.375 percent
    B. 8.735 percent
    C. 8.25 percent
    D. 8.35 percent

33. The lender negotiated a $55,000 loan and charged three discount points. What was the cash outflow of the lender?
    A. $56,560
    B. $56,650
    C. $53,530
    D. $53,350

Advanced Level

34. One lender charges 6.5 percent interest and the second lender charges 7 percent. How much money will the borrower save the first year on a $150,000 loan if he goes with the first lender?
    A. $500
    B. $650
    C. $750
    D. $850

35. The buyers secured an $82,000 loan at 9.25 percent interest for 30 years. Their monthly payment is $674.59. How much of their first payment will be applied to the principal balance?
    A. $42.51
    B. $64.51
    C. $632.08
    D. $785.55

36. The listing price of a property was $135,000. The buyer made an offer of 90 percent of the listing price, which was accepted by the sellers. The property appraised for $135,000, and the buyers secured an 85 percent loan at 9 percent interest for 30 years. How much interest will be paid in the first payment?
    A. $774.56
    B. $747.56
    C. $860.62
    D. $839.24

37. This month's interest payment is $585.70. If the buyer secured a 90 percent loan at an 8.75 percent annual rate of interest, what was the sale price?
    A. $80,325
    B. $80,235
    C. $89,250
    D. $89,500

38. A borrower secured an $80,000 loan at 8.25 percent interest, and the lender's cash outflow was $77,600. What was the effective yield to the lender?
    A. 8.50 percent
    B. 8.625 percent
    C. 8.375 percent
    D. 8.85 percent

PROPERTY TAX MATH FORMULAS

The calculation of real estate property taxes involves two math formulas. Taxes are computed on the assessed value, which is a percentage of the market value. The assessed value is then multiplied by the tax rate to give the annual property tax.

> Example: The market value of a property is $70,000 and it is assessed at 40 percent of the market value. If the tax rate is $5.50 per $100, what is the annual property tax?

The word *per* in a math question means divide. Thus, $5.50 ÷ $100 = 0.055 tax rate.

$$\frac{\$28,000 \text{ Assessed Value}}{\$70,000 \mid 40\%}$$

Market Value × Assessment Rate

$$\frac{\$1,540 \text{ Annual Property Taxes}}{\$28,000 \mid 0.055}$$

Assessed Value × Tax Rate

Market Value × Assessment Rate = Assessed Value

Assessed Value ÷ Market Value = Assessment Rate

Assessed Value ÷ Assessment Rate = Market Value

Assessed Value × Tax Rate = Annual Property Taxes

Annual Property Taxes ÷ Assessed Value = Tax Rate

Annual Property Taxes ÷ Tax Rate = Assessed Value

The above formulas can also use the appraised value instead of the market value of the property.

The tax rate can also be expressed as mills, which means 1/1,000 of a dollar. Thus, whenever you see the tax rate expressed as mills, divide that number by 1,000.

> Example: If the tax rate is 55 mills, that means 55 ÷ 1,000 = 0.055 for the tax rate. If the tax rate is 555 mills, that means 555 ÷ 1,000 = 0.555 for the tax rate.

PROPERTY TAX QUESTIONS

Beginner Level

39. Jimmy's property appraised for $125,000. If the assessment rate is 100 percent and the tax rate is $1 per $100, what are the annual property taxes?
    A. $1,250
    B. $1,520
    C. $1,350
    D. $1,550

Intermediate Level

40. If the market value of a property is $169,000, it is assessed at 35 percent, and the tax rate is $4.25 per $100, what are the monthly property taxes?
    A. $2,513.88
    B. $2,531.88
    C. $409.49
    D. $209.49

41. The appraised value of a property is $52,350. It is assessed at 38 percent of the appraised value and the tax rate is 95 mills. What are the quarterly property taxes?
    A. $472.45
    B. $1,889.83
    C. $1,998.83
    D. $1,589.83

Advanced Level

42. The market value of a property is $65,000 and is assessed for 45 percent of its value. If the owner's semiannual tax bill was $511.88, what was the tax rate per $100?
    A. $3.50
    B. 350 mills
    C. $1.75
    D. 175 mills

43. Mr. and Mrs. Homeowner received a semi-annual tax bill of $984.38. Property in the jurisdiction is assessed at one-fourth the market value. If the tax rate is $4.50 per $100, what is the estimated market value of the property?
    A. $43,750
    B. $175,000
    C. $195,000
    D. $53,750

APPRAISAL MATH FORMULAS

The appraisal formulas reviewed in this section are the income, the cost, and the gross rent multiplier approaches to appraising. This section also includes a review of capital gains, appreciation, and depreciation of property.

The income approach to appraising is used to convert the annual net operating income of investment property into a value by dividing it by the capitalization rate.

Please note that the appraiser will use the *market rent*, which is also known as the *economic rent*, to determine the potential gross income. The market rent is the rental income that real estate could command in the market at any given time versus *contract rent*, which is the income generated under the current lease contract. An appraiser has two options for computing the value of the property using the income approach to appraising. In the first example, the formula is

Potential Gross Income + Additional Income – Vacancy Rate =
Effective Gross Income

Example: Three apartments rent for $450 per month, three for $500 per month, and two for $550 per month. There is a 5 percent vacancy rate, $300 in monthly expenses, and $125 per month additional income. If the owner wants a 10 percent return on her investment, how much can she pay for the property?

$$3 \times \$450 \times 12 = \$16,200$$
$$3 \times \$500 \times 12 = \$18,000$$
$$2 \times \$550 \times 12 = \underline{\$13,200}$$

$47,400 Potential Gross Income

$$\$125 \times 12 = \underline{+\quad 1,500 \text{ Additional Income}}$$

$48,900

$$\underline{-\quad 5\% \text{ Vacancy Rate}}$$

$46,455 Effective Gross Income

$$\$300 \times 12 = \underline{-\quad 3,600 \text{ Expenses}}$$

$42,855 Annual Net Operating Income

$42,855 Annual Net Operating Income ÷

$428,550	10%
Value	Cap Rate

The second option is to use the following formula:

Potential Gross Income – Vacancy Rate + Additional Income =
Effective Gross Income

$$3 \times \$450 \times 12 = \$16,200$$
$$3 \times \$500 \times 12 = \$18,000$$
$$2 \times \$550 \times 12 = \underline{\$13,200}$$

$$\$47,400 \text{ Potential Gross Income}$$
$$-\quad \underline{5\% \text{ Vacancy Rate}}$$
$$\$45,030$$
$$\$125 \times 12 = \quad \underline{+ 1,500 \text{ Additional Income}}$$
$$\$46,530 \text{ Effective Gross Income}$$
$$\$300 \times 12 = \quad \underline{- 3,600 \text{ Expenses}}$$
$$\$42,930 \text{ Annual Net Operating Income}$$

$42,930 Annual Net Operating Income ÷	
$429,300	10%
Value	Cap Rate

In this chapter review, we will use the first formula to compute the value under the income approach to appraising. Please check with your instructor to determine which method is used in your state.

The cost approach to appraising is used to determine the value of special-purpose properties, but it can also be used to appraise new buildings.

Example: The replacement cost of a building is $125,000. It has an annual depreciation of 10 percent, and a site value of $35,000. What is the value of the property?

$$\$125,000 \quad \text{Replacement Cost}$$
$$-\quad \underline{10\% \quad \text{Depreciation Rate}}$$
$$\$112,500$$
$$\underline{+ 35,000 \quad \text{Site Value}}$$
$$\$147,500 \quad \text{Property Value}$$

Replacement Cost
– Depreciation Rate
+ Site Value
Property Value

The gross rent multiplier formula is used to appraise small income-producing properties, such as a single-family home or duplex that is investment property (use monthly rent). If this method is used to determine the value of a small shopping center, it is called the *gross income multiplier* and the annual rent is used.

Example: An appraiser has determined that the gross rent multiplier of a house that rents for $650 is 110. What is the value of the property?

$$\frac{\text{\$71,500 Value}}{110 \quad | \quad \text{\$650}}$$

×

Gross Rent Multiplier × Rent

Gross Rent Multiplier × Monthly Rent = Value
Value ÷ Gross Rent Multiplier = Monthly Rent
Value ÷ Monthly Rent = Gross Rent Multiplier

Gross Income Multiplier × Annual Rent = Value
Value ÷ Gross Income Multiplier = Annual Rent
Value ÷ Annual Rent = Gross Income Multiplier

A capital gain is the profit that an owner makes when selling an asset, such as real estate.

Example: Harry purchased a property for $90,000. He made $22,500 worth of improvements. Three years later, he sold the property for $130,000 and paid a 6 percent commission. What were his capital gains on the sale?

Step 1
$ 90,000   Original Investment
+ 22,500   Improvements
$112,500   Adjusted Basis

Step 2
$$\frac{\text{\$7,800 Commission \$}}{\text{\$130,000} \quad | \quad 6\%}$$
Sales Price × Commission %

Step 3
$130,000 – 7,800 = $122,200 Adjusted (Net) Sale Price (The sale price minus selling expenses equals the adjusted sale price)

Step 4
$122,200   Adjusted Sale Price
–112,500   Adjusted Basis
$ 9,700   Capital Gains

Original Investment
+ Improvements
Adjusted Basis

Selling Price
– Selling Expenses
Adjusted Sale Price

Adjusted Sale Price
– Adjusted Basis
Capital Gains

The above formula is for computing the capital gains on an owner's principal place of residence. Under the new tax laws, which became effective May 7, 1997, first-time homebuyers may make a penalty-free withdrawal of up to $10,000 from their tax-deferred individual retirement fund or IRA for a down payment. Homeowners whose gain exceeds the maximum for exclusion must pay tax on the amount over the exclusion ($500,000 for married homeowners who file jointly, $250,000 for single filers).The exclusion can be taken more than once. However, the home must have been used as a principal place of residence for two of the preceding five years.

Appraisal math may deal with the appreciation or depreciation of property value.

Example: Mr. and Mrs. Homeowner paid $80,000 for their property. This year, their property appreciated in value 10 percent. What is the value of the property today?

$88,000 Appreciated Value

Original	100%
Investment	+ 10% Appreciation Rate
$80,000	× 110% Appreciated %

Appreciated Value

Original	100%
Investment	+ Appreciation Rate
$80,000	× Appreciated %

Example: Mr. and Mrs. Homeowner paid $80,000 for their property. This year their property depreciated in value 10 percent. What is the value of their property?

$72,000 Depreciated Value

Original	100%
Investment	− 10% Appreciation Rate
$80,000	× 90%Depreciated %

Depreciated Value

Original	100%
Investment	− Depreciation Rate
$80,000	× Depreciated %

APPRAISAL QUESTIONS

Beginner Level

44. An apartment building with a $90,000 net operating income and an 8 percent cap rate has a value of
    A. $1,000,000.
    B. $1,125,000.
    C. $1,500,000.
    D. $1,720,000.

45. An apartment building has a semiannual net income of $48,000 and has been appraised for $1,250,000. What is the cap rate?
    A. 3.84 percent
    B. 4.38 percent
    C. 7.68 percent
    D. 7.86 percent

46. Last year Don's apartment building had a effective gross income of $55,575 and expenses of $5,500. If the cap rate is 10 percent, what is the value?
    A. $555,555
    B. $555,750
    C. $500,000
    D. $500,750

47. If the gross rent multiplier of a property is 112 and the rent is $600 monthly, what is the value of the property?
    A. $76,200
    B. $62,700
    C. $27,600
    D. $67,200

48. Three years ago, Keith paid $150,000 for a three-bedroom home. The property has appreciated at 5 percent each year. What is the value of the property today?
    A. $172,500
    B. $173,644
    C. $175,464
    D. $179,300

49. Two years ago, Ashley paid $175,000 for a house. Since that time, the property has depreciated 3 percent each year. What is the value of the property today?
    A. $164,500
    B. $164,658
    C. $185,500
    D. $185,657

Intermediate Level

50. The replacement cost of a building is $250,000. It has an annual depreciation of 8 percent, a site value of $50,000, and annual taxes of $3,950. What is the value of the property?
    A. $230,000
    B. $276,050
    C. $280,000
    D. $283,950

51. A building has a semiannual effective gross income of $250,000. If the annual expenses are 20 percent of the effective gross income, what is the net operating income?
    A. $500,000
    B. $200,000
    C. $100,000
    D. $400,000

52. Three years ago, Ms. Owner paid $165,000 for her property. During her period of ownership, she added a family room valued at $16,500 and $10,000 worth of other improvements. If she sells the property for $240,000 and pays a 7 percent commission, what capital gains may she exclude?
    A. $25,300
    B. $31,700
    C. $37,100
    D. $48,500

53. Mr. Howard purchased a home for $250,000. He added a tennis court at a cost of $10,000. Two years later, he sold his property for $325,000 and paid a 7 percent commission plus $250 in attorney fees. If he buys another property for $350,000, how much capital gains will he exclude?
    A. $22,750
    B. $42,000
    C. $42,250
    D. $42,520

Advanced Level

54. The rent collected in a 12-unit building is as follows: three apartments, $550; three apartments, $600; three apartments, $650. There is a vacancy rate of 4 percent, additional annual income of $2,400, and annual expenses of $5,000. With a cap rate of 9 percent, how much should the buyer pay for this property?
    A. $661,244
    B. $698,534
    C. $717,866
    D. $773,422

55. Five apartments rent for $550 per month, and five others for $600 per month. There is an 8 percent vacancy rate and monthly expenses of $250. If a buyer wants to yield an 8 percent return, what should he pay for the property?
    A. $790,375
    B. $765,000
    C. $756,000
    D. $790,735

56. A property is now worth $117,978. If it has appreciated 6 percent each year for the past two years, what was the original investment?
    A. $111,300
    B. $105,000
    C. $104,245
    D. $110,899

57. A property is now worth $98,250. If it has depreciated in value 5 percent each year for the past two years, what was the original investment?
    A. $103,421
    B. $103,241
    C. $108,864
    D. $108,320

SETTLEMENT MATH FORMULAS

To prorate an expense means to divide or distribute it proportionately. The settlement sheet is a history of the buyer's and seller's debits and credits in a sales transaction. If the entry is a debit, the party owes it at the closing table. If the entry is a credit, the party receives it at the closing table. The following worksheet shows the normal entries on a settlement sheet. Discount points can be paid by buyer or seller, so read the question carefully.

Settlement Date: February 18, 2005	Buyer's Statement		Seller's Statement	
	Debit	Credit	Debit	Credit
Sales Price	DB			CS
Earnest Money Deposit		CB		
New Loan		CB		
Interest—New Loan	DB			
Loan Balance			DS	
Assumed Loan		CB	DS	
Interest—Assumed Loan	CB		DS	
Purchase-Money Mortgage		CB	DS	
Interest—Purchase-Money Mortgage	DB			CS
Commission			DS	
Property Taxes—Paid in Advance	DB			CS
Property Taxes—Paid in Arrears		CB	DS	
Assumed Insurance Policy	DB			CS
Credit Report	DB			
Origination Fees	DB			
Survey	DB			
Title Expenses	DB			
Appraisal Fee	DB			
Recording Fee	DB			
Transfer Fee			DS	

Discount points (Could be a DS or DB. Read the question to determine how it is to be entered.)

A 360-day or 365-day year may be used to to compute interest, taxes, insurance, and so forth. Please check to determine how they are computed in your state.

To compute proration problems, use a 360-day year, with each month having 30 days, unless the question states otherwise. Each proration question has a beginning date, prorate date, and ending date.

- The beginning date is always January 1, unless the question states otherwise.

- The prorate date is normally the closing date, but can be the date of the sale.

- The ending date is December 30, unless the question states otherwise.

■ If paid in arrears, count from the beginning date to the prorate date, then debit the seller and credit the buyer.

■ If paid in advance, count from the prorate date to the ending date, then credit the seller and debit the buyer.

■ When the borrower is assuming the loan, the seller will owe from the first of the month through the closing date. The buyer will owe till the end of the month.
Example: Closing date – August 14 (365-day year)
   The seller will owe interest from August 1 through 14, or 14 days.
   The buyer will owe 17 days' interest. (31 – 14 = 17 days)

■ When the borrower is securing a *new loan*, the borrower will owe interest from the closing date through the end of that month.
Example: Closing date – September 23 (365-day year)
   The buyer will owe 7 days' interest at the closing table.
   (30 – 23 = 7 days)

Principal and interest payments are made in arrears. If the buyer's loan closed on September 23, the first PI payment would not be due until November 1. The interest for the month of October would be paid in the November 1 payment.

The following chart can be used if a 365-day year is needed to work the question.

Month	Number of Days	Month	Number of Days
January	31	July	31
February	28*	August	31
March	31	September	30
April	30	October	31
May	31	November	30
June	30	December	31

*Remember, if the question states that it is a leap year, February will have 29 days.

Example: The property taxes of $1,250 have been paid for the year. If the property closes on June 23, how much is credited to the seller on the settlement sheet?

Step 1   January 1   The taxes have been paid, so count from the prorate
         June 23   date to the ending date and credit the seller, debit
                          the buyer.
         December 30   June 23 to June 30   =   7 days
                          July through December = 180 days
                          Total   = 187 days CS, DB

Step 2 $1,250 ÷ 360 = $ 3.47 daily tax rate
Step 3   × 187 days
                          $ 648.89 CS, DB

SETTLEMENT MATH QUESTIONS

(Use a 360-day year unless the question says otherwise.)

Beginner Level

58. On January 1 the seller paid the $2,345 in taxes for the current year. If he sold the property on June 23 of that same year, how much would he be credited at closing? (Use a 360-day year.)
    A. $1,158.78
    B. $1,218.10
    C. $1,293.53
    D. $1,772.50

59. Mr. and Mrs. Rinehart live in a county were taxes are paid in arrears and 360 days are used to compute the property tax bill. They sold their house on April 13. If the annual tax bill is $3,355, how much will be credited the buyer on the settlement statement for taxes for this year?
    A. $946.57
    B. $959.96
    C. $2,407.78
    D. $2,441.84

Intermediate Level

60. Semiannual property taxes of $450 were paid only for the first half of the year. The property sold on July 11 and closed on September 19. If the taxes were prorated between the buyer and seller as of the date of sale, which of the following is TRUE?
    A. $252.50 CS, DB
    B. $252.50 DS, CB
    C. $27.50 DS, CB
    D. $497.50 CS, DB

61. A buyer negotiated a $75,000 loan at 8 percent interest for 30 years, with the first payment due in arrears on April 1. If the closing takes place on February 26, how much interest must the buyer pay on the day of closing?
    A. $566.78
    B. $656.78
    C. $56.68
    D. $66.68

Advanced Level

62. Mr. Meade's offer of $295,000 was accepted and he secured an 80 percent loan at 7 percent for 25 years. The closing took place on January 5 and his first PITI payment is due March 1. Using a 365-day year, how much interest would Mr. Meade be debited on the closing statement?
    A. $226.30
    B. $1,176.76
    C. $1,276.67
    D. $1,652.00

63. The buyer assumed a loan of $50,000 at 8.25 percent interest. Payments are due on the first of the month, in arrears. The last payment was made on April 1 and the closing took place on April 20. Which of the following is TRUE?
    A. $119.60 CS, DB
    B. $119.60 DB, CS
    C. $229.20 CS, DB
    D. $229.20 DS, CB

64. The buyer had a 20 percent down payment on a property she purchased for $89,500. She must also pay a 1 percent origination fee, $350 for title insurance, and one discount point. How much money will the buyer owe at the closing?
    A. $18,966
    B. $19,682
    C. $17,423
    D. $20,350

65. After the borrower made his payment on September 1, his loan balance was $12,259. His monthly payment is $124.34 per month paid in arrears on the first of the month. The interest rate on the loan is 9 percent. On October 1, he paid the lender for the October 1 payment, then paid off the entire mortgage balance. If the prepayment penalty was 2 percent, his prepayment penalty charge was approximately
    A. $244.53.
    B. $245.18.
    C. $232.40.
    D. $247.93.

INSURANCE PRORATION

Sometimes the buyer assumes the seller's insurance policy. Insurance is always paid in advance; thus, this entry is a debit to the buyer and a credit to the seller. The following shows a very simple way to compute the number of days to prorate when more than one calendar year is involved.

■ The beginning date is the date the policy was written.

■ The prorate date is the closing date.

■ The ending date will be for the term of the policy and will end at midnight, one day prior to the date the policy was written.

Example: If a one-year policy was written on June 15, 2005, it would end at midnight 365 days later.

Beginning Date	June 15, 2005
Prorate Date	November 23, 2005
Ending Date	June 14, 2006
Nov. 23–30	= 7 days
December–May	= 180 days
June	= 14 days
Total	202 days

$425 ÷ 360 = $1.1805 × 201 = $237.28 CS, DB

INSURANCE PRORATION QUESTIONS

(Use a 360-day year unless the question says otherwise.)

Beginner Level

66. Amy purchased a new home. Her one-year premium began on September 14, 2005 and cost $504. Her company transferred her. The buyer assumed her policy at the closing on January 25, 2006. How much will be credited to Amy on the closing statement?
    A. $183.40
    B. $138.40
    C. $320.60
    D. $319.20

Advanced Level

67. The lender required Tajasi to insure 100 percent of the value of improvements. The appraiser determihed her property value, including the site, to be $335,000. The site was 20 percent of the value. Tajasi purchased a two-year insurance premium that began on the closing date of November 15, 2006. The premium was $879. Her company transferred her July 11, 2007, and the buyer assumed her policy. Which of the following will be entered on the HUD-1 statement?
    A. $288.13 CS, DB
    B. $288.13 DB, CS
    C. $589.26 CS, DB
    D. $590.87 DB, CS

AREA MATH FORMULAS

The following are the formulas and rules that you must know to compute area math questions.

■ The area of a rectangle or square is found by multiplying length × width.

■ The area of a triangle is found by multiplying ½ base × height.

■ The area of a circle is found by multiplying π (3.1416) × radius squared.

■ The area of a trapezoid is found by adding the parallel lines, dividing by 2, and then multiplying by the height.

■ To compute square feet, multiply length × width.

■ To compute cubic feet, multiply length × width × height.

■ There are 9 square feet in 1 square yard.

■ To convert square feet to square yards, divide by 9.

■ There are 27 cubic feet in 1 cubic yard.

■ To convert cubic feet to cubic yards, divide by 27.

■ To convert square feet to acres, divide by 43,560.

■ To convert acres to square feet, multiply by 43,560.

■ There are 5,280 feet in 1 mile.

■ The front footage is the first dimension in a lot size.

Example: A lot measures 200' × 250' and sells for $55,000. Another lot in that same area measuring 150' × 175' would likely sell for what price?

Step 1   A = 200' × 250'
         A = 50,000 square feet

Step 2 $55,000 ÷ 50,000 = $1.10 per sq. ft.

Step 3   A = 150' × 175'
         A = 26,250 square feet

Step 4   26,250 × $1.10 = $28,875

Example: How many square feet are in a triangular-shaped area that has a base of 60' and a height of 130'?

A = ½(b) × h

Step 1   A = ½(60') × 130'
         A = 30' × 130'
         A = 3,900 square feet

130'

60'

Example: A circle has a diameter of 90'. How many square feet does it contain? (The radius is one-half of the diameter.)

$$A = \pi r2$$

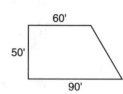

Step 1   A = 3.1416 × 45' × 45'
          A = 6,361.74 square feet

How many square yards does it contain?

6,361.74 ÷ 9 = 706.86 square yards

Example: The two parallel sides of a trapezoid are 60' and 90'. The height is 50'. How many square feet does it contain?

A = [(parallel lines) ÷ 2] × h

Step 1   A = [(60' + 90') ÷ 2] × 50'
          A = 75' × 50'
          A = 3,750 square feet

How many acres does it contain?

3,750 ÷ 43,560 = 0.0861 acres

Example: A storage room that measures 20' × 30' × 10' contains how many cubic feet?

V = L × W × H

Step 1   V = 20' × 30' × 10'
          V = 6,000 cubic feet

How many cubic yards does it contain?

6,000 ÷ 27 = 222.22 cubic yards

AREA MATH QUESTIONS

Beginner Level

68. If a circular property has a diameter of 50'
    and costs $120 per square foot, what is the
    cost of the property?
    A. $235,620
    B. $942,480
    C. $1,235,620
    D. $2,356,200

69. The N½ of the SW¼ of the NE¼ sold for
    $2,500 per acre. What was the selling price?
    A. $10,000
    B. $20,000
    C. $40,000
    D. $50,000

70. A lot contains 9/10 of an acre. What is the
    depth of the lot if the front measures 150'?
    A. 216.36'
    B. 261.36'
    C. 322.67'
    D. 323.67'

Intermediate Level

71. A two-story house measures 25' × 50'. A one-
    story family room was added that measures
    20' × 20'. At a cost of $9.95 per square yard
    for carpet and $2.50 per square yard for
    installation, how much will it cost to carpet
    the house and family room?
    A. $2,282.50
    B. $36,105.00
    C. $20,542.50
    D. $4,011.67

72. The rooms in Sandy's house measures as
    follows: living room, 20' × 25'; dining room,
    18' × 20'; bedroom, 14' × 26'; bedroom, 15'
    × 15'; bedroom, 12' × 14'. The carpet she has
    selected cost $9.95 per square yard. How
    much more will it cost her to carpet the entire
    house?
    A. $732.39
    B. $836.91
    C. $950.77
    D. $1,787.68

73. A rectangular lot measures 200' × 300'.
    Property in the area is selling for $150,000
    per acre. If the broker charges 8 percent, how
    much is she paid?
    A. $16,529
    B. $15,290
    C. $16,730
    D. $19,243

74. A building measures 30' × 80' × 15'. B made
    an offer of $35 per square foot on the prop-
    erty. The owner made a counteroffer of $2.75
    per cubic foot. How much more will it cost B
    if he accepts the counteroffer?
    A. $18,000
    B. $15,000
    C. $17,000
    D. $16,000

Advanced Level

75. A buyer purchased a property that is one mile
    square and another that measures 511.23'
    × 511.23'. At a cost of $2,000 an acre, how
    much did she pay for the property?
    A. $1,291,999
    B. $1,921,999
    C. $1,733,435
    D. $1,373,435

76. How many cubic yards of concrete must a
    builder buy to pour a sidewalk that measures
    45' × 3.25' and is five inches thick?
    A. 60.9375
    B. 2.2571
    C. 0.4167
    D. 6.7708

77. Using the dimensions in the following diagram, what is the approximate cost to purchase at $4,000 per acre?
    A. $3,214
    B. $6,428
    C. $9,213
    D. $12,856

78. How many square feet of living area are in the following house?
    A. 2,087.5
    B. 2,150.0
    C. 2,775.0
    D. 2,990.5

ADDITIONAL PRACTICE

Beginner Level

79. Mr. Stewart's home is valued at $250,000 and is insured for 80 percent of its value. The one-year insurance policy was purchased on January 12, 2005 at a cost of $550. The property was sold and the buyer assumed his policy on December 23, 2006. How much will Mr. Stewart be credited at the closing?
    A. $522.50
    B. $432.70
    C. $27.50
    D. $29.03

80. The seller's net after paying a 6 percent commission was $355,000. The approximate sale price of the property was
    A. $377,660.
    B. $379,850.
    C. $376,300.
    D. $381,720.

81. Agent Mary works for XYZ Realty in Illinois and she referred a buyer to Agent Paul, who works for ABC Realty in Georgia. For the referral, Mary is to receive 25 percent of Paul's commission. The buyer purchased a $350,000 home and the 7 percent commission was split as follows: listing broker, 2 percent; listing agent, 2 percent; selling broker, 1.5 percent; selling agent, 1.5 percent. How much was Mary paid for the referral?
    A. $24,500.00
    B. $7,000.00
    C. $5,250.50
    D. $1,312.50

82. Agent Keith works for JKJ Realty in North Dakota and she referred a buyer to Agent Kenzie, who works for ASD Realty in South Dakota. Keith's check was for $2,062.50 or 25 percent of Kenzie's portion. The 7 percent commission was split as follows: listing broker, 2 percent; listing agent, 2 percent; selling broker, 1.5 percent; selling agent, 1.5 percent. What was the sale price of the property?
    A. $500,000
    B. $550,000
    C. $600,000
    D. $650,000

83. A property was listed for $450,000. Sam's offer of 95 percent of the list price was accepted. He had a 20 percent down payment and secured a 30-year fixed rate loan at 6.75% interest. How much interest will he pay the first month of the loan?
    A. $1,923.75
    B. $3,847.50
    C. $7,695.00
    D. $23,085.00

84. Building B had a net operating income of $75,230, expenses of $4,900, additional income of $2,500, and a cap rate of 8 percent. What is the effective gross income?
    A. $77,730
    B. $79,500
    C. $80,130
    D. $82,630

85. A lot is 275 feet deep. It contains ⅔ of an acre. What is the length of the lot?
    A. 158.4'
    B. 106.5'
    C. 290.04'
    D. 105.6'

Intermediate Level

86. Four years ago, Carl purchased a property for $148,000. For three years, it appreciated 4 percent each year, but the fourth year it depreciated 4 percent. What was the approximate value of the property at the end of the fourth year?
    A. $159,020
    B. $159,130
    C. $159,820
    D. $159,900

87. Carol paid $135,500 for her property. Taxes in her community are assessed at 80 percent of the market value. If the tax rate is 700 mills per $100, how much will be escrowed for taxes for her monthly PITI payment?
    A. $63.00
    B. $63.23
    C. $75.60
    D. $75.88

88. Mr. and Mrs. Lloyd pay $137.81 in monthly property taxes. If the tax rate is $3.50 per $100 and the assessment rate is 35 percent, what is the value of the property?
    A. $153,998.69
    B. $143,997.45
    C. $166,532.72
    D. $134,997.54

89. An agent is managing a 15-unit apartment building and is paid 9 percent of the gross income. She leases five apartments for $500, five for $550, and five for $600. There is a 3 percent vacancy rate and additional income of $450 per month. The monthly operating expenses are $1,749 and the owner is generating an 8 percent return on the investment. What is the effective gross income on the building?
    A. $99,000
    B. $96,030
    C. $80,442
    D. $101,430

90. Four units are renting for $450 each per month. There is a 5 percent vacancy factor, and annual expenses are $3,547. The owner wants an 8 percent return on her investment and the property has additional monthly income of $464. What is the effective gross income of the property?
    A. $21,796
    B. $21,976
    C. $20,984
    D. $26,088

91. Mr. and Mrs. Ben-Hur secured a loan with a 75 percent loan-to-value ratio. The interest rate was 7.125 percent and the term was for 30 years. The first month's interest payment was $477.82. What was the appraised value of the property?
    A. $107,300
    B. $80,475
    C. $103,700
    D. $79,239

92. Ms. Feldkamp wants to receive a net of $82,000 after selling her home. She has an existing mortgage of $32,500 and will have selling expenses of $444. If the broker is to receive a 7 percent commission, what is the LEAST offer that she can accept for the property?
    A. $122,990.08
    B. $122,515.08
    C. $123,595.70
    D. $123,959.70

93. A homeowner has a property valued at $125,000 that is assessed at 35 percent of its value. If the local tax rate is 6,400 mills per $100 of the assessed value, what are the monthly taxes?
    A. $280.00
    B. $140.33
    C. $480.00
    D. $233.33

Advanced Level

94. Ms. Wilson offered 90 percent of the $120,900 list price of a property. Her offer was accepted and the lender agreed to negotiate an 80 percent loan at 8 percent interest for 30 years. Ms. Wilson had a $5,000 earnest money deposit, paid $350 for title expenses, $250 attorney fees, and had other expenses of $749. How much money does she need to close on the property?
    - A. $18,111
    - B. $23,111
    - C. $10,159
    - D. $15,159

95. Mr. Smiley sold his property for $99,500. He paid a real estate commission of 6 percent, paid an attorney $250, paid a transfer tax of $99.50, paid his existing mortgage of $50,140, and agreed to a purchase-money mortgage of $10,000. What were his net proceeds at the closing?
    - A. $43,050.40
    - B. $33,040.50
    - C. $53,040.50
    - D. $33,050.40

96. An owner of a fourplex has one unit that rents for $450 a month, one unit that rents for $475 per month, and two units that rent for $500 per month. The vacancy rate is 4 percent and the monthly expenses average $350. If the return on the property is 10 percent, what is the value?
    - A. $218,260
    - B. $118,260
    - C. $189,760
    - D. $179,760

97. A house is now worth $105,000. The lot is now worth $50,000. If the house depreciated 4 percent each year for the past two years and the lot appreciated 6 percent each year for the past two years, what was the approximate combined original value of the house and lot?
    - A. $156,544
    - B. $113,932
    - C. $109,375
    - D. $170,112

98. Mr. and Mrs. First Time Homebuyers purchased a property for $79,000. They had to make a 10 percent down payment, and they negotiated a 30-year fixed rate loan for 7 percent. They paid $1,000 in earnest money, a 0.5 percent origination fee, $670 in other closing costs, and $25 per month for hazard insurance. How much cash did the buyer need to bring to closing?
    - A. $8,225.50
    - B. $8,432.50
    - C. $7,950.50
    - D. $7,225.50

99. Ms. Singleton assumed the seller's insurance policy on June 24, 2006. The owner paid $649.50 for a three-year policy on April 30, 2005. Which of the following is TRUE? (Use a 360-day year.)
    - A. $249.90 DS, CB
    - B. $249.90 CB, DS
    - C. $399.00 CS, DB
    - D. $399.00 DB, CS

100. On September 20, 2006, Ms. Huwel closed on her new home, for which she paid $160,000, and she insured 80 percent of its value. Her premium on the two-year policy was $3.75 per $1,000. On November 11, 2007, she sold the property, and the buyer assumed the policy. How much will the buyer be debited at the closing, using a 360-day year?
    - A. $480.00
    - B. $273.99
    - C. $205.34
    - D. $274.01

ANSWERS

1. **(B)**

$$\frac{\$15{,}750}{\$225{,}000 \mid 7\%}$$
$$\times$$

$$\frac{\$12{,}375}{\$225{,}000 \mid 5.5\%}$$
$$\times$$

$$\begin{array}{r} \$15{,}750 \\ -\,12{,}375 \\ \hline \mathbf{\$3{,}375} \end{array}$$

2. **(C)**

$$\frac{\$21{,}000 \div}{\mathbf{\$300{,}000} \mid 7\%}$$

3. **(D)**

2% + 1.5% = 3.5% Anne's share
6% − 3.5% = 2.5% Broker's share

$$\frac{\mathbf{\$4{,}375}}{\$175{,}000 \mid 2.5\%}$$
$$\times$$

4. **(D)**

$8,225 \times 2 = \$16,450$ total commission paid

$$\frac{\div\,\$16{,}450}{\$235{,}000 \mid \mathbf{0.07\ or\ 7\%}}$$

5. **(B)**

$$\frac{\$7{,}500}{\$125{,}000 \mid 6\%}$$
$$\times$$

$$\frac{\mathbf{\$3{,}000}}{\$7{,}500 \mid 40\%}$$
$$\times$$

6. **(C)**

7% − 2% − 1.5% = 3.5% to the broker

$$\frac{\mathbf{\$6{,}650}}{\$190{,}000 \mid 3.5\%}$$
$$\times$$

7. **(A)**

$$\frac{\$12{,}750}{\$425{,}000 \mid 3\%}$$
$$\times$$

$12,750 + 2,995 = \mathbf{\$15,745}$

8. **(C)**

$$\frac{\$6{,}000}{\$100{,}000 \mid 6\%}$$
$$\times$$

$$\frac{\$5{,}000}{\$100{,}000 \mid 5\%}$$
$$\times$$

$$\frac{\$2{,}000}{\$50{,}000 \mid 4\%}$$
$$\times$$

$$\begin{array}{r} \$\ 6{,}000 \\ 5{,}000 \\ +\ 2{,}000 \\ \hline \mathbf{\$13{,}000} \end{array}$$

9. **(D)**

$2,500 × 2 = $5,000

$5,000 ÷ **$71,428.57** | 7%

10. **(D)**

$3,500 ÷ $5,933.33 | 60%

÷ $5,833.33 $83,333 | **0.07 or 7%**

11. **(A)**

100% – 6% = 94% Seller's percent

$470,000 ÷ **$500,000** | 94%

12. **(B)**

100% – 6% = 94% Seller's percent

$200,000 ÷ **$212,756.95** | 94%

13. **(D)**

100%	$149,850
– 6%	+ 550
94%	$150,400

$150,400 ÷ **$160,000** | 94%

14. **(A)**

100%	$20,000
– 7%	35,250
93%	+ 400
	$55,650

$55,650 ÷ **$59,838.71** | 93%

15. **(C)**

100%	$104,500
– 6.5%	+ 12%
93.5%	$117,040

$117,040 ÷ **$125,176.47** | 93.5%

16. **(D)**

25' × 50' = 1,250 sq. ft.
1,250 × $15.50 = $19,375 Annual rent

$1,356.25 $19,375 | 7%
×

17. **(B)**

$1,200
× 12
$14,400

$1,152 $14,400 | 8%
×

18. **(A)**

$$\$550 \times 12 \times 5 = \$\ 33,000$$
$$\$600 \times 12 \times 5 = \$\ 36,000$$
$$\$650 \times 12 \times 5 = \underline{\$\ 39,000}$$
$$\$108,000$$

$$\begin{array}{c} \mathbf{\$7,290} \\ \hline \$108,000 \mid 6.75\% \\ \times \end{array}$$

19. **(D)**

$$\begin{array}{r} \$1,500,000 \\ -\ 850,000 \\ \hline \$\ 650,000 \end{array}$$

$$\begin{array}{c} \$26,000 \\ \hline \$650,000 \mid 4\% \\ \times \end{array}$$

$$\$1,200 \times 12 = \$14,400$$

$$\begin{array}{r} \$26,000 \\ +\ 14,400 \\ \hline \mathbf{\$40,400} \end{array}$$

20. **(B)**

$$\$500 \times 12 \times 5 = \$\ 30,000$$
$$\$575 \times 12 \times 15 = \$103,500$$
$$\$133,500$$

$$\$133,500 \times 6 = \$801,000$$

$$\begin{array}{c} \mathbf{\$48,060} \\ \hline \$801,000 \mid 6\% \\ \times \end{array}$$

21. **(A)**

$$\begin{array}{r} 575 \\ \times\ 12 \\ \hline \$6,900 \end{array}$$

$$\begin{array}{r} \$389,250 \\ -225,000 \\ \hline \$164,250 \end{array}$$

$$\begin{array}{c} \$8,623 \\ \hline \$164,250 \mid 5.25\% \\ \times \end{array}$$

$$\begin{array}{r} \$8,623 \\ +\ 6,900 \\ \hline \mathbf{\$15,523} \end{array}$$

22. **(D)**

$$\begin{array}{r} \$\ 425 \\ \times\ 12 \\ \hline \$5,100 \end{array}$$

$$\begin{array}{r} \$9,321 \\ -5,100 \\ \hline \$4,221 \end{array}$$

$$\begin{array}{c} \$4,221 \div \\ \hline \$70,350 \mid 6\% \\ \times \end{array}$$

$$\begin{array}{r} \$175,000 \\ +\ 70,350 \\ \hline \mathbf{\$245,350} \end{array}$$

23. **(C)**

$$\$800 \times 12 = \$9,600$$

$$\begin{array}{r} \$49,600 \\ -\ 9,600 \\ \hline \$40,000 \end{array}$$

$$\begin{array}{c} \$40,000 \div \\ \hline \$1,000,000 \mid 4\% \end{array}$$

$$\begin{array}{r} \$1,000,000 \\ +\ 1,000,000 \\ \hline \mathbf{\$2,000,000} \end{array}$$

24. **(C)**

$$\begin{array}{c} \div \$131,250 \\ \hline \$175,000 \mid \mathbf{0.75\ or\ 75\%} \end{array}$$

25. **(D)**

$$\begin{array}{c} \$82,250 \div \\ \hline \mathbf{\$102,812.50} \mid 80\% \end{array}$$

26. **(A)**

$$\begin{array}{c} \mathbf{\$790} \\ \hline \$79,000 \mid 1\% \\ \times \end{array}$$

27. **(B)**

$$\frac{\$17,640 \div}{\mathbf{\$252,000} \mid 7\%}$$

28. **(B)**

$4,387.50 \times 2 = \$8,775$ annual interest

$$\frac{\$8,775 \div}{\mathbf{\$135,000} \mid 6.5\%}$$

29. **(A)**

$$\frac{\$3,800}{\$190,000 \mid 2\%} \qquad \frac{\mathbf{\$1,710}}{\$3,800 \mid 45\%}$$
$$\qquad\quad \times \qquad\qquad\qquad \times$$

30. **(B)**

$$\begin{array}{r} \$1,340.63 \\ \times \quad 4 \\ \hline \$5,362.52 \end{array} \qquad \frac{\div 5,362.52}{\$65,000 \mid \mathbf{8.25\%}}$$
$$\qquad\qquad\qquad\qquad\qquad \times$$

31. **(C)**

$$\begin{array}{r} \$3,000 \\ +2,000 \\ \hline \$5,000 \end{array} \qquad \frac{\div \$5,000}{\$100,000 \mid \mathbf{0.05 \text{ or } 5 \text{ points}}}$$

32. **(A)** $0.125 \times 3 = 0.375$
    $8\% + 0.375 = \mathbf{8.375\%}$

33. **(D)**

$$\begin{array}{r} \$55,000 \\ - \quad 3\% \\ \hline \mathbf{\$53,350} \end{array} \quad \text{or} \quad \frac{\$1,650}{\$55,000 \mid 3\%} \qquad \begin{array}{r} \$55,000 \\ - \quad 1,650 \\ \hline \mathbf{\$53,350} \end{array}$$
$$\qquad\qquad\qquad\qquad\qquad \times$$

34. **(C)**

$$\frac{\$9,750}{\$150,000 \mid 6.5\%} \qquad \frac{\$10,500}{\$150,000 \mid 7\%} \qquad \begin{array}{r} \$10,500 \\ - \quad 9,750 \\ \hline \$ \quad 750 \end{array}$$
$$\qquad\quad \times \qquad\qquad\qquad\quad \times$$

35. **(A)**

$$\frac{\$7,585}{\$82,000 \mid 9.25\%} \qquad \$7,585 \div 12 = \$632.08 \qquad \begin{array}{r} \$674.59 \\ - \quad 632.08 \\ \hline \$ \quad \mathbf{42.51} \end{array}$$
$$\qquad\quad \times$$

36. **(A)**

$$\frac{\$121,500}{\$135,000 \mid 90\%} \qquad \frac{\$103,275}{\$121,500 \mid 85\%} \qquad \begin{array}{c} \$9,294.75 \div 12 = \mathbf{\$774.56} \\ \hline \$103,275 \mid 9\% \end{array}$$
$$\qquad\quad \times \qquad\qquad\qquad\quad \times \qquad\qquad\qquad\qquad \times$$

37. **(C)**

$$\begin{array}{r} \$\ 585.75 \\ \times\ \ \ \ \ 12 \\ \hline \$7,028.40 \end{array}$$

$7,028.40 ÷	
$80,324.57	8.75%
×	

$80,324.57 ÷	
$89,249.52	90%
×	

38. **(B)**

$$\begin{array}{r} \$80,000 \\ -\ 77,600 \\ \hline \$\ 2,400 \end{array}$$

÷ 2,400	
$80,000	3 pts.
×	

$0.125 \times 3 = 0.375$
$8.25\% + 0.375 = \mathbf{8.625\%}$

39. **(A)**

$\$1 \div 100 = 0.01$ Tax rate

$1,250	
$125,000	0.01
×	

40. **(D)**

$\$4.25 \div 100 = 0.0425$

$59,150	
$169,000	35%
×	

$2,513.875 ÷ 12 = **$209.49**	
$59,150	0.0425
×	

41. **(A)**

$95 \div 1,000 = 0.095$

$19,893	
$52,350	38%
×	

$1,889.83 ÷ 4 = **$472.45**	
$19,893	0.095
×	

42. **(A)**

$29,250	
$65,000	45%
×	

$$\begin{array}{r} \$511.88 \\ \times\ \ \ \ \ 2 \\ \hline \$1,023.75 \end{array}$$

÷ $1,023.76	
$29,250	0.035

$$\begin{array}{r} 0.035 \\ \times\ 100 \\ \hline \mathbf{\$3.50} \end{array}$$

43. **(B)**

$\$4.50 \div 100 = 0.045$
$\$984.38 \times 2 = \$1,968.76$

$1,968.76 ÷	
$43,750	0.045

$43,750 ÷	
$175,000	25%

44. **(B)**

$90,000 ÷	
$1,125,000	0.08 (8%)
×	

45. **(C)**

$\$48,000 \times 2 = \$96,000$

÷ $96,000	
$1,250,000	**0.0768 or 7.68%**

46. **(D)**

$$\begin{array}{r} \$55,575 \\ -\ 5,500 \\ \hline \$50,075 \end{array}$$

$50,075 ÷	
$500,750	10%

47. **(D)**

$$\frac{\text{\textbf{\$67,200}}}{112 \mid \$600}$$
$$\times$$

48. **(B)** $150,000 + 5\% + 5\% + 5\% = \$173,643.75$ or **\$173,644**

49. **(B)** $175,000 - 3\% - 3\% = \$164,657.50$ or **\$164,658**

50. **(C)**

$250,000	$230,000
$-$ 8%	$+$ 50,000
$230,000	**$280,000**

51. **(D)**

$250,000	$500,000
$\times$ 2	$-$ 20%
$500,000	**$400,000**

52. **(C)**

$ 65,000	$240,000	$223,200
$+$ 16,500	$-$ 7%	$-$ 191,500
$+$ 10,000	$223,200	**$ 31,700**
$+$191,000		

53. **(B)**

$250,000	$325,000	$302,000
$+$ 10,000	$-$ 7%	$-$ 260,000
$260,000	$302,250	**$ 42,000**
	$-$ 250	
	$302,000	

54. **(A)**

$550 × 12 × 3 = $19,800	$64,800	$67,200	$64,512	$59,512 ÷	
$600 × 12 × 3 = $21,600	$+$ 2,400	$-$ 4%	$-$ 5,000	**$661,244**	0.09%
$650 × 12 × 3 = $23,400	$67,200	$64,512	$59,512		
$64,800					

55. **(C)**

5 × $550 × 12 = $33,000	
5 × $600 × 12 = $36,000	
$69,000	
$-$ 8%	
$63,480	$60,480 ÷
$250 × 12 = $-$ 3,000	**$756,000** 8%
$60,480	

56. **(B)**

$117,978 ÷			$111,300 ÷	
$111,300	100%		**$105,000**	100%
	+ 6%			+ 6%
	106%			106%

57. **(C)**

$98,250 ÷			$103,421 ÷	
$103,421	100%		**$108,864**	100%
	+ 5%			+ 5%
	95%			95%

58. **(B)**

January 1   The taxes were paid in advance, so count from June 23 through December 30.
June 23   June 30 − 23 = 7 days
December 30 July through December = 30 × 6 = 180 days
             180 + 7 = 187 days
             $2,345 ÷ 360 = $6.5139 daily tax
             187 × $6.5139 = **$1,218.10** credit to seller at closing

59. **(B)**

January through March	90 days
April 13	+13 days
Total	103 days

$3,355 ÷ 360 = $9.32 per day
103 × $9.32 = **$959.96**

60. **(C)** July 1 − 11 = 11 days
$450 ÷ 180 = $2.50

$ 2.50
× 11
$27.50 DS, CB

61. **(D)**

February 26	February 30 − 26 = 4 days		$6,000 ÷ 360		$16.67
February 30			$75,000	8%	× 4
				×	**$66.68**

62. **(B)**

$236,000			$16,520		$16,520 ÷ 365 = $45.26 (31 − 5 = 26 days)
$295,000	80%		$236,000	7%	× 26
	×			×	**$1,176.76**

63. **(D)**

April 1	April 1 – 20 = 20 days	$4,125 ÷ 360	= $11.46	$11.46
April 20		$50,000	8.25%		× 20
		×		**$229.20**

64. **(B)**

$71,600	$89,500	$716	$ 716 discount points
$89,500	80%	−71,600	$71,600	1%	716 original fee
×	$17,900	×	350 insurance
			+17,900 down payment
			$19,682

65. **(A)**

$1,103.31 ÷ 12 = $91.94	$124.34	$12,259.00	**$244.53**
$12,259	9%	− 91.94	− 32.40	$12,226.60	2%
×	$ 32.40	$12,226.60	×

66. **(D)**

Beginning Date:	September 14, 2005
Prorate Date:	January 25, 2006
Ending Date:	September 13, 2006
	January 25–30 = 5 days
	February–August = 210 days
	September = 13 days
	Total = 228 days
	$504 ÷ 360 = $1.40 × 228 = **$319.20**

67. **(C)**

Beginning Date:	November 15, 2005
Prorate Date:	July 11, 2006
Ending Date:	November 14, 2006 *2008*
	July 11–13 = 19 days
	August 2006–October 2007 = 450 days
	November = 14 days
	Total = 483 days
	$890 ÷ 720 = $1.22 × 483 = **$589.26**

68. **(A)**   A = 3.1416 × 25' × 25'
A = 1,963.5 sq. ft. ÷ $120 = **$235,620**

69. **(D)**   640 ÷ 4 ÷ 4 ÷ 2 = 20 acres (See page 201 for explanation)
20 × $2,500 = **$50,000**

70. **(B)**   9 ÷ 10 = 90%
43,560 × 90% = 39,204
39,204 ÷ 150 = **261.36**

71. **(D)**

A = 25' × 50'	A = 20' × 20'	2,500	2,900 ÷ 9 =	322.222
A = 1,250 sq. ft.	A = 400 sq. ft.	+ 400	$9.95 + 2.50 =	× 12.45
× 2		2,900		**$4,011.67**
2,500				

72. **(D)**

20' × 25' = 500 sq. ft.   1,617 ÷ 9 = 179.6667 square yards
18' × 20' = 360 sq. ft.   179.667 × $9.95 = **$1,787.68** for entire house
14' × 26' = 364 sq. ft.
15' × 15' = 225 sq. ft.
12' × 14' = 168 sq. ft.
Total   1,617 sq. ft.

73. **(A)**   200' × 300' = 60,000 sq. ft. ÷ 43,560 = 1.3774 acres
1.3774 × $150,000 = $206,610
$206,610 × 8% = **$16,528.80 or $16,529**

74. **(B)**

A = 30' × 80'	V = 30' × 80' × 15'	$99,000
A = 2,400 sq. ft.	V = 36,000 cubic ft.	−84,000
× $35	× $2.75	**$15,000**
$84,000	$99,000	

75. **(A)**   5,280 × 5,280 = 27,878,400
27,878,400 ÷ 43,560 = 640
511.23 × 511.23 = 261,356.1129
261,356.1129 ÷ 43,560 = 5.9999
640 + 5.9999 = 645.9999
645.9999 × $2,000 = **$1,291,999**

76. **(B)**

5" ÷ 12" = 0.4167'   60.9423 ÷ 27 = **2.2571 cubic yds**.
V = 45' × 3.25' × 0.4167'
V = 60.9423 cubic ft.

77. **(B)**

A = [(300' + 400') ÷ 2)] × 200'   70,000 ÷ 43,560 = 1.6070 acres
A = (700' ÷ 2) × 200'   1.6070 × $4,000 = $6,427.91 or **$6,428**
A = 350' × 200'
A = 70,000 sq. ft.

78. **(A)** $A = 35' \times 40'$

$A = 1,400$ sq. ft.

$A = [(15' + 40') \div 2 \times 25']$

$A = 687.5$ sq. ft.

```
  1,400
+ 687.5
────────
  2,087.5
```

79. **(C)**

Beginning Date:	January 12, 2005
Prorate Date:	December 23, 2006
Ending Date:	January 11, 2006

December 30–23 = 7 days

January 1–11 = 11 days

Total = 18 days

$550 \div 360 = 1.5277 \times 18 = $**$27.50**

80. **(A)**

$100\% - 6\% = 94\%$

```
          │  $355,000 ÷
──────────┼──────────────
$377,659.57│   94%
```

81. **(D)**

```
      $5,250                    $1,312.50
───────────────          ─────────────────
$350,000 │ 1.5%          $5,250  │  25%
      ×                        ×
```

82. **(B)**

```
   $2,062.50 ÷                $8,250 ÷
───────────────          ─────────────────
$8,250  │  25%           $550,000 │  1.5%
```

83. **(A)**

```
    $427,500        100% − 20% =       $342,000              $23,085
───────────────     80% Loan      ───────────────     ───────────────
$450,000 │ 95%                     $427,500 │ 80%       $427,500 │ 6.75%
      ×                                  ×                    ×
```

$23,085 \div 12 = $**$1,923.75**

84. **(C)** $75,230 net operating income

$+\ \ 4,900$ expenses

$80,130 effective gross income

85. **(D)** $43,560 \div 3 = 14,520 \times 2 = 29,040$ sq. ft.

$29,040 \div 275' = $**105.60 ft.**

OR $2 \div 3 = 0.6667$

$43,560 \times 0.6667 = 29,041.45$ sq. ft.

$29,041.45 \div 275' = $**105.6052 ft.**

86. **(C)**

$$\frac{\$153,920}{\$148,000 \mid 104\%}\times \qquad \frac{\$160,076.80}{\$153,920 \mid 104\%}\times \qquad \frac{\$166,479.87}{\$160,076.80 \mid 104\%}\times \qquad \frac{\mathbf{\$159,820.68}}{\$164,479.87 \mid 96\%}\times$$

87. **(B)**

700 mills $\div$ 1,000 = 0.7 $\div$ 100 = 0.007 tax rate $\qquad \frac{\$108,400}{\$135,500 \mid 80\%}\times \qquad \frac{\$758.80}{\$108,400 \mid 0.007}\times$

$$\$758.80 \div 12 = \mathbf{\$63.23}$$

88. **(D)**

$$\frac{\$137.81 \times 12 = \$1,653.72}{\$3.50 \div 100 = 0.035} \qquad \frac{\$1,653.72 \div}{\$47,249.14 \mid 0.035} \qquad \frac{\$47,249.14 \div}{\mathbf{\$134,997.54} \mid 35\%}$$

89. **(D)**

$5 \times \$500 \times 12 = \$30,000$
$5 \times \$550 \times 12 = \$33,000$
$5 \times \$600 \times 12 = \$36,000$
Total PGI = \$99,000

$99,000	$450 × 12 = $5,400	$ 96,030
− 3%		+ 5,400
$96,030		**$101,430**

90. **(D)**

$4 \times \$450 \times 12 = \$21,600$ PGI
$\underline{\qquad - \qquad 5\% \text{ VR}}$
$\$20,520$
$\$464 \times 12 = \quad \underline{+ \; 5,568 \quad \text{AI}}$
$\mathbf{\$ \, 26,088} \;\; \mathbf{EGI}$

91. **(A)**

$477.82 × 12 = $5,733.84 Annual Interest $ $\quad \dfrac{\$5,733.84 \div}{\$80,475 \mid 7.125\%} \qquad \dfrac{\$80,475 \div}{\mathbf{\$107,300} \mid 75\%}$

92. **(C)**

100%	$82,000	$114,944 ÷
− 7%	32,500	**$123,595.70** | 93%
93%	+ 444	
	$114,944	

93. **(D)**

6,400 mills $\div$ 1,000 = 6.40 $\div$ 100 = 0.064 $\qquad \dfrac{\$43,750}{\$125,000 \mid 35\%}\times \qquad \dfrac{\$2,800}{\$43,750 \mid 0.064}\times$

$$\$2,800 \div 12 = \mathbf{\$233.33}$$

94. **(A)**

$108,810	
$120,900	90%

$\times$

$87,048	
$108,810	80%

$\times$

Debits	Credits
$108,810	$87,048
350	5,000
250	
749	
$110	
$110,159	$92,048

$110,159 - 92,048 = \textbf{\$18,111}$

95. **(B)**

Debits	Credits
$ 5,970.00	$99,500
250.00	
99.50	
50,140.00	
10,000.00	
$66,459.50	$99,500

$5,970	
$99,500	6%

$\times$

$99,500 - 66,459.50 = \textbf{\$33,040.50}$

96. **(D)**

$1 \times \$450 \times 12 = \ \$ 5,400$
$1 \times \$475 \times 12 = \ \$ 5,700$
$2 \times \$500 \times 12 = \ \underline{\$12,000}$

$23,100	PGI
$-$ 4%	VR
$22,176	EGI
$350 \times 12 = -$ 4,200	EXP
$17,975	ANOI
$17,976 $\div$	
$179,760	10%

97. **(D)**

$105,000 $\div$	
$109,375	100%
	$-$ 4%
	96%

$109,375 $\div$	
$113,932.29	100%
	$-$ 4%
	96%

$53,000 $\div$	
$50,000	100%
	$+$ 6%
	106%

$56,180 $\div$	
$53,000	100%
	$+$ 6%
	106%

$113,932.29 + 56,180 = \textbf{\$170,112.29}$

98. **(A)**

Debits	Credits
$79,000.00	$71,100
355.50	1,000
670.00	$72,100
300.00	
$80,325.50	

$79,000
$- \quad 10\%$
$71,100

$355.50	
$71,100	0.5%
×	

$$\$25 \times 12 = \$300$$
$$\$80,325.50 - 72,100 = \mathbf{\$8,225.50}$$

99. **(C)**

$$\$649.50 \div 1,080 = 0.60$$

Beginning Date:	April 30, 2006
Prorate Date:	June 24, 2006
Ending Date:	April 29, 2008

June 24–June 30 = 6 days

July 2006–April 29, 2008 = 659 days

Total = 665 days

$$\$665 \times 0.60 = \mathbf{\$399 \ CS, \ DB}$$

100. **(C)**

$128,000

$160,000	80%
×	

$$\$3.75 \div 1.000 = 0.00375$$

$480

$128,000	0.00375
×	

$$\$480 \div 720 = 0.6667$$

Beginning Date:	September 20, 2006
Prorate Date:	November 11, 2007
Ending Date:	September 19, 2008

November 11–November 30 = 19 days

December 2007–August 2008 = 270 days

September 2008 = 19 days

Total = 308 days

$$\$308 \times 0.6667 = \mathbf{\$205.35}$$

Broker Simulation Questions

In 2009, all broker candidates taking the AMP licensing exam will be required to pass a multiple-choice state law section and a section on national law, which features simulation exercises. The purpose of the simulation format is to provide realistic scenarios to determine a level of competency that goes beyond the recall of information.

The scenario topics include the following:

- Advertising
- Agency/Non-Agency Relationships*
- Disclosures (including stigmatized property)
- Document Preparation
- Environmental Issues
- Ethics
- Fair Housing*
- Finance
- Negotiation
- Property Representations*
- Representation of Services
- Risk Management
- Training/Supervision of Licensees*
- Trust Accounts*
- Valuation

The starred topics must appear on every exam. Ethics must be addressed in four exercises; residential properties should make an appearance in three exercises; commercial, two; property management, one; and in the remaining two, property type is unspecified.

The purpose of the simulation exam is to measure a person's ability to use and apply judgment, common sense, and situational ethics in running a business. The simulation exam is very different from a multiple-choice exam, which measures the ability to remember and identify facts. It is important to review the material on the listed topics, which will be covered on the exam. It is essential to know the laws and ethical standards in order to apply good judgment and common sense.

A primary issue and a property type—residential, commercial, property management, or unspecified—will be designated in each simulation. The opening narrative will identify the office environment and pose a specific problem that the broker is to resolve. Each party will be identified as the broker, cooperating broker, agent, client, customer, etc. Students should read carefully to look for additional information as they move to each new section.

The simulation exercise includes two main sections: Information Gathering (IG) and Decision Making (DM). In the Information Gathering section, the goal is to gather all the facts that a broker would want to know before making a decision. In the Decision Making section, judgment, common sense, and the ability to consider ethical implications are measured. Students should be certain to read all instructions and options carefully before selecting an answer. Once an answer has been selected, it CANNOT be changed.

Simulation Test Format

Each selection the student makes has a point total (from −3 to +3) associated with it; the total of all the points from all the student's individual selections determines the student's final score. The testing service determines a passing score by assessing what basic level of knowledge a competent practitioner should be able to demonstrate; it is possible to score at this level even if a few incorrect answers are selected or if some correct selections are omitted.

Item Scoring:

+ 3: **the best selection**

+ 2: very important, critical information

+ 1: correct, but not necessarily the best of the available choices

  0: information could be available but is usually not included

− 1: not necessary; not relevant

− 2: very bad choice; licensee could do damage to the public

− 3: **the worst selection**

Most of the choices on your exam will **be weighted + 2, +1,** − **2, or** −1.

Computing the Minimum Pass Level (MPL)

The Information Gathering and Decision Making sections will each have a minimum pass level (MPL).

Example: The IG scenario contains 12 options.

2 options are weighted: +2   If you selected these, you would have 4 points.

4 options are weighted: +1   If you selected these, you would have 4 points.

2 options are weighted: –2   If you selected these, a total of 4 points would be deducted.

4 options are weighted: –1   If you selected these, a total of 4 points would be deducted.

If you selected all the options weighted +2 and +1, you could score a maximum of 8 points.

The testing service has determined that the MPL for this section is 6. So, the options selected must add up to 6, once both positive (from options scored +1 and +2) and negative point totals (from options scored –1 and –2) are considered.

Example: The DM section contains 5 options.

1 option is weighted: +2   If you selected this option, you would have 2 points.

2 options are weighted: +1   If you selected these options, you would have 2 points.

1 option is weighted: –1   If you selected this option, 1 point would be deducted.

2 options are weighted: –2   If you selected these options, 4 points would be deducted.

This section would have a maximum of 4 points. The testing service has set an MPL of 3 for this section.

Keep in mind that it is the *total raw score* for both the Information Gathering and Decision Making sections on the *entire exam* that determines whether you pass; students must meet or exceed the minimum passing level in both Information Gathering and Decision Making.

<table>
<tr>
<td colspan="2">

SCENARIO WILL BE DISPLAYED HERE.

This section will tell you to "Choose only one option"
or "Select as <u>many</u> responses as appropriate" to gather information.

</td>
</tr>
<tr>
<td>

Possible selections will be displayed here.

☐ Option 1

☐ Option 2

☐ Option 3

☐ Option 4

☐ Option 5

☐ Option 6

☐ Option 7

☐ Option 8

</td>
<td>

When you check an answer on the left, a response will appear here. <u>When an answer has been checked, it CANNOT be changed, so choose your answers very carefully.</u> You may receive additional information here upon making a selection.

When you finish making selections, click "Go to Next Section."

A popup will read **"You have chosen to continue to the next section. You will not be able to make any additional selections in this section. Are you sure you want to continue?"**

The two options will be OK and Cancel. To move to the next section, click "OK." To make additional selections in this section, click "Cancel."

</td>
</tr>
</table>

Click the Time button to display how much time you are spending on the question.

Go to Next section.	Time

<table>
<tr>
<td colspan="2">

**CAROLINE IS STUDYING FOR HER AMP BROKER'S EXAM.
WHAT SHOULD SHE DO TO PREPARE FOR THE EXAM?**

SELECT ALL THE ITEMS from the list that you consider to be correct,
then click the "GO TO NEXT SECTION" button to continue.

</td>
</tr>
<tr>
<td>

☐ Ask brokers who recently passed the exam which questions they remember from the exam.

</td>
<td>

If selected: Score –3
Please note: The points will not be revealed in the software.

</td>
</tr>
<tr>
<td>

☐ Study state laws.

</td>
<td>

If selected: Score +3

</td>
</tr>
<tr>
<td>

☐ Study the Canon of Ethics.

</td>
<td>

If selected: Score +2

</td>
</tr>
<tr>
<td>

☐ Learn how to analyze simulation scenarios.

</td>
<td>

If selected: Score +2

</td>
</tr>
<tr>
<td>

☐ Study *Your Guide to Passing the AMP Real Estate Exam* book.

</td>
<td>

If selected: Score +3

</td>
</tr>
<tr>
<td>

☐ Do nothing. Active agents know how to pass an exam.

</td>
<td>

If selected: Score –3

</td>
</tr>
</table>

Go to Next section.	Time

Maximum Points: 10   Minimum Pass Level: 8

Learn to analyze answers in the Information Gathering section for the most significant answers.

Of course, the scenario questions will be more complicated than this example!

State Law

The state law portion of the exam will contain 40 multiple-choice questions. A score of 75 percent is required to pass this section. The state laws are found on the Real Estate Commission's Web site and should be read to prepare for the portion of the exam. **The national simulation and the state portion of the exam must be passed to earn the broker's license.**

Key Points of the Major Topics

Residential, Commercial, and Property Management Topics will be covered.

Advertising

1. Real estate advertisements must follow state advertising laws. Generally, the name of the broker or brokerage must appear in the ads of any listed property.

2. The Equal Housing Opportunity logo must be included in ads.

3. Ads cannot be discriminatory in any way.

4. Truth-in-Lending guidelines must be followed when advertising one- to four-family residential purchases, new loans, refinancing, consolidation loans, and all loans of $25,000 or less for private consumers.

5. Regulation Z requires full disclosure when trigger items are used in an ad. Trigger items in advertising include the interest rate, number of payments, down payment, term of the loan, and monthly payments. If a trigger item is used in an ad, the full disclosure that is required includes the annual percentage rate (APR), the terms of repayment, and the amount of down payment.

6. A "blind ad" is one in which consumers are led to believe they will be calling a for-sale-by-owner property because the name of the brokerage or principal broker is not in the ad, but upon calling, the sellers identify their brokerage firm or that they are licensees. Blind ads are illegal in most states.

7. Advertising cannot be false, misleading, or deceptive.

Agency/Non-Agency Relationships

See Chapter 1, pages 11–12 for review.

Disclosures

1. Be sure to have available all state-mandated disclosure documents, such as Consumer Guide to Agency Relationships, Agency Disclosure, Dual Agency Disclosure, Property Disclosure and Lead-Based-Paint Disclosure forms, and other applicable disclosure documents.

Document Preparation

1. Be sure your company is using current forms.

2. Train agents to never leave a space blank. If the requested information does not apply in a particular situation or transaction, agents should write N/A in the blank.

3. Set up a system to review listing, sales, property disclosure, agency disclosure, and any other documents related to the transaction.

4. Documents need to be legible.

Environmental Issues

See pages 51 and 63.

Ethics

Review the National Association of REALTORS® Code of Ethics.

Fair Housing

See pages 26–29.

Finance

See Chapter 5.

Negotiation

See page 81.

Property Representations

See pages 12, 14, 51, 80, and 86.

Representation of Services

1. Clients and customers have the right to know the services they can expect from the brokerage and agents.

2. Agents need to know the company's business model. Options might include fee for service, flat fee, limited service, online companies, franchise, agent owner, buyer agency, seller agency, and independently owned.

3. The company's business model must comply with state and federal laws.

Risk Management

See pages 93–94.

Update your broker policy manual at least once a year.

Training/Supervision of Licensees

See pages 170–171.

1. Develop a system to review files of each listing and sales contract.

2. Implement a system for storage of documents according to your state's laws.

<u>Trust Accounts</u>

See pages 88 and 168.

<u>Valuation</u>

See pages 10, 29, 31, 32, and 63.

1. A buyer working with an agent makes an offer on a property offered for sale by owner. The offer is contingent on the buyer's securing an FHA loan. Does this loan have to follow RESPA guidelines?
   A. No, because FHA and VA loans do have to meet HUD guidelines, but not RESPA guidelines.
   B. No, because the offer was made by a buyer working with a broker.
   C. Yes, because an FHA loan is guaranteed by the government.
   D. Yes, because it is a single-family residential property.

2. Which of the following is a typical characteristic of an FHA or VA loan?
   A. They are backed by the government and are not assumable.
   B. The down payment on these loans can normally be financed.
   C. Prepayment penalties cannot be charged on these loans.
   D. Typically, these loans must be repaid within 15 years.

3. The current market interest rate is 17 percent. Mr. and Mrs. Homeowner want to transfer their property to their daughter. The loan balance is $75,000. The property can be transferred if the loan does NOT contain a(n)
   A. alienation clause.
   B. acceleration clause.
   C. defeasance clause.
   D. nondisturbance clause.

4. Mr. Buyer purchased two parcels of land. One was one mile square and the other contained ten acres. If the land cost $2,500 an acre, what was the cost of the land?
   A. $1,265,000
   B. $1,625,000
   C. $1,526,000
   D. $1,600,000

5. An offer has been accepted on a property. After the title search, who gives an opinion of title?
   A. An attorney
   B. The seller
   C. The buyer
   D. The broker

6. Mr. and Mrs. Buyer just purchased their first house, which sits on five acres. They intend to keep goats on the property. Which of the following would allow or disallow them to keep goats?
   A. Federal ordinances
   B. State ordinances
   C. Zoning
   D. Neighbors

7. A buyer made an offer of $250,000 on a property with no contingencies and the offer was accepted. The buyer planned to build a shopping center, but never mentioned it to the agent. Just before the closing, the buyer discovered that he could not build the shopping center. What is the status of the sales contract?
   A. Valid
   B. Void
   C. Voidable
   D. Unenforceable

8. A disabled person moved into an apartment and at his own expense lowered the light switches, lowered the kitchen cabinets, installed handrails, and widened the doorways. At the expiration of the lease, which of the following would the tenant LEAST LIKELY have to return to its original condition?
   A. Light switches
   B. Kitchen cabinets
   C. Handrails
   D. Doorways

9. Which of the following BEST defines physical depreciation?
   A. Functional obsolescence caused by a poor design
   B. External obsolescence caused by any outside factor
   C. Deterioration caused by the age of the building
   D. Deterioration caused by normal wear and tear of the property

10. Which of the following must be disclosed when an agent is showing a house?
    A. Mortgage balance
    B. The asking price of other homes in the neighborhood
    C. That the property is in a flood plain zone
    D. Original cost of the property

11. What type of interest is normally computed on a residential loan?
    A. Simple
    B. Compound
    C. Annual
    D. Monthly

12. Which of the following is an example of an emblement?
    A. A stand of walnut trees
    B. A field of corn
    C. An apple orchard
    D. A vineyard

13. A buyer's agent is usually considered to be in what relationship to the seller?
    A. Client
    B. Customer
    C. Agency
    D. Subagency

14. A mortgage document and mortgage note are
    A. nonnegotiable instruments.
    B. debt-releasing documents.
    C. used by mortgagors to secure liens on a property.
    D. standard security instruments.

15. Who is the optionee in an option contract?
    A. Vendor
    B. Vendee
    C. Lessor
    D. Lessee

16. *J* sells a property to *H*, then *H* leases it back to *J*. At the conclusion of this transaction, what is the status of *J*'s interest in the property?
    A. Fee simple absolute
    B. Fee simple defeasible
    C. A freehold interest
    D. A nonfreehold interest

17. Which of the following is a physical characteristic of real estate?
    A. Mobility
    B. Scarcity
    C. Uniqueness
    D. Transferability

18. Which of the following normally purchases mortgages in the secondary mortgage market?
    A. Mortgage banking companies, savings and loans, commercial banks, and mutual saving banks
    B. Fannie Mae, Ginnie Mae, and Freddie Mac
    C. Federal Housing Administration
    D. Department of Veterans Affairs

19. Broker Alma had a listing agreement to sell Noah's house. Noah found a buyer for the house and Alma collected the brokerage fee. The type of listing agreement Alma had is a(n)
    A. exclusive-right-to-sell listing.
    B. exclusive agency listing.
    C. open listing.
    D. net listing.

20. The federal Truth-in-Lending Act
    A. requires a lender to estimate a borrower's loan closing charges on all mortgages.
    B. regulates advertising that contains information regarding mortgage terms.
    C. prevents brokers from using phrases like "FHA-VA financing available" in classified ads.
    D. dictates that all mortgage loan applications be made on specially prepared government forms.

21. Recording a deed provides the greatest benefit for the
    A. grantor.
    B. public.
    C. attorney.
    D. grantee.

22. Which of the following documents is only signed by the seller(s) in the transaction?
    A. Purchase agreement
    B. Listing agreement
    C. Option
    D. Warranty deed

23. The ability to pay for a home is the foremost consideration in choosing a home. What is the second consideration?
    A. Specification
    B. Age
    C. Improvements
    D. Location

24. The most important test in determining whether something is a fixture is
    A. the weight and/or size.
    B. its amount of utilization.
    C. its method of attachment.
    D. the intention of the party who attached it.

25. A section of real estate
    A. contains 460 acres.
    B. is 1 mile square.
    C. contains 43,560 acres.
    D. is numbered to indicate either north or south.

26. Mr. and Mrs. Mark have decided to list their house. Thirty minutes before the sales agent was scheduled to arrive, Mrs. Mark had to leave for an emergency. Mr. Mark stayed for the appointment and reached an agreement for the listing price of the property, which he owns in severalty. Who must sign the listing agreement?
    A. Mr. Mark now
    B. Mrs. Mark when she returns
    C. Mr. and Mrs. Mark before the listing is placed in the MLS
    D. Mr. and Mrs. Mark should sign the listing agreement as soon as their schedules permit

27. Which of the following is NOT necessary in a listing contract?
    A. The signature of all parties on the deed
    B. The signature of the sellers
    C. The signature of the broker
    D. The signature of the buyer

28. Mr. and Mrs. Hampton own their property as tenants by the entirety. The agent secured the signature of one spouse on the listing contract. Which of the following is TRUE?
    A. Both signatures are required.
    B. One spouse can sign because they each have an equal interest in the property.
    C. Only one spouse is required to sign because they are married.
    D. If it's an open listing, the agent has the proper signature.

29. A real estate tax lien takes priority over which of the following?
    A. Encroachment
    B. Encumbrance
    C. Mortgage lien
    D. Deed restrictions

30. The principles of appraising include which of the following?
    A. Reserves for replacement
    B. Operating expense ratio
    C. Highest and best use
    D. Holding period

31. Agents of Happy Valley Realty recently sold a home for $143,500. The brokerage charged the sellers a 6.5 percent commission paid. The broker paid the agent who secured the buyer 25 percent of the commission and the listing agent 30 percent of the commission collected. How much was the listing salesperson paid?
    A. $3,731
    B. $2,332
    C. $2,798
    D. $6,529

32. Harold is curious to know how much money his son and daughter-in-law still owe on their mortgage loan. He knows that the interest portion of their last monthly payment was $291.42. If they are paying interest at the rate of 8.25 percent, what was the outstanding balance of their loan before that last payment was made?
    A. $43,713.00
    B. $42,388.36
    C. $36,427.50
    D. $34,284.70

33. David's home on Dove Street is valued at $65,000. Property in their area is assessed at 60 percent of its value, and the local tax rate is $2.85 per hundred. How much are David's monthly taxes?
    A. $1,111.50
    B. $926.30
    C. $111.15
    D. $92.63

34. Andrew leases the 12 apartments in the Overton Arms for a total monthly rental of $3,000. If this figure represents an 8 percent annual return on Andrew's investment, what was the original cost of the property?
    A. $450,000
    B. $360,000
    C. $45,000
    D. $36,000

35. A broker receives a check for earnest money from a buyer and deposits the money in an escrow or trust account. He does this to protect himself from the charge of which of the following?
    A. Commingling
    B. Novation
    C. Lost or stolen funds
    D. Embezzlement

36. By paying the debt after a foreclosure sale, the mortgagor has the right to regain the property. What is this right called?
    A. Acceleration
    B. Redemption
    C. Reversion
    D. Recovery

37. Helen grants a life estate to her grandson and stipulates that, upon his death, the title will pass to her son-in-law. What is the second estate called?
    A. Estate in reversion
    B. Estate in remainder
    C. Estate for years
    D. Estate in recapture

38. Under joint tenancy
    A. there is a right of survivorship.
    B. only two people can own real estate.
    C. the fractional undivided interest may be different.
    D. the estate is inheritable.

39. In some states, a lender holds title to the mortgaged land. These states are known as
    A. title-theory states.
    B. lien-theory states.
    C. statutory share states.
    D. dower rights states.

40. The borrower's offer of $190,000 was accepted. She has a 10 percent down payment and would like to avoid paying for private mortgage insurance. Is there a loan that would allow her to accomplish her goal?
    A. Yes, she can borrow $19,000 from a private source, tell the lender she has a 20 percent down payment instead of a 10 percent down payment, and avoid private mortgage insurance.
    B. Yes, if the seller will negotiate a purchase-money mortgage for $19,000 and agree to be in a second lien position on the property, she can avoid private mortgage insurance.
    C. No, because all borrowers must pay private mortgage insurance when negotiating any type of loan.
    D. No, because private mortgage insurance is always paid when a borrower has less than a 20 percent down payment.

41. Which of the following is NOT an example of a subdivision rule and regulation?
    A. The agreement that the property cannot be sold and used as a waste disposal site
    B. The agreement that a tree house cannot be built on the property
    C. The agreement that walls and fences shall not exceed four feet in height
    D. The agreement that no structure of a temporary character shall be constructed on any lot

42. Which of the following is NOT an example of an appurtenance that would transfer when the property is sold?
    A. Easement
    B. Lease
    C. Deed restriction
    D. License

43. A couple wants to list a home they have lived in for 38 years because they have decided to move to Florida before the winter storms arrive. The listing agent is aware that zoning may change in the area, which would greatly increase the value of their property. The agent should
    A. say nothing in case the zoning does not change.
    B. inform the sellers of all the facts she has regarding the zoning change and let them make the decision about listing the property.
    C. list the property because she has a buyer that has already shown interest, and if it sells, then the sellers will be in Florida before the winter storms.
    D. list the property and say nothing because if the zoning does change, the listing contract will be void anyway.

44. Which of the following is NOT a depreciation factor when assessing the value of a property?
    A. A house with four bedrooms located on the second floor and the bath located on the first floor
    B. A hog farm located one-half mile down the road from a $250,000 home
    C. A house located next to a city park
    D. A house, which cost $50,000 to build 40 years ago, with major cracks in the foundation

45. What is a tenancy at will?
    A. A tenancy created by the consent of the landlord
    B. A tenancy that expires on a specific date
    C. A tenancy created by the death of the owner
    D. A tenancy created by the testator

46. The value of a piece of land
    A. is the present worth of future benefits.
    B. includes a measure of past expenditures.
    C. is what a buyer pays for the property.
    D. is the same as the market price.

47. A seller wants to net $65,000 on his house after paying the broker's fee of 6 percent. What will the gross selling price be?
    A. $69,149
    B. $68,900
    C. $67,035
    D. $66,091

48. Wilma is buying a condominium in a new subdivision and obtaining financing from a local savings and loan association. Which of the following BEST describes Wilma?
    A. Vendor
    B. Mortgagee
    C. Grantor
    D. Mortgagor

49. All of the following terminate an offer EXCEPT
    A. revocation of the offer before acceptance.
    B. death of the offeror before acceptance.
    C. a counteroffer by the offeree.
    D. an offer from a third party.

50. Ellen is purchasing a house under a contract for deed. Until the contract is paid, Ellen has
    A. legal title to the premises.
    B. no interest in the property.
    C. a legal life estate in the premises.
    D. equitable title in the premises.

51. Broker Len receives a deposit with a written offer that includes a ten-day acceptance clause. On the fifth day, and prior to acceptance by Carla, the seller, the buyer, Fergus, notifies the broker he is withdrawing his offer and demands that his deposit be returned. In this situation
    A. Fergus cannot withdraw the offer; it must be held open for the full ten days.
    B. Fergus has the right to revoke his offer and secure the return of the deposit at any time before he is notified of Carla's acceptance.
    C. Len notifies Carla that Fergus is withdrawing his offer, and Len and Fergus each retain one-half of the deposit.
    D. Len declares the deposit forfeited and retains it for his services and commission.

52. Amanda and George are joint tenants. George sells his interest to Percy. What is the relationship of Amanda and Percy with respect to the land?
    A. They are automatically joint tenants.
    B. They are tenants in common.
    C. There is no relationship because the sale from George to Percy of joint tenancy property is ineffective.
    D. Each owns a divided one-half interest.

53. A homeowner who always maintains his house has just discovered that he has termite infestation. This is an example of
    A. incurable physical obsolescence.
    B. possible curable physical obsolescence.
    C. possible curable economic obsolescence.
    D. incurable internal obsolescence.

54. When appraising property, the appraiser considers which of the following?
    A. The original price paid for the property, if purchased within three years
    B. The reconciliation of the values determined by the different methods of appraising
    C. The average cost of the comparable properties, after adjustments are made
    D. The cost for updating the subject property, other than the cost of replacing the carpet

55. When appraising a property, the appraiser determines the most probable price that a buyer would be willing to pay for a property. This is known as a(n)
    A. objective value/fair market value.
    B. subjective value/fair market value.
    C. plottage value.
    D. use value.

56. On Monday, Victor receives an offer from Leona for $12,000 on a vacant lot he has for sale. On Tuesday, Victor rejects the offer, counteroffers at $13,000, and gives Leona three days to accept. On Friday, Leona rejects the counteroffer and Victor then accepts Leona's original offer. Under these conditions there is
    A. a valid agreement because Leona accepted Victor's offer exactly as it was made.
    B. not a valid agreement because Leona's offer was rejected, and once rejected, it cannot later be accepted.
    C. a valid agreement because Leona accepted before Victor advised her that the offer was withdrawn.
    D. not a valid agreement because Victor's offer was not accepted within 72 hours.

57. Due to the economic growth in an area, a house designed by a famous architect is now in a flight pattern from the nearby airport. This is an example of
    A. external obsolescence, and the owners could receive compensation through inverse condemnation.
    B. external obsolescence, and the owners will not under any circumstances receive any compensation.
    C. functional obsolescence because of the poor design.
    D. functional obsolescence because of the noise from the planes.

58. In an appurtenant easement the property burdened by the easement is known as a
    A. prescriptive estate.
    B. dominant estate.
    C. condemned estate.
    D. servient estate.

59. Which of the following is NOT found in the appraisal report?
    A. Date of the inspection
    B. Condition of the subject property
    C. Adjustments of the subject property
    D. Signature of the appraiser

60. Unless stated otherwise in the listing contract, the buyer should receive on the purchase of a property
    A. air rights, surface rights, and subsurface rights.
    B. air rights and surface rights.
    C. air rights and subsurface rights.
    D. air rights and mineral rights.

61. A house sold for $84,500 and the commission rate was 7 percent. If the commission is split 60/40 between the selling broker and the listing broker, and each broker splits his share of the commission evenly with his salesperson, how much will the listing salesperson earn from the sale of the house, according to the sales contract?
    A. $1,774
    B. $1,183
    C. $1,020
    D. $2,366

62. Justin Time and Lotta Time enter into a purchase agreement with Henry and Susan Date to buy the Date's house for $84,500. The buyers pay $2,000 in earnest money and obtain a new mortgage of $67,600. The purchase agreement provides for a March 15, 2005, closing. The buyers and sellers prorate 2005 taxes of $1,880.96, which have been prepaid. The Times have closing costs of $1,250 and the Dates have closing costs of $850. How much cash must the buyers bring to the closing? (Use a 360-day year.)
    A. $17,239.09
    B. $17,639.09
    C. $16,541.87
    D. $19,639.09

63. If a mortgage on a house is 80 percent of the appraised value and the mortgage interest of 8 percent amounts to $460 per month, what is the appraised value of the house?
    A. $86,250
    B. $71,875
    C. $69,000
    D. $92,875

64. A building is 100 feet by 150 feet and sits on a lot valued at $25,000. If the replacement cost of the property is $25 per square foot and it has depreciated 5 percent, what is the value of the property?
    A. $375,000
    B. $381,250
    C. $481,250
    D. $318,250

65. Broker Mary took a listing and later discovered that her client had previously been declared incompetent by a court of law. The listing is now
    A. binding, as the broker was acting as the owner's agent in good faith.
    B. of no value to the broker because it is void.
    C. the basis for recovery of a commission if the broker produces a buyer.
    D. renegotiable.

66. Perry defaulted on his home mortgage loan payments, and the lender obtained a court order to foreclose on the property. At the foreclosure sale, however, Perry's house sold for only $29,000; the unpaid balance on the loan at the time of foreclosure was $40,000. What must the lender do to recover the $11,000 Perry still owes?
    A. Sue for damages
    B. Sue for specific performance
    C. Seek a judgment by default
    D. Seek a deficiency judgment

67. All of the following are exemptions to the federal Fair Housing Act of 1968 EXCEPT the
    A. sale of a single-family home where the listing broker does not advertise the property.
    B. rental of a unit in an owner-occupied, three-family dwelling where no advertisement is placed in the paper.
    C. restriction of noncommercial lodgings by a private club to members of that club.
    D. property is a state or local housing program designed specifically for the elderly.

68. A broker holds a listing on a vacant lot measuring 100' by 125' at a listing price of $250 per front foot. The commission that the broker will collect is 8 percent. If the property sells for its full asking price, what will be the broker's fee?
    A. $2,500
    B. $2,000
    C. $1,500
    D. $1,250

69. Sal has been offering Cathay's house for sale at the price of $47,900. Mr. and Mrs. Cortez, an Hispanic couple, saw the house and were interested in purchasing it. When Mrs. Cortez asked Sal what the price of the house was, Sal said $53,000. Under the federal Fair Housing Act of 1968, such a statement is
    A. legal because all that is important is that Mr. and Mrs. Cortez be given the right to buy the house.
    B. legal because the representation was made by broker Sal and not by Cathay.
    C. illegal because the difference in the offering price and the quoted price was greater than $5,000.
    D. illegal because the terms of the sale were changed for Mr. and Mrs. Cortez.

70. The market rent for a duplex is $650 per month per unit. If the GRM is 125, what is the value of the property?
    A. $81,250
    B. $162,500
    C. $126,500
    D. $216,500

71. House keys are considered to be
    A. personal property because they are movable.
    B. personal property because they are not attached.
    C. real property because sale contracts stipulate that they will be transferred.
    D. real property because of the adaptation to the real estate.

72. In the lease agreement, a tenant has agreed to build out space to meet her needs at her expense. The chattel fixtures that she adds to the property are the
    A. property of the landlord upon the expiration of the lease because they are now attached to the property.
    B. tenants' as long as they are removed from the property on or before the expiration of the lease and she leaves the property in good repair.
    C. tenants' as long as they are removed from the property on or before the expiration of the lease because she paid for them.
    D. property of the landlord automatically upon their addition, and the property must be left in good repair.

73. *A*, *B*, and *C* are co-owners of property. When *C* dies testate, *A* and *B* are the devisees to her one-third interest in the property. How do they own the property?
    A. Joint tenancy
    B. Tenancy in common
    C. Severalty
    D. Partnership tenancy

74. Which of the following is an example of a freehold inheritable estate?
    A. Life estate
    B. Dower estate
    C. Estate at will
    D. Fee simple defeasible estate

75. Frances moved into a condominium that boasted of many common facilities, including a swimming pool, tennis courts, and a putting green. Under a typical condominium arrangement, these common elements are owned by
    A. an association of homeowners in the condominium.
    B. a corporation in which Frances and the owners of the other units own stock.
    C. Frances and the owners of the other units in the form of an undivided percentage interest.
    D. Frances and the owners of the other units in the form of divided interests.

76. In a graduated-payment loan
    A. mortgage payments decrease.
    B. mortgage payments balloon in five years.
    C. mortgage payments increase for a period of time and then level out.
    D. the interest rate on the loan adjusts annually.

77. Jack feels that he has been the victim of an unfair discriminatory practice by a local broker. His complaint must be filed with HUD within
    A. 3 months of the alleged discrimination.
    B. 6 months of the alleged discrimination.
    C. 9 months of the alleged discrimination.
    D. 12 months of the alleged discrimination.

78. A mortgage using both real and personal property as security is a
    A. blanket mortgage.
    B. package mortgage.
    C. dual mortgage.
    D. wraparound mortgage.

79. If a buyer obtains a mortgage for $50,000 with four points, how much will she be charged by the lender at closing for the points?
    A. $6,000
    B. $200
    C. $2,000
    D. $600

80. A borrower obtained a second mortgage loan for $7,000. The loan called for payments of $50 per month, including 6 percent interest over a period of five years, with the final installment made as a balloon payment including the remaining outstanding principal. What type of loan is this?
    A. Fully amortized loan
    B. Straight loan
    C. Partially amortized loan
    D. Accelerated loan

81. Michael bought property in a secluded area adjacent to the Atlantic Ocean. Shortly thereafter, he noticed that people from town often walked along the shore in front of his property. He later learned that the locals had been walking along this beach for years. Michael went to court to try to stop people from walking along the water's edge in front of his property. Michael is likely to be
   A. unsuccessful because the local citizens were walking there before he bought the property, and thus had an easement.
   B. unsuccessful because under the doctrine of littoral rights, he owns the property only to the high-water mark, and the public can use the land beyond that mark.
   C. successful because of the doctrine of riparian rights.
   D. successful because he has the right to control access to his own property.

82. All of the following are true about the concept of adverse possession EXCEPT
   A. the person taking possession of the property must do so without the consent of the owner.
   B. occupancy of the property by the person taking possession must be continuous over a specified period.
   C. the person taking possession of the property must compensate the owner at the end of the adverse possession period.
   D. the person taking possession of the property may end up owning the property.

83. Reconciliation is an appraisal term used to describe the
   A. appraiser's determination of a property's highest value.
   B. average values for properties similar to the one being appraised.
   C. appraiser's analysis and comparison of the results of each appraisal approach.
   D. method used to determine a property's most appropriate capitalization rate.

84. In consideration of $15,000, Jim gives Charles the right to purchase certain described real estate for $200,000. If Charles enters into an agreement to purchase it within 60 days, Charles is a(n)
   A. optionor.
   B. escrowee.
   C. optionee.
   D. grantor.

85. When a mortgage loan has been paid in full, which of the following is the MOST important thing for the borrower to do?
   A. Put the paid note and all canceled papers in a safe-deposit box
   B. Arrange to receive and pay future real estate tax bills
   C. Be sure the mortgagor signs a satisfaction of mortgage
   D. Record the satisfaction of mortgage

86. Normally, the priority of general liens is determined by the
   A. order in which they are filed or recorded.
   B. order in which the cause of action arose.
   C. size of the claim.
   D. court.

87. When property is held in tenancy by the entirety
   A. the owners must be husband and wife.
   B. either owner may sell his or her own interest separately to a third party by signing a quitclaim deed.
   C. there is no right of survivorship.
   D. the property may be partitioned.

88. The practice of directing potential buyers of one race into one area and potential buyers of another race into a second area is known as
   A. canvassing.
   B. blockbusting.
   C. redlining.
   D. steering.

89. A broker who is entitled to collect a commission when the sellers sell their own property has a(n)
   A. exclusive-agency listing contract with the sellers.
   B. net listing contract with the sellers.
   C. exclusive-right-to-sell listing contract with the sellers.
   D. open listing contract with the sellers.

90. Sheila, a broker, listed a property under a valid written listing agreement. After the sale was completed, the owner refused to pay the broker's fee. Which of the following can Sheila do?
   A. She can take the seller to court and sue for the commission.
   B. She is entitled to a lien on the seller's property for the amount of the commission.
   C. She can go to court and stop the transaction until she is paid.
   D. She can collect the commission from the buyer.

91. All of the following are tests for determining a fixture EXCEPT
   A. intent of the parties.
   B. size of the item.
   C. method of attachment of the item.
   D. adaptation of the item to the particular real estate.

92. When real estate is sold under an installment land contract, possession is usually given to the buyer. The vendee's interest in the property is
   A. a legal title interest.
   B. an equitable title interest.
   C. kept by the seller until the full purchase price is paid.
   D. held by the mortgagee until the full purchase price is paid.

93. To start a condominium, a developer usually files which of the following?
   A. Judgment
   B. Lien
   C. Certificate
   D. Declaration

94. George agrees to buy Elaine's real estate for $53,000. George signs a sales contract and deposits $5,300 earnest money with broker Stuart. Elaine is unable to show good title, and George demands the return of his earnest money as provided in the contract. What should Stuart do?
   A. Deduct his commission and return the balance to George
   B. Deduct his commission and pay the balance to Elaine
   C. Return the entire amount of the earnest money to George
   D. Pay the entire amount to Elaine to dispose of as she sees fit

95. If the annual rate of interest on a mortgage loan is 8.5 percent, and the monthly interest payment is $201.46, what is the principal amount of the loan?
   A. $2,417.52
   B. $28,441.41
   C. $2,844.14
   D. $14,270.00

96. All of the following are contracts between an agent and a principal EXCEPT
   A. open listing.
   B. net listing.
   C. multiple listing.
   D. exclusive listing.

97. Mary and Dudley enter into a contract wherein Dudley will build a structure on some vacant land. Dudley begins work and finds that because of the nature of the soil, the supports for the structure must be dug much deeper than he had thought. The additional work will cause Dudley to lose money on the project. Under these circumstances
   A. Dudley does not have to continue with the contract, under the doctrine of impossibility.
   B. Dudley does not have to continue with the contract because Mary does not have the right to force Dudley to lose money.
   C. Dudley can force Mary to renegotiate the contract because of Dudley's mistake, if the mistake was reasonable.
   D. Dudley is liable for breach of contract if he fails to perform, and the fact that the job is more difficult than Dudley had expected is irrelevant.

98. Allen offers to sell Naomi certain undeveloped land in the country and represents to her that a new freeway will run right by the land, even though Allen knows that the plans for the new freeway have been dropped. Naomi, relying on the representation, purchases the land from Allen. Under these circumstances
    A. Allen can be forced to proceed with the sale even though there was fraud.
    B. the contract is voidable at the option of Allen.
    C. the misrepresentation automatically voids the contract.
    D. Naomi must purchase the property and cannot sue Allen for fraud.

99. If the market value of a house is $84,500, the assessment ratio is 35 percent, and the tax rate is 30 mills, what are the monthly taxes?
    A. $887.25
    B. $942.50
    C. $73.94
    D. $87.72

100. Richard seeks relief from zoning regulations on the ground of nonconforming use. Effective arguments to the zoning authorities would include all of the following EXCEPT that
    A. the nonconforming use existed prior to the passing of the zoning ordinance.
    B. he would earn more by using the property for purposes that do not conform with the zoning ordinance.
    C. the nonconforming use didn't harm the public health, safety, and welfare.
    D. conforming to the zoning ordinance would create an undue hardship.

101. Jimmy and his neighbor both own irregularly shaped lots. To create a bird sanctuary, Jimmy would like to purchase part of his neighbor's property. If Jimmy has the properties surveyed, all of the following terms would most likely be found in the survey EXCEPT
    A. datum.
    B. monument.
    C. point of beginning.
    D. linear distance.

102. An option contract
    A. sets a time limit to keep an offer open.
    B. is an open-end agreement.
    C. does not set the sale price for the property.
    D. transfers title when it is signed by the seller.

103. What is the legal procedure or action that may be brought by either the buyer or the seller to enforce the terms of a contract?
    A. Injunction
    B. Suit for specific performance
    C. Lis pendens
    D. Attachment

104. In an option to purchase real estate, the optionee
    A. must purchase the property, but may do so at any time within the option period.
    B. has no obligation to purchase the property.
    C. as a matter of right is limited to a refund of the option consideration if the option is exercised.
    D. is the prospective seller of the property.

105. Which of the following contracts would become void on the death of one of the principals in the contract?
    A. Listing contracts and offers
    B. Listing contracts and sales contracts
    C. Listing contracts and deeds
    D. Listing contracts and mortgage

106. Lot A measured 200' × 300' sold for $30,000 per acre. Lot B located down the street measures 150' × 200'. If it sells for the same price, Lot A, what is the price of Lot B?
    A. $21,780
    B. $20,661
    C. $41,322
    D. $51,229

107. A borrower negotiated a $25,000 term mortgage for one year. His semiannual interest was $875. What was the interest rate?
    A. 3.5 percent
    B. 4.0 percent
    C. 5.0 percent
    D. 7.0 percent

108. The seller left the closing table with a check for $145,250. She paid a 6 percent commission to the brokerage. What was the sale price of the property?
    A. $153,965
    B. $154,521
    C. $155,418
    D. $155,525

109. A seller netted $275,500 after paying a 6.5 percent commission and $5,000 in other closing costs. What was the sale price?
    A. $280,500
    B. $285,500
    C. $295,000
    D. $300,000

110. An investment property has annual expenses of $15,000 and the annual net operating income is $50,000. If the value is $500,000, what is the cap rate?
    A. 1 percent
    B. 10 percent
    C. 15 percent
    D. 20 percent

ANSWERS

For additional information please refer to the page number in parentheses.

1. **(D)** RESPA covers one- to four-family residential loans financed by a federally related mortgage loan. (119)

2. **(C)** Prepayment penalties cannot be charged on FHA or VA mortgages. (146–47)

3. **(A)** The alienation clause in a mortgage document allows the lender to call the note due and payable on the conveyance of the property. (154)

4. **(B)** 640 + 10 = 650 acres × $2,500 = $1,625,000 (1 mile square = 640 acres). (3)

5. **(A)** An attorney gives an opinion of title and issues a title certificate. (109)

6. **(C)** The local zoning laws regulate the type of animals that can be kept on a property. (60)

7. **(A)** A contract with no contingencies is a valid, enforceable contract. (56)

8. **(D)** The tenant would least likely be responsible for returning the doorways to their original width. (91)

9. **(D)** Deterioration caused by normal wear and tear of the property best describes depreciation. (8)

10. **(C)** Any material fact or property defect must be disclosed to potential buyers of a property. (13)

11. **(A)** The lender normally computes simple interest on residential loans. (154)

12. **(B)** Emblements are crops that require annual planting. The crop that has been harvested is an emblement. (16)

13. **(B)** The seller is normally considered to be the customer to a buyer's agent. (46)

14. **(D)** By definition of mortgage document and mortgage note. (116)

15. **(B)** In an option contract, the optionee is the vendee or buyer. (58)

16. **(D)** In this sale-leaseback transaction *J* is the lessee and has a nonfreehold interest in the property. (22 & 84)

17. **(C)** Heterogeneity, immobility, and durability are the physical characteristics of real estate. Heterogeneity, or nonhomogeneity, means that every parcel of land is unique. (16)

18. **(B)** Fannie Mae, Ginnie Mae, and Freddie Mac buy and sell mortgages on the secondary market. (148)

19. **(A)** In an exclusive-right-to-sell listing, the broker collects a commission even if the seller sells the property. (18)

20. **(B)** Truth-in-Lending requires the disclosure of the cost of financing the loan expressed as an APR, and regulates the advertising of mortgage loans. (149)

21. **(D)** It is to the benefit of the buyer to give constructive notice to the world that she or he is the owner of the property. (113)

22. **(D)** A deed is a transfer of title, and the party currently holding title is required to sign. (115)

23. **(D)** The location of the property affects its price today and in the future. People purchase homes because of their preference for certain locations. (16)

24. **(D)** Courts have held that the intention of the parties is the most important factor in determining when an item is a fixture. (17)

25. **(B)** A section of land is one mile square. (3)

26. **(A)** Mr. Mark owns the property in severalty, and he is the only party who must sign the listing. (19)

27. **(D)** The buyer is not a party to the listing contract. (19)

28. **(A)** Both signatures are required on the listing because it is owned as tenancy by the entirety. (23)

29. **(C)** Real estate taxes and special assessments take priority over all other liens. (113)

30. **(C)** The highest and best use of the property is its most profitable use. (29)

31. **(C)** $\$143,500 \times 6.5\% = \$9,327.50$ $\$9,327.50 \times 0.30 = \$2,798.25$ (191)

32. **(B)** $\$291.42 \times 12 = \$3,497.04$ $\$3,497.04 \div 8.25\% = \$42,388.36$ (199)

33. **(D)** $\$2.85 \div 100 = 0.0285$ $\$65,000 \times 60\% = \$39,000$ $\$39,000 \times 0.0285 = \$1,111.50$
    $\$1,111.50 \div 12 = \$92.625$ (202)

34. **(A)** $\$3,000 \times 12 = \$36,000$ $\$36,000 \div 8\% = \$450,000$ (205)

35. **(A)** All money received in a fiduciary relationship must be placed in an escrow account to prevent commingling. (168)

36. **(B)** The equitable right of redemption is the owner's right to regain property before foreclosure. The statutory right of redemption is the owner's right to regain the property after foreclosure. (153)

37. **(B)** The son-in-law is a remainderman and his interest is an estate in remainder. (22)

38. **(A)** Joint tenancy is characterized by right of survivorship. (23)

39. **(A)** By definition of title-theory state. (143)

40. **(B)** If the seller would lend her $19,000 as a purchase-money mortgage, she could avoid private mortgage insurance. (141)

41. **(A)** This is an example of a deed condition placed on the property by a grantor that is binding on all future owners. (21)

42. **(D)** A license is the revocable permission for a temporary land use granted to another, but it does not transfer with the property. (6)

43. **(B)** The agent must inform the sellers of all facts that she has regarding the possible zoning change and the consequences of their decision should they accept any offers on the property before the decision about the zoning is finalized. (12)

44. **(C)** Depreciation does not occur because a house is located next to a city park. (8)

45. **(A)** A tenancy at will is a lease that is created at the consent of the landlord. (82)

46. **(A)** By definition of value. (29)

47. **(A)** 100% – 6% = 94% $65,000 ÷ 94% = $69,148.94 (190–191)

48. **(D)** Wilma is the borrower or the mortgagor. (144)

49. **(D)** An offer from a third party does not terminate an offer. (59)

50. **(D)** When the legal title in the property is held by another party, the buyer's interest is an equitable interest. (141)

51. **(B)** An offer can be withdrawn at any time prior to acceptance. (59)

52. **(B)** When a joint tenant sells an interest in a property, the new owner becomes a tenant in common with the other joint tenants. (23)

53. **(B)** Unless termite infestation has been present on a property for an extended period of time, it is curable. Because the question states that the homeowner always maintained his house and the termite infestation was just discovered, then the physical obsolescence is probably curable. (8)

54. **(B)** Appraisers reconcile the values as determined by the different methods of appraising, but they do not consider any of the factors in the other answers. (31)

55. **(A)** The appraiser determines the most probable price that a buyer will pay for the property. This is known as the fair market value and should be an objective value. (29)

56. **(B)** Once an offer has been rejected it cannot be accepted later. (20)

57. **(A)** A change outside the property has affected the property's value. This is external obsolescence, and the owners could receive compensation through inverse condemnation. (9)

58. **(D)** In an appurtenant easement, the servient estate is burdened by the easement and the dominant estate benefits from it. (5)

59. **(C)** Adjustments are never made in the subject property, only in the comparable properties. (30)

60. **(A)** Any rights that are not being transferred should be in the listing contract. (15)

61. **(B)** $84,500 × 7% = $5,915 $5,915 × 40% = $2,366 $2,366 ÷ 2 = $1,183 (191)

62. **(B)**

Debit	Credit
$84,500.00	$ 2,000
$ 1,489.09	$67,600
$ 1,250.00	$69,600
$87,239.09	

Jan. 1
March 15—Count from March 15 through Dec. 30 = 285 days
Dec. 30

$1,880.96 ÷ 360 = $5.22489 per day
$5.22489 × 285 days = $1,489.09

$87,239.09 – $69,600 = $17,639.09 (210–211)

63. **(A)** $460 × 12 = $5,520 $5,520 ÷ 80% = $69,000 $69,000 ÷ 80% = $86,250 (198)

64. **(B)** A = 100 × 150 = 15,000 sq. ft.
15,000 square feet × $25 = $375,000
– 5%
$356,250
+ 25,000
$381,250 (205)

65. **(B)** The listing agent should enter into the listing agreement with the guardian of the incompetent party. (19)

66. **(D)** By definition of deficiency judgment. (152)

67. **(A)** Single-family homeowners under certain circumstances can discriminate when selling their property, but an owner who does cannot use the services of a broker. (28)

68. **(B)** 100' × $250 = $25,000 $25,000 × 8% = $2,000 (215)

69. **(D)** It is discriminatory to change the terms of the listing agreement. (26)

70. **(B)** $650 × 2 = $1,300   125 × $1,300 = $162,500 (205–206)

71. **(D)** House keys are adapted to the use of a specific property and are considered real property. (17)

72. **(B)** Trade fixtures must be removed from the property on or before the lease expires. The tenant is responsible for any damage caused by the removal of the fixtures. Those that are not removed become the property of the landlord. (17)

73. **(B)** Tenancy in common is an inheritable estate. When C wrote her will she made the other co-owners her devisees. (23)

74. **(D)** Fee simple absolute and fee simple defeasible estates are freehold inheritable estates. (22)

75. **(C)** Common areas are owned by the condo owners in an undivided percentage interest. (24)

76. **(C)** By definition of graduated-payment mortgage. (145)

77. **(D)** Complaints must be filed with HUD within one year. (28)

78. **(B)** By definition of package mortgage. (145)

79. **(C)** $50,000 × 4% = $2,000 (198)

80. **(C)** By definition of partially amortized loan. (144)

81. **(B)** By definition of littoral rights. (15)

82. **(C)** The adverse possessor does not compensate the owner at the end of the adverse possession period. (122)

83. **(C)** By definition of reconciliation. (31)

84. **(C)** Charles is the buyer and thus the optionee. (58)

85. **(D)** The satisfaction of mortgage or mortgage release needs to be recorded to release the lender's interest in the property. (112)

86. **(A)** The priority of liens is usually determined by the order in which they are filed or recorded. (112)

87. **(A)** Tenancy by the entirety involves a husband and wife who own property. (23)

88. **(D)** By definition of channeling and steering. (26)

89. **(C)** By definition of exclusive-right-to-sell listing. (18)

90. **(A)** The broker must sue the seller for the commission. (19)

91. **(B)** The size of an item is not one of the tests to determine if it is a fixture. (16)

92. **(B)** The buyer's interest in the property in a land contract is an equitable title interest. (141)

93. **(D)** To develop a condominium community, the developer must file a declaration. (24)

94. **(C)** The earnest money check should be returned to the buyer. The broker must pursue the seller for the commission. (13)

95. **(B)** $201.46 × 12 = $2,417.52 $2,417.52 ÷ 8.5% = $28,441.41 (198)

96. **(C)** The multiple-listing service is an agreement between brokers, not between an agent and a principal. (18)

97. **(D)** Because there were no contingencies in the contract, Dudley must fulfill the contract. (13)

98. **(A)** Allen committed fraud in selling the property. However, if Naomi still chooses to buy the property upon the discovery of that fact, Allen must sell. (56)

99. **(C)** $30 \div 1,000 = 0.03$ $\$84,500 \times 35\% = \$29,575$ $\$29,575 \times 0.03 = \$887.25$ $\$887.25 \div 12 = \$73.94$
(202)

100. **(B)** The fact that Richard could earn more money is not a valid reason to grant relief from zoning regulations. (60)

101. **(A)** A datum is a point, line, or surface from which elevations are measured to determine the heights of structures or grades of streets and would not be found in a survey between two neighbors' properties. (2)

102. **(A)** By definition, option contract. (58)

103. **(B)** By definition, suit for specific performance. (57)

104. **(B)** The optionee (buyer) has no obligation to purchase the property. The buyer has purchased an option on the property, and is not entitled to a refund of the option money if the buyer does not purchase it. (58)

105. **(A)** Listing contracts and offers would terminate on the death of either party. (19)

106. **(B)** $150' \times 200' = 30,000$ square feet
$30,000 \div 43,560 = 0.6887$ acres
$\$30,000 \times 0.6887 = \$20,661$ (215)

107. **(D)** $\$875 \times 2 = \$1,750$ annual interest
$\$1,750 \div \$25,000 = 0.07 = 7\%$ (198)

108. **(B)** $100\% - 6\% = 94\%$
$\$145,250 \div 94\% = \$154,521$ (191)

109. **(D)** $\$275,500 + \$5,000 = \$280,500$
$100\% - 6.5\% = 93.5\%$
$\$280,500 \div 93.5\% = \$300,000$ (191)

110. **(B)** $\$50,000 \div \$500,000 = 0.1 = 10\%$ (205)

1. A house sold for $137,500, and the buyers secured an FHA mortgage. The required down payment was set at 3 percent for the first $50,000 and 5 percent for any amount over $50,000. What was the amount of the mortgage?
   A. $1,500
   B. $4,375
   C. $133,125
   D. $131,625

2. After a neighborhood had been hit by vandals on a number of occasions, Nolan offered to pay $100 to anyone providing information leading to the arrest and conviction of the guilty party. Shortly thereafter, Eileen supplied the needed information and received the reward. This is an example of a(n)
   A. gift.
   B. option.
   C. unilateral contract.
   D. voidable contract.

3. Broker Kate pays her salespeople 20 percent of the commission for listing property and 40 percent of the commission for selling it. The commission rate is 5 percent. What was the selling price of a house if the salesperson who both listed and sold it received $3,600?
   A. $120,000
   B. $200,000
   C. $72,000
   D. $100,000

4. Which of the following is a loan in which only interest is payable during the term of the loan and all principal is payable at the end of the loan period?
   A. Amortized loan
   B. Flexible loan
   C. Fixed installment loan
   D. Term loan

5. A property owned solely by one spouse
   A. is owned in trust.
   B. is owned in severalty.
   C. is immune from seizure by creditors.
   D. cannot be homesteaded.

6. When a property fails to sell at a court foreclosure for an amount sufficient to satisfy the mortgage debt, the mortgagee may usually sue for which of the following?
   A. Judgment by default
   B. Deficiency judgment
   C. Satisfaction of mortgage
   D. Damages

7. Joe is purchasing a parcel of real estate registered as Torrens property. In connection with the purchase
   A. Joe should have an attorney review the abstract and render an opinion about prior transfers.
   B. the Torrens certificate is proof of ownership.
   C. Joe should check for adverse possession.
   D. the execution of the deed transfers title.

8. Sam is purchasing property from Harry and taking a quitclaim deed. Under the assurances of such a deed, Sam can be certain that
   A. Harry has a good title to the property.
   B. Harry's interest at that time in the property is being transferred to Sam.
   C. Harry will convey after-acquired title.
   D. there are no liens against the property that adversely affect marketable title.

9. Seller Henry and Broker Walter enter into an open listing agreement. Under such an agreement, Henry
   A. must inform Walter of all potential buyers.
   B. does not have to pay Walter a commission if Henry finds a buyer.
   C. must pay Walter a commission if Henry or Walter finds a buyer.
   D. must pay Walter a commission if anyone but Henry finds a buyer.

10. When a buyer signs a purchase agreement and the seller accepts, the buyer acquires an interest in the real estate, prior to closing, known as
    A. equitable title.
    B. equitable rights.
    C. statutory rights.
    D. servient tenement.

11. All of the following are intended to convey title to real estate that has been sold EXCEPT
    A. warranty deed.
    B. deeds of trust.
    C. trustee's deed.
    D. deed in lieu of foreclosure.

12. The ABC Real Estate Company listed a property at $4.50 per square foot. The land dimensions were 50 feet by 137 feet. If the commission rate was set at 7.25 percent, how much did the seller pay the ABC Real Estate Company?
    A. $1,005.50
    B. $2,234.81
    C. $22,348.12
    D. $10,055.00

13. To purchase a home, a buyer obtained a $142,500 mortgage at 7.75 percent interest for 25 years. The mortgage was closed on June 15, with the first P&I payment in arrears due on August 1. At the closing, which of the following occurred?
    A. The buyer paid a $460.16 interest adjustment.
    B. The seller paid a $460.16 interest adjustment.
    C. The seller paid a $920.31 interest adjustment.
    D. The buyer paid a $920.31 interest adjustment.

14. To be valid, a deed must be signed by which of the following?
    A. Grantors
    B. Attorney at law
    C. Grantees
    D. Broker

15. In order to have a valid conveyance, all of the following are necessary EXCEPT
    A. legal capacity to execute.
    B. recital of consideration.
    C. designation of any limitations.
    D. proof of heirship.

16. Which of the following discriminatory acts is exempted from the federal Fair Housing Act?
    A. Rental of rooms in an owner-occupied one- to four-family dwelling
    B. Alteration of the terms or conditions of mortgage
    C. Property for sale above $250,000
    D. Property sold on an installment sales contract

17. Thornton Enterprises manages a number of income-producing properties for a large landholder in the city. The management agreement provides that the property manager shall be responsible for finding new tenants and maintaining the properties. The fee Thornton Enterprises may charge for its services is MOST LIKELY a percentage of the
    A. net income earned from the properties.
    B. gross income earned from the properties.
    C. total expenses incurred in maintaining the properties.
    D. ROI.

18. On a settlement statement, the commission owed to the broker is a
    A. debit to the sellers.
    B. debit to the buyers.
    C. credit to the sellers and a debit to the buyers.
    D. credit to the buyers.

19. Mike and Joyce entered into an agreement to sell a rental property they own. The closing is to take place September 15. On September 1, Mike and Joyce received a rent payment for the month of September from the tenant. Under the terms of the purchase agreement, the buyers are entitled to any rent received covering the period subsequent to the closing. At the closing, the prepaid rent will appear as a
    A. credit to the sellers and a debit to the buyers.
    B. debit to the sellers and a credit to the buyers.
    C. credit to the buyers.
    D. debit to the sellers.

20. Under the provisions of the Real Estate Settlement Procedures Act, certain disclosures are required from the
    A. seller in a residential real estate transaction.
    B. buyer in a residential real estate transaction.
    C. lender in a residential real estate transaction.
    D. closer in a residential real estate transaction.

21. Which of the following real estate documents will LEAST LIKELY be recorded at the county recorder's office?
    A. Contract for deed
    B. Long-term lease
    C. Option agreement
    D. Purchase agreement

22. Salesperson Harry is proposing an advertisement for a house on which he obtained a listing for broker Wallace. In the ad, Harry
    A. need not show Wallace's name if Harry's phone number appears.
    B. must show his association with Wallace.
    C. must show the sale price of the property.
    D. All of the above

23. Broker Sally obtained a listing agreement on the sale of Hamilton's house. A buyer was found and purchase agreements signed. It is Sally's duty to make sure that the buyer
    A. will make a loan application.
    B. has a copy of all written agreements.
    C. is qualified for the mortgage.
    D. has inspected the home.

24. Sellers Fred and Margaret have executed three open listings with three brokers around town. All three brokers would like to place "For Sale" signs on the seller's property. Under these circumstances
    A. a broker does not have to obtain the seller's permission before placing a sign on the property.
    B. only one For Sale sign may be placed on the property at one time.
    C. upon obtaining the seller's written consent, all can place signs on the property.
    D. the first listing broker must consent to all signs.

25. For a parcel of real estate to have value, it must have
    A. utility.
    B. scarcity.
    C. transferability.
    D. All of the above

26. Under the income approach to estimating the value of real estate, the capitalization rate is the
    A. rate at which the property increases in value.
    B. rate of return the property earns on an investment.
    C. rate of capital required to keep a property operating by its most effective method.
    D. maximum rate of return allowed by law on an investment.

27. Robert was asked to value a single-family home in order to determine the proposed sale price. Robert found five comparable houses that had recently sold. Adjustments to the sale prices of the comparables should be made to reflect differences in
    A. location, physical condition, and amenities of the property.
    B. gross rent multiplier of other properties.
    C. expired properties.
    D. current listed properties.

28. The final step in the appraisal process is to
    A. make copies for the lender.
    B. create an invoice.
    C. adjust the subject property.
    D. reconcile the differences.

29. If a landlord breaches the lease and the unit is uninhabitable, what action can the tenant take?
    A. Suit for possession
    B. Constructive eviction
    C. Tenancy at sufferance
    D. Covenant of quiet possession

30. How can tenancy at sufferance be created?
    A. By failure to surrender possession
    B. By payment of rent
    C. By bringing an unlawful detainer action
    D. By giving 30 days' written notice

31. If the title will pass to a third party upon the death of the life tenant, what was the third party's interest in the property?
    A. Remainder interest
    B. Reversionary interest
    C. Conditional interest
    D. Redemption interest

32. What is the interest of the grantee when real estate is conveyed only for as long as specified conditions are met?
    A. Defeasible fee
    B. Indefeasible fee
    C. Restrictive fee
    D. Base fee

33. FHA insurance regulations state that the
    A. FHA set the interest rate.
    B. buyer and/or seller may pay the points.
    C. mortgage insurance premium be paid by the seller.
    D. closing costs be paid by the buyer.

34. The United States uses both lien theory and title theory in mortgage law. Under the title theory the
    A. mortgagor has title to the property.
    B. mortgagee has title to the property.
    C. mortgagor and mortgagee jointly hold title.
    D. buyer holds title in trust.

35. Brokers who conspire to set commission rates or enter into an agreement to allocate a specific market are subject to which of the following?
    A. Sherman Antitrust Act
    B. Law of agency
    C. Blue-sky laws
    D. Securities Act of 1933

36. Which of the following affect the control and regulation of land use?
    A. Public and private land-use controls
    B. Zoning ordinances
    C. Deed restrictions
    D. All of the above

37. Under a percentage lease, the lessee pays $400 per month plus 2.75 percent of gross sales. Last month's gross sales were $198,210. How much is the rent?
    A. $5,450.78
    B. $5,850.78
    C. $5,540.78
    D. $5,580.78

38. What type of lease requires the lessee to pay taxes, insurance, and repairs?
   A. Net lease
   B. Percentage lease
   C. Variable lease
   D. Gross lease

39. After signing a lease, the lessor obtains which of the following interests in real estate?
   A. Freehold estate
   B. Leased fee interest
   C. Leasehold interest
   D. Remainderman interest

40. If the market value of a property is $72,000 and it is assessed at 67 percent of value, what are the monthly taxes if the tax rate for the area is $6.50 per $100 of the assessed value?
   A. $3,157.38
   B. $4,857.50
   C. $261.30
   D. $485.75

41. A $50,000 mortgage on a property represents an 80 percent loan-to-value ratio. If the real estate was assessed at 82 percent, the taxes were based on $4 per $100 of assessed value, and the taxes were $2,050 annually, what was the sale price of the home?
   A. $62,500
   B. $51,250
   C. $41,000
   D. $50,000

42. Which of the following is a method of foreclosure that does not require civil action?
   A. Judicial foreclosure
   B. Strict foreclosure
   C. Sheriff's foreclosure
   D. Nonjudicial foreclosure

43. If a home sells for $65,900, and the mortgage requires a 40 percent down payment and a 1 percent origination fee plus $450 in closing costs, how much does the buyer need to close?
   A. $26,623.60
   B. $27,205.40
   C. $27,173.59
   D. $26,360.00

44. If a building is 200 feet wide, 300 feet long, and five stories high (each story 12 feet in height), how much does the building cost at $0.79 per cubic foot?
   A. $237,000
   B. $275,982
   C. $568,880
   D. $2,844,000

45. Prorated items that represent prepaid expenses of the seller should be shown on the settlement statement as a
   A. credit to the seller and debit to the buyer.
   B. debit to the seller and credit to the buyer.
   C. credit to the buyer.
   D. debit to the seller.

46. A mortgagor can get direct financing from all of the following EXCEPT
   A. mortgage banking companies.
   B. savings and loan associations.
   C. commercial banks.
   D. Ginnie Mae.

47. After the statute of limitations has run out, a contract that has been breached is which of the following?
   A. Unenforceable
   B. Rescinded
   C. Terminated
   D. Discharged

48. In the event the parties to a contract wish to delete a provision in the printed agreement form, they should
   A. execute a supplement to the purchase agreement.
   B. cross out the provisions to be deleted.
   C. have their signatures notarized.
   D. arrive at an oral agreement to make the changes.

49. A licensed real estate broker
   A. becomes an agent of the vendee upon obtaining a valid listing.
   B. can disclose any truthful information received from the principal.
   C. becomes an agent of the vendor when a buyer is found.
   D. must disclose all material facts to the principal.

50. How many acres are in the S½ of the NW¼ of the SE¼ of a section?
    A. 10
    B. 20
    C. 40
    D. 120

51. Greg listed his home with the XYZ Brokerage Company under an open listing agreement. After the sale of the property, a dispute arose between XYZ Brokerage and Sunday Brokerage; each claimed to be entitled to a commission. In this situation, the commission should be paid to the broker who
    A. listed the property.
    B. advertised the property.
    C. obtained the first offer.
    D. was the procuring cause of the sale.

52. Broker Sam has an exclusive-right-to-sell listing with Ned. While Ned is out of town on business, Sam finds a buyer who is interested in the house if Ned will take a purchase money mortgage. However, the buyer must have a commitment from the seller prior to Ned's scheduled return to the city. Under these circumstances
    A. Sam may enter into a binding agreement on behalf of Ned.
    B. Sam may collect a commission even if the transaction falls through due to Ned's absence from the city.
    C. the buyer is deemed to have an option until Ned signs.
    D. Sam must obtain the signature of Ned in order to get a commission.

53. Sandy and Gary, who are not married, jointly own a parcel of real estate. Each owns an undivided interest. Sandy's share is two-thirds and Gary's share is one-third. This form of ownership is
    A. tenancy in common.
    B. joint tenancy.
    C. tenancy by the entirety.
    D. community property ownership.

54. Jay, an unmarried man, signed a contract to purchase real estate. The contract included a clause providing that Jay's liability would terminate and his deposit be refunded if a duplicate of the contract signed by the seller is not delivered to him within two days of the contract date. Owner Saul signed the contract the next day. On the third day the broker attempted to deliver the signed copy to Jay, but learned that he had since died as the result of an accident. In these circumstances
    A. because the seller had accepted the offer within the time limit, the estate of the deceased buyer is liable for completion of the contract.
    B. the contract, by its terms, is void.
    C. death cancels all real estate contracts.
    D. the broker can collect a commission from the seller.

55. Sam leases a property to Henry under an oral one-year lease. If Henry defaults, Sam may
    A. not bring court action because of parol evidence rule.
    B. not bring court action because of the statute of frauds.
    C. bring a court action because one-year leases need not be in writing to be enforced.
    D. bring a court action because the statute of limitations does not apply to oral leases.

56. Acceleration is a term associated with which of the following?
    A. Listings
    B. Sales contracts
    C. Mortgages
    D. Leases

57. The federal Fair Housing Act of 1968 makes it illegal to discriminate because of
    A. age.
    B. marital status.
    C. public assistance.
    D. religion.

58. Barclay owns a large parcel of undeveloped property, in severalty, very near a large urban area. Developer Longworth, who believes the property could be developed for commercial purposes, enters into an agreement with Barclay to purchase the property. Longworth insists that Barclay's wife sign the deed. The purpose of obtaining Mrs. Barclay's signature is to
    A. terminate any rights Mrs. Barclay may have in the property.
    B. defeat any curtesy rights.
    C. provide the developer with a sale-leaseback agreement.
    D. subordinate Barclay's wife's interest to that of Longworth.

59. Broker Allen enters into a listing agreement with seller Bennett wherein Bennett will receive $12,000 from the sale of a vacant lot and Allen will receive any sale proceeds over and above that amount. The type of listing agreement into which Allen and Bennett entered is
    A. called a gross listing.
    B. a highly popular method of listing property in most states.
    C. called an exclusive agency.
    D. called a net listing.

60. If the annual net income from certain commercial property is $22,000, and the capitalization rate is 8 percent, what is the value of the property using the income approach?
    A. $275,000
    B. $176,000
    C. $200,000
    D. $183,000

61. If a storage tank that measures 12' × 9' × 8' was designed to store natural gas, and the cost of natural gas is $1.82 per cubic foot, what does it cost to fill the tank to one-half its capacity?
    A. $864.00
    B. $1,572.48
    C. $786.24
    D. $684.58

62. A real estate sales contract becomes valid or in effect when it has been signed by which of the following?
    A. Buyer
    B. Buyer and seller
    C. Seller
    D. Broker and seller

63. Sandy and Chris enter into an agreement wherein Chris will mow Sandy's lawn every two weeks during the course of the summer. Shortly thereafter, Chris decides to go into a different business. George would like to assume Chris's duties mowing the lawn. Sandy agrees and enters into a new contract with George. Sandy and Chris tear up the original agreement. This is known as a(n)
    A. assignment.
    B. novation.
    C. secondary agreement.
    D. sublease.

64. All of the following situations are in violation of the federal Fair Housing Act of 1968 EXCEPT the
    A. refusal of property manager Joe Kelley to rent an apartment to a Catholic couple who are otherwise qualified.
    B. general policy of the Locust Loan Company, which avoids granting home improvement loans to individuals in "changing" neighborhoods.
    C. intentional neglect of broker Harvey Hall to show a black family any property listings of homes in all-white neighborhoods.
    D. insistence of Agnes Taylor, a widow, on renting her spare bedroom only to another woman.

65. If a house sold for $140,000, and the buyer obtained an FHA mortgage in the amount of $136,500, how much money would be paid for four points?
    A. $5,420
    B. $5,460
    C. $5,600
    D. $5,640

66. What is a tenancy at will?
    A. Tenancy with the consent of the landlord
    B. Tenancy that expires on a specific date
    C. Tenancy created by the death of the owner
    D. Tenancy created by the testator

67. Which of the following BEST describes a datum?
    A. Undersized or fractional section
    B. Imaginary line from which heights are measured
    C. Primary township
    D. Imaginary line that measures longitude

68. A licensed salesperson is authorized by law to
    A. sign a closing statement.
    B. collect a commission directly from a principal for performing assigned duties.
    C. advertise listed property under the salesperson's own name.
    D. act under the supervision of a real estate broker.

69. Which of the following BEST describes steering?
    A. Leading prospective homeowners to or away from certain areas
    B. Refusing to make loans to persons in certain areas
    C. A requirement to join MLS
    D. Practice of setting commissions

70. In establishing priorities for liens
    A. a mechanic's lien is always first in priority.
    B. the date on which the lien was recorded determines priority.
    C. the date on which the debt was incurred determines priority.
    D. a broker's lien is automatically in first priority.

71. A management agreement usually covers which of the following items?
    A. Statement of owner's purpose
    B. Estoppel certificates
    C. Joint and several liability
    D. Waiver of subrogation

72. If either party to a real estate sales contract defaults, usually the other party can
    A. bring an action of adverse possession.
    B. declare the sale canceled and has no legal recourse.
    C. serve notice of redemption.
    D. sue for specific performance.

73. The taxes for 2005 are $743.25 and have not been paid. If the sale is to be closed on August 12, 2005, which of the following is TRUE? (Use a 360-day year.)
    A. $284.91 DS, CB
    B. $458.32 DS, CB
    C. $284.91 CB, DS
    D. $458.32 CS, DB

74. The supply of mortgage credit for single-family homes is regulated by the Federal Reserve System through the use of which of the following?
    A. Reserve requirements and discount rates
    B. Federal National Mortgage Association
    C. Federal Housing Administration
    D. Housing and Urban Development Corporation

75. In estimating the value of commercial property, what is the appraiser's most important consideration?
    A. Reproduction cost
    B. Net income
    C. Gross rent multiplier
    D. Gross income

76. All of the following are examples of a specific lien EXCEPT
    A. real estate taxes.
    B. an IRS lien.
    C. a mortgage.
    D. a mechanic's lien.

77. Which of the following types of ownership are characterized by the right of survivorship?
    A. Joint tenancy and tenancy by the entireties
    B. Joint tenancy and severalty
    C. Joint tenancy and tenancy in common
    D. Joint tenancy and condominium tenancy

78. The type of ownership that blends severalty and tenancy in common ownership is a
   A. periodic tenancy.
   B. condominium.
   C. cooperative.
   D. life estate.

79. If *K* grants a life estate to *L* based on the life of *M*, and *L* dies before *M*, what is the status of the life estate?
   A. It belongs to *K* in fee simple absolute ownership.
   B. It belongs to *K*'s remainderman.
   C. It belongs to *M* and the heirs of *M*.
   D. It belongs to *L*'s heirs until the death of *M*.

80. A subdivision has a deed restriction that does not allow tree houses. An architect moves into the subdivision and builds a tree house in the back yard. How many neighbors will it take to enforce the deed restriction and what action should be taken?
   A. 75 percent of the neighbors must sign a petition that will be given to the local zoning board for enforcement.
   B. Only one neighbor needs to take action through the local zoning board.
   C. Only one neighbor needs to take action through the court system.
   D. 75 percent of the neighbors must take action through private court action.

81. A developer discovers that a proposed swimming pool in a condominium community meets all local zoning requirements except for the side yard line on one side of the clubhouse. What should the developer do?
   A. Because it's only on one side of the clubhouse, no action is necessary on the part of the developer.
   B. The developer should file for a variance with the local zoning board.
   C. The developer should file for a nonconforming use with the local zoning board.
   D. The developer should continue with the construction and later file for an adverse possession claim to the property.

82. A lot is valued at $75,000. The two-story house measures 30' × 50' and is valued at $100 a square foot. If the owner is willing to pay a 6 percent commission, the agent should list the property for at least what amount?
   A. $375,000
   B. $389,350
   C. $397,500
   D. $398,936

83. Which of the following situations would terminate a listing agreement without legal liability?
   A. Death of the agent
   B. Destruction of the broker's office
   C. Death of the seller
   D. Bankruptcy of the agent

84. An exclusive listing is usually an
   A. executory bilateral contract.
   B. exculpatory bilateral contract.
   C. executed unilateral contract.
   D. executed implied contract.

85. An agent listed a property for $89,000 and five days later received an offer of $89,000. Which of the following is TRUE?
   A. The seller must accept the offer because it is for the listed price.
   B. The buyer cannot withdraw the offer because it is for the listed price.
   C. The seller does not have to accept the offer or pay the broker's commission unless she or he accepts the offer.
   D. The buyer may withdraw the offer prior to its acceptance.

86. A contract that stipulates an offer can be accepted within a specified time and contains a specified price and specified terms, which may or may not include the right of assignment, in return for the payment of consideration is known as a(n)
   A. sales contract.
   B. lease.
   C. offer.
   D. option.

87. Which of the following statements is NOT true?
    A. A land contract is also known as an installment contract.
    B. If a time for performance is not stated in a contract, the duties are expected to be performed within a reasonable time.
    C. An equitable title is transferred when the deed is signed by the grantor at the closing table.
    D. Liquidated damages are agreed to in advance by the buyer and seller to compensate one party if the other does not live up to the contract.

88. Which of the following is NOT false?
    A. An earnest money deposit is necessary to create a legally binding contract.
    B. The death of the agent will affect the status of listing contracts.
    C. If "time is of the essence" is found in a contract, then the contract must be performed within the time limit specified.
    D. A contract entered into under duress, undue influence, or misrepresentation is void.

89. Because the cost of clean-up and removal of hazardous waste can be greater than the value of the property, an agent is expected to have
    A. technical expertise in possible hazardous substances.
    B. technical expertise in the area of asbestos, which is present in so many buildings.
    C. taken a class on how to identify asbestos, because it is present in so many buildings.
    D. a basic knowledge of hazardous substances and be aware of environmental issues in a real estate transaction.

90. The primary objectives of a property manager are to
    A. generate the highest net operating income of the property while maintaining and preserving the owner's investment.
    B. secure tenants by offering the lowest possible rents that the budget allows.
    C. negotiate contracts with service providers that give the manager the most advantageous kickbacks.
    D. cut expenses in any way necessary to generate a profit for the owner.

91. A lease with a definite beginning, a definite ending, and no notice is required to terminate the lease is a(n)
    A. estate for years.
    B. periodic tenancy.
    C. estate at will.
    D. estate at sufferance.

92. A tenant entered into a three-year lease that was an estate for years agreement. On termination of the lease agreement, the tenant remained in possession of the property. Which of the following is TRUE?
    A. If the landlord accepted payment for another month, the original lease automatically renewed for another term.
    B. The landlord could evict the tenant or treat the holdover tenant as a periodic tenancy.
    C. The tenant had the right to remain in the property because the landlord did not give proper notice.
    D. The tenant had the right to remain in the property because the landlord does not have it rented to anyone anyway.

93. Which of the following is NOT a requirement for a valid lease?
    A. Offer and acceptance
    B. Description of the leased premises
    C. Capacity to contract
    D. An option agreement

94. A property leases for $700 per month, plus 4 percent of all gross sales of more than $350,000. How much were the gross sales if the total rent paid for the year was $14,975?
    A. $414,375
    B. $164,375
    C. $356,375
    D. $514,375

95. A homeowner purchased a first principal place of residence for $69,000. In the next five years, she made $10,000 worth of improvements. The property sold for $109,000 and a 6 percent commission was paid. Which of the following is TRUE regarding the capital gains?
    A. The adjusted basis is $102,460.
    B. The capital gain is $23,460.
    C. The capital gain is $33,460.
    D. The adjusted basis is $89,000.

96. Which of the following is TRUE regarding the refinancing of property?
    A. A title search is conducted, the property is appraised, and the borrower must requalify for the loan.
    B. The general rule of thumb is that a property should be refinanced when there is a 1 percent interest differential.
    C. If the borrowers have divorced, only one party's income will still be considered because only one name is now on the deed.
    D. If the borrowers have divorced, both parties' income will still be considered because both names are on the deed.

97. What is the priority of the following liens?
    A. IRS liens, then property taxes
    B. IRS liens, then special assessments
    C. First mortgage, then property taxes
    D. Property taxes, then first mortgage

98. A borrower purchased mortgagee's title insurance on a property. After the final payment was made on the mortgage, a title defect was found. The borrower may have recourse through the
    A. previous owner if a general warranty deed was transferred at the closing.
    B. previous owner if a quitclaim deed was transferred at the closing.
    C. title insurance company because a title policy was secured when the property was purchased.
    D. title insurance company even though a mortgagee's title insurance was secured when the property was purchased.

99. What is the MAJOR DIFFERENCE between constructive notice and actual notice?
    A. Constructive notice is direct knowledge, while actual notice is legal notice.
    B. Constructive notice is documented at an attorney's office, while actual notice is documented through the newspapers.
    C. Constructive notice provides protection because it is recorded by an attorney, while actual notice can be recorded by an agent.
    D. Constructive notice is notice that the law presumes we have, while actual notice is what a party actually knows.

100. Which of the following is NOT true regarding RESPA?
    A. RESPA requirements apply when a residential purchase is financed by a federally related mortgage loan.
    B. RESPA was enacted to eliminate kickbacks and other referral fees that increase the cost of settlement.
    C. RESPA requires that a good-faith estimate of settlement costs be provided to the buyer within two days of loan application.
    D. The settlement statement must be made available for inspection by the borrower at or before settlement.

101. Robert and Dorothy, no longer needing their large house, decide to sell the house and move into a cooperative apartment building. Under the cooperative form of ownership, Robert and Dorothy will
    A. become stockholders in a corporation.
    B. never lose their apartment if they pay their share of the cooperative's taxes.
    C. take out a new mortgage on their unit.
    D. receive a 20-year lease for their unit.

102. Which of the following is NOT an example of a legal description?
    A. Geodetic survey
    B. Lot and block
    C. Metes and bounds
    D. Torrens system

103. Carrie is buying a single-family home for investment purposes. The appraiser will MOST LIKELY use which method to appraise the property?
    A. Income
    B. GIM
    C. Cost
    D. Market data

104. In appraising a residential property, the appraiser would make a
    A. positive adjustment to the subject property if the subject property had an amenity the comparable did not.
    B. negative adjustment to the subject property if the subject property had an amenity the comparable did not.
    C. positive adjustment to the comparable property if the subject property had an amenity the comparable did not.
    D. negative adjustment to the comparable property if the comparable property did not have an amenity the subject property had.

105. Which of the following terms is associated with real estate property taxes?
    A. Caveat emptor
    B. Caveat venditor
    C. Annuit coeptis
    D. Ad valorem

106. The closing date was scheduled for October 31 and the seller made her mortgage payment on October 1. The loan balance after the October 1 payment was $125,000 and the interest rate was 8 percent. If there were no prepayment penalties, the loan payoff would be
    A. $135,000.00.
    B. $8,333.33.
    C. $125,833.33.
    D. $124,166.67.

107. The sellers accepted an offer of $510,000 for their property. On closing their mortgage balance was $200,000, the commission paid was 6 percent, and they had $5,000 in other closing costs. The net to the sellers is
    A. $30,600.
    B. $274,400.
    C. $310,000.
    D. $479,400.

108. On April 1 a borrower made her monthly payment principal and interest payment of $212.47 and her loan balance was $6,945.23. On May 1 she made another principal and interest payment and paid off the loan. If the interest rate was 10 percent, what was her payoff?
    A. $6,790.64
    B. $6,887.35
    C. $6,250.71
    D. $6,125.99

109. A lender charged $4,000 in discount points on a $100,000 loan. How many discount points were charged?
    A. 1
    B. 10
    C. 4
    D. 40

110. A borrower negotiated a 90 percent loan and the lender is charging two points. If his offer of $190,000 is accepted, what is the minimum cash he will need to close?
    A. $22,420
    B. $19,000
    C. $25,239
    D. $22,240

ANSWERS

For additional information please refer to the page number in parentheses.

1. **(D)** $137,500 – 50,000 = $87,500
    $50,000 × 3% = $1,500
    $87,500 × 5% = $4,375
    $4,375 + 1,500 = $5,875
    $137,500 – 5,875 = $131,625 (198)

2. **(C)** Nolan is the only party bound to the contract; therefore, it is a unilateral contract. (56)

3. **(A)** 20% + 40% = 60%
    $3,600 ÷ 60% = $6,000
    $6,000 ÷ 5% = $120,000 (191)

4. **(D)** By definition of term loan. (146)

5. **(B)** Ownership in severalty is ownership by one party. (23)

6. **(B)** A deficiency judgment allows a mortgagee to sue for the balance owned when the security for a loan is insufficient to satisfy the debt. (152)

7. **(B)** The Torrens system is a method of registering land, and the Torrens certificate is proof of ownership. (113)

8. **(B)** A title transferred by a quitclaim deed provides no warranties. It transfers whatever interest the grantor has in the property. (115)

9. **(B)** In an open listing, the seller retains the right to sell the property and not pay a commission to the broker. (18)

10. **(A)** The buyer's interest in the property when legal title is held by another party is known as equitable title. (57)

11. **(D)** A deed in lieu of foreclosure conveys title to the lender, but it does not indicate the sale of property. (115)

12. **(B)** A = 50' × 137'

    A = 6,850 sq. ft.
    6,850 × $4.50 = $30,825
    $30,825 × 7.25% = $2,234.81 (191 & 215)

13. **(A)** The buyer owes interest from June 15 through June 30, or 15 days.
    $142,500 × 7.75% = $11,043.75
    $11,043.75 ÷ 360 = $30.6770
    $30.6770 × 15 = $460.16 (210)

14. **(A)** To transfer a title, a deed is signed by the grantors. (115)

15. **(D)** Proof of heirship is not one of the requirements for a valid deed. (114-115)

16. **(A)** The rental of rooms in an owner-occupied one- to four-family dwelling is exempt from the federal Fair Housing Act. No broker can be used and the owner cannot discriminate in advertising. (28)

17. **(B)** Property managers are usually paid a percentage of the gross income. (194)

18. **(A)** The commission is a debit to the seller on a settlement sheet. (210)

19. **(B)** The sellers owe the remaining month's rent to the buyer. (210)

20. **(C)** RESPA requires that the lender make the proper disclosures. (119)

21. **(D)** A purchase agreement would least likely be recorded at the county recorder's office. (113)

22. **(B)** State laws require that all listed property be advertised through the broker. (20)

23. **(B)** State laws require that parties receive a copy of all contracts they sign. (57)

24. **(C)** If consent is secured from the seller, all the brokers in the open listing can place signs on the property. (Some states require written consent.) (18)

25. **(D)** DUST is the acronym to remember the characteristics of value. Demand, utility, scarcity, and transferability make real estate valuable. (31)

26. **(B)** By definition of capitalization rate. (204)

27. **(A)** Adjustments are made in the amenities of the comparable properties. (30)

28. **(D)** The final step in the appraisal process is to reconcile the difference to arrive at the value. (31)

29. **(B)** If the property is uninhabitable, the tenant may leave the property. This is known as constructive eviction. (92)

30. **(A)** Tenancy at sufferance is created when the tenant refuses to surrender possession of the property upon the expiration of the lease. (82)

31. **(A)** By definition of remainder interest. (22)

32. **(A)** A fee simple defeasible title is transferred when the real estate is conveyed with specified conditions. (22)

33. **(B)** The buyer and/or seller may pay the points in FHA-insured loans. (147)

34. **(B)** In title-theory states, the lender has title to the property. (143)

35. **(A)** The Sherman Antitrust Act and state laws prohibit price fixing. (171)

36. **(D)** All are examples of public and private land-use controls. (13)

37. **(B)** $198,210 \times 2.75\% = \$5,450.78$
$\$5,450.78 + 400 = \$5,850.78$ (195)

38. **(A)** By definition of net lease. (83)

39. **(B)** The landlord's interest is a leased fee interest, while the tenant's interest is a leasehold interest. (81)

40. **(C)** $6.50 ÷ 100 = 0.065
$72,000 × 67% = $48,240
$48,240 × 0.065 = $3,135.60
$3,135.60 ÷ 12 = $261.30 (202)

41. **(A)** $50,000 ÷ 80% = $62,500 (202)

42. **(D)** Nonjudicial foreclosure does not involve civil action. The lender is allowed to foreclose by advertisement. (143)

43. **(B)**

Debit	Credit
$65,900.00	$39,540.00
395.40	
450.00	
$66,745.40	$39,540.00

$65,900 × 40% = $26,360
$65,900 – 26,360 = $39,540
$39,540 × 1% = $395.40
$66,745.40   Debits – $39,540.00 Credits = $27,205.40 (210)

44. **(D)** V = 200' × 300' × 12' = 720,000 cu. ft.
720,000 × 0.79 = $568,880 × 5 = $2,844,000 (215)

45. **(A)** Prepaid expenses are a credit to the seller and a debit to the buyer. (210)

46. **(D)** Ginnie Mae does not negotiate loans. (148)

47. **(A)** A contract not performed within the statutory time period is unenforceable. (56)

48. **(A)** To delete a provision in an agreement, the parties should execute a supplement to the purchase agreement. (123)

49. **(D)** A broker is required by the law of agency to disclose all material facts to the principal. (13)

50. **(B)** 640 ÷ 4 ÷ 4 ÷ 2 = 20 acres (3)

51. **(D)** The party who is the procuring cause of the sale should be paid the commission. (172)

52. **(D)** An agent cannot accept offers for a seller unless authorized to do so by the seller through a power of attorney or other legal document. (13)

53. **(A)** Tenancy in common ownership allows unequal shares of the real estate. (23)

54. **(B)** The signed contract was not received by the buyer within two days and on the death of the buyer became void. (20)

55. **(C)** Leases for less than one year need not be in writing and are enforceable. (55)

56. **(C)** An acceleration clause in the mortgage allows the lender to call the entire mortgage balance due and payable. (155)

57. **(D)** Religion is a protected class under the federal Fair Housing Act. (26)

58. **(A)** Longworth wants to assure that Mrs. Barclay has released her dower rights to the property. (22)

59. **(D)** By definition of net listing. (18)

60. **(A)** $22,000 ÷ 8% = $275,000 (204)

61. **(C)** V = 12' × 9' × 8' = 864 cu. ft.
       864 × $1.82 = $1,572.48 ÷ 2 = $786.24 (215)

62. **(B)** The sales contract becomes valid when signed by the buyer and seller. (56)

63. **(B)** By definition of novation. (57)

64. **(D)** A homeowner can rent a spare bedroom and discriminate because of gender. (28)

65. **(B)** $136,500 × 4% = $5,460 (198)

66. **(A)** A tenancy at will is a lease for an uncertain duration that is created with the consent of the landlord. (82)

67. **(B)** By definition of datum. (2)

68. **(D)** An agent can work only under the authority of a broker. (167)

69. **(A)** By definition of steering. (28)

70. **(B)** Unless there are unusual circumstances, the date on which the lien was recorded determines priority. (112-113)

71. **(A)** A management agreement must contain a statement of the owner's purpose. (80)

72. **(D)** By definition of specific performance. (57)

73. **(B)** Count from January 1 through August 12 for 222 days.
       $743.25 ÷ 360 = $2.0645 $2.0645 × 222 = $458.32 DS, CB (202)

74. **(A)** The purpose of the Federal Reserve is to regulate the flow of money by regulating reserve requirements and discount rates. (140)

75. **(B)** The annual net operating income is used to compute the value of the property. (204)

76. **(B)** An IRS lien is a general lien against real and personal property. (112)

77. **(A)** By definition of joint tenancy and tenancy by the entireties. (23)

78. **(B)** When an owner purchases a condominium, the air space is owned in severalty; whereas the land and the improvements on the land are owned by all members in the condominium community as tenancy in common. (24)

79. **(D)** *L* has been granted a life estate pur autre vie based on the life of *M*. Should *L* predecease *M*, *L*'s heirs inherit the life estate as long as *M* is alive. (22)

80. **(C)** Only one neighbor is necessary to enforce the deed restrictions through court action. (13)

81. **(B)** A variance may be granted to relieve the harshness of a zoning ordinance. (60)

82. **(D)** 100% – 6% = 94%
    A = 30' × 50' = 1,500 × 2 = 3,000 sq. ft.
    3,000 × $100 = $300,000
    $300,000 + 75,000 = $375,000
    $375,000 ÷ 94% = $398,936.17 or $398,936 (191 & 215)

83. **(C)** Upon the death of either the principal broker or the seller, the listing is void. (19)

84. **(A)** A listing contract is an executory contract in that something remains to be performed by one or more parties. It is a bilateral contract because all parties are bound to the contract. (56)

85. **(D)** An offer can be rescinded at any time prior to its acceptance. The seller does not have to accept a full price offer, but a commission is due the broker. (20)

86. **(D)** By definition of option contract. (58)

87. **(C)** The legal title is transferred to the buyer at the closing, not equitable title. (57)

88. **(C)** When time is of the essence is stated in a contract, it means that the contract must be performed within the specified time limit. Any party that does not perform within the proper time period is liable for breach of contract. (59)

89. **(D)** Agents are not expected to be experts in the area of hazardous substances, but should have a basic knowledge so all parties in the transaction can make informed decisions. (90)

90. **(A)** The objectives of a property manager are to generate the highest net operating income from a property while maintaining, modernizing, and preserving the owner's interest. (92)

91. **(A)** By the definition of estate for years. (82)

92. **(B)** If the tenant remains in possession of the property after the expiration of the lease, the landlord may evict the tenant or accept payment from the tenant and create a periodic tenancy. (82)

93. **(D)** A lease does not have to contain an option agreement to be valid. (58 & 81)

94. **(D)** $700 × 12 = $8,400
    $14,975 – $8,400 = $6,575
    $6,575 ÷ 4% = $164,375
    $164,375 + $350,000 = $514,375 (195)

95. **(B)** $69,000 + $10,000 = $79,000 adjusted basis
    $109,000 – 6% = $102,460 net to seller
    $102,460 – $79,000 = $23,460 capital gains (206)

96. **(A)** When a property is refinanced, a title search is conducted, the property is appraised, the borrower must qualify for the loan, and closing costs must be paid. (151)

97. **(D)** Property taxes and special assessments are paid before all other liens. (113)

98. **(A)** If a general warranty deed was given, there may be recourse through the previous owner. (110 & 115)

99. **(D)** By definitions of constructive and actual notice. (113)

100. **(C)** The good-faith estimate must be given to the buyer within three business days of loan application. (119)

101. **(A)** When purchasing a cooperative, the owner receives stock in the company (cooperative) and a proprietary lease for the apartment. (25)

102. **(D)** The Torrens system is a system of land registration, not a legal description. (7)

103. **(D)** The appraiser would use the market data approach to determine value. (30)

104. **(C)** If the subject property has an amenity that the comparable does not, then the appraiser makes a positive adjustment (adds) to the comparable property. (30)

105. **(D)** Property taxes are also called *ad valorem* taxes. (108)

106. **(C)** $125,000 × 8% = $10,000
$10,000 ÷ 12 = $833.33
$125,000 + $833.33 = $125,833.33 (210)

107. **(B)** $510,000 × 6% = $30,600
$510,000 − $200,000 − $30,600 − 5,000 = $274,400 (190)

108. **(A)** $6,945.23 × 10% = $694.52 ÷ 12 = $57.88
$212.47 − $57.88 = $154.59
$6,945.23 − $154.59 = $6,790.64 (191 & 198)

109. **(C)** $4,000 ÷ $100,000 = 0.04 = 4 percent or 4 points (198)

110. **(A)** $190,000 × 90% = $171,000
$171,000 × 2% = $3,420
$190,000 − $171,000 = $19,000
$19,000 + $3,420 = $22,420 (198)

STATE-SPECIFIC
QUESTIONS TO KNOW

Before you take your exam, be sure you can answer these questions about your state.

1. Is an agency disclosure form used in your state? ____yes ____no

    If yes, when must it be given to the buyer, seller, landlord, tenant? _____

2. Is a dual agency disclosure form used in your state? ____yes ____no

    If yes, when is it required to be disclosed? _____

3. Is designated agency offered in your state? ____yes ____no

4. Is a property disclosure statement used in your state? ____yes ____no

    If yes, when is it given to the buyer? _____

5. How long are transaction files kept in your state? _____

6. Does your company have a buyer agency agreement? ____yes ____no

    If yes, please read to determine how the buyer agent will be compensated.

7. Does your state have a law regarding stigmatized properties? ____yes ____no

    If yes, please review the legal duties when dealing with a stigmatized property.

8. Does your broker's listing agreement contain a broker protection clause? ____yes ____no

    If yes, what is the standard time frame for the clause? _____

9. Does your state require property management agreements to be in writing? ___yes ___no

10. Does your state have a Landlord-Tenant Act? ____yes ____no

    If yes, can the security deposits be placed in an interest-bearing account? ___yes ___no

11. In your community, who pays for the survey? ____seller ____buyer

12. In your community, who pays for the lender's title policy? ____seller ____buyer

13. Is your state a lien-theory, a title-theory, or an intermediate-theory state? _____

14. Under your state law, when must the earnest money check be deposited into the escrow account? _____

15. In your state, under what conditions may the earnest money check be withdrawn from the escrow account? _____

16. If the broker's license is suspended or revoked, what is the status of the sales associate's license? _____

Web Site Directory

Alabama Real Estate Commission
www.arec.state.al.us

Americans with Disabilities Act
www.usdoj.gov/crt/ada/adahom1.htm

American Society of Home Inspectors
www.ashi.com

Appraisal Foundation
www.appraisalfoundation.org

Appraisal Institute
www.appraisalinstitute.org

Building Owners and Managers Association
www.boma.org

Department of Housing and Urban Development
www.hud.gov

Department of Veterans Affairs
www.va.gov

Environmental Protection Agency
www.epa.gov

Fannie Mae
www.fanniemae.com

Federal Emergency Management Agency
www.fema.gov

Federal Reserve
www.federalreserve.gov

Freddie Mac
www.freddiemac.com

Georgia Real Estate Commission
www.grec.state.ga.us

Ginnie Mae
www.ginniemae.gov

Illinois Office of Banks and Real Estate
www.state.il.us/obr

Internal Revenue Service
www.irs.gov

Institute of Real Estate Management
www.irem.org

Lead Safe USA
www.leadsafeusa.com

Missouri Real Estate Commission
pr.mo.gov/realestate.asp

Montana
mt.gov/DLI/BSD/license/bsd_boards/rre_board/board_page.asp

National Association of Exclusive Buyer Agents
www.naeba.com

National Association of Home Builders
www.nahb.com

National Association of Independent Fee Appraisers
www.naifa.com

National Association of Real Estate Brokers
www.nareb.com

National Association of REALTORS®
www.realtor.org

National Association of Residential Property Managers
www.narpm.com

National Fair Housing Advocate Online
www.fairhousing.com

Nebraska
www.nrec.state.ne.us

Nevada Real Estate Division
www.red.state.nv.us

New Hampshire Real Estate Commission
www.nh.gov/nhrec

North Dakota
www.realestatend.org

Real Estate Buyer's Agent Council
www.rebac.net

Real Estate News
www.inman.com

South Dakota
www.state.sd.us/SDREC

U.S. Department of Justice, Antitrust Division
www.usdoj.gov/atr

U.S. Farm Service Agency
www.fsa.usda.gov

Wyoming Real Estate Commission
realestate.state.wy.us

IRS Form **8300**	**Report of Cash Payments Over $10,000**	FinCEN Form **8300**
(Rev. December 2004)	**Received in a Trade or Business**	(Rev. December 2004)
OMB No. 1545-0892	▶ See instructions for definition of cash.	OMB No. 1506-0018
Department of the Treasury	▶ Use this form for transactions occurring after December 31, 2004. Do not use prior versions after this date.	Department of the Treasury
Internal Revenue Service	**For Privacy Act and Paperwork Reduction Act Notice, see page 5.**	Financial Crimes Enforcement Network

1 Check appropriate box(es) if: **a** ☐ Amends prior report;   **b** ☐ Suspicious transaction.

Part I   **Identity of Individual From Whom the Cash Was Received**

2 If more than one individual is involved, check here and see instructions . . . . ▶ ☐

3 Last name   **4** First name   **5** M.I.   **6** Taxpayer identification number

7 Address (number, street, and apt. or suite no.)   **8** Date of birth . ▶   M M D D Y Y Y Y   (see instructions)

9 City   **10** State   **11** ZIP code   **12** Country (if not U.S.)   **13** Occupation, profession, or business

14 Identifying document (ID)   **a Describe ID** ▶ ....   **b Issued by** ▶ ....   **c Number** ▶

Part II   **Person on Whose Behalf This Transaction Was Conducted**

15 If this transaction was conducted on behalf of more than one person, check here and see instructions . . . . . ▶ ☐

16 Individual's last name or Organization's name   **17** First name   **18** M.I.   **19** Taxpayer identification number

20 Doing business as (DBA) name (see instructions)   Employer identification number

21 Address (number, street, and apt. or suite no.)   **22** Occupation, profession, or business

23 City   **24** State   **25** ZIP code   **26** Country (if not U.S.)

27 Alien identification (ID)   **a Describe ID** ▶ ....   **b Issued by** ▶ ....   **c Number** ▶

Part III   **Description of Transaction and Method of Payment**

28 Date cash received   M M D D Y Y Y Y   **29** Total cash received $ _____ .00   **30** If cash was received in more than one payment, check here . . . ▶ ☐   **31** Total price if different from item 29 $ _____ .00

32 Amount of cash received (in U.S. dollar equivalent) (must equal item 29) (see instructions):

a U.S. currency $ _____ .00 (Amount in $100 bills or higher $ _____ .00)

b Foreign currency $ _____ .00 (Country ▶ _____)

c Cashier's check(s) $ _____ .00   Issuer's name(s) and serial number(s) of the monetary instrument(s) ▶

d Money order(s) $ _____ .00

e Bank draft(s) $ _____ .00

f Traveler's check(s) $ _____ .00

33 Type of transaction

a ☐ Personal property purchased   **f** ☐ Debt obligations paid

b ☐ Real property purchased   **g** ☐ Exchange of cash

c ☐ Personal services provided   **h** ☐ Escrow or trust funds

d ☐ Business services provided   **i** ☐ Bail received by court clerks

e ☐ Intangible property purchased   **j** ☐ Other (specify in item 34) ▶

34 Specific description of property or service shown in 33. Give serial or registration number, address, docket number, etc. ▶ ....

Part IV   **Business That Received Cash**

35 Name of business that received cash   **36** Employer identification number

37 Address (number, street, and apt. or suite no.)   Social security number

38 City   **39** State   **40** ZIP code   **41** Nature of your business

42 Under penalties of perjury, I declare that to the best of my knowledge the information I have furnished above is true, correct, and complete.

Signature ▶ _____ Authorized official   Title ▶ _____

43 Date of signature   M M D D Y Y Y Y   **44** Type or print name of contact person   **45** Contact telephone number   ( )

IRS Form **8300** (Rev. 12-2004)   Cat. No. 62133S   FinCEN Form **8300** (Rev. 12-2004)

IRS Form 8300 (Rev. 12-2004)   Page **2**   **FinCEN Form 8300** (Rev. 12-2004)

Multiple Parties
(Complete applicable parts below if box 2 or 15 on page 1 is checked)

Part I   Continued—Complete if box 2 on page 1 is checked

3 Last name		**4** First name	**5** M.I.	**6** Taxpayer identification number

7 Address (number, street, and apt. or suite no.)		**8** Date of birth . . ▶ (see instructions)	M M D D Y Y Y Y

9 City	**10** State	**11** ZIP code	**12** Country (if not U.S.)	**13** Occupation, profession, or business

14 Identifying document (ID)	**a Describe ID ▶** .... **c Number ▶**	**b Issued by ▶** ....

3 Last name		**4** First name	**5** M.I.	**6** Taxpayer identification number

7 Address (number, street, and apt. or suite no.)		**8** Date of birth . . ▶ (see instructions)	M M D D Y Y Y Y

9 City	**10** State	**11** ZIP code	**12** Country (if not U.S.)	**13** Occupation, profession, or business

14 Identifying document (ID)	**a Describe ID ▶** .... **c Number ▶**	**b Issued by ▶** ....

Part II   Continued—Complete if box 15 on page 1 is checked

16 Individual's last name or Organization's name	**17** First name	**18** M.I.	**19** Taxpayer identification number

20 Doing business as (DBA) name (see instructions)	Employer identification number

21 Address (number, street, and apt. or suite no.)	**22** Occupation, profession, or business

23 City	**24** State	**25** ZIP code	**26** Country (if not U.S.)

27 Alien identification (ID)	**a Describe ID ▶** .... **c Number ▶**	**b Issued by ▶** ....

16 Individual's last name or Organization's name	**17** First name	**18** M.I.	**19** Taxpayer identification number

20 Doing business as (DBA) name (see instructions)	Employer identification number

21 Address (number, street, and apt. or suite no.)	**22** Occupation, profession, or business

23 City	**24** State	**25** ZIP code	**26** Country (if not U.S.)

27 Alien identification (ID)	**a Describe ID ▶** .... **c Number ▶**	**b Issued by ▶** ....

Comments – Please use the lines provided below to comment on or clarify any information you entered on any line in Parts I, II, III, and IV

_____

_____

_____

_____

_____

IRS Form 8300 (Rev. 12-2004)   **FinCEN Form 8300** (Rev. 12-2004)

Section references are to the Internal Revenue Code unless otherwise noted.

Important Reminders

● Section 6050I (26 United States Code (U.S.C.) 6050I) and 31 U.S.C. 5331 require that certain information be reported to the IRS and the Financial Crimes Enforcement Network (FinCEN). This information must be reported on IRS/FinCEN Form 8300.

● Item 33 box i is to be checked only by clerks of the court; box d is to be checked by bail bondsmen. See the instructions on page 5.

● For purposes of section 6050I and 31 U.S.C. 5331, the word "cash" and "currency" have the same meaning. See *Cash* under *Definitions* on page 4.

General Instructions

Who must file. Each person engaged in a trade or business who, in the course of that trade or business, receives more than $10,000 in cash in one transaction or in two or more related transactions, must file Form 8300. Any transactions conducted between a payer (or its agent) and the recipient in a 24-hour period are related transactions. Transactions are considered related even if they occur over a period of more than 24 hours if the recipient knows, or has reason to know, that each transaction is one of a series of connected transactions.

Keep a copy of each Form 8300 for 5 years from the date you file it.

Clerks of Federal or State courts must file Form 8300 if more than $10,000 in cash is received as bail for an individual(s) charged with certain criminal offenses. For these purposes, a clerk includes the clerk's office or any other office, department, division, branch, or unit of the court that is authorized to receive bail. If a person receives bail on behalf of a clerk, the clerk is treated as receiving the bail. See the instructions for Item 33 on page 5.

If multiple payments are made in cash to satisfy bail and the initial payment does not exceed $10,000, the initial payment and subsequent payments must be aggregated and the information return must be filed by the 15th day after receipt of the payment that causes the aggregate amount to exceed $10,000 in cash. In such cases, the reporting requirement can be satisfied either by sending a single written statement with an aggregate amount listed or by furnishing a copy of each Form 8300 relating to that payer. Payments made to satisfy separate bail requirements are not required to be aggregated. See Treasury Regulations section 1.6050I-2.

Casinos must file Form 8300 for nongaming activities (restaurants, shops, etc.).

Voluntary use of Form 8300. Form 8300 may be filed voluntarily for any suspicious transaction (see *Definitions*) for use by the IRS, even if the total amount does not exceed $10,000.

Exceptions. Cash is not required to be reported if it is received:

● By a financial institution required to file Form 104, Currency Transaction Report.

● By a casino required to file (or exempt from filing) Form 103, Currency Transaction Report by Casinos, if the cash is received as part of its gaming business.

● By an agent who receives the cash from a principal, if the agent uses all of the cash within 15 days in a second transaction that is reportable on Form 8300 or on Form 104, and discloses all the information necessary to complete Part II of Form 8300 or Form 104 to the recipient of the cash in the second transaction.

● In a transaction occurring entirely outside the United States. See Publication 1544, Reporting Cash Payments Over $10,000 (Received in a Trade or Business), regarding transactions occurring in Puerto Rico, the Virgin Islands, and territories and possessions of the United States.

● In a transaction that is not in the course of a person's trade or business.

When to file. File Form 8300 by the 15th day after the date the cash was received. If that date falls on a Saturday, Sunday, or legal holiday, file the form on the next business day.

Where to file. File the form with the Internal Revenue Service, Detroit Computing Center, P.O. Box 32621, Detroit, MI 48232.

Statement to be provided. You must give a written or electronic statement to each person named on a required Form 8300 on or before January 31 of the year following the calendar year in which the cash is received. The statement must show the name, telephone number, and address of the information contact for the business, the aggregate amount of reportable cash received, and that the information was furnished to the IRS. Keep a copy of the statement for your records.

Multiple payments. If you receive more than one cash payment for a single transaction or for related transactions, you must report the multiple payments any time you receive a total amount that exceeds $10,000 within any 12-month period. Submit the report within 15 days of the date you receive the payment that

causes the total amount to exceed $10,000. If more than one report is required within 15 days, you may file a combined report. File the combined report no later than the date the earliest report, if filed separately, would have to be filed.

Taxpayer identification number (TIN). You must furnish the correct TIN of the person or persons from whom you receive the cash and, if applicable, the person or persons on whose behalf the transaction is being conducted. You may be subject to penalties for an incorrect or missing TIN.

The TIN for an individual (including a sole proprietorship) is the individual's social security number (SSN). For certain resident aliens who are not eligible to get an SSN and nonresident aliens who are required to file tax returns, it is an IRS Individual Taxpayer Identification Number (ITIN). For other persons, including corporations, partnerships, and estates, it is the employer identification number (EIN).

If you have requested but are not able to get a TIN for one or more of the parties to a transaction within 15 days following the transaction, file the report and attach a statement explaining why the TIN is not included.

Exception: *You are not required to provide the TIN of a person who is a nonresident alien individual or a foreign organization if that person does not have income effectively connected with the conduct of a U.S. trade or business and does not have an office or place of business, or fiscal or paying agent, in the United States. See* Publication 1544 *for more information.*

Penalties. You may be subject to penalties if you fail to file a correct and complete Form 8300 on time and you cannot show that the failure was due to reasonable cause. You may also be subject to penalties if you fail to furnish timely a correct and complete statement to each person named in a required report. A minimum penalty of $25,000 may be imposed if the failure is due to an intentional or willful disregard of the cash reporting requirements.

Penalties may also be imposed for causing, or attempting to cause, a trade or business to fail to file a required report; for causing, or attempting to cause, a trade or business to file a required report containing a material omission or misstatement of fact; or for structuring, or attempting to structure, transactions to avoid the reporting requirements. These violations may also be subject to criminal prosecution which, upon conviction, may result in imprisonment of up to 5 years or fines of up to $250,000 for individuals and $500,000 for corporations or both.

Definitions

Cash. The term "cash" means the following:

• U.S. and foreign coin and currency received in any transaction.

• A cashier's check, money order, bank draft, or traveler's check having a face amount of $10,000 or less that is received in a designated reporting transaction (defined below), or that is received in any transaction in which the recipient knows that the instrument is being used in an attempt to avoid the reporting of the transaction under either section 6050I or 31 U.S.C. 5331.

Note. Cash does not include a check drawn on the payer's own account, such as a personal check, regardless of the amount.

Designated reporting transaction. A retail sale (or the receipt of funds by a broker or other intermediary in connection with a retail sale) of a consumer durable, a collectible, or a travel or entertainment activity.

Retail sale. Any sale (whether or not the sale is for resale or for any other purpose) made in the course of a trade or business if that trade or business principally consists of making sales to ultimate consumers.

Consumer durable. An item of tangible personal property of a type that, under ordinary usage, can reasonably be expected to remain useful for at least 1 year, and that has a sales price of more than $10,000.

Collectible. Any work of art, rug, antique, metal, gem, stamp, coin, etc.

Travel or entertainment activity. An item of travel or entertainment that pertains to a single trip or event if the combined sales price of the item and all other items relating to the same trip or event that are sold in the same transaction (or related transactions) exceeds $10,000.

Exceptions. A cashier's check, money order, bank draft, or traveler's check is not considered received in a designated reporting transaction if it constitutes the proceeds of a bank loan or if it is received as a payment on certain promissory notes, installment sales contracts, or down payment plans. See Publication 1544 for more information.

Person. An individual, corporation, partnership, trust, estate, association, or company.

Recipient. The person receiving the cash. Each branch or other unit of a person's trade or business is considered a separate recipient unless the branch receiving the cash (or a central office linking the branches), knows or has reason to know the identity of payers making cash payments to other branches.

Transaction. Includes the purchase of property or services, the payment of debt, the exchange of a negotiable instrument for cash, and the receipt of cash to be held in escrow or trust. A single transaction may not be broken into multiple transactions to avoid reporting.

Suspicious transaction. A transaction in which it appears that a person is attempting to cause Form 8300 not to be filed, or to file a false or incomplete form. The term also includes any transaction in which there is an indication of possible illegal activity.

Specific Instructions

You must complete all parts. However, you may skip Part II if the individual named in Part I is conducting the transaction on his or her behalf only. For voluntary reporting of suspicious transactions, see Item 1 below.

Item 1. If you are amending a prior report, check box 1a. Complete the appropriate items with the correct or amended information only. Complete all of Part IV. Staple a copy of the original report to the amended report.

To voluntarily report a suspicious transaction (see *Definitions*), check box 1b. You may also telephone your local IRS Criminal Investigation Division or call 1-800-800-2877.

Part I

Item 2. If two or more individuals conducted the transaction you are reporting, check the box and complete Part I for any one of the individuals. Provide the same information for the other individual(s) on the back of the form. If more than three individuals are involved, provide the same information on additional sheets of paper and attach them to this form.

Item 6. Enter the taxpayer identification number (TIN) of the individual named. See *Taxpayer identification number (TIN)* on page 3 for more information.

Item 8. Enter eight numerals for the date of birth of the individual named. For example, if the individual's birth date is July 6, 1960, enter 07 06 1960.

Item 13. Fully describe the nature of the occupation, profession, or business (for example, "plumber," "attorney," or "automobile dealer"). Do not use general or nondescriptive terms such as "businessman" or "self-employed."

Item 14. You must verify the name and address of the named individual(s). Verification must be made by examination of a document normally accepted as a means of identification when cashing checks (for example, a driver's license, passport, alien registration card, or other official

document). In item 14a, enter the type of document examined. In item 14b, identify the issuer of the document. In item 14c, enter the document's number. For example, if the individual has a Utah driver's license, enter "driver's license" in item 14a, "Utah" in item 14b, and the number appearing on the license in item 14c.

Note. You must complete all three items (a, b, and c) in this line to make sure that Form 8300 will be processed correctly.

Part II

Item 15. If the transaction is being conducted on behalf of more than one person (including husband and wife or parent and child), check the box and complete Part II for any one of the persons. Provide the same information for the other person(s) on the back of the form. If more than three persons are involved, provide the same information on additional sheets of paper and attach them to this form.

Items 16 through 19. If the person on whose behalf the transaction is being conducted is an individual, complete items 16, 17, and 18. Enter his or her TIN in item 19. If the individual is a sole proprietor and has an employer identification number (EIN), you must enter both the SSN and EIN in item 19. If the person is an organization, put its name as shown on required tax filings in item 16 and its EIN in item 19.

Item 20. If a sole proprietor or organization named in items 16 through 18 is doing business under a name other than that entered in item 16 (e.g., a "trade" or "doing business as (DBA)" name), enter it here.

Item 27. If the person is not required to furnish a TIN, complete this item. See *Taxpayer Identification Number (TIN)* on page 3. Enter a description of the type of official document issued to that person in item 27a (for example, "passport"), the country that issued the document in item 27b, and the document's number in item 27c.

Note. You must complete all three items (a, b, and c) in this line to make sure that Form 8300 will be processed correctly.

Part III

Item 28. Enter the date you received the cash. If you received the cash in more than one payment, enter the date you received the payment that caused the combined amount to exceed $10,000. See *Multiple payments* under *General Instructions* for more information.

Item 30. Check this box if the amount shown in item 29 was received in more than one payment (for example, as installment payments or payments on related transactions).

IRS Form 8300 (Rev. 12-2004)   Page **5**   **FinCEN Form 8300** (Rev. 12-2004)

Item 31. Enter the total price of the property, services, amount of cash exchanged, etc. (for example, the total cost of a vehicle purchased, cost of catering service, exchange of currency) if different from the amount shown in item 29.

Item 32. Enter the dollar amount of each form of cash received. Show foreign currency amounts in U.S. dollar equivalent at a fair market rate of exchange available to the public. The sum of the amounts must equal item 29. For cashier's check, money order, bank draft, or traveler's check, provide the name of the issuer and the serial number of each instrument. Names of all issuers and all serial numbers involved must be provided. If necessary, provide this information on additional sheets of paper and attach them to this form.

Item 33. Check the appropriate box(es) that describe the transaction. If the transaction is not specified in boxes a–i, check box j and briefly describe the transaction (for example, "car lease," "boat lease," "house lease," or "aircraft rental"). If the transaction relates to the receipt of bail by a court clerk, check box i, "Bail received by court clerks." This box is only for use by court clerks. If the transaction relates to cash received by a bail bondsman, check box **d**, "Business services provided."

Part IV

Item 36. If you are a sole proprietorship, you must enter your SSN. If your business also has an EIN, you must provide the EIN as well. All other business entities must enter an EIN.

Item 41. Fully describe the nature of your business, for example, "attorney" or "jewelry dealer." Do not use general or nondescriptive terms such as "business" or "store."

Item 42. This form must be signed by an individual who has been authorized to do so for the business that received the cash.

Comments

Use this section to comment on or clarify anything you may have entered on any line in Parts I, II, III, and IV. For example, if you checked box b (Suspicious transaction) in line 1 above Part I, you may want to explain why you think that the cash transaction you are reporting on Form 8300 may be suspicious.

Privacy Act and Paperwork Reduction Act Notice. Except as otherwise noted, the information solicited on this form is required by the Internal Revenue Service (IRS) and the Financial Crimes Enforcement Network (FinCEN) in order to carry out the laws and regulations of the United States Department of the Treasury. Trades or businesses, except for clerks of criminal courts, are required to provide the information to the IRS and FinCEN under both section 6050I and 31 U.S.C. 5331. Clerks of criminal courts are required to provide the information to the IRS under section 6050I. Section 6109 and 31 U.S.C. 5331 require that you provide your social security number in order to adequately identify you and process your return and other papers. The principal purpose for collecting the information on this form is to maintain reports or records which have a high degree of usefulness in criminal, tax, or regulatory investigations or proceedings, or in the conduct of intelligence or counterintelligence activities, by directing the Federal Government's attention to unusual or questionable transactions.

You are not required to provide information as to whether the reported transaction is deemed suspicious. Failure to provide all other requested information, or providing fraudulent information, may result in criminal prosecution and other penalties under Title 26 and Title 31 of the United States Code.

Generally, tax returns and return information are confidential, as stated in section 6103. However, section 6103 allows or requires the IRS to disclose or give the information requested on this form to others as described in the Code. For example, we may disclose your tax information to the Department of Justice, to enforce the tax laws, both civil and criminal, and to cities, states, the District of Columbia, to carry out their tax laws. We may disclose this information to other persons as necessary to obtain information which we cannot get in any other way. We may disclose this information to Federal, state, and local child support agencies; and to other Federal agencies for the purposes of determining entitlement for benefits or the eligibility for and the repayment of loans. We may also provide the records to appropriate state, local, and foreign criminal law enforcement and regulatory personnel in the performance of their official duties. We may also disclose this information to other countries under a tax treaty, or to Federal and state agencies to enforce Federal nontax criminal laws and to combat terrorism.

The IRS authority to disclose information to combat terrorism expired on December 31, 2003. Legislation is pending that would reinstate this authority. "In addition, FinCEN may provide the information to those officials if they are conducting intelligence or counter-intelligence activities to protect against international terrorism."

You are not required to provide the information requested on a form that is subject to the Paperwork Reduction Act unless the form displays a valid OMB control number. Books or records relating to a form or its instructions must be retained as long as their contents may become material in the administration of any law under Title 26 or Title 31.

The time needed to complete this form will vary depending on individual circumstances. The estimated average time is 21 minutes. If you have comments concerning the accuracy of this time estimate or suggestions for making this form simpler, you can write to the Tax Products Coordinating Committee, Western Area Distribution Center, Rancho Cordova, CA 95743-0001. Do not send this form to this office. Instead, see *Where To File* on page 3.

abandonment. The voluntary and permanent cessation of use or enjoyment with no intention to resume or reclaim one's possession or interest. May pertain to an easement or a property.

abrogation. Tenants cannot sign away their rights in advance of signing the lease.

abstract of title. A condensed version of the history of title to a particular parcel of real estate, as recorded in the county clerk's records; consists of a summary of the original grant and all subsequent conveyances and encumbrances affecting the property.

abutting. The joining, reaching, or touching of adjoining land. Abutting parcels of land have a common boundary.

accelerated depreciation. A method of calculating for tax purposes the depreciation of income property at a faster rate than would be achieved using the straight-line method. Note that any depreciation taken in excess of that which would be claimed using the straight-line rate is subject to recapture as ordinary income to the extent of gain resulting from the sale. *See also* straight-line method.

acceleration clause. A provision in a written mortgage, note, bond, or conditional sales contract that, in the event of default, the whole amount of principal and interest may be declared to be due and payable at once.

accretion. An increase or addition to land by the deposit of sand or soil washed up naturally from a river, lake, or sea.

accrued depreciation. The actual depreciation that has occurred to a property at any given date; the difference between the cost of replacement new (as of the date of appraisal) and the present appraised value.

acknowledgment. A declaration made by a person to a notary public, or other public official authorized to take acknowledgments, that an instrument was executed by that person as a free and voluntary act.

actual eviction. The result of legal action originated by a lessor, whereby a defaulted tenant is physically ousted from the rented property pursuant to a court order. *See also* eviction.

actual notice. Express information or fact; that which is known; actual knowledge.

adjustable-rate mortgage. A mortgage in which the interest rate changes at predetermined intervals. The mortgage has caps or a ceiling that limits the amount it can change at the predetermined intervals.

administrator. The party appointed by the county court to settle the estate of a deceased person who died without leaving a will.

ad valorem tax. A tax levied according to value; generally used to refer to real estate tax. Also called the general tax.

adverse possession. The right of an occupant of land to acquire title against the real owner, where possession has been actual, continuous, hostile, visible, and distinct for the statutory period.

affidavit. A written statement signed and sworn to before a person authorized to administer an oath.

agent. One who represents or has the power to act for another person (called the principal). The authorization may be express or implied. A fiduciary relationship is created under the law of agency when a property owner, as the principal, executes a listing agreement or management contract authorizing a licensed real estate broker to be the owner's agent.

agreement of sale. A written agreement whereby the purchaser agrees to buy certain real estate and the seller agrees to sell, upon terms and conditions set forth in the agreement.

air lot. A designated airspace over a piece of land. Air lots, like surface property, may be transferred.

air rights. The right to use the open space above a property, generally allowing the surface to be used for another purpose.

alienation. The act of transferring property to another. Alienation may be voluntary, such as by gift or sale, or involuntary, such as through eminent domain or adverse possession.

alienation clause. The clause in a mortgage or deed of trust that states that the balance of the secured debt becomes immediately due and payable at the mortgagee's option if the property is sold by the mortgagor. In effect, this clause prevents the mortgagor from assigning the debt without the mortgagee's approval.

alluvion.   New deposits of soil as the result of accretion.

amenities.   The tangible and intangible features that increase the value or desirability of real estate.

Americans with Disabilities Act.   The ADA is a federal law that became effective in 1992. It is designed to eliminate discrimination against individuals with disabilities by mandating equal access to jobs, public accommodations, public transportation, telecommunications, and government services.

amortization.   The liquidation of a financial burden by installment payments.

amortized loan.   A loan in which the principal as well as the interest is payable in monthly or other periodic installments over the term of the loan.

antitrust laws.   The laws designed to preserve the free enterprise of the open marketplace by making illegal certain private conspiracies and combinations formed to minimize competition. Violations of antitrust laws in the real estate business generally involve either price fixing (brokers conspiring to set fixed compensation rates) or allocation of customers or markets (brokers agreeing to limit their areas of trade or dealing to certain areas or properties).

appraisal.   An estimate of the quantity, quality, or value of something. The process through which conclusions of property value are obtained; also refers to the report setting forth the process of estimation and conclusion of value.

appraised value.   An estimate of a property's present worth.

appreciation.   An increase in the worth or value of a property due to economic or related causes that may prove to be either temporary or permanent; opposite of depreciation.

appurtenant.   Belonging to; incident to; annexed to. For example, a garage is appurtenant to a house, and the common interest in the common elements of a condominium is appurtenant to each apartment. Appurtenances pass with the land when the property is transferred.

arbitration.   A means of settling a controversy between two parties through the medium of an impartial third party whose decision on the controversy (it is agreed) will be final and binding.

assemblage.   The process of merging two or more parcels of real estate to create one parcel.

assessment.   The imposition of a tax, charge, or levy, usually according to established rates.

assignment.   The transfer in writing of rights or interest in a bond, mortgage, lease, or other instrument.

assumption of mortgage.   The transfer of title to property to a grantee wherein he assumes liability for payment of an existing note secured by a mortgage against the property; should the mortgage be foreclosed and the property sold for a lesser amount than that due, the grantee-purchaser who has assumed and agreed to pay the debt secured by the mortgage is personally liable for the deficiency. Before a seller may be relieved of liability under the existing mortgage, the lender must accept the transfer of liability for payment of the note.

attachment.   The method by which a debtor's property is placed in the custody of the law and held as security pending outcome of a creditor's suit.

attorney-in-fact.   The holder of a power of attorney.

attorney's opinion of title.   An instrument written and signed by the attorney who examines the title, stating the attorney's opinion as to whether a seller may convey good title.

automatic extension.   A clause in a listing agreement that states that the agreement will continue automatically for a certain period of time after its expiration date. In many states, use of this clause is discouraged or prohibited.

avulsion.   The sudden removal of land by natural forces, such as an earthquake.

balloon payment.   The final payment of a mortgage loan that is considerably larger than the required periodic payments because the loan amount was not fully amortized.

bargain and sale deed.   A deed that carries with it no warranties against liens or other encumbrances, but that does imply that the grantor has the right to convey title. Note that the grantor may add warranties to the deed at his or her discretion.

base line. One of a set of imaginary lines running east and west and crossing a principal meridian at a definite point, used by surveyors for reference in locating and describing land under the rectangular survey system (or government survey method) of property description.

bench mark. A permanent reference mark or point established for use by surveyors in measuring differences in elevation.

beneficiary. 1. The person for whom a trust operates, or in whose behalf the income from a trust estate is drawn. 2. A lender who lends money on real estate and takes back a note and deed of trust from the borrower.

bequest. A provision in a will providing for the distribution of personal property.

bilateral contract. A contract in which each party promises to perform an act in exchange for the other party's promise to perform.

bill of sale. A written instrument given to pass title to personal property.

binder. An agreement that may accompany an earnest money deposit for the purchase of real property as evidence of the purchaser's good faith and intent to complete the transaction.

blanket mortgage. A mortgage covering more than one parcel of real estate, providing for each parcel's partial release from the mortgage lien upon repayment of a definite portion of the debt.

blockbusting. The illegal practice of inducing homeowners to sell their properties by making representations regarding the entry or prospective entry of minority persons into the neighborhood.

blue-sky laws. The common name for those state laws that regulate the registration and sale of investment securities.

branch office. A secondary place of business apart from the principal or main office from which real estate business is conducted. A branch office generally must be run by a licensed real estate broker working on behalf of the broker operating the principal office.

breach of contract. The failure, without legal excuse, of one of the parties to a contract to perform according to the contract.

broker. One who buys and sells for another for a commission. *See also* real estate broker.

brokerage. The business of buying and selling for another for a commission.

budget loan or budget mortgage. A loan in which the monthly payments made by the borrower cover not only interest and a payment on the principal, but also one-twelfth of such expenses as taxes, insurance, assessments, and similar charges. The monthly payment is called a *PITI payment.*

buffer zone. A zone or space between two different use districts. An example of a buffer zone would be a park between a residential district and a commercial district.

building code. An ordinance specifying minimum standards of construction of buildings for the protection of public safety and health.

building line. A line fixed at a certain distance from the front and/or sides of a lot beyond which no structure can project; a setback line used to ensure a degree of uniformity in the appearance of buildings and unobstructed light, air, and view.

building restrictions. The limitations on the size or type of property improvements established by zoning acts or by deed or lease restrictions.

bulk zoning. Bulk zoning controls the density of the development on land to avoid overcrowding.

bundle of legal rights. The theory that land ownership involves ownership of all legal rights to the land such as possession, control within the law, and enjoyment, rather than ownership of the land itself.

buydown mortgage. A mortgage in which the interest rate is reduced by paying interest in advance. A temporary buydown is for the initial years of the loan. A permanent buydown is for the life of the loan.

capacity of parties. The legal ability of persons to enter into a valid contract. Most persons have full capacity to contract, and are said to be competent parties.

capital gains. A tax on the profits realized from the sale of a capital asset.

capital improvement. Any improvement that is made to extend the useful life of a property or add to its value.

capital investment. The initial capital and the long-term expenditures made to establish and maintain a business or investment property.

capitalization. The process of converting into present value (or obtaining the present worth of) a series of anticipated future periodic installments of net income. In real estate appraising, it usually takes the form of discounting. The formula is expressed:

Income ÷ Rate = Value

capitalization rate. The rate of return a property will produce on the owner's investment.

cash flow. The net spendable income from an investment, determined by deducting all operating and fixed expenses from the gross income. If expenses exceed income, a negative cash flow is the result.

casualty insurance. A type of insurance policy that protects a property owner or other person from loss or injury sustained as a result of theft, vandalism, or similar occurrences.

caveat emptor. A Latin phrase meaning "Let the buyer beware."

caveat venditor. A Latin phrase meaning "Let the seller beware."

certificate of eligibility. A certificate given by the federal government to qualified veterans to show their remaining eligibility for a VA-guaranteed loan.

certificate of occupancy. A certificate of occupancy is issued after the building is inspected to make sure it complies with building codes.

certificate of reasonable value. A certificate issued by the Veterans Administration certifying the value, as determined by an approved VA appraiser, of property secured by a VA mortgage.

certificate of reduction. A document issued by the lender to verify the loan balance.

certificate of sale. The document generally given to a purchaser at a tax foreclosure sale. A certificate of sale does not convey title; generally it is an instrument certifying that the holder received title to the property after the redemption period had passed and that the holder paid the property taxes for that interim period.

certificate of title. A statement of opinion on the status of the title to a parcel of real property based on an examination of specified public records.

cession deed. The type of deed used when land is donated to the government.

chain of title. The succession of conveyances from some accepted starting point whereby the present holder of real property derives his or her title.

chattel. Personal property.

City Planning Commission. A local governmental organization designed to direct and control the development of land within a municipality.

cloud on title. A claim or encumbrance that may affect title to land.

codicil. An addition to a will that alters, explains, adds to, or confirms the will, but does not revoke it.

coinsurance clause. A clause in insurance policies covering real property that requires the policyholder to maintain fire insurance; coverage is generally equal to at least 80 percent of the property's actual replacement cost.

collateral. Something of value given or pledged to a lender as security for a debt or obligation.

commercial property. A classification of real estate that includes income-producing property such as office buildings, restaurants, shopping centers, hotels, and stores.

commingled property. That property of a married couple that is so mixed or commingled that it is difficult to determine whether it is separate or community property. Commingled property becomes community property.

commingling. The illegal act of a real estate broker who mixes the money of other people with that of his or her own; by law, brokers are required to maintain a separate trust account for the funds of other parties held temporarily by the broker.

commission. The payment made to a broker for services rendered, such as in the sale or purchase of real property; usually a percentage of the selling price of the property.

common elements. Those parts of a property that are necessary or convenient to the existence, maintenance, and safety of a condominium, or are normally used in common by all of the condominium residents. All condominium owners have an undivided ownership interest in the common elements.

common law. The body of law based on custom, usage, and court decisions.

community property. A system of property ownership based on the theory that each spouse has an equal interest in the property acquired by the efforts of either spouse during marriage.

Community Reinvestment Act. A part of the Housing and Community Development Act passed in 1977. The purpose of the act is to prevent the practice of redlining and disinvestment by lenders in certain areas of a city.

comparables. The properties listed in an appraisal report that are substantially equivalent to the subject property.

competent parties. Those persons who are recognized by law as being able to contract with others; usually those of legal age and sound mind.

condemnation. A judicial or administrative proceeding to exercise the power of eminent domain, by which a government agency takes private property for public use and compensates the owner.

conditional-use permit. A permit granted that allows the holder to build a special-purpose property that is inconsistent with zoning in the area. A conditional permit is generally issued to allow buildings for the good of the public such as hospitals and houses of worship in a residential area.

condominium. The absolute ownership of an apartment or a unit, generally in a multiunit building, based on a legal description of the airspace that the unit actually occupies, plus an undivided interest in the ownership of the common elements that are owned jointly with the other condominium unit owners. The entire tract of real estate included in a condominium development is called a *parcel*, or *development parcel*. One apartment or space in a condominium building or a part of a property intended for independent use and having lawful access to a public way is called a *unit*. Ownership of one unit also includes a definite undivided interest in the common elements.

conformity. The maximum value is achieved when the property is in harmony with its surroundings.

consideration. Something of value that induces one to enter into a contract. Consideration may be "valuable" (money or commodity) or "good" (love and affection).

constructive eviction. 1. Acts done by the landlord that so materially disturb or impair the tenant's enjoyment of the leased premises that the tenant is effectively forced to move out and terminate the lease without liability for any further rent. 2. A purchaser's inability to obtain clear title.

constructive notice. Notice given to the world by recorded documents. All persons are charged with knowledge of such documents and their contents, whether or not they have actually examined them. Possession of property is also considered constructive notice that the person in possession has an interest in the property.

contingency. A provision in a contract that requires completion or that a certain event must occur before the contract becomes binding.

contract. An agreement entered into by two or more legally competent parties by the terms of which one or more of the parties, for a consideration, undertakes to do or to refrain from doing some legal act or acts. A contract may be either unilateral, where only one party is bound to act, or bilateral, where all parties to the instrument are legally bound to act as prescribed.

contract for deed. A contract for the sale of real estate wherein the sales price is paid in periodic installments by the purchaser, who is in possession although title is retained by the seller until final payment. Also called an *installment contract* or a *land contract*.

contract for exchange of real estate. A contract of sale of real estate in which the consideration is paid wholly or partly in property.

contract rent. Rental income received under the current lease agreement. See market rent.

contribution. The value of any part of the property is measured by its effect on the value of the whole.

conventional insured mortgage. A mortgage (loan) wherein the borrower has less than a 20 percent down payment. The lender may require that the borrower purchase private mortgage insurance to reduce the lender's risk.

conventional life estate. A life estate created by the grantor rather than by law.

conventional mortgage. A mortgage (loan) where real property is used as security for the payment of the debt and the loan is not insured through FHA or guaranteed by VA.

conventional uninsured mortgage.   A mortgage (loan) wherein the borrower has a 20 percent or greater down payment and the lender accepts the creditworthiness of the borrower and the property as security for the loan.

conversion.   The process of changing from one form of ownership to another, such as apartment use to condo use.

conveyance.   A written instrument that evidences transfer of some interest in real property from one person to another.

cooperative.   A residential multiunit building whose title is held by a trust or corporation, which is owned by and operated for the benefit of persons living within the building, who are the beneficial owners of the trust or stockholders of the corporation, each having a proprietary lease.

corporation.   An entity or organization created by operation of law whose rights of doing business are essentially the same as those of an individual. The entity has continuous existence until dissolved according to legal procedures.

correction lines.   Used in the government survey to compensate for the curvature of the earth.

cost approach.   The process of estimating the value of a special purchase property. The formula is reproduction or replacement cost minus depreciation plus land equals value.

counseling.   The business of providing people with expert advice on a subject, based on the counselor's extensive, expert knowledge of the subject.

counteroffer.   A new offer made as a reply to an offer received, having the effect of voiding the original offer, which cannot be accepted thereafter unless revived by the offeror's repeating it.

covenant.   A promise to do or refrain from doing an act. The covenants found in a general warranty deed are seisin, encumbrances, further assurance, quiet enjoyment, and warranty forever.

covenant of quiet enjoyment.   1. In a deed, this covenant assures that the grantee and the grantee's heirs have the right to the property free from interference from the acts or claims of third parties. 2. In a lease, this covenant assures the tenants' right of possession without interference from the landlord or third parties.

cul-de-sac.   A dead-end street that widens sufficiently at the end to permit an automobile to make a U-turn.

curable depreciation.   When the cost of fixing the property does not exceed the value of the property.

curtesy.   A life estate, usually a fractional interest, given by some states to the surviving husband in real estate owned by his deceased wife. Many states have abolished curtesy.

cycle.   A recurring sequence of events that regularly follow one another, generally within a fixed interval of time. The cycle of real estate is growth, stability, decline, and restoration.

datum.   A horizontal plane from which heights and depths are measured.

dba.   Doing business as.

debenture.   A note or bond given as evidence of debt and issued without security.

debt.   Something owed to another; an obligation to pay or return something.

debt service.   A borrower's periodic payment, comprising principal and interest, on the unpaid balance of a mortgage.

decreasing returns.   When adding improvements to the land does not produce a proportional increase in the property value.

deed.   A written instrument that, when executed, and delivered, conveys title to or an interest in real estate.

deed in trust.   A three-party instrument in which the trustor conveys legal title to the trustee for the benefit of the beneficiary. That trustee has full power to sell, mortgage, and subdivide a parcel of real estate. The beneficiary controls the trustee's use of these powers under the provisions of the trust agreement.

deed of reconveyance.   The instrument used to reconvey title to a trustor under a deed of trust once the debt has been satisfied.

deed of trust.   An instrument used to create a mortgage lien by which the mortgagor conveys his or her title to a trustee, who holds it as security for the benefit of the note holder (the lender); also called a *trust deed*.

deed restrictions. The clauses in a deed limiting the future uses of the property. Deed restrictions may impose a vast variety of limitations and conditions, such as limiting the density of buildings, dictating the types of structures that can be erected, and preventing buildings from being used for specific purposes or from being used at all.

default. The nonperformance of a duty, whether arising under a contract or otherwise; failure to meet an obligation when due.

defeasance. A provision or condition in a deed or in a separate instrument that, being performed, renders the instrument void.

defeasible fee estate. An estate in land in which the holder has fee simple title subject to being divested on the happening of a specified condition. Two categories: 1. fee simple determinable or special limitation and 2. fee simple subject to a condition subsequent.

deficiency judgment. A personal judgment levied against the mortgagor when a foreclosure sale does not produce sufficient funds to pay the mortgage debt in full.

delinquent taxes. Those unpaid taxes that are past due.

delivery. The legal act of transferring ownership. Documents such as deeds and mortgages must be delivered and accepted to be valid.

delivery in escrow. Delivery of a deed to a third person until the performance of some act or condition by one of the parties.

demand. The willingness of a number of people to accept available goods at a given price; often coupled with supply.

density zoning. The zoning ordinances that restrict the average maximum number of houses per acre that may be built within a particular area, generally a subdivision.

depreciation. 1. In appraisal, a loss of value in property due to all causes, including physical deterioration, functional depreciation, and economic obsolescence. 2. In real estate investment, an expense deduction for tax purposes taken over the period of ownership of income property.

descent. The hereditary succession of an heir to the property of a relative who dies intestate.

designated agent. An agent who has been appointed by a broker to act for a specific principal or client.

determinable fee estate. A defeasible fee estate in which the property automatically reverts to the grantor upon the occurrence of a specified event or condition. Also known as *special limitation*.

devise. A transfer of real estate by will or last testament. The donor is the devisor and the recipient is the devisee.

diminishing returns. The principle of diminishing returns applies when a given parcel of land reaches its maximum percentage return on investment, and further expenditures for improving the property yield a decreasing return.

discount points. An added loan fee charged by a lender to make the yield on a lower-than-market-value FHA or VA loan competitive with higher-interest conventional loans.

discount rate. The rate of interest a commercial bank must pay when it borrows from its Federal Reserve bank. Consequently, the discount rate is the rate of interest the banking system carries within its own framework. Member banks may take certain promissory notes that they have received from customers and sell them to their district Federal Reserve bank for less than face value. With the funds received, the banks can make further loans. Changes in the discount rate may cause banks and other lenders to reexamine credit policies and conditions.

dispossess. To oust from land by legal process.

dominant tenement. A property that includes in its ownership the appurtenant right to use an easement over another's property for a specific purpose.

dower. The legal right or interest recognized in some states that a wife acquires in the property her husband held or acquired during their marriage. During the lifetime of the husband, the right is only a possibility of an interest; on his death, it can become an interest in land. Many states have abolished dower.

dual agency. This occurs when an agent represents both parties in the same transaction. Both parties are clients.

due diligence.   Reasonable care and protection agents owe any party that is their client (buyer, seller, principal broker, owner of the property in a property management agreement); the obligation of a person to use good-faith efforts to perform the terms of a contract, such as the buyer's responsibility to make efforts to obtain financing if that was a term of the sales contract.

due-on-sale clause.   A clause in a mortgage allowing the lender the right to implement the acceleration clause in the mortgage if the borrower transfers title to the property.

duress.   The use of unlawful constraint that forces action or inaction against a person's will.

earnest money deposit.   An amount of money deposited by a buyer under the terms of a contract.

easement.   A right to use the land of another for a specific purpose, such as for a right-of-way or utilities; an incorporeal interest in land. An easement appurtenant passes with the land when conveyed.

easement by necessity.   An easement allowed by law as necessary for the full enjoyment of a parcel of real estate; for example, a right of ingress and egress over a grantor's land.

easement by prescription.   An easement acquired by continuous, open, uninterrupted, exclusive, and adverse use of the property for the period of time prescribed by state law.

easement in gross.   An easement that is not created for the benefit of any land owned by the owner of the easement but that attaches personally to the easement owner. For example, a right to an easement granted by Eleanor Franks to Joe Fish to use a portion of her property for the rest of his life would be an easement in gross.

economic life.   The period of time over which an improved property will earn an income adequate to justify its continued existence.

economic obsolescence.   The impairment of desirability or useful life arising from factors external to the property such as economic forces or environmental changes that affect supply and demand relationships in the market. Loss in the use and value of a property arising from the factors of economic obsolescence is to be distinguished from loss in value from physical deterioration and functional obsolescence, both of which are inherent in the property. Also referred to as *locational obsolescence* or *environmental obsolescence*.

emblements.   Those growing crops produced annually through the tenant's own care and labor, and that he or she is entitled to take away after the tenancy is ended. Emblements are regarded as personal property even prior to harvest, so if the landlord terminates the lease, the tenant may still reenter the land and remove such crops. If the tenant terminates the tenancy voluntarily, however, he or she is not generally entitled to the emblements.

eminent domain.   The right of a government or municipal quasi-public body to acquire property for public use through a court action called *condemnation*, in which the court determines that the use is a public use and determines the price or compensation to be paid to the owner.

employee status.   One who works as a direct employee of an employer. The employer is obligated to withhold income taxes and Social Security taxes from the compensation of his or her employees. *See also* independent contractor.

employment contract.   A document evidencing formal employment between employer and employee or between principal and agent. In the real estate business, this generally takes the form of a listing agreement or management agreement.

encroachment.   A fixture, or structure, such as a wall or fence that invades a portion of a property belonging to another.

encumbrance.   Any lien such as a mortgage, tax, or judgment lien, an easement, a restriction on the use of the land, or an outstanding dower right that may diminish the value of the property.

Equal Credit Opportunity Act. The ECOA is a federal act that prohibits discrimination by lenders on the basis of race, color, religion, sex, national origin, age, or marital status in any aspect of a credit transaction.

equalization. The raising or lowering of assessed values for tax purposes in a particular county or taxing district to make them equal to assessments in other counties or districts.

equitable lien. A lien that arises out of common law, wherein the parties have agreed in writing that a certain property will be held as security for a debt.

equitable right of redemption. The right of a defaulted borrower to redeem her or his property before foreclosure upon full payment of the outstanding debt as well as accrued interest and related costs prior to the foreclosure.

equitable title. The interest held by a vendee under a contract for deed or a sales contract; the equitable right to obtain absolute ownership to property when legal title is held in another's name; and an insurable interest.

equity. The interest or value that an owner has in a property over and above any mortgage indebtedness.

erosion. The gradual wearing away of land by water, wind, and general weather conditions; the diminishing of property caused by the elements.

errors and omissions insurance. An insurance that protects brokers from loss due to errors, mistakes, and negligence.

escalation clause. A clause found in a mortgage or lease that allows the payment to adjust over the life of the mortgage or lease.

escheat. The reversion of property to the state in the event the owner thereof dies without leaving a will and has no heirs to whom the property may pass by lawful descent.

escrow. The closing of a transaction through a third party, called an *escrow agent* or *escrowee*, who receives certain funds and documents to be delivered on the performance of certain conditions in the escrow agreement.

estate for years. An interest for a certain, exact period of time in property leased for a specified consideration.

estate in land. The degree, quantity, nature, and extent of interest that a person has in real property.

estate in severalty. An estate owned by one person.

estoppel certificate. A legal instrument executed by a mortgagor showing the amount of the unpaid balance due on a mortgage and stating that the mortgagor has no defenses or offsets against the mortgagee at the time of execution of the certificate. Also called a *certificate of no defense*.

ethical. Conforming to professional standards of conduct.

eviction. A legal process to oust a person from possession of real estate.

evidence of title. A proof of ownership of property, which is commonly a certificate of title, a title insurance policy, an abstract of title with lawyer's opinion, or a Torrens registration certificate.

exchange. A transaction in which all or part of the consideration for the purchase of real property is the transfer of like-kind property (that is, real estate for real estate).

exclusive-agency buyer agency agreement. A buyer brokerage agreement wherein the broker is entitled to a payment only if he or she locates the property the buyer purchases. The buyer can find property without the services of the agent.

exclusive-agency listing. A listing contract under which the owner appoints a real estate broker as his or her exclusive agent for a designated period of time to sell the property on the owner's stated terms for a commission. However, the owner reserves the right to sell without paying anyone a commission by selling to a prospect who has not been introduced or claimed by the broker.

exclusive buyer agency agreement. An exclusive-agency agreement wherein the buyer is legally bound to compensate the agent whenever the buyer purchases a property of the type described in the contract. This is true even if the buyer finds the property.

exclusive-right-to-sell listing.   A listing contract under which the owner appoints a real estate broker as the owner's exclusive agent for a designated period of time to sell the property on the owner's stated terms and agrees to pay the broker a commission when the property is sold, whether by the broker, the owner, or another broker.

exculpatory clause.   A "hold harmless" clause that may be found in contracts excusing a party for injuries to another.

executed contract.   A contract in which all parties have fulfilled their promises and thus performed the contract.

execution.   The signing and delivery of an instrument. Also, a legal order directing an official to enforce a judgment against the property of a debtor.

executor.   The male designated in a will to handle the estate of the deceased.

executory contract.   A contract under which something remains to be done by one or more of the parties.

executrix.   The female designated in a will to handle the estate of the deceased. The probate court must approve any sale of property by the executrix.

expenses.   The short-term costs that are deducted from an investment property's income, such as minor repairs, regular maintenance, and renting costs.

expressed contract.   An oral or written contract in which the parties state their terms and express their intentions in words.

familial status.   A protected class under federal fair housing law. A landlord cannot refuse to rent to a head of the household with minor children or to a pregnant woman.

federal Fair Housing Act.   The term for Title VIII of the Civil Rights Act enacted in 1968 that prohibits discrimination based on race, color, sex, religion, or national origin in the sale and rental of residential property.

Federal Home Loan Bank System.   A system created by the Federal Home Loan Bank Act of 1932 to provide for a central reserve credit system for savings institutions engaged in home mortgage finance (predominantly savings and loans). The system is divided into 12 federal home loan bank districts with an FHLB in each district. The FHLBs maintain a permanent pool of credit to maintain liquidity of members or to provide means for mortgage lending when local funds are insufficient. Three sources of funds are available for the operation of the FHLB: 1. capital stock, 2. deposits of member institutions, and 3. consolidated obligations sold on the market. When member associations need funds, they obtain money by borrowing from FHLB. The FHLB Board supervises the system. The board is composed of three members appointed by the president of the United States with the advice and consent of the Senate.

Federal Home Loan Mortgage Corporation.   A member of the secondary mortgage market that primarily buys conventional loans.

Federal Housing Administration (FHA).   A federal administrative body created by the National Housing Act in 1934 to encourage improvement in housing standards and conditions, to provide an adequate home financing system through the insurance of housing mortgages and credit, and to exert a stabilizing influence on the mortgage market.

federal income tax.   An annual tax based on income, including monies derived from the lease, use, or operation of real estate.

Federal National Mortgage Association (FNMA).   "Fannie Mae" is the popular name for this federal agency that creates a secondary market for existing mortgages. FNMA does not loan money directly, but rather buys VA, FHA, and conventional loans.

Federal Reserve banks.   The government controls banks located in each of the 12 Federal Reserve districts, established by the Federal Reserve Act of 1913. The Board of Governors, working closely with the president and the U.S. Treasury, controls the Federal Reserve. The Federal Reserve system (through the 12 central banks) supervises and examines members' commercial banks; clears and collects checks drawn on commercial banks; and may influence the cost, supply, and availability of money.

fee simple absolute. The highest form of ownership recognized by law. Also known as *fee simple* or *ownership in fee.*

fee simple defeasible with a special limitation. Also known as a *fee simple determinable estate.* An estate created with a special limitation. Title would automatically revert back to the grantor or the grantor's heirs if the estate ceased to be used for the special limitation.

fee simple estate. The maximum possible estate or right of ownership of real property continuing forever. Sometimes called a *fee* or *fee simple absolute.*

fee simple subject to a condition subsequent. A de-feasible fee estate in which the grantor reserves right of reentry to the property when the condition of ownership is violated.

FHA appraisal. A Federal Housing Administration (FHA) evaluation of a property as security for a loan. Includes study of the physical characteristics of the property and surroundings; the location of the property; the prospective borrower's ability and willingness to repay a loan; and the mortgage amount and monthly payments.

FHA loan. A loan insured by the FHA and made by an approved lender in accordance with the FHA's regulations.

fiduciary relationship. A relationship of trust and confidence, as between trustee and beneficiary, attorney and client, and principal and agent.

financing statement. *See* Uniform Commercial Code.

first mortgage. A mortgage that creates a superior voluntary lien on the property mortgaged relative to other charges or encumbrances against same.

fixture. An article that was once personal property, but has been so affixed to real estate that it has become real property.

floor area ratio (FAR). The FAR indicates the relationship between a building area and land, or the relationship between the square footage of the building and the square footage of the land.

forcible entry and detainer. A summary proceeding for restoring to possession of land one who is wrongfully kept out or has been wrongfully deprived of the possession.

foreclosure. A legal procedure whereby property used as security for a debt is sold to satisfy the debt in the event of default in payment of the mortgage note or default of other terms in the mortgage document. The foreclosure procedure brings the rights of all parties to a conclusion and passes the title in the mortgaged property to either the holder of the mortgage or a third party who may purchase the realty at the foreclosure sale, free of all encumbrances affecting the property subsequent to the mortgage.

formal will. A will written by an attorney, with two subscribing witnesses and with necessary language. Such a will may appoint the executor of the estate as independent agent and avoid the necessity of a bond.

fractional sections. An oversized or undersized section that is not exactly one mile by one mile is a fractional section; used only in the government or rectangular survey.

fraud. A misstatement of a material fact made with intent to deceive or made with reckless disregard of the truth and that actually does deceive.

freehold estate. An estate in land in which ownership is for an indeterminate length of time, in contrast to a leasehold estate.

front feet. A unit of linear measurement of the side of a property that faces the street.

functional obsolescence. The impairment of functional capacity or efficiency. Functional obsolescence reflects the loss in value brought about by factors that affect the property, such as overcapacity, inadequacy, or changes in the design. The inability of a structure to perform adequately the function for which it is currently employed.

future interest. A person's present right to an interest in real property that will not result in possession or enjoyment until some time in the future, such as a reversion or right of reentry.

gap. A defect in the chain of title of a particular parcel of real estate; a missing document or conveyance that raises doubt as to the present ownership of the land.

general agent. A party authorized to perform all acts of the principal's affairs within the continued operation of a particular job or business.

general contractor. A construction specialist who enters into a formal construction contract with a landowner or master lessee to construct a real estate building or project. The general contractor often contracts with several subcontractors specializing in various aspects of the building process to perform individual jobs.

general lien. A lien on all real and personal property owned by a debtor.

general partnership. *See* partnership.

general tax. *See* ad valorem tax.

general warranty deed. A deed that states that the title conveyed therein is good from the sovereignty of the soil to the grantee therein; no one else can claim the property.

GI-guaranteed mortgage. *See* VA loan.

government lot. Those fractional sections in the rectangular (government) survey system that are less than one full quarter-section in area.

Government National Mortgage Association (GNMA). "Ginnie Mae," a federal agency and division of HUD that operates special assistance aspects of federally aided housing programs and participates in the secondary market through its mortgage-backed securities pools.

graduated lease. A lease that provides for periodic step increases in the rental payments.

graduated payment mortgage. A loan in which smaller payments are made in the early years and larger payments at some predetermined time. This may create negative amortization.

grant. The act of conveying or transferring title to real property.

grant deed. A type of deed that includes three basic warranties: 1. the owner warrants the right to convey the property; 2. the owner warrants that the property is not encumbered other than with those encumbrances listed in the deed; and 3. the owner promises to convey any after-acquired title to the property. Grant deeds are popular in states that rely heavily on title insurance.

grantee. A person to whom real estate is conveyed; the buyer.

granting clause. That portion of the deed that states the grantor's intention to transfer title and type of ownership interest conveyed.

grantor. A person who conveys real estate by deed; the seller.

gross lease. A lease of property under which a landlord pays all property charges regularly incurred through ownership, such as repairs, taxes, insurance, and operating expenses. Most residential leases are gross leases.

gross rent multiplier (GRM). A figure used as a multiplier of the gross rental income of a property to produce an estimate of the property's value.

ground lease. A lease of land only, on which the tenant usually owns a building or is required to build his or her own building as specified in the lease. Such leases are usually long-term net leases; a tenant's rights and obligations continue until the lease expires or is terminated through default.

growing-equity mortgage. A loan in which the monthly payments increase, with the increased amount being applied directly to the outstanding principal balance, thus decreasing the loan term.

guaranteed sale plan. An agreement between broker and seller that if the seller's real property is not sold before a certain date, the broker will purchase it for a specified price.

guardian. One who guards or cares for another person's rights and property. A guardian has legal custody of the affairs of a minor or a person incapable of taking care of his own interests, called a *ward*.

habendum clause. The deed clause beginning "to have and to hold" that defines or limits the extent of ownership in the estate granted by the deed.

heir. One who might inherit or succeed to an interest in land under the state law of descent when the owner dies without leaving a valid will.

highest and best use. That possible use of land that will produce the greatest net income and thereby develop the highest land value.

holdover tenancy. A tenancy whereby a lessee retains possession of leased property after the lessee's lease has expired and the landlord, by continuing to accept rent from the tenant, agrees to the tenant's continued occupancy as defined by state law.

holographic will. A will that is written, dated, and signed in the handwriting of the maker, and that does not need to be notarized or witnessed to be valid.

homeowners insurance policy. A standardized package insurance policy that covers a residential real estate owner against financial loss from fire, theft, public liability, and other common risks.

homeowners warranty program. An insurance program offered to buyers by some brokerages, warranting the property against certain defects for a specified period of time.

homestead. The land, and the improvements thereon, designated by the owner as the owner's homestead and, therefore, protected by state law from forced sale by certain creditors of the owner.

HUD. The Department of Housing and Urban Development, which regulates FHA and GNMA.

hypothecation. A pledge of property to the lender without giving up possession rights.

implied contract. A contract under which the agreement of the parties is demonstrated by their acts and conduct.

implied grant. A method of creating an easement. One party may be using another's property for the benefit of both parties; for example, a sewer on a property.

improvement. 1. Improvements on land—any structure, usually privately owned, erected on a site to enhance the value of the property; for example, buildings, fences, and driveways. 2. Improvements to land—usually a publicly owned structure, such as a curb, sidewalk, or sewer.

income approach. The process of estimating the value of an income-producing property by capitalization of the annual net income expected to be produced by the property during its remaining useful life.

increasing returns. When increased expenditures for improvements to a given parcel of land yield an increasing percentage return on investment, the principle of increasing returns applies.

incurable depreciation. The cost of fixing the property will be more than the increase in value or the corrections are not physically possible.

indefeasible fee. A title that cannot be defeated. Example: fee simple absolute.

indemnification. An agreement to compensate someone for a loss.

independent contractor. One who is retained to perform a certain act, but who is subject to the control and direction of another only as to the end result and not as to how he or she performs the act. Unlike an employee, an independent contractor pays for all his or her expenses, income and Social Security taxes, and receives no employee benefits. Many real estate salespeople are independent contractors.

index lease. A lease in which the rental payment is tied to some agreed-on index, such as the Consumer Price Index or the Wholesale Price Index.

industrial property. All land and buildings used or suited for use in the production, storage, or distribution of tangible goods.

installment contract. *See* contract for deed.

installment sale. A method of reporting income received from the sale of real estate when the sales price is paid in two or more installments over two or more years. If the sale meets certain requirements, a taxpayer can postpone reporting such income to future years when the taxpayer's other income may be lower.

insurable title. A title to land that a title company will insure.

insurance. The indemnification against loss from a specific hazard or peril through a contract (called a *policy*) and for a consideration (called a *premium*).

intangible property. Personal property that cannot be physically "touched," such as stock or lease.

interest. A charge made or paid by a lender for the use of money.

interim financing. A short-term loan usually made during the construction phase of a building project, often referred to as a *construction loan*.

inter vivos trust. A living trust created by an owner during the owner's lifetime.

intestate. The condition of a property owner who dies without leaving a will. Title to such property will pass to the owner's heirs as provided in the state law of descent.

invalid. In regard to contracts, it means having no legal force or effect.

invalidate. To render null and void.

investment.   Money directed toward the purchase, improvement, and development of an asset in expectation of income or profits. A good financial investment has the following characteristics: safety, regularity of yield, marketability, acceptable denominations, valuable collateral, acceptable duration, required attention, and potential appreciation.

involuntary alienation.   The transfer of property against an owner's will. Example: foreclosure.

involuntary lien.   A lien that is placed on the property without the consent of the owner.

IRS tax lien.   A general, statutory, involuntary lien on all real and personal property owned by a debtor.

joint tenancy.   The ownership of real estate between two or more parties who have been named in one conveyance as joint tenants. Upon the death of a joint tenant, that tenant's interest passes to the surviving joint tenant or tenants by the right of survivorship.

joint venture.   The joining of two or more people to conduct a specific business enterprise. On the one hand, a joint venture is similar to a partnership in that it must be created by agreement between the parties to share in the losses and profits of the venture. On the other hand, it is unlike a partnership in that the venture is for one specific project only, rather than for a continuing business relationship.

judgment.   The official decision of a court on the respective rights and claims of the parties to an action or suit. When a judgment is entered and recorded with the county recorder, it usually becomes a general lien on the property.

judgment clause.   A provision that may be included in notes, leases, and contracts by which the debtor, lessee, or obligor authorizes any attorney to go into court to confess a judgment against the debtor for a default in payment. Also called a *cognovit*.

judicial sale.   A type of foreclosure in which the lender enforces the acceleration clause in the mortgage and files a suit to foreclose on the property.

laches.   An equitable doctrine used by courts to bar a legal claim or prevent the assertion of a right because of undue delay, negligence, or failure to assert the claim or right.

land.   The earth's surface extending downward to the center of the earth and upward infinitely into space.

land contract.   The seller finances the property instead of a traditional lender. The seller holds title until final payment is made.

landlocked.   Property that does not have access to a public road to enter (ingress) or leave (egress) the land. This situation may create an easement by necessity.

latent defect.   A hidden defect in the property.

law of agency.   *See* agent.

lawyer's opinion of title.   *See* attorney's opinion of title.

lease.   A contract between a landlord (the lessor) and a tenant (the lessee) transferring the right to exclusive possession and use of the landlord's real property to the lessee for a specified period of time and for a stated consideration (rent). By state law, leases for longer than a certain period of time (generally one year) must be in writing to be enforceable.

leased fee interest.   The landlord's retained interest in the leased property is the leased fee interest.

leasehold estate.   A tenant's right to occupy real estate during the term of a lease, generally considered to be a personal property interest.

leasehold interest.   The tenant's interest in the leased property is the leasehold interest.

lease option.   This lease gives the tenant the option right to purchase the property within or at the end of the lease.

lease purchase.   The tenant leases property for a period of time with the intention of purchasing it.

legal description.   A description of a specific parcel of real estate sufficient for an independent surveyor to locate and identify it. The most common forms of legal description are rectangular survey; metes and bounds; and lot, block (plat), and subdivision.

legality of object.   An element that must be present in a valid contract. All contracts that have for their object an act that violates the laws of the United States, or the laws of a state to which the parties are subject, are illegal, invalid, and not recognized by the courts.

legal life estate.   A life estate created by law; dower, curtesy, and homestead.

legatee. A person who receives personal or real property under a will.

lessee. The tenant who leases a property.

lessor. One who leases property to a tenant.

leverage. The use of borrowed money to finance the bulk of an investment.

levy. To assess; to seize or collect. To levy a tax is to assess a property and set the rate of taxation. To levy an execution is to seize officially the property of a person to satisfy an obligation.

license. 1. A privilege or right granted to a person by a state to operate as a real estate broker or salesperson. 2. The revocable permission for a temporary use of land—a personal right that cannot be sold.

lien. A right given by law to certain creditors to have their debt paid out of the property of a defaulting debtor, usually by means of a court sale.

lienee. The party whose property is subject to a lien.

lienor. The party holding the lien right.

lien-theory state. A state in which the mortgage gives the mortgagee the right to place a lien on the property and the mortgagor retains title to the property.

life estate. An interest in real or personal property that is limited in duration to the lifetime of its owner or some other designated person.

life tenant. A person in possession of a life estate.

liquidated damages. An amount predetermined by the parties to a contract as the total compensation the aggrieved party will receive should the other party breach the contract.

liquidity. The ability to sell an asset and convert it into cash at a price close to its true value.

lis pendens. Latin for "action pending," which is recorded to give constructive notice that an action affecting the property (lawsuit) has been filed, but a judgment has not been decreed. A lis pendens notice renders the property unmarketable.

listing agreement. A contract between a landowner (as principal) and a licensed real estate broker (as agent) by which the broker is employed as agent to sell real estate on the owner's terms within a given time, for which service the landowner agrees to pay a commission.

listing broker. The broker in a multiple-listing situation from whose office a listing agreement is initiated, as opposed to the selling broker, from whose office negotiations leading up to a sale are initiated. The listing broker and the selling broker may, of course, be the same person. *See also* multiple listing.

littoral rights. 1. A landowner's claim to use water in large lakes and oceans adjacent to the landlord's property. 2. The ownership's rights to land bordering these bodies of water up to the high-water mark.

loan-to-value. The relationship between the amount of a loan and the appraised value of a property. It is expressed as a percentage of the appraised value.

lock-in clause. 1. The lender's agreement to lock in an interest rate for a specified time period. 2. A condition in a promissory note that prohibits prepayment of the note.

lot-and-block description. A description of real property that identifies a parcel of land by reference to lot and block numbers within a subdivision, as identified on a subdivided plat duly recorded in the county recorder's office.

management agreement. A contract between the owner of income property and a management firm or individual property manager outlining the scope of the manager's authority.

marketable title. A good or clear salable title reasonably free from risk of litigation over possible defects; also called a *merchantable title*.

market-date approach. That approach in analysis that is based on the proposition that an informed purchaser would pay no more for a property than the cost to him of acquiring an existing property with the same utility. This approach is applicable when an active market provides sufficient quantities of reliable data that can be verified from authoritative sources. The approach is relatively unreliable in an inactive market or in estimating the value of properties for which no real comparable sales data are available. It is also questionable when sales data cannot be verified with principals to the transaction. Also referred to as the *market comparison* or *direct sales comparison approach*.

market price. The actual selling price of a property.

market rent.   Also known as *economic rent*; the rental income that real estate could command in the market at any given time, versus *contract rent*, which is the income generated under the current lease contract.

market value.   The highest price that a property will bring in a competitive and open market under all conditions requisite to a fair sale. The price at which a buyer would buy and a seller would sell, each acting prudently and knowledgeably, and assuming the price is not affected by undue stimulus.

master deed.   A document that legally establishes the condominium regime. It is referred to as a *condominium declaration* and fully describes each unit and common elements as well as specific essential elements of ownership that govern its operation.

master plan.   A master plan provides the guidelines for the future development of a community.

mechanic's lien.   A statutory lien created in favor of contractors, laborers, and materialmen who have performed work or furnished materials in erecting or repairing a building.

metes-and-bounds description.   A legal description of a parcel of land that begins at a well-marked point and follows the boundaries, using direction and distances around the tract back to the place of beginning.

mill.   One-tenth of 1¢ (0.001). Some states use a mill rate to compute real estate taxes; for example, a rate of 52 mills would be 0.052 tax for each dollar of assessed valuation of a property.

millage rate.   A property tax rate obtained by dividing the total assessed value of all the property in the tax district into the total amount of revenue needed by the taxing district. This millage rate is then applied to the assessed value of each property in the district to determine individual taxes.

ministerial acts.   Acts performed by a licensee for a consumer that are informative in nature, but do not rise to the level of active representation, such as responding to inquiries about a property's price range or providing other facts.

misrepresentation.   To represent falsely; to give an untrue idea of a property. May be accomplished by omission or concealment of a material fact.

money judgment.   A court judgment ordering payment of money rather than specific performance of a certain action. *See also* judgment.

money market.   Those institutions—such as banks, savings and loan associations, and life insurance companies—whose function it is to supply money and credit to borrowers.

month-to-month tenancy.   A periodic tenancy; the tenant rents for one period at a time. In the absence of a rental agreement (oral or written), a tenancy is generally considered to be month to month.

monument.   A fixed natural or artificial object used to establish real estate boundaries for a metes-and-bounds description.

mortgage.   A conditional transfer or pledge of real estate as security for a loan. Also, the document creating a mortgage lien.

mortgage bankers.   A firm or individual who originates loans for sale to other investors.

mortgage broker.   A mortgage broker is a firm or person who brings borrowers and lenders together, and the finders' fee is normally paid by the lender, but could be paid by the borrower.

mortgagee.   The lender who receives a pledge from a borrower to repay a loan.

mortgage lien.   A lien or charge on a mortgagor's property that secures the underlying debt obligations.

mortgagor.   One who, having all or part of title to property, pledges that property as security for a debt; the borrower.

multiple listing.   An exclusive listing (generally, an exclusive-right-to-sell) with the additional authority and obligation on the part of the listing broker to distribute the listing to other brokers in the multiple-listing organization.

municipal ordinances.   The laws, regulations, and codes enacted by the governing body of a municipality.

mutual rescission.   The act of putting an end to a contract by mutual agreement of the parties.

negative amortization.   A loan in which the loan balance increases with each payment rather than decreasing because the payment amount is not sufficient to cover the interest.

negligence.   Carelessness and inattentiveness resulting in violation of trust. Failure to do what is required.

net income. The gross income of a property minus operating expenses (not including debt service).

net lease. A lease requiring the tenant to pay not only rent, but also all costs incurred in maintaining the property, including taxes, insurance, utilities, and repairs.

net listing. A listing establishing a price, which must be expressly agreed on, below which the owner will not sell the property and at which price the broker will not receive a commission; the broker receives the excess over and above the net listing price as commission.

nonconforming loan. A loan that does not meet secondary market standards.

nonconforming use. A use of property that is permitted to continue after a zoning ordinance prohibiting it has been established for the area. Also, a use of property that is not conforming to current zoning because of a change in zoning, such as property being used for residential purposes, but currently zoned commercial.

nondisturbance clause. A clause found in a lease that protects the tenant. If the landlord defaults on payments to the lender, the lender has the right to collect rent from the tenant. If the tenant pays the lender, the tenant cannot be evicted.

nonhomogeneity. A lack of uniformity; dissimilarity. As no two parcels of land are exactly alike, real estate is said to be unique or nonhomogeneous.

nonjudicial foreclosure. Also known as *foreclosure by advertisement* because it is a foreclosure procedure where the lender does not have to involve the courts.

nonrecourse loan. A loan in which the property being pledged as collateral is the sole security for the loan. The borrower cannot be held personally liable for the note.

notarize. To certify or attest to a document, as by a notary.

notary public. A public official authorized to certify and attest to documents, take affidavits, take acknowledgments, administer oaths, and perform other such acts.

note. An instrument of credit given to attest a debt.

notice of abandonment. An instrument filed to release a recorded declaration of homestead.

novation. Substituting a new contract for an old one and the release of liability.

obligee/promisee. The lender in the note.

obligor/promissor. The borrower in a note.

obsolescence. To be obsolete; as used in appraising the loss of value because it is outdated or less useful.

offer and acceptance. The two components of a valid contract; a "meeting of the minds."

officer's deed. A deed by sheriffs, trustees, guardians, and the like.

one hundred-percent-commission plan. A salesperson compensation plan whereby the salesperson pays the salesperson's broker a monthly service charge to cover the costs of office expenses and receives 100 percent of the commissions from the sales that he or she negotiates.

open buyer agency agreement. A nonexclusive agency contract between a broker and a buyer wherein the buyer may enter into similar agreements with an unlimited number of brokers; the broker is paid who locates the property the buyer purchases.

open-end mortgage. A mortgage loan that is expandable by increments up to a maximum dollar amount, all of which is secured by the same original mortgage.

open listing. A listing contract under which the broker's commission is contingent on the broker's producing a ready, willing, and able buyer before the property is sold by the seller or another broker; the principal (owner) reserves the right to list the property with other brokers.

open mortgage. An open mortgage is a mortgage without a prepayment clause. FHA-insured and VA-guaranteed mortgages are open mortgages.

option. The right to purchase property within a definite time at a specified price. No obligation to purchase exists, but the seller is obligated to sell if the option holder exercises right to purchase.

optionee. The party that receives and holds an option.

optionor. The party that grants or gives an option.

ownership. The exclusive right to hold, possess, or control and dispose of a tangible or intangible thing. Ownership may be held by a person, corporation, or political entity.

package mortgage.   A method of financing in which the loan that finances the purchase of a home also finances the purchase of certain items of personal property, such as a washer, dryer, refrigerator, stove, and other specified appliances.

participation financing.   A mortgage in which the lender participates in the income of the mortgaged venture beyond a fixed return, or receives a yield on the loan in addition to the straight interest rate.

partnership.   An association of two or more individuals who carry on a continuing business for profit as co-owners. Under the law, a partnership is regarded as a group of individuals, rather than as a single entity. A general partnership is a typical form of joint venture, in which each general partner shares in the administration, profits, and losses of the operation. A limited partnership is a business arrangement whereby the operation is administered by one or more general partners and funded by limited or silent partners who are by law responsible for losses only to the extent of their investment.

party wall.   A wall that is located on or at a boundary line between two adjoining parcels for the use of the owners of both properties.

patent defect.   A defect that can be found by normal inspection of the property.

payee.   The party that receives payment.

payor.   The party that makes payment to another.

percentage lease.   A lease commonly used for retail property in which the rental is based on the tenant's gross sales at the premises; often stipulates a base monthly rental plus a percentage of any gross sales above a certain amount.

periodic estate.   An interest in leased property that continues from period to period—week to week, month to month, or year to year.

personal property.   Those items, called chattels, that are not classified as real property; tangible and movable objects.

physical deterioration.   A reduction in utility resulting from an impairment of physical condition. For purposes of appraisal analysis, it is most common and convenient to divide physical deterioration into curable and incurable components.

plat.   A map of a town, section, or subdivision indicating the location and boundaries of individual properties.

plat book.   A record of recorded subdivisions of land.

plottage.   The value that is created when two or more tracts of land are merged into a single, larger one.

point.   A unit of measurement used for various loan charges. One point equals 1 percent of the amount of the loan. *See also* discount points.

point of beginning.   The starting point of the survey situated in one corner of the parcel in a metes-and-bounds legal description. All metes-and-bounds descriptions must follow the boundaries of the parcel back to the point of beginning.

police power.   The government's right to impose laws, statutes, and ordinances to protect the public health, safety, and welfare, including zoning ordinances and building codes.

power of attorney.   A written instrument authorizing a person (the attorney-in-fact) to act on behalf of the maker to the extent indicated in the instrument.

premises.   The specific section of a deed that states the names of the parties, recital of consideration, operative words of conveyance, legal property description, and appurtenance provisions.

prepayment penalty.   A charge imposed on a borrower by a lender for early payment of the loan principal to compensate the lender for interest and other charges that would otherwise be lost.

prepayment privilege clause.   The statement of the terms upon which the mortgagor may pay the entire or stated amount of the mortgage principal at some time prior to the due date.

prescription.   The right or easement to land that is acquired by adverse possession or "squatter's rights." It must be acquired under certain conditions as required by law.

prescriptive title.   A title that is acquired by an adverse possession claim.

price fixing.   *See* antitrust laws.

primary mortgage market.   The market where a person or business goes to negotiate a loan.

principal.   1. A sum lent or employed as a fund or investment, as distinguished from its income or profits. 2. The original amount (as in a loan) of the total due and payable at a certain date. 3. A main party to a transaction—the person for whom the agent works.

principal meridian.   One of 35 north and south survey lines established and defined as part of the rectangular (government) survey system.

principle of conformity.   The appraisal theory stating that buildings that are similar in design, construction, and age to other buildings in the area have a higher value than they would in a neighborhood of dissimilar buildings.

principle of substitution.   The appraisal theory that states that no one will pay more for a property than the cost of buying or building a similar property; or, in the case of investments, the price of a substitute investment.

priority.   The order of position or time. The priority of liens is generally determined by the chronological order in which the lien documents are recorded; tax liens, however, have priority even over previously recorded liens.

private mortgage insurance (PMI).   Insurance written by a private company (not government) that protects a lender against loss if a borrower defaults.

probate.   The formal judicial proceeding to prove or confirm the validity of a will.

procuring cause.   The effort that brings about the desired result. Under an open listing, the broker who is the procuring cause of the sale receives the commission.

progression.   When a small structure is placed in an area of larger more expensive structures, the value of the smaller structure will increase.

property management.   The operation of the property of another for compensation. Includes marketing of space; advertising and rental activities; collection, recording, and remitting of rents; maintenance of the property; tenant relations; hiring of employees; keeping proper accounts; and rendering periodic reports to the owner.

property tax.   Those taxes levied by the government against either real or personal property. The right to tax real property in the United States rests exclusively with the states, not with the federal government.

proprietary lease.   A lease given by the corporation that owns a cooperative apartment building to the shareholder, giving the shareholder (tenant) the right to occupy one of the units.

proration.   The proportionate division or distribution of expenses of property ownership between two or more parties. Closing statement prorations generally include taxes, rents, insurance, interest charges, and assessments.

prospectus.   A printed advertisement, usually in pamphlet form, presenting a new development, subdivision, business venture, or stock issue.

public utility easement.   A right granted by a property owner to a public utility company to erect and maintain poles, wires, and conduits on, across, or under the owner's land for telephone, electric power, gas, water, or sewer installation.

puffing.   An exaggerated opinion, many times in regards to a property's amenity.

pur autre vie.   A term meaning for the life of another. A life estate pur autre vie is a life estate that is measured by the life of a person other than the grantee.

purchase-money mortgage.   A note secured by a mortgage or deed of trust given by a buyer, as mortgagor, to a seller, as mortgagee, as part of the purchase price of the real estate.

pyramiding.   Obtaining additional investment property by borrowing against the equity of existing investments.

qualification.   The act of determining the prospect's needs, abilities, and urgency to buy and then matching these with available properties.

quiet enjoyment.   A covenant in a deed that the title being given is good against third parties.

quiet title lawsuit.   A suit to clear up any defects or clouds on a title.

quitclaim deed.   A conveyance by which the grantor transfers whatever interest the grantor has in the real estate without warranties or obligations.

range.   A strip of land six miles wide, extending north and south and numbered east and west according to its distance from the principal meridians in the rectangular survey system (government survey method) of land description.

ready, willing, and able buyer. One who is prepared to buy property on the seller's terms and is ready to take positive steps to consummate the transaction.

real estate. Land; a portion of the earth's surface extending downward to the center of the earth and upward infinitely into space, including all things permanently attached thereto, whether by nature or by man; any and every interest in land.

real estate broker. Any person, partnership, association, or corporation that sells (or offers to sell), buys (or offers to buy), or negotiates the purchase, sale, or exchange of real estate, or that leases (or offers to lease) or rents (or offers to rent) any real estate or the improvements thereon for others and for compensation or valuable consideration. A real estate broker may not conduct business without a real estate broker's license.

real estate investment trust (REIT). Trust ownership of real estate wherein a group of individuals purchases certificates of ownership in the trust, which purchases property and distributes the profits back to the investors free of corporate income tax.

Real Estate Settlement Procedures Act (RESPA). The federal law ensuring that the buyer and seller in a real estate transaction have knowledge of all settlement costs when the purchase of a one- to four-family residential dwelling is financed by a federally related mortgage loan. Federally related loans include those made by savings and loans, insured by the FHA or VA, administered by HUD, or intended to be sold by the lender to an agency.

reality of consent. An element of all valid contracts. Offer and acceptance in a contract are usually taken to mean that reality of consent is also present. This is not the case if any of the following are present, however: mistake, misrepresentation, fraud, undue influence, or duress.

real property. Real property, or real estate as it is often called, consists of land, anything affixed to it so as to be regarded as a permanent part of the land, that which is appurtenant to the land, and that which is immovable by law.

REALTOR®. A registered trademark term reserved for the sole use of active members of local REALTOR® boards affiliated with the National Association of REALTORS®.

receiver. The court-appointed custodian of property involved in litigation, pending final disposition of the matter before the court.

reconciliation. The final step in the appraisal process, in which the appraiser reconciles the estimates of value received from the market-data, cost, and income approaches to arrive at a final estimate of market value for the subject property.

recording. The act of entering or recording documents affecting or conveying interests in real estate in the recorder's office established in each county. Until recorded, a deed or mortgage generally is not effective against subsequent purchases or mortgage liens.

recovery fund. A fund established in some states from real estate license funds to cover claims of aggrieved parties who have suffered monetary damage through the actions of a real estate licensee.

rectangular survey system. A system established in 1785 by the U.S. government, providing for surveying and describing land by reference to principal meridians and base lines.

redemption period. A period of time established by state law during which a property owner has the right to redeem his or her real estate from a foreclosure or tax sale by paying the sales price, interest, and costs. Many states do not have mortgage redemption laws.

redlining. The illegal practice of some institutions of denying loans or restricting their number for certain areas of a community.

regression. When a large structure is placed in an area of smaller, less expensive structures, the value of the larger structure will decrease.

release. To relinquish an interest in or claim to a parcel of property.

reliction. When water recedes, new land is acquired by reliction.

relocation service. An organization that aids a person in selling a property in one area and buying another property in another area.

remainder. The remnant of an estate that has been conveyed to take effect and be enjoyed after the termination of a prior estate, such as when an owner conveys a life estate to one party and the remainder to another.

remainder interest. A third party who has a future ownership interest in the property upon the death of the life tenant. *See* life estates.

rent. A fixed, periodic payment made by a tenant of a property to the owner for possession and use, usually by prior agreement of the parties.

rent control. The regulation by the state or local government agencies restricting the amount of rent landlords can charge their tenants.

rent schedule. A statement of proposed rental rates, determined by the owner or the property manager or both, based on a building's estimated expenses, market supply, and demand and the owner's long-range goals for the property.

replacement cost. The cost of construction at current prices of a building having utility equivalent to the building being appraised but built with modern materials and according to current standards, design, and layout. The use of the replacement cost concept presumably eliminates all functional obsolescence, and the only depreciations to be measured are physical deterioration and economic obsolescence.

reproduction cost. The cost of construction at current prices of an exact duplicate or replica using the same materials, construction standards, design, layout, and quality of workmanship and embodying all the deficiencies, superadequacies, and obsolescences of the subject building.

rescission. The termination of a contract by mutual agreement of the parties.

reservation in a deed. The creation by a deed to property of a new right in favor of the grantor. Usually involves an easement, life estate, or a mineral interest.

restriction. A limitation on the use of real property, generally originated by the owner or subdivider in a deed.

reverse mortgage. A mortgage that allows senior homeowners 62 years of age or older to release a percent of the equity in their property without making monthly payments. The loan is repaid when the borrower no longer resides in the property.

reversion. The remnant of an estate that the grantor holds after the grantor has granted a life estate to another person; the estate will return or revert to the grantor; also called a *reverser*.

reversionary right. An owner's right to regain possession of leased property upon termination of the lease agreement.

rezoning. The process involved in changing the existing zoning of a property or area.

right of first refusal. A potential buyer's right to meet the terms of the sales contract.

right of survivorship. *See* joint tenancy.

riparian rights. An owner's rights in land that borders on or includes a stream, river, lake, or sea. These rights include access to and use of the water.

sale and leaseback. A transaction in which an owner sells his or her improved property and, as part of the same transaction, signs a long-term lease to remain in possession of the premises.

sales comparison approach. Also known as the *market approach to appraising*. It is used to appraise residential property or vacant land that will be used for residential purposes. It is based on the principle of substitution.

sales contract. A contract containing the complete terms of the agreement between buyer and seller for the sale of a particular parcel or parcels of real estate.

salesperson. A person who performs real estate activities while employed by, or associated with, a licensed real estate broker.

sandwich lease. The lessee's interest in a sublease is the sandwich lease.

satisfaction. A document acknowledging the payment of a debt.

secondary mortgage market. A market for the purchase and sale of existing mortgages, designed to provide greater liquidity for mortgages; also called the *secondary money market*.

section. A portion of a township under the rectangular survey system (government survey method). A township is divided into 36 sections numbered 1 to 36. A section is a square with mile-long sides and an area of 1 square mile or 640 acres.

security deposit. A payment made by the tenant that the landlord holds during the lease term and that may be kept wholly or in part on default or destruction of the premises by the tenant.

selling broker. *See* listing broker.

separate property. The real property owned by a husband or wife prior to their marriage.

servient tenement.   The land on which an easement exists in favor of an adjacent property (called a *dominant estate*); also called a *servient estate*.

setback.   The amount of space local zoning regulations require between a lot line and a building line.

severalty.   The ownership of real property by one person only, also called *sole ownership*.

severance.   The process of changing real property to personal property.

shared participation mortgage.   A type of participation mortgage in which the lender shares in the appreciation of the mortgage property when the property is sold.

situs.   The personal preference of people for one area over another, not necessarily based on objective facts and knowledge.

sole ownership.   *See* severalty.

special agent.   A party authorized to perform with limited authority given by the principal.

special assessment.   A tax or levy customarily imposed against only those specific parcels of real estate that will benefit from a proposed public improvement, such as a street or sewer.

special warranty deed.   A deed in which the grantor warrants or guarantees the title only against defects arising during the period of the grantor's tenure and ownership of the property and not against defects existing before that time, generally using the language, "by, through, or under the grantor but not otherwise."

specific lien.   A lien affecting or attaching only to a certain, specific parcel of land or piece of property.

specific performance suit.   A legal action brought in a court of equity in special cases to compel a party to carry out the terms of a contract. The basis for an equity court's jurisdiction in breach of a real estate contract is the fact that land is unique and mere legal damages would not adequately compensate the buyer for the seller's breach.

sponsoring broker.   A duly licensed real estate broker who employs a salesperson. Under law, the broker is responsible for the acts of the broker's salespeople.

squatter's rights.   Those rights acquired through adverse possession. By "squatting" on land for a certain statutory period under prescribed conditions, one may acquire title by limitations. If an easement only is acquired, instead of title to the land itself, one has title by prescription.

statute of frauds.   The part of a state law that requires that certain instruments, such as deeds, real estate sales contracts, and certain leases, be in writing in order to be legally enforceable.

statue of limitation.   That law pertaining to the period of time within which certain actions must be brought to court.

statutory lien.   A lien imposed on property by statute, such as a tax lien, in contrast to a voluntary lien that an owner places on the owner's own real estate, such as a mortgage lien.

statutory right of redemption.   In some states, defaulted borrowers have the statutory right of redemption, which allows them to buy back their property after the foreclosure sale by paying the sales price, interest, and costs.

steering.   The illegal practice of channeling home seekers to particular areas, either to maintain the homogeneity of an area or to change its character in order to create a speculative situation.

stigmatized property.   A property is considered stigmatized or undesirable because of events that have occurred on the property.

straight-line method.   A method of calculating depreciation for tax purposes, computed by dividing the adjusted basis of a property less its estimated salvage value by the estimated number of years of remaining useful life.

strict foreclosure.   A foreclosure procedure in which the lender secures title and all equity to the property.

subagent.   An agent of an agent. The broker is the agent of the principal. The salesperson is a subagent of the principal.

subcontractor.   *See* general contractor.

subdivision.   A tract of land divided by the owner, known as the *subdivider*, into blocks, building lots, and streets according to a recorded subdivision plat, which must comply with local ordinances and regulations.

subletting.   The leasing of premises by a lessee to a third party for part of the lessee's remaining term. *See also* assignment.

subordination. A relegation to a lesser position, usually in respect to a right or security.

subrogation. The substitution of one creditor for another, with the substituted person succeeding to the legal rights and claims of the original claimant. Subrogation is used by title insurers to acquire rights to sue from the injured party to recover any claims they have paid.

substitution. An appraisal principle that states that the maximum value of a property tends to be set by the cost of purchasing an equally desirable and valuable substitute property, assuming that no costly delay is encountered in making the substitution.

suit for partition. A legal action to divide the ownership interests in a property.

suit for possession. A court suit initiated by a landlord to evict a tenant from leased premises after the tenant has breached one of the terms of the lease or has held possession of the property after the lease's expiration.

suit for specific performance. A legal action brought by either a buyer or a seller to enforce performance of the terms of a contract.

suit to quiet title. A legal action intended to establish or settle the title to a particular property, especially when there is a cloud on the title.

summation appraisal. An approach under which value equals estimated land value plus reproduction costs of any improvements, after depreciation has been subtracted.

supply. The amount of goods available in the market to be sold at a given price. The term is often coupled with demand.

surety bond. An agreement by an insurance or bonding company to be responsible for certain possible defaults, debts, or obligations contracted for by an insured party; in essence, a policy insuring one's personal and/or financial integrity. In the real estate business, a surety bond is generally used to ensure that a particular project will be completed at a certain date or that a contract will be performed as stated.

survey. The process by which boundaries are measured and land areas are determined; the on-site measurement of lot lines, dimensions, and positions of buildings on a lot, including the determination of any existing encroachments or easements.

syndicate. A combination of two or more persons or firms to accomplish a joint venture of mutual interest. Syndicates dissolve when the specific purpose for which they were created has been accomplished.

tacking. Combining successive periods of property use; associated with adverse possession claims.

tangible property. Property that can be seen and touched.

taxation. The process by which a government or municipal quasipublic body raises monies to fund its operation.

tax deed. An instrument, similar to a certificate of sale, given to a purchaser at a tax sale. *See also* certificate of sale.

taxes. A compulsory contribution required by the government from persons, corporations, and other organizations, according to a law, for the general support of the government and for the maintenance of public services.

tax lien. A charge against property created by operation of law. Tax liens and assessments take priority over all other liens.

tax rate. The rate at which real property is taxed in a tax district or county. For example, in a certain county, real property may be taxed at a rate of 56¢ per dollar of assessed valuation.

tax sale. A court-ordered sale of real property to raise money to cover delinquent taxes.

tax shelters. Allow a taxpayer to reduce current tax liability by offsetting income from one source with losses from another source.

tenancy at sufferance. The tenancy of a lessee who lawfully comes into possession of a landlord's real estate, but who continues to occupy the premises improperly after the lessee's lease rights have expired.

tenancy at will. An estate that gives the lessee the right to possession until the estate is terminated by either party; the term of this estate is indefinite.

tenancy by the entirety. The joint ownership, recognized in some states, of property acquired by husband and wife during marriage. Upon the death of one spouse, the survivor becomes the owner of the property.

tenancy in common.   A form of co-ownership by which each owner holds an undivided interest in real property as if that owner was the sole owner. Each individual owner has the right to partition. Unlike a joint tenancy, there is no right of survivorship between tenants in common.

tenant.   One who holds or possesses lands or tenements by any kind of right or title.

tenement.   Everything that may be occupied under a lease by a tenant.

termination (lease).   The cancellation of a lease by action of either party. A lease may be terminated by expiration of term, surrender and acceptance, constructive eviction by lessor, or option when provided in lease for breach of covenants.

termination (listing).   The cancellation of a broker-principal employment contract; a listing may be terminated by death or insanity of either party, expiration of listing period, mutual agreement, sufficient written notice, or the completion of performance under the agreement.

term mortgage.   A nonamortized loan in which the borrower makes periodic interest payments to the lender and the principal balance is due on maturity. Also known as a *straight mortgage.*

testamentary trust.   A trust created through a will after a property owner's death.

testate.   Having made and left a valid will.

testator.   A male willmaker.

testatrix.   A female willmaker.

time is of the essence.   A phrase in a contract that requires the performance of a certain act within a stated period of time.

time-share estate.   A fee simple interest in an interval ownership of property for a specified time period. The owner's occupancy is limited to the time period purchased.

time-share use.   The right to use and occupy the property for a certain number of years. A time-share use may be conveyed by a lease or license.

title.   The legal evidence of ownership rights to real property.

title insurance.   Insurance that is designed to indemnify the holder for loss sustained for reason of defects in a title, up to and including the policy limits.

title-theory states.   A state in which a security instrument gives the mortgagee the title to the property.

Torrens system.   A method of evidencing title by registration with the proper public authority, generally called the registrar. Named for its founder, Sir Robert Torrens.

township.   The principal unit of the rectangular (government) survey system. A township is a square with 6-mile sides and an area of 36 square miles.

township lines.   The lines running at six-mile intervals parallel to the base lines in the rectangular (government) survey system.

trade fixtures.   The articles installed by a tenant under the terms of a lease and removable by the tenant before the lease expires. These remain personal property and are not true fixtures.

transaction broker.   A person who represents neither party in a transaction. Both parties are treated as customers.

transfer taxes.   Real estate transfer taxes or RETT are state, county, and/or municipal sales taxes most often used as general revenue.

trust.   A fiduciary arrangement whereby property is conveyed to a person or institution, called a *trustee,* to be held and administered on behalf of another person, called a *beneficiary.*

trust deed.   An instrument used to create a mortgage lien by which the mortgagor conveys his or her title to a trustee, who holds it as security for the benefit of the note holder (the lender); also called a *deed of trust.*

trustee.   One who as agent for others handles money or holds title to their land.

trustee's deed.   A deed executed by a trustee conveying land held in a trust.

trustor.   A borrower in a deed of trust; a grantor in a deed in trust.

Truth-in-Lending Act.   Also known as Regulation Z, this act requires that the lender disclose the true cost of credit to individual borrowers for certain types of loans. It also regulates the advertisement of creditors.

unconventional mortgage.   An unconventional mortgage (loan) is backed by the government to reduce the lender's risk. Examples: FHA-insured loans and VA-guaranteed loans.

unenforceable contract.   A contract in which neither party can sue the other to force performance, such as a contract missing the signature of the person authorized to perform.

undivided interest.   An interest in a property that cannot be physically divided. *See* tenancy in common.

Uniform Commercial Code (UCC).   A codification of commercial law adopted in most states that attempts to make uniform all laws relating to commercial transactions including chattel mortgages and bulk transfers. Security interests in chattels are created by an instrument known as a *security agreement*. Article 6 of the code regulates bulk transfers—the sale of a business as a whole, including all fixtures, chattels, and merchandise.

unilateral contract.   A one-sided contract wherein one party makes a promise in order to induce a second party to do something. The second party is not legally bound to perform; however, if the second party does comply, the first party is obligated to keep the promise.

unity of ownership.   The four unities that are traditionally needed to create a joint tenancy—unity of title, unity of time, unity of interest, and unity of possession.

universal agent.   An agent that represents a principal in all activities; such as someone given full power of attorney.

useful life.   In real estate investment, the number of years a property will be useful to the investors.

usury.   The practice of charging more than the rate of interest allowed by law.

valid contract.   A contract that complies with all the essentials of a contract and is binding and enforceable on all parties to it.

valid deed.   An enforceable deed that has a competent grantor and grantee, consideration, conveyance, legal description of land, signature of grantor, acknowledgment, delivery, and acceptance.

valid lease.   An enforceable lease that has the following essential parts: lessor and lessee with contractual capacity, offer and acceptance, legality of object, description of the premises, consideration, signatures, and delivery. Leases for more than one year must also be in writing.

VA loan.   A mortgage loan on approved property made to a qualified veteran by an authorized lender and guaranteed by the Department of Veterans Affairs to limit possible loss by the lender.

variance.   The permission obtained from zoning authorities to build a structure or conduct a use that is expressly prohibited by the current zoning laws; an exception from the zoning ordinances.

vendee.   The buyer or purchaser.

vendor.   The seller.

voidable contract.   A contract that seems to be valid on the surface, but may be rejected or disaffirmed by one of the parties.

void contract.   A contract that has no legal force or effect because it does not meet the essential elements of a contract.

voluntary lien.   A lien that is created intentionally by the property owner, such as a mortgage.

voluntary transfer.   *See* alienation.

waiver.   The intentional or voluntary relinquishment of a known claim or right.

warranty deed.   A deed in which the grantor fully warrants good clear title to the premises. Used in most real estate deed transfers, a warranty deed offers the greatest protection of any deed.

warranty of habitability.   In a lease, this warranty requires that the landlord keep the property in good condition, that is to maintain the property, equipment, and to comply with state and local codes.

waste.   An improper use or an abuse of a property by a possessor who holds less than fee ownership, such as a tenant, life tenant, mortgagor, or vendee. Such waste generally impairs the value of the land or the interest of the person holding the title or the reversionary rights.

will.   A written document, properly witnessed, providing for the transfer of title to property owned by the deceased, called the *testator*.

wraparound mortgage.   A method of refinancing in which the new mortgage is placed in a secondary, or subordinate, position. In essence, it is an additional mortgage in which another lender refinances a borrower by lending an amount over the existing first-mortgage amount without disturbing the existence of the first mortgage.

writ of attachment.   Action taken by a creditor wherein the court retains custody of the property while a lawsuit is being decided, thus preventing the debtor from transferring unsecured real estate before a judgment is rendered. This ensures that the property will be available to satisfy the judgment.

writ of execution.   A court order that authorizes and directs the proper officer of the court (usually the sheriff) to sell the property of a defendant as required by the judgment or decree of the court.

year-to-year tenancy.   A periodic tenancy in which rent is collected from year to year.

zoning ordinance.   An exercise of police power by a municipality to regulate and control the character and use of property.

INDEX

This appendix was created to provide a review of key real estate concepts in the days or hours prior to your exam. The pages can be easily removed and carried with you from classroom to home to office. The review terms follow the outline of this book. For additional terms, please review your glossary before your exam.

CHAPTER 1—LISTING PROPERTY

Listing—Page 1

1. The *metes-and-bounds legal description* describes the land by metes (distance) and bounds (direction).

2. A *bench mark* is a permanent reference point placed by a government survey team to establish elevation or altitude above sea level.

3. The *lot-and-block* method of legal description is used to record subdivided land. *Contiguous lots* are adjacent to each another.

4. The *government, rectangular*, or *geodetic survey* is based on a system of imaginary lines. Principal meridian lines run north and south; base lines run east and west.

5. The largest area in the government survey is called a *check* and is 24 miles by 24 miles. Checks are divided into *townships*, which are 6 miles by 6 miles. Townships are divided into *sections*, which are 1 mile by 1 mile. Each section contains 640 acres. Oversized or undersized sections are called *fractional sections*. *Correction lines* are adjustments for the earth's curvature.

6. In computing the *gross living area* (GLA) of a building, use only the area above grade or ground level. Do not include the garage, porch, or patio.

7. The measure of a property along the street or water line is called the *front footage*.

8. The word *appurtenant* means attached. *Tangible* (touchable) appurtenances include personal property or fixtures that may or may not pass in the deed. *Intangible* (cannot touch) appurtenances include rights and privileges that belong to the land and pass in the deed.

9. An *easement* is the right to *use* the land of another; it does not include possession rights.

10. The parcel of land that *benefits* from an appurtenant easement is known as the *dominant estate*. The parcel of land *burdened* by the easement is known as the *servient estate*.

11. Personal gross easements terminate on the death of the easement owner and do not transfer when the property is sold. Commercial gross easements, such as a utility easement, transfer when the property is sold.

12. An *easement by necessity* is created for a landlocked property to provide the access rights of ingress (entry) and egress (exit).

13. An *easement by prescription* is created when a claimant uses another's property for a statutory period of time and follows the proper legal proceedings to secure the easement.

14. A *license* is a personal *privilege* to enter the land of another and use it for a specific purpose. It can be revoked at any time and terminates on the death of either party or the sale of the land.

15. An *encumbrance* is any claim, lien, or liability that affects the value or the use of a property.

16. *Building codes* are established to ensure the health, safety, and welfare of property owners. A *certificate of occupancy* is issued when a building meets code requirements.

17. A *building permit* is issued for construction of a new building or other improvement, substantial repair of an existing structure, or demolition of a building.

18. *Constructive* or *legal notice* gives notice to the world of the ownership of property. A recorded deed provides constructive notice and protects the owner in regard to third parties.

19. *Actual notice* is express or direct knowledge gained by reading, hearing, or seeing.

20. Property taxes (*ad valorem taxes*) and special assessments take priority over all other property liens.

21. The signatures of all parties named on a deed must be on the listing agreement.

22. Commission rates are *negotiable* between the principal and broker. The *Sherman Antitrust Act* prohibits collusive acts designed to restrict competition.

Services to the Seller—Page 10

1. When the owner of property hires a broker to find a buyer, an *agency relationship* is created. The *owner* (*principal*) delegates to the *broker* (*agent*) the right to act on the owner's behalf, creating a fiduciary relationship of trust and confidence.

2. Representing only *one* party in a transaction creates a *single agency*. Representing *both* parties creates a *dual agency*. A dual

agency must be *disclosed in writing* to all parties. In a dual agency, both parties would have client status.

3. A *facilitator* or *transaction broker* does not represent either party in the transaction. Both parties are treated as customers.

4. A *designated seller's agent* would be the agent representing only the seller. A *designated buyer's agent* would be the agent representing only the buyer.

5. *Ministerial acts* are those acts that a licensee may perform for a consumer that are informative in nature and do not rise to the level of active representation.

6. A *general agency* is created when the principal delegates a broad range of powers to the agent. A *special agency* is created when the principal delegates only a specific act or business transaction with detailed instructions.

7. In an *express agency*, the parties state the contract's terms and express their intention either orally or in writing. An *implied agency* occurs when the actions or conduct of the parties communicate that there is an agreement.

8. The acronym *COALD* represents the duties of the agent to the principal: care, obedience, accountability, loyalty, and disclosure.

9. A *listing agreement* is a *personal service contract* employing the brokerage firm to find a ready, willing, and able buyer. Most states require that the listing agreement be in writing to be enforceable.

10. In an *exclusive-right-to-sell listing*, one broker is hired to list and sell the property. If the seller gives the listing broker permission to work with cooperating brokers, then other brokers may sell the property. If the property sells during the listing term, the seller must pay the commission even if the seller finds the buyer.

11. In an *exclusive-agency listing*, the seller retains the right to sell the property and authorizes one broker to list the property. If the seller grants the listing broker authority to place the property in the MLS, then other brokers may sell the property. If the seller secures the buyer, no commission is due. If a broker secures the buyer, a commission must be paid.

12. In an *open listing*, the seller enters into listing agreements with any number of brokerage firms and also retains the right to sell the property. If the seller secures the buyer, no commission is due. If a broker secures the buyer, a commission must be paid.

13. A *net listing* stipulates that the seller will receive a specified amount of money and anything over that amount is the broker's commission. Net listings are illegal in most states.

14. A *listing contract* is considered an *employment contract*. If a seller does not accept a full list price offer, a commission is due the broker because the broker procured a ready, willing, and able buyer.

15. A party should immediately receive a copy of any document the party has just signed.

16. A broker should keep copies of all records pertaining to the property. State laws determine how long they are kept.

17. A *latent defect* is a hidden defect; a *patent defect* is obvious.

18. A *deed condition* creates a conditional fee estate. If the condition is breached, the title may revert to the grantor or the grantor's heirs.

19. A *covenant* is a promise between two or more parties in which they agree to perform or not to perform specified acts.

20. A seller or landlord must provide a lead-based paint disclosure statement on residential properties built prior to 1978. On acceptance of an offer, purchasers must be given ten days to inspect the property. This right may be waived.

21. *Real estate* is the land and all attachments to the land. *Real property* is land, all attachments, plus the bundle of legal rights that are inherent in its ownership.

22. *Personal property* includes movable items not attached to the real estate. Real property can become personal property by *severance* from the land.

23. *Fructus naturales*, or fruits of nature, do not require annual cultivation and are considered *real property*.

24. Crops that require annual planting are known as *emblements* and are considered *personal property*.

25. A *fixture* is personal property that has become affixed to the land or improvements so that it becomes real property. A *trade fixture* is personal property owned by a tenant, is attached to rented space, and is used in conducting a business. Trade fixtures generally become the property of the landlord if not been removed prior to the expiration of the lease.

26. *Riparian rights* are granted to owners of land along a river, stream, or lake. Land adjoining navigable rivers is usually owned to the *water's edge*; land adjoining nonnavigable streams and lakes is owned to the *center* of the stream or lake.

27. *Littoral rights* are granted to owners of land that borders on large, navigable lakes, seas, and oceans. Ownership is to the mean high-water mark.

28. An owner is entitled to all increases in land that result from *accretion*, the deposit of soil by water's action. These deposits are called *alluvion* or *alluvium*. When water recedes, the new land is acquired by *reliction*. *Avulsion* is the sudden loss of land, while *erosion* is the gradual wearing away of land.

29. The courts use four tests to determine if an item is real or personal property: (1) intention, (2) method of annexation, (3) adaptation to real estate, and (4) agreement.

Forms of Ownership—Page 21

1. An *estate in land* refers to a party's legal interests or rights to a property. To be an estate, an interest must be possessory or may become possessory in the future. An easement is not an estate in land because it does not allow for the possession of the property.

2. *Freehold estates* include fee estates and life estates. A freehold estate exists for an uncertain duration. Nonfreehold estates include leasehold estates, which are based on calendar time.

3. *Fee simple absolute* is the highest ownership recognized by law. This possessory interest is freely transferable, of indefinite duration, and is an inheritable estate.

4. The two types of fee simple defeasible estates (title can be defeated) are special limitation and condition subsequent. When a title is transferred by special limitation with the possibility of reverter, the grantee has ownership interests "so long as" the property is used for that particular purpose.

5. When a title is transferred by condition subsequent with a right of reentry, the grantee ownership is "on the condition that," which means there is an action or activity that the grantee must not perform. This deed condition is binding on the future owners of the property.

6. A *conventional life estate* is a freehold estate that is created by the grantor. It is not inheritable and is limited in duration to the life of the life tenant(s).

7. The *life tenant* has full enjoyment of the ownership as long as alive. On the death of the life tenant, the property reverts to the grantor or to a remainderman. The grantor's future interest is called a *reversionary interest*. The future interest of the remainderman is a *remainder interest*.

8. A life estate based on the life of a third party is called a *life estate pur autre vie*.

9. The life tenant has the right to sell, mortgage, or lease the property, but cannot allow the property to go to *waste*. A lease or deed signed by the life tenant becomes *void* on the death of the life tenant.

10. Dower, curtesy, and homestead are legal life estates that are created by law. *Dower* is a wife's interest in real estate owned by her husband. *Curtesy* is a husband's interest in real estate owned by his wife. A *homestead* protects the owner from certain creditors.

11. *Severalty* means the title to real estate is owned by one party: an individual, a corporation, or a government body.

12. Characteristics of *tenancy in common* ownership are each tenant holds an undivided fractional interest; interests may be unequal; unity of possession; each co-owner can sell, convey, mortgage, or transfer his or her interest without the consent of the other owners; and it is an inheritable estate.

13.   *Joint tenancy* is a concurrent form of ownership characterized by right of survivorship. There must be unities of time, interest, and possession for joint tenancy to be created. Each joint tenant has the right to sell, mortgage, or lease an interest without the consent of the other owners.

14.   If one joint tenant sells his or her property, the new owner would be a tenant in common with the other joint tenants.

15.   When cotenants cannot voluntarily agree to the termination of their co-ownership, a *suit for partition* can be filed in which the court dissolves the relationship.

16.   *Tenancy by the entirety* is recognized in some states and allows a husband and wife to each have an equal, undivided interest in the property that is characterized by survivorship.

17.   A *trust* is established to manage a property for the owner. The three parties in a trust agreement are the trustor, the trustee, and the beneficiary.

18.   *Community property states* regard any property acquired during marriage as obtained by mutual effort. When one spouse dies, the surviving spouse automatically owns one-half of the community property. *Separate property*, owned, inherited, or received as a gift by either spouse before or during marriage, can be sold or mortgaged without the signature of the nonowning spouse.

19.   A *partnership* is an association of two or more persons who establish a business for profit as co-owners. *General partners* are personally liable for business losses and obligations and are responsible for the operation of the business. *Limited partners* are liable for business losses only to the extent of their investment and do not participate in the operation of the business.

20.   To create a condominium community, the developer must record a *declaration of condominium*. The *master deed* allows the land to be converted to condominium use. The *bylaws* govern the operation of the homeowners' association.

21.   A party purchasing a residential condominium owns airspace in a unit and is a tenant in common with other community members in the land and improvements. A *limited common area* is owned by all but is limited to the use of the condo owners.

22.   Each condo owner is required to pay a homeowners' association fee to cover maintenance, insurance, and reserve funds. If the fee is not paid, the condo could be sold at foreclosure.

23.   In a *cooperative*, a corporation owns the property in severalty. Owners purchase *stock* in the company and receive a *proprietary lease*. Both are considered personal property. The maintenance fee includes each co-op owner's share of the corporations' expenses.

24.   Should a co-op owner default on a payment, the other shareholders are expected to pay. A co-op owner who defaults or breaches

the lease may be *evicted*. If the co-op defaults on a payment to the lender, the lender can foreclose on the entire property.

25. *Time-sharing* allows for an *interval ownership* or *use* by multiple purchasers of the property. When a time-share *estate* is conveyed, the owner *holds a deed* to the property. When a time-share *use* is conveyed, the buyer has the *right to occupy* the property for a stipulated time.

Fair Housing Laws—Page 26

1. The *Civil Rights Act of 1866* prohibits discrimination based on race in real estate and personal transactions. There are no *exceptions* to this law and *no limits on punitive damages* for racial discrimination.

2. A landlord must make *reasonable accommodations* in rules, policies, practices, and services to afford the disabled person equal opportunity to use and enjoy a dwelling. An owner *cannot refuse* to permit a disabled person to modify a dwelling, and the disabled person may be required to restore the unit to its original condition.

3. After March 12, 1991, multifamily dwellings must be designed to allow accessibility to the building and through units by persons in wheelchairs. New apartments built *with elevators* must be entirely accessible; the ground level of new apartment buildings *without elevators* must be accessible.

4. *Jones v. Mayer* is a 1968 Supreme Court case that upheld the Civil Rights Act of 1866.

5. Currently, federal fair housing laws prohibit discrimination based on *race, color, religion, sex, national origin, familial status*, and *disability*. Many state laws are stricter than federal regulations. Failure to comply with these laws is a criminal act and grounds for disciplinary action.

6. *Blockbusting* (*panic peddling*) occurs when an agent induces owners to sell because minority groups are *moving into* a neighborhood. *Steering* (*channeling*) occurs when an agent directs *buyers into or out of* certain neighborhoods. These activities are illegal.

7. *Familial status* protects the head of a household responsible for a minor child or children, or a pregnant woman from discriminatory practices. Housing occupied or intended to be *solely* occupied by persons aged 62 or older is exempt from the law. If 80 percent of the units are occupied by someone 55 years of age or older, then the building also is exempt.

8. The *sale or rental of a single-family home* is exempt if the owner who is not occupying a home has only one sale in 24 months; no more than three homes are owned at any one time; the services of a broker or any other person engaged in the business of selling or leasing real estate are not used; and no discriminatory advertising is used.

9. A one- to four-family dwelling is exempt if the *owner occupies one of the units, no discriminatory advertising* is used, and a *broker is not used*. A *nonprofit religious organization* can discriminate on a religious basis, so long as membership in the organization is not discriminatory; a *nonprofit private club* may restrict rentals or occupancy of lodgings to members, so long as membership in the nonprofit private club is not discriminatory.

10. Complaints for violations of the federal Fair Housing Act may be *filed with HUD* or taken directly to a *federal district court* or to the *Attorney general of the United States*. An aggrieved party must file a complaint within one year of the discriminatory act.

11. Any person who fails to attend or provide testimony at a hearing or fails to answer lawful inquiries may be fined up to $100,000 and/or imprisoned for up to one year. An offender can be fined up to $11,000 for the first offense, $27,500 for the second offense within five years, and $55,000 for the third offense within seven years. Penalties for intimidation are up to $1,000 and/or up to one year in jail. Penalties for bodily injury are up to $10,000 and/or up to 10 years in jail; for death, the penalty can be any jail term up to life.

12. Refusing to make loans or issue insurance policies in specific areas for reasons other than the financial qualifications of the applicant is known as *redlining*. Redlining is illegal.

13. A *disability* is a *physical or mental impairment* or *history* of such impairment that substantially limits one or more of a person's major life activities. The law *does not protect* anyone using illegal drugs or controlled substances.

14. Real estate ads should state *no discriminatory preference* or limitation on account of race, color, national origin, sex, familial status, or handicap. Ads should describe property, not people.

Assessment of Property Value—Pages 8 and 29

1. The purpose of an appraisal is to *estimate* the market value, or most *probable price* that a buyer will pay for the property in an arm's-length transaction. *Market price* is the actual selling price of the property. *Cost* is the actual dollars spent to produce an asset. Value, price, and cost could be the same, but they are usually different.

2. *Competition* is the interaction of supply and demand. Excess profits attract competition.

3. *Conformity* is the maximum value achieved when the property is in harmony with its surroundings.

4. *Contribution* is the value of any part of the property, measured by its effect on the value of the whole.

5. *Highest and best use* is the most reasonable, probable, and profitable use of the property.

6. *Increasing returns* is when money spent on an improvement increases the property value. (Remodeling the kitchen will usually increase the property's value.)

7. *Decreasing returns* is when adding improvements to the land does not produce a proportional increase in property values. (A swimming pool may not increase a property's value.)

8. *Plottage* is the value that is created when two or more tracts of land are merged into a single, larger one; while *assemblage* is the process of merging the parcels of real estate.

9. *Progression* occurs when the value of a modest home increases if surrounded by larger, more expensive properties.

10. *Regression* occurs when a large, more expensive home is adversely affected if surrounded by smaller, more modest homes.

11. *Substitution* is the foundation for all approaches to appraising; the maximum value of a property tends to be set by the cost of purchasing an equal substitute property.

12. *Supply* is the amount of goods available in the market, and *demand* is the need for the good.

13. In the *market data approach* to appraising, the subject property's value is estimated by comparing recent sales of similar properties. The property with the fewest adjustments is used to determine the market value. Adjustments are always made to the values of the *comparable properties.*

14. The *income* or *capitalization approach* is used to appraise investment property. The appraiser estimates the present worth of future rights to the income the property generates.

15. The *cost approach* is used to appraise unique properties such as a house of worship, post office, library, or hospital.

16. *Replacement cost* is the dollar amount required to construct improvements of equal utility using current materials. *Reproduction cost* is the dollar amount required to construct an exact duplicate of the subject property.

17. *Situs (location)* is a major factor in determining the value of a property.

18. *Depreciation* causes a property to lose value. Depreciation may be curable (reasonable and economically feasible to correct) or *incurable* (not economically feasible to correct).

19. *Physical depreciation* is caused by lack of maintenance and ordinary wear and tear.

20. *Functional obsolescence* occurs because of the absence or inadequacies of features in design or construction.

21. *External* or *environmental obsolescence* is incurable and occurs because of factors located outside the property.

22.   *Market data* is used by the appraiser to determine value. *General data* would be appropriate for many properties. *Specific data* refers to information regarding the subject and comparable properties.

23.   When making adjustments to the values of comparable properties, remember:

SBA—Subject Better, Add; CBS—Comparable Better, Subtract

Zoning—Page 60

1.   *Public controls* include the inherent right of the state to regulate land use for the health, safety, and welfare of the public. Such controls include land-use planning, zoning ordinances, subdivision regulations, building codes, and environmental protection legislation.

2.   *Private restrictions* are placed on real estate by the developer to control and maintain the desirable quality and character of a subdivision or property. *One neighbor* can enforce a deed restriction through court action.

3.   Municipalities and counties develop a *master plan* to guide long-term development. *Zoning ordinances* implement the master plan and regulate land use and structures. Zoning powers are given to the local government *by state enabling acts*.

4.   *Land use* is regulated by dividing the land into residential, commercial, industrial, and agricultural use districts. A *buffer zone* separates two different use districts.

5.   *Bulk zoning* controls density or the ratio of land area to structure area. *Aesthetic zoning* requires that new buildings conform to certain types of architectural styles. *Incentive zoning* requires that the street floors of office buildings be used for retail space.

6.   When zoning changes, zoning boards must make decisions on *nonconforming properties*. An owner may be allowed to continue a nonconforming use of a property until the property is sold or destroyed.

7.   A *variance* may be granted if the zoning creates an unnecessary hardship on the owner and the variance is not detrimental to zoning.

8.   When a special-purpose property, such as a library, is to be built, a *conditional-use permit* must be secured.

CHAPTER 2—SELLING PROPERTY

Services to the Buyer—Page 45

1. In the *exclusive buyer agency*, the broker is due a commission whenever a property is purchased.

2. In an *exclusive-agency buyer* agency, the broker is entitled to payment *only* if the broker locates the property purchased by the buyer.

3. In an *open buyer agency*, the buyer may have contracts with several agents, and *pays only* the broker who finds suitable property.

4. The bundle of rights allows the owner to possess, enjoy, control, exclude, and dispose of the property.

5. Assessing the buyer's price range depends on three basic factors: (1) *stable income*, (2) *net worth*, and (3) *credit history*.

6. A loan underwriter evaluates a loan application to determine the desirability of the loan.

7. The *mortgage-to-income ratio (housing-to-income ratio)* is the ratio of the monthly housing expense to gross monthly income.

8. The *debt service ratio* is the sum of the total monthly debt payments in relationship to the borrower's gross monthly income.

9. Real estate property taxes also are known as *ad valorem* taxes.

10. Homeowners *may deduct* the interest payments made on loans for first and second homes that meet qualifications, certain loan origination fees and loan discount points, loan prepayment penalties, and real estate property taxes.

11. A *capital gain* is the profit realized from the sale or exchange of an asset.

12. *Married homeowners* who file jointly may exclude up to $500,000 from capital gains tax for profits on the sale of a principal residence. Single filers may exclude up to $250,000 from capital gains tax for profits on the sale of a principal residence. If the capital gain exceeds the exclusion, capital gains tax must be paid on the excess amount.

13. The exclusion can be taken more than once. The home must have been used as a principal place of residence for two of the preceding five years.

14. *Depreciation*, or *cost recovery*, is a form of tax deduction. It allows an investor to recover the cost of an income-producing property used in a trade or business.

15. The cost of the improvements may be depreciated or deducted over an arbitrary period of time. *Land cannot be depreciated.*

16. The Internal Revenue Code Section 1031 allows investors to *trade like-kind property*. If no boot, which is cash or its equivalent, is

involved in the trade, it is a tax-free exchange. If boot is involved, tax must be paid on the boot.

Contracts—Page 54

1. A valid and enforceable contract must contain the following essential elements: *legally competent parties, offer and acceptance, proper legal form, legal purpose, consideration, reality of consent,* and *the signature(s) of the party or parties authorized to perform.*

2. To *offer* means to put forward for acceptance, rejection, or consideration. An offer becomes a contract when accepted without changes.

3. The *offeror* makes the offer; the *offeree* receives it.

4. The terms of the offer must be clear and definite and have a time frame for acceptance. An offer can be *revoked at any time before acceptance.* Offers may be terminated by notice of revocation, death or insanity of either party, or a counteroffer.

5. If any change is made in an offer, the original offer is void. If a *counteroffer* is made, the legal positions of the parties are reversed.

6. Only *one* party is obligated to perform in a *unilateral* contract. Open listings and options are unilateral contracts.

7. *Both* parties are obligated to perform in a *bilateral contract.* Exclusive listings, leases, and sales contracts are bilateral contracts.

8. In an *express contract*, the parties have specifically agreed, either orally or in writing, to enter into a contract.

9. In an *implied contract*, the parties by their actions or conduct enter into a contract.

10. One or both parties still have *duties to perform* in an *executory contract.*

11. In an *executed contract*, all parties have *fulfilled* their obligations.

12. A contract is *valid* when it meets all the essential elements and is enforceable.

13. A contract is *void* if it is missing an essential element and is unenforceable by either party.

14. A contract is *voidable* if it can be rescinded by one or both parties. Contracts entered into under duress, undue influence, misrepresentation, fraud, or with a minor or an incompetent person are voidable by the innocent party.

15. A contract is *unenforceable* if neither party can sue to force performance of the contract.

16. *Time is of the essence* means the contract must be performed within the time limit specified.

17. An *assignment* is a transfer of rights and/or duties from one contract to another or from one person to another person.

18. *Novation* means a new contract has been substituted for another; it releases liability from the original contract.

19. Any *ambiguities* in a contract will be construed *against* its writer. To add or delete a provision in a contract, an addendum should be signed by the parties.

20. *Contingencies* require the completion of a certain act or promise before the contract is binding.

21. In a sales contract, land contract, or trust deed the buyer's interest in the property is an *equitable title*. Legal title is held by another party, and the buyer has an insurable interest in the property.

22. A *liquidated damages* clause requires that compensation be paid if one party breaches the contract.

23. *Caveat emptor* means "let the buyer beware." *Caveat venditor* means "let the seller beware."

24. In an *option* agreement the owner (optionor) agrees to keep open an offer to sell or lease real property for a specified time. The owner receives option money that may or may not apply toward the purchase price.

25. An *option contract* binds the optionor to sell should the optionee exercise the option.

26. An option contract should contain the names and addresses of the parties, identification of the property, sales price, date of the expiration of the option, method of notice by which the option is to be exercised, and provisions for forfeiture of the option money if the option is not exercised. It may contain a clause forbidding assignment.

27. An option contract is a *unilateral contract*. An option that has been *exercised* is a *bilateral contract*.

28. In a land contract, the seller is the *vendor* and the buyer is the *vendee*. Typically, the seller retains legal title to the property until the final payment is made. A land contract is also known as a *contract for deed, an installment contract, articles of agreement for warranty deed, bond for title*, or *an agreement of sale*.

Zoning and Insurance—Page 60

1. The right of property subdivision can be regulated by the government or by private controls, such as *deed restrictions*.

2. *State enabling acts* allow municipal governments to create zoning and planning boards to evaluate current needs and to project for future growth in a stable manner.

3. *Special study zones* are used to control development in high-risk flood-prone or geological areas.

4. *Performance standards* regulate air, noise, and water pollution.

5. Agents must *disclose material facts* that would affect the value of a property, such as zoning, property taxes, land-use restrictions, and special assessments.

6. A property may become *stigmatized* because an undesirable event has occurred on the property or near the property. Brokers should seek legal counsel when dealing with such properties.

7. If a property was built prior to 1978, a seller must fill out a *lead-based paint disclosure*.

8. Buyers normally buy *homeowners insurance* to protect against loss due to destruction of the premises, injury to others, and theft of personal property.

9. Most homeowners insurance policies require that the owner maintain insurance equal to at least *80 percent of the replacement cost* of the dwelling.

10. Buyers may hire their own property inspector. Lenders normally require a survey, pest inspection, flood certification, and environmental inspection before closing.

11. An *encroachment* is an unauthorized intrusion onto the real property of another. A survey is the best way for a buyer to determine if there are any encroachments.

CHAPTER 3—PROPERTY MANAGEMENT

Page 79

1. A *written management agreement* should stipulate the relationship between the property manager and the owner (employer-employee, principal-agent, or trustor-trustee), how compensation will be computed, and owners' and managers' rights and responsibilities.

2. The property manager has a fiduciary relationship with the owner. The *objectives* of a manager are to *generate the highest net operating income while maintaining the property*.

3. The *property manager* has a *fiduciary relationship* with the *owner*, which includes the duties of care, obedience, accounting, loyalty, and disclosure.

4. The *duty of care* means to use care and skill while managing the property and binding the owner to contracts and to be responsible in every way to the owner.

5. The *duty of obedience* means to carry out, in good faith, the owner's instructions. The property manager should immediately terminate the relationship if asked to do something illegal or unethical.

6. The *duty of accounting* means to maintain and accurately report to the owner the status of all funds received on behalf of or from the property owner. The manager may not commingle funds.

7. The *duty of loyalty* means to put the property owner's interests first and act without self-interest in every transaction.

8. The *duty of disclosure* means to keep the owner informed of all material facts regarding the management of the property.

9. A *lease* gives the tenant the right to exclusive occupancy of the property and is considered personal property.

10. An *estate for years* (*tenancy for years*) has a *definite time period* and *no notice* is needed to terminate. When the ending date arrives, the tenant is to vacate the premises.

11. An *estate from period to period* (*periodic tenancy*) has an *indefinite time period*. This lease automatically renews until proper notice is given.

12. An *estate at will* (*tenancy at will*) gives the tenant the right to possess the property *with the consent of the landlord*. The lease can be terminated at any time by either party.

13. An *estate at sufferance* (*tenancy at sufferance*) is created when the tenant remains in possession of the property after the lease expires *without the consent of the landlord*. If the landlord gives permission to a tenant to remain on the property, a *holdover tenancy* is created.

14. A lease agreement can be oral or written. The owners' right to retake the property after the expiration of the lease is a *reversionary right*. Oral leases for 12 months and under are enforceable.

15. The lessor's interest is called a *leased fee interest*, and the lessee's interest is called a *leasehold interest*.

16. By an *implied covenant of quiet enjoyment*, the lessor guarantees that the lessee will have exclusive possession and the landlord will not interfere with the tenant's possession or use of the property.

17. A tenant is usually evicted because of nonpayment of rent, unlawful use of the premises or noncompliance with health and safety codes. Filing a suit for possession is known as *actual eviction*.

18. The *warranty of habitability* requires that the landlord keep the property in good condition. If the landlord breaches the lease agreement and the tenant must leave the premises, the tenant may sue for *constructive eviction*.

19. A tenant who transfers *all the leasehold interests assigns the lease*, creating a new landlord-tenant relationship between the lessor and the assignee. The lessor now expects payment from the assignee.

20. A *sublease* is created when a *tenant transfers less than all the leasehold interests* to a new tenant. In a sublease, there are two landlord-tenant relationships. One between the lessor and lessee in the original lease, and a second relationship between the lessee and the sublessee. The lessee can charge more rent and keep the profit. The lease between the sublessor and the sublessee is called a *sandwich lease*.

21. In a *lease option*, the tenant has the option to purchase a property at a specified price within a certain period.

22. In a *lease purchase*, the tenant agrees to purchase the property at a specified price within a certain period, usually the end of the lease.

23. In a *gross (straight) lease*, the tenant pays a *fixed rental amount* and the owner pays all other ownership expenses for the property. The tenant normally pays for utilities.

24. The tenant who enters into a *net lease* agrees to pay ownership expenses such as property taxes, insurance, and maintenance.

25. In a *percentage lease*, a commercial tenant agrees to pay a fixed base rental fee plus a percentage of the gross income in excess of a predetermined minimum amount of sales.

26. In a *sale-leaseback*, the grantor sells the property to the grantee and then leases it back.

27. A *graduated lease* allows for a periodic step-up of rent payments and may be used to attract tenants to a property that is difficult to rent.

28. In times of *inflation*, the property manager may negotiate an *index lease*, wherein the rent is tied to an index outside the control of

either the landlord or the tenant. Index leases contain an *escalation clause* that allows the lease payment to change based on the index.

29. Leases may be *terminated* by the expiration of the term of the lease, proper notice as defined in the lease, surrender and acceptance, abandonment, merger, or destruction or condemnation of the property. *The death of the lessor or lessee does not automatically terminate a lease.*

30. Should the property be sold, the grantee takes the title subject to all existing leases and cannot make any changes until each lease expires.

31. Tenants should be aware that they cannot use their space in such a way as to *infringe on the rights of others* in the building or the community.

32. The property manager will development the budget comparison statement, profit and loss report, and the operating budget. Most owners require that the property manager create a *monthly report of income and expenses.*

33. Only the *interest portion* of each mortgage payment should be deducted as an expense on the profit and loss statement.

34. The *return on investment (ROI)* is the ratio of the property's net income after taxes (ATCF) to the money invested (equity). The ROI also may be computed on a before-tax basis.

35. Material facts that a property manager should disclose to the tenant include location and return of security deposits, building rules, procedure for paying the rent, penalties for late payments, process for maintenance requests, and steps for renewal and termination of the lease.

36. A *leasing agent* is an independent contractor, and his or her primary function is to show the property, follow up on prospective tenants, and lease the property.

37. The four goals of a *life safety* program are (1) Preventing emergencies and security breaches by installing smoke detectors, sprinkler systems, paging systems, closed-circuit television, video camera, and security alarms. (2) Detecting a breach as early as possible. (3) Containing or confining the damage or intrusion. (4) Counteracting the damage by prompt and proper action.

38. The Uniform Residential Landlord and Tenant Act *does not allow abrogation* where tenants sign away their rights in advance of signing the lease.

39. The *Americans with Disabilities Act (ADA)* is intended to enable individuals with disabilities to become a part of the mainstream by mandating equal access to public accommodations, jobs, public transportation, telecommunications, and government services. Private clubs and religious organizations are exempt.

40. ADA stipulates that employers with *15 or more employees* adopt nondiscriminatory employment procedures for the disabled, includ-

ing making reasonable accommodations to allow a qualified person to perform job functions.

41. ADA requires that existing architectural and communication barriers be removed, if this can be accomplished in a readily achievable manner. Priority 1: *Get the party to the door*. Priority 2: *Provide equal access to all areas where goods and services are available to the public*. Priority 3: *Make restroom facilities accessible*. Priority 4: *Provide free access to all remaining areas*.

42. *Preventive maintenance* preserves the physical building and eliminates costly problems before major repairs become necessary.

43. *Corrective maintenance* includes keeping the building's equipment, utilities, and amenities functioning properly.

44. *Routine maintenance* includes maintenance of the common areas and grounds and the physical cleanliness of the building.

45. *New construction maintenance* occurs to meet the needs of the tenant, such as installing new carpeting or remodeling the property.

46. Property managers must be aware of state laws regulating *security deposits* and send the owner a *monthly report of income and expenses*.

47. Property managers must have a working knowledge of hazardous substances and the laws regulating owners. A *hazardous waste* is a *byproduct of a manufactured item*; a *hazardous substance* may include *everyday items such as household cleaning products*.

CHAPTER 4—SETTLEMENT/TRANSFER OF OWNERSHIP

Page 107

1. Home ownership may provide the following *tax deductions*: mortgage interest payments on qualified residential first and second homes, real estate property taxes, certain loan discount points, certain loan origination fees, loan prepayment penalties, and casualty losses to real estate not covered by insurance.

2. *Tax shelters* reduce current tax liability by offsetting income from one source with losses from another source.

3. *Income* may be classified as *active income* generated by salaries and commissions; *portfolio activity* generated by interest, dividends, royalties, gains, or losses from the sale of portfolio assets; and *passive income* generated by nonmaterial participation of rental income or income from limited partnerships.

4. A *capital gain* is a taxable profit that is realized from the sale of a capital asset.

5. A *capital improvement* is any improvement made to extend the useful life of a property or add to its value.

6. A *deed* transfers the title from the grantor to the grantee. The *title* is found within the deed and is used to show ownership of land.

7. A *title search* is conducted to ensure that the buyer and the lender receive a marketable title or one that would not place either party in a position of legal liability.

8. Easements, restrictions, violations of zoning ordinances, lis pendens notices, mortgages, liens, federal tax liens, property tax liens, and encroachments could render a title *unmarketable*. Slight encroachments usually *do not* render a title unmarketable.

9. *Title insurance* protects the policyholder against losses that arise from defects in the title. Prior defects and liens found in the title search, defects known to the buyer, and changes in zoning are not covered in a title policy. *Standard coverage* includes protection against forged documents, missing heirs, incompetent grantors, incorrect marital statements, improperly delivered deeds, and defects found in public records.

10. An *owner's (mortgagor's) title policy* is issued for the market value of the property and benefits the owner. A *lender's (mortgagee's) title policy* covers the loan balance and decreases as the balance is reduced.

11. A *cloud on title* is any claim that creates a defect of title or casts doubt on the title's validity.

12. When a title insurance company makes a payment to settle a claim, the company requires that a policyholder *subrogate* any rights to the claim. *Subrogation* is the substitution of one creditor for another. This gives the title insurance company the right to sue the guilty party to recover any monies it paid to settle a title claim.

13. A *title search* is carried out by a lawyer, abstractor, or title insurance company. It is a condensed legal history of all transactions affecting the property.

14. A *lien* is a legal right that a creditor has in the borrower's property.

15. A *general lien* is a claim against all property of the lienee. A *specific lien* is a claim against one particular property.

16. A *voluntary lien* is established intentionally by the lienee. An *involuntary lien* is placed on the property without any action on the part of the owner.

17. A voluntary or involuntary lien may be statutory or equitable. A *statutory lien* is created by law, such as a judgment. An *equitable lien* is created by the court based on "fairness."

18. Property taxes are specific, involuntary liens.

19. *Special assessments* are levied for the improvements made to property and are specific and statutory. They may be either voluntary or involuntary liens.

20. A *mortgage lien* or *deed of trust* is a voluntary lien on real estate that secures the loan for the lender until the debt is paid in full.

21. A *mechanic's lien* is placed on the property by a party who performed labor or furnished material to improve the property. Generally, a mechanic's lien becomes effective on the day the work began or the materials were delivered.

22. A *judgment* is a decision by the court on the respective rights and claims of the parties in a suit. It is a general, involuntary, equitable lien on real and personal property in the county where the judgment is rendered.

23. A creditor may seek a *writ of attachment*, which allows the court to retain custody of the property while a suit is being decided. This prevents the debtor from transferring the real estate before a judgment is rendered.

24. A *lis pendens notice* gives constructive notice that an action affecting the property has been filed in court and that a future lien may be placed on the property. A lis pendens notice renders a property unmarketable.

25. An *IRS tax lien* is a general, statutory, involuntary lien on all real and personal property of the citizen who owes taxes. It does not supersede previously recorded liens.

26. The *priority of liens* is generally as follows: *real estate taxes and special assessments; senior lien; junior liens in the order of recording.*

27. Under the *Torrens system* of land registration, the title does not transfer and encumbrances are not effective until the proper documents are registered at the Torrens office.

28. A *deed* is the written instrument that transfers the title from the grantor to the grantee. The *essential elements* of a valid deed are the name of the grantor, a grantee who is identified with reasonable certainty, consideration, a granting clause or habendum clause that defines the extent of ownership, limitations placed on the conveyance, an accurate legal description, the signature of the grantor, and delivery and acceptance by the grantee.

29. Most states require that a deed be *acknowledged and attested* before it can be recorded. *Acknowledgment* verifies that the person voluntarily signed the document and verifies the *identity* of the signer.

30. A *general warranty deed* is the *best* type of deed for the *buyer* to receive because it binds the seller to covenants back to the origins of the property.

31. The usual *covenants* found in a general warranty deed are the *covenant of seisin*, which promises that the grantor owns the property and has the right to convey title; the *covenant against encumbrances*, which promises that the property is free from liens and encumbrances except those stated in the deed; the *covenant of quiet enjoyment*, which promises that the grantor has a superior title to the property; the *covenant of further assurance*, which promises that the grantor will obtain and deliver any instrument needed to make the title good; and the *covenant of warranty forever*, which promises that the grantor will compensate the grantee for any loss sustained if the title fails in the future.

32. With a *special warranty deed*, the grantor's *liabilities are limited* to the grantor's period of ownership.

33. A *bargain and sale deed* makes no express promises or warranties against encumbrances. This deed *implies* that the owner holds title and has possession of the property.

34. A *quitclaim* deed provides the buyer with the *least protection* because it provides no promises or warranties. The grantee has no legal recourse against the grantor should a title defect be found in the future.

35. *Quitclaim deeds* are used to convey title, to release interests in real estate, or to correct errors found in a deed.

36. A reconveyance deed is used in a deed in trust or a deed of trust to reconvey the title to the trustor.

37. *Administrator's, executor's, sheriff's,* and *guardian's deeds* are examples of deeds executed pursuant to court order.

38. Most states have imposed a *transfer tax*, which is normally paid by the seller.

39. The *Real Estate Settlement Procedures Act (RESPA)* requires the disclosure of settlement costs. Disclosures must be made on loans that are financed by federally related mortgages.

40. RESPA *applies* to first and second liens for the purchase or refinancing of one- to four-family dwellings. RESPA *does not apply* to a land contract; a purchase-money mortgage where the seller is financing the property; or a loan assumption where the lender charges less than $50 for the assumption.

41. RESPA requires that *within three business days* of loan application, the applicants must receive a copy of *Settlement Costs and You*, and a *good-faith estimate* of the settlement costs. The *Uniform Settlement Statement (HUD Form 1)* must be used to itemize all debits and credits. RESPA does not allow the lender *to receive kickbacks* from service providers.

42. Lenders *cannot* charge a fee for the preparation of the settlement statement. The settlement statement must be made available to the borrower for inspection one day prior to closing, with copies to the buyer and seller at the closing.

43. When a contract is *rescinded*, it is canceled, terminated, or annulled and the parties are returned to their legal positions before they entered into the contract.

44. The right of the government to take property for public use and pay just compensation to the owner is called *eminent domain*. The government exercises this right by the *process of condemnation*.

45. *Taxation* is the right of the government to charge the owner of real estate a fee to raise funds to meet public needs.

46. When a property owner dies intestate and the government can find no heirs, the property *escheats (reverts)* to the state or county.

47. A party who has open, notorious, hostile, and continuous use of another's property for a statutory period may acquire title to the property by *adverse possession*. The rights of the party in possession are called *squatter's rights*.

48. Periods of ownership by different squatters can be combined, which is known as *tacking*.

49. To acquire a title through adverse possession, the claimant must file a suit to quiet title. The title received by the squatter is called a *title by prescription*.

50. A *license* is a personal, revocable, nonassignable right to use the land of another for a specific purpose. It is void on the death of either party or the sale of the property.

51. A *syndicate* is formed when two or more people unite and pool their resources to own, develop, and/or operate an investment.

52. The main advantage of a *real estate investment trust (REIT)* is that investors can avoid double taxation when certain requirements are met.

53. A *security* is created when a party joins with others in the expectation of making a profit from the efforts of others. Securities sold *interstate* are regulated by the *Securities and Exchange Commission*. Securities sold *intrastate* (within state lines) are regulated by *blue-sky laws*.

CHAPTER 5—FINANCING

Page 139

1. The *primary mortgage market* includes savings and loan associations, mutual savings banks, commercial banks, insurance companies, mortgage bankers, mortgage brokers, credit unions, pension funds, and the Rural Economic and Community Development agency, formerly the Farmers Home Administration.

2. *Savings and loans* are an important source of funds for single-family home loans.

3. *Commercial banks* have specialized in short-term loans, but they are becoming more active in the negotiation of long-term residential loans.

4. *Insurance companies* specialize in large-scale, long-term loans that finance commercial and industrial properties. They may require an equity kicker or participation financing, meaning they become a partner with the borrower.

5. *Mortgage bankers* originate loans with money from insurance companies, pension funds, or individuals. They package and sell mortgages and continue to service a loan after it is sold. *Mortgage brokers* are financial middlemen between borrowers and lenders.

6. *Credit unions* are a source of funds for their members.

7. The *Rural Economic and Community Development* agency negotiates loans to people in rural areas for the purchase of property, to operate farms, and to purchase farm equipment. These loans can be originated through a private lender or directly from the agency.

8. In a *purchase-money mortgage*, the seller agrees to finance a portion or the entire purchase price. At the closing, the seller pays off the existing mortgage and "takes back" a mortgage on the property sold. Purchase-money mortgages usually create a junior lien on the property.

9. When a property is purchased *subject to the mortgage*, the original borrower or obligor remains liable for the debt. When a third party *assumes the mortgage*, the third party becomes primarily liable for the debt, and the original borrower is secondarily liable.

10. The *Federal Reserve* stabilizes the economy by controlling the money supply and credit available in the country. It does this by (1) creating money, (2) regulating reserve requirements, and (3) setting the discount rate of interest it charges for loans to member banks.

Types of Loans—Page 146

1. A *security instrument* protects the lender's interest by providing collateral for the loan. *Trust deeds and mortgages* are standard security instruments. A *land contract* also is a security instrument.

2. In a *lien-theory state*, the borrower receives the deed to the property, and the lender establishes a lien position by recording the note and mortgage.

3. In a *title-theory state*, the law construes the lender to have legal title to the property and the borrower to have an equitable title.

4. Under a *deed of trust*, the borrower transfers legal title to the trustee, who holds the title for the benefit of the beneficiary (the lender). When the borrower has made the final payment to the lender, the lender's interest in the property has been defeated. The lender sends the proper documents to the trustee, who uses a deed of reconveyance to convey the title to the trustor.

5. Under a deed of trust, should the *borrower default* on the loan, the lender notifies the trustee. The borrower is given a time frame in which to make the payments current, pay a reinstatement fee, and reinstate the delinquent loan. If the borrower cannot, the trustee advertises and sells the property in a *foreclosure by advertisement*. This avoids the judicial foreclosure process found in lien-theory states.

6. A *mortgage* is a *pledge of property* to the lender as security for the payment of the debt. The *mortgagor* is the *borrower* and the *mortgagee* is the *lender*.

7. A *note* is *evidence of the debt* and states the terms of repayment. The *borrower* is the *obligor*, or *promissor*, because of the obligation to repay the debt. The *lender* is the *obligee/promisee*.

8. A *conventional mortgage* is *not* backed by the government, and it can be insured or uninsured.

9. In conventional financing, if a borrower has a 20 percent or greater down payment, the lender may accept the creditworthiness of the borrower and the security of the property to ensure the payment of debt. If a borrower has less than a 20 percent down payment, the lender may require that the borrower purchase *private mortgage insurance (PMI)*. Should the borrower default, the lender may foreclose. At the foreclosure sale, if the property sells for less than the mortgage balance, the PMI pays the lender up to the amount covered in the policy.

10. An *unconventional mortgage* is backed by the government. Examples: FHA-insured and VA-guaranteed loans.

11. To *amortize* means to repay a loan in periodic payments that include principal *and* interest.

12. In a *fully amortized loan*, the principal balance is zero at the end of the loan term. In a *partially amortized loan*, the principal and interest payments do not pay off the entire loan. In a *nonamortized loan*, periodic interest payments are made to the lender, but no part of the payments is applied to the principal balance.

13. A *construction loan* is an example of a *term mortgage*. The borrower receives the money in stages, called *draws*, and during

construction the payments to the lender are only for interest. When the construction is complete, the borrower must have secured long-term financing and will pay off the entire principal balance.

14.   An *adjustable-rate mortgage (ARM)* contains an *escalation clause* that allows the interest to adjust over the loan term. ARMs are tied to an index. The premium charged by the lender and added to the index to determine the interest charged is called the *margin*, which remains *constant* over the life of an ARM. A cap sets the maximum limit the interest rate can increase and the maximum limit of rate change at each adjustment interval.

15.   In a *graduated-payment mortgage*, the borrower makes lower monthly payments for the first few years and then larger payments. If the lower monthly payments do not cover all the interest charges, the lender will add the unpaid interest to the principal balance. This creates negative amortization, which means the borrower owes more than the original loan amount.

16.   In a *growing-equity mortgage*, there are periodic increases in the monthly payment that are applied directly to the principal, thus reducing the term of the loan.

17.   In a *shared-appreciation mortgage*, the lender agrees to originate the loan at below-market interest rates in return for a guaranteed share of the appreciation the borrower will realize when the property is sold.

18.   A *reverse mortgage* allows elderly homeowners to borrow against the equity in their homes and receive monthly payments, a lump sum, a line of credit, or a combination of any of these terms. The loan becomes due when the borrower no longer permanently resides in the property.

19.   A *package mortgage* includes both real and personal property and is usually used in the sale of new homes in a subdivision or in resort condominium sales.

20.   A *blanket mortgage* covers more than one tract of land and contains a partial release clause that allows the borrower to obtain a release of any one lot or parcel.

21.   A *wraparound mortgage* is a junior loan that wraps around an existing senior loan when the original loan is assumable.

22.   A *buydown mortgage* allows the borrower to "buy down" the interest rate, thus reducing the monthly payment for a number of years.

23.   A *budget mortgage* includes principal, interest, taxes, and insurance payments. The tax and insurance portions of each payment are paid from an escrow account.

24.   In 1934 *FHA* was established to encourage improvements in housing standards, to encourage lenders to make loans, and to exert a stabilizing influence on the mortgage market. *FHA does not negotiate loans.*

25. With an FHA-insured loan, the borrower must purchase a mortgage insurance premium (MIP). A minimum cash down payment is required, which may be a gift. Interest rates are negotiable, and FHA does not set income limits for borrowers. *No prepayment penalties* are allowed on FHA-insured loans.

26. One of the purposes of the VA is to make loans available for *qualified veterans and unremarried widows or widowers of veterans.* The VA *guarantees loans* but normally does not make loans.

27. A *qualified veteran* can negotiate a loan with 100 percent loan-to-value ratio or with a minimum down payment. A qualified person can secure a VA-guaranteed loan on a *one- to four-family dwelling* when the property will be *owner-occupied.*

28. Though the limit on the amount of loan that a veteran can obtain is determined by the lender, there is a limit that the VA will guarantee, based on a sliding scale of the value of the property. A veteran must apply for a *certificate of eligibility*, which establishes the maximum guarantee entitlement of the veteran. The VA also issues a *certificate of reasonable value (CRV)* for the property being purchased, which states the current market value based on a VA-approved appraisal and places a ceiling on the amount of a VA loan allowed. A veteran is not required to have a down payment unless the purchase price exceeds the amount cited in the CRV.

29. At the closing, the borrower or seller must pay a *funding fee* to the VA. This is a percentage of the loan amount and depends on the eligibility status and down payment of the veteran. The fee may be financed as a part of the loan. Discount points may be paid by the buyer or seller. No prepayment penalties are allowed on a VA loan.

30. A VA loan is *assumable* with VA approval. Another qualified veteran's certificate of eligibility may replace the existing certificate. The original borrower is granted *novation* by the lender, and full eligibility may be reinstated by the VA. If a nonveteran assumes the loan, the original borrower remains liable.

Secondary Mortgage Markets, Lending Guidelines, and Laws—Page 148

1. The *secondary mortgage markets* were created to stabilize the source of funds for lenders on the primary markets, especially when money is in short supply.

2. The *Federal National Mortgage Association*, or *Fannie Mae*, is a government-sponsored enterprise (GSE) chartered by Congress. Fannie Mae buys mortgages on the secondary market, pools them, and sells them as mortgage-backed securities to investors on the open market.

3. The *Government National Mortgage Association*, or *Ginnie Mae*, was created when Fannie Mae was reorganized in 1968. Ginnie Mae specializes in high-risk and special assistance programs and has the management and liquidating functions of the old Fan-

nie Mae. The Ginnie Mae passthrough certificate provides for a monthly "passthrough" of principal and interest payments directly to the certificate holder.

4. The *Federal Home Loan Mortgage Corporation*, or *Freddie Mac*, was established to assist *savings and loans* as a secondary market for conventional mortgages, and is a publicly owned corporation. Freddie Mac purchases mortgages, pools them, and sells bonds in the open market as mortgage-backed securities.

5. For a *loan application*, the lender requires a copy of the purchase and sale agreement; the residence, employment, and credit histories of the borrower; income information; a report of the borrower's assets and liabilities; and a copy of a gift letter, if applicable.

6. The *loan origination fee* covers the administrative costs of making the loan and is a percentage of the loan amount.

7. The *loan commitment letter* states that the loan has been approved pending a satisfactory title report, mortgagee's title insurance, homeowner's insurance policy, survey, verification of job status, affidavit of marital status, copy of the settlement sheet of the house sold, verification of bank accounts, payoff of a particular bill, inspection reports required by the lender, and repairs required by the appraiser.

8. *State usury laws* limit the maximum interest rate that a lender can charge on certain types of loans. Usury laws do not set interest rates.

9. The *Truth-in-Lending Act (Regulation Z)* requires that lenders disclose the *true cost of credit* expressed as an *APR* or *annual percentage rate*.

10. *Finance fees* that must be disclosed include loan fees, finders' fees, service charges, interest and discount points. Fees that *do not have* to be disclosed include attorneys' fees, escrow fees, appraisals, surveys, inspections fees, title fees, and closing expenses. (RESPA does require the disclosure of these fees.)

11. Regulation Z covers all *one- to four-family* real estate financing for residential borrowers who are natural persons, but not loans that are used for business, commercial, or agricultural purposes; personal property credit transactions involving more than $25,000; and loans to the owner of a dwelling containing more than four housing units.

12. A borrower negotiating a home improvement loan or refinancing (but not a first mortgage or trust deed) has a *three-day right of rescission* in which to cancel the transaction.

13. Truth-in-Lending requires *full disclosure* by the lender if the following *trigger items* are used in an ad: monthly payment, number of payments, down payment, finance charges and the term of payment. If any of these items are used, the ad *must include* the purchase price; required down payment; number, amounts, and due dates of all payments; and the annual percentage rate.

14. Regulation Z defines a *creditor* as a person or an institution that extends consumer credit more than 25 times a year or more than five times a year if the transaction involves a dwelling as security. The credit must be subject to a finance charge or payable in more than four installments by written agreement.

15. The *Equal Credit Opportunity Act* prohibits discrimination based on race, color, religion, national origin, sex, marital status, age, or source of income in the granting of credit. Loan qualification is based on income, net worth, job stability, and credit rating.

16. Lenders have *30 days* to inform a rejected applicant of the reasons why credit was denied.

17. The *Community Reinvestment Act* was passed to prevent redlining and disinvestment in central city areas.

Common Clauses and Terms in Mortgage Instruments—Page 153

1. The prepayment privilege clause found in an *open mortgage* allows a borrower to pay off the loan before the end of the term. Because of early repayment, some lenders charge a prepayment penalty, which is computed as a percentage of the remaining mortgage balance.

2. The *interest* is a *charge for the use of money*.

3. When the mortgage is paid, the lender must release its interest in the property. In lien-theory states, a *mortgage release* or *satisfaction piece* is recorded to release the lender's interest.

4. In title-theory states, a *defeasance clause* provides that the lender release its interest when the loan is paid in full.

5. If the mortgage document was a *trust deed*, the *reconveyance deed must be recorded* to release the lender's title interest.

6. A *due-on-sale* clause in a mortgage allows the lender to collect full payment from the mortgagor when the property is sold. Mortgages may also contain an *alienation clause*, stipulating that if the property is conveyed to any party, the lender can collect full payment.

7. In a *subordination agreement* a lender with a first lien position agrees to take a second lien position on the property.

8. Notes, mortgages, and security instruments contain an *acceleration clause* that allows the lender to call the note payable in advance of the loan term. Default of the mortgage, destruction of the premises, or the sale of the property to another party may accelerate the payments.

9. The *default clause* in a mortgage allows the lender to foreclose if there is a nonperformance of a duty or obligation on the part of the borrower.

10. *Foreclosure* is the legal process whereby a property is sold as security for the payment of a debt. State and local laws regulate foreclosure proceedings.

11. *Foreclosure by judicial sale* requires that the lender go to court and prove that the borrower has defaulted. The judge orders an appraisal of the property and sets a sale date. Creditors are notified and the property is advertised. When the sale of the property is confirmed, the owner's rights to the property have been foreclosed.

12. An *equitable right of redemption* is the defaulted borrower's right to redeem the property before confirmation of the foreclosure. A *statutory right of redemption* is the defaulted borrower's right to redeem the property *after* confirmation of the foreclosure.

13. *Nonjudicial foreclosure* is used in states where the mortgage contains a *power-of-sale clause* that allows the lender to sell the property without going to court. The defaulted borrower has a specified time to pay delinquent payments and costs, after which the property is advertised and sold.

14. *Strict foreclosure* allows the lender to foreclose after appropriate notice has been given to the delinquent borrower and the proper papers have been filed. If full payment is not made, the property is sold, and the lender keeps all equity.

15. In a *nonrecourse loan*, the borrower is not held *personally responsible* for the note because the property is adequate collateral.

16. The process of *rescission* means the contract has been canceled, and the parties have returned to the legal positions they were in before they entered the contract.

CHAPTER 6—PROFESSIONAL RESPONSIBILITIES/FAIR PRACTICE/ADMINISTRATION

Page 167

1. For a salesperson to be *operative* in the real estate business, a broker must *sponsor* the salesperson's license. The salesperson is authorized to perform real estate activities on behalf of and in the name of the broker.

2. An *independent contractor* pays the contractor's own income tax and Social Security and may not receive any employee benefits from the broker. The broker can regulate the working hours, office routine, and attendance at meetings of *employees* and may *withhold* income, Social Security, FICA, and state taxes.

3. A *trust account*, also known as an *escrow* or *impound account*, is set up by a broker to hold the money of others. State laws regulate the establishment, maintenance, and auditing of the account(s) that a broker is required to have.

4. *Commingling* a client's money with a broker's personal or business account is not allowed in most states. *Embezzlement* or using someone else's money is illegal.

5. *State laws* determine the length of time that brokers must keep complete and accurate records of all business transactions.

6. Disputes within the office may be settled by company polices and procedures. Disputes between REALTORS® will be settled by arbitration. Disputes between non-REALTORS® may be settled through the court system.

7. In some states, if the broker's license is *suspended or revoked*, all of the licenses held by that broker are immediately suspended until those licensees associate with another broker.

8. Federal and state antitrust laws *do not allow* groups of brokers to fix commission rates among or between them. Payments of commissions are *negotiated* between brokers and their clients.

9. Each broker should have a *written agreement* with the broker's licensees on how commissions will be divided. A salesperson may receive a commission *only* from her or his broker.

10. Most state laws *require* that an agent be licensed at the time of the transaction, have an employment contract (listing), and be the procuring cause of the sale to earn a commission. When the brokerage firm has secured a qualified buyer, the broker is due a commission.

11. If a *buyer agency* relationship has been created, agreement should state who is responsible for the payment of the commission.

12. A broker operating a real estate office must maintain *accurate accounting records* showing the receipt and disbursement of funds at settlement and including commissions paid to and from other brokers.

13. A broker who operates an office should maintain *adequate insurance coverage*, including errors and omissions insurance, which insures a licensee against mistakes made during the normal conduct of business. The cost of the insurance coverage usually is paid by the licensee.

14. Listed properties should be advertised through the broker.

15. Parties should receive a copy of all documents they sign.

16. Each person engaged in a trade or business who receives *more than $10,000 in cash* in one transaction, or in two or more related transactions, must file *Form 8300* with the Internal Revenue Service. The form must be filed by the 15th day after the date the cash was received. A copy of the form must be kept for five years.